Pietro Rossi (Ed.)
The Boundaries of Europe

Discourses on Intellectual Europe

Published on behalf of ALLEA
Series Editor: Günter Stock, President of ALLEA

Volume 1

The Boundaries of Europe

From the Fall of the Ancient World to the Age of Decolonisation

Edited by
Pietro Rossi

DE GRUYTER
AKADEMIE FORSCHUNG

ISBN 978-3-11-055507-3
e-ISBN (PDF) 978-3-11-042072-2
e-ISBN (PUB) 978-3-11-042083-8
ISSN 2364-1398
eISSN 2364-2947

Library of Congress Cataloging-in-Publication Data
A CIP catalog record for this book has been applied for at the Library of Congress.

Bibliographic information published by the Deutsche Nationalbibliothek
The Deutsche Nationalbibliothek lists this publication in the Deutsche Nationalbibliografie; detailed bibliographic data are available in the Internet at http://dnb.dnb.de.

© 2017 Walter de Gruyter GmbH, Berlin/Boston
This volume is text- and page-identical with the hardback published in 2015.
Cover: www.tagul.com
Typesetting: Michael Peschke, Berlin
Printing: CPI books GmbH, Leck

♾ Printed on acid free paper
Printed in Germany

www.degruyter.com

Foreword by Series Editor Günter Stock

There is a debate on the future of Europe that is currently in progress, and with it comes a perceived scepticism and lack of commitment towards the idea of European integration that increasingly manifests itself in politics, the media, culture and society. The question, however, remains as to what extent this reported scepticism truly reflects people's opinions and feelings about Europe. We all consider it normal to cross borders within Europe, often while using the same money, as well as to take part in exchange programmes, invest in enterprises across Europe, and appeal to Europe institutions if national regulations, for example, do not meet our expectations.

In this discourse, the European Academies of Sciences and Humanities can play a special role. Due to their long-standing tradition of preserving, securing and making available the cultural heritage of Europe, the Academies are in a prime position to show and promote Europe's intellectual and cultural richness. This is truly Europe's most valuable asset: the traditions of enlightenment, which need to be reinvented and revitalised every day, gathering and sharing knowledge, and, above all, a culture of diversity. And to the members of All European Academies (ALLEA), it is both possible and necessary to look at what others have called the soul or spirit of Europe in a more systematic way.

On this principle, the essay collections in the ALLEA book series *Discourses on Intellectual Europe* pursue the question of an intrinsic or quintessential European identity – a question which lies at the heart of the discourse on European integration. As Robert Schuman said, "the European spirit signifies being conscious of belonging to a cultural family and to have a willingness to serve that community in the spirit of total mutuality, without any hidden motives of hegemony". *Discourses on Intellectual Europe* is one way ALLEA seeks to actively contribute to the preservation of this spirit.

From an academic point of view, *Discourses on Intellectual Europe* also shows that perspectives from all disciplines and the social sciences and humanities in particular can and must play an important role in this debate. In addition to English as the widely accepted modern *lingua franca*, each essay is printed in the original language in order to reflect Europe's linguistic diversity.

The Boundaries of Europe is grounded on the premise that in order to identify what holds Europe together, we must first understand the boundaries that have defined Europe over the last centuries and today, whether geographic, cultural, or historical. I wish to express my sincere gratitude to the editors and authors who generously contributed their expertise to this first volume.

I hope that these essays will inspire readers to consider Europe not simply as a collection of countries, but as a shared heritage, a spirit, a place where knowledge is sought after for the benefit of all.

Günter Stock
President, All European Academies

Contents

Foreword by Series Editor Günter Stock —— v

Pietro Rossi
Premessa —— 1
Foreword —— 14

Arnaldo Marcone
Il Mediterraneo da "mare nostrum" a frontiera tra civiltà —— 27
The Mediterranean from "Mare Nostrum" to Frontier between Civilisations —— 42

Franco Cardini
L'Europa e l'Islam: incontri e scontri —— 57
Europe and Islam: Encounters and Confrontations —— 76

Bo Stråth
The Conquest of the North —— 95

Manfred Hildermeier
Die Ausdehnung nach Osten —— 111
The Expansion towards the East —— 125

Markus Koller
Europa und das Osmanische Reich —— 139
Europe and the Ottoman Empire —— 157

Alberto Masoero
La Russia tra Europa e Asia —— 175
Russia between Europe and Asia —— 192

John H. Elliott
Europe and the Atlantic —— 209

Massimo L. Salvadori
L'Europeizzazione del mondo e il suo declino —— 223
The Europeanisation of the World: Its Rise and Decline —— 241

The Authors —— 257

Pietro Rossi
Premessa

1

Al pari delle altre "regioni" del globo in cui si è insediata la specie umana, occupate da quelle che – con un termine tanto equivoco quanto insostituibile – chiamiamo "civiltà", anche l'Europa ha i suoi confini: confini nel tempo e confini nello spazio. Con la differenza che i confini nel tempo sono soltanto confini *a quo*, non potendosi ovviamente sapere se e quando avrà luogo la pur sovente proclamata *finis Europae*, mentre i confini nello spazio sono più definibili, essendo dati dai limiti dell'espansione della civiltà europea a nord come a sud, a est come a ovest, e sono confini sia terrestri sia marittimi.

Le due specie di confini, per quanto teoricamente distinte, s'intrecciano e, in qualche misura, si condizionano. Ciò vale in modo particolare per quanto riguarda i primi inizi dell'Europa come costruzione storico-culturale. L'antichità greco-romana conosceva il termine "Europa", del quale si avvaleva sia per designare la mitica fanciulla rapita da Zeus e da lui trasportata in volo fino a Creta, sia per indicare una delle tre parti della terra insieme all'Asia e alla Libia (cioè a quella che sarà poi chiamata Africa). Ma quell'Europa era ben differente, come collocazione e come estensione, dallo spazio geografico che intendiamo oggi: per gli antichi Greci era costituita dalla Grecia stessa e dai paesi a nord, cioè dalle terre che si affacciano sul Ponte Eusino fino all'odierno Don, più tardi forse fino al Volga. Il fatto è che allora l'Europa semplicemente non esisteva. La storia antica ha avuto il proprio centro di gravità nel Mediterraneo e nelle regioni ad esso circostanti; le sue città sono sorte sulle coste del mare (o di fiumi nella vicinanza del mare), e questo è stato anche il veicolo principale dei commerci e degli scambi culturali, così com'è stato il teatro delle guerre, di quelle tra le colonie greche o tra Atene e l'impero persiano, e poi dello scontro epocale tra la potenza romana e quella punica. È pur vero che il suo ambito territoriale si verrà estendendo al di là delle Alpi, fino alla Britannia, e verso i deserti africani, e che il suo limite sud-orientale rimarrà sempre fluido; ma le metropoli dell'antichità – da Atene a Alessandria, da Roma a Cartagine, infine ancora a Costantinopoli – erano affacciate sul *mare nostrum* o edificate in prossimità di esso. Città come Treviri o Colonia si collocavano invece alla periferia dell'impero; erano luoghi d'incontro con popoli estranei a quel mondo e a quella civiltà; e molte altre erano soprattutto colonie fondate per presidiare il *limes* dell'impero.

Come ebbe a scrivere nel 1935 Marc Bloch, "l'Europa è sorta esattamente quando l'impero romano è crollato". Ma forse anche la relazione di contemporaneità che questa formula suggerisce è fuorviante, nel senso che il crollo dell'impero è stato sì condizione preliminare della nascita dell'Europa, una *conditio sine qua non*, ma non è stato il suo antecedente immediato. La tarda antichità ha avuto ancora a lungo il proprio centro di gravità nel Mediterraneo; dopo le invasioni barbariche e la divisione dell'impero tra Occidente e Oriente sono state le flotte bizantine ad assicurare gli scambi tra le diverse province e la difesa delle loro coste. Perché l'Europa potesse nascere occorreva un'altra, ancor più decisiva condizione: la separazione politica ed economica tra le regioni costiere, settentrionali e meridionali, del Mediterraneo. Ciò è avvenuto qualche secolo più tardi, tra la fine del VII e l'inizio dell'VIII secolo, quando dalla penisola araba gli eserciti islamici hanno invaso e occupato stabilmente i paesi del Nord Africa, spingendosi fino nel cuore della penisola iberica. Un libro divenuto celebre, più volte discusso ma mai confutato nella sua tesi centrale, *Mahomet et Charlemagne* di Henri Pirenne (apparso postumo nel '37), ha messo in luce il carattere pluri-continentale dell'impero romano, che "non conosce né Asia, né Africa, né Europa", e che è riuscito a sopravvivere per secoli alle ondate migratorie dei nuovi popoli provenienti dalle foreste del Settentrione e dalle steppe dell'Oriente. La formazione del primo nucleo dell'Europa, di un'Europa distinta e in concorrenza con l'impero bizantino – cioè del Sacro Romano Impero – è stata resa possibile dalla perdita delle coste settentrionali dell'Africa, la quale ha fatto sì che venisse meno la funzione tradizionale del Mediterraneo come luogo di comunicazione e di scambio. Una nuova religione, diversa dai culti antichi per quanto anch'essa fondata sul monoteismo di radice ebraica, veniva a contrapporsi al Cristianesimo, reclamando e imponendo l'adesione alla nuova fede.

Che l'impero carolingio, con il rapporto ambiguo da esso instaurato con il papato, abbia costituito il nucleo dell'Europa, non vuol però dire affatto che questa esistesse già allora. Ciò che esisteva era piuttosto – come ha affermato Pirenne, e sulla sua scia anche Lucien Febvre e tanti altri – un'area continentale, sempre più isolata dalle correnti di traffico del Mediterraneo orientale controllate da Costantinopoli: in quest'area il substrato preromano si era fuso con i coloni di origine romana e con gli invasori di stirpe germanica, dando luogo a un *melting pot* unito dalla comunanza della fede cristiana. Essa faceva ancora parte della "Romània", una parte dai limiti geografici incerti, soprattutto verso est e verso sud, che si era costituita politicamente a spese di invasori precedenti, i Sassoni a est e i Longobardi nella penisola italiana. La sua base era una dinastia cresciuta all'ombra di quella merovingia; la sua consacrazione fu un atto di grande valore simbolico, cioè l'assunzione della corona imperiale, benedetta dal papato. Gran parte di quella che nel corso dei secoli diventerà l'Europa rimaneva al di fuori di questo nucleo; anzi, alla morte di Carlo Magno il nucleo stesso si frantumerà, e la corona imperiale passerà da una dinastia germanica all'altra, senza comportare un potere effettivo; anche l'alleanza con il papato andrà soggetta ad alterne vicende.

Più che di Europa, per i secoli dall'VIII al X si può parlare di una *respublica Christiana* nella quale l'emergere del papato come potenza politica supplisce, o cerca di supplire, alla frammentazione del potere propria della società feudale. I rapporti di dominio e di sudditanza assumono, nel vuoto delle istituzioni, un carattere personale; diventano rapporti tra il signore e il feudatario, tra vassalli maggiori e minori, tra proprietari terrieri e servi. Soltanto verso il Mille la rinascita delle città e la loro rivendicazione di autonomia avvieranno un processo di riorganizzazione politica, che consentirà la formazione di una fascia urbana che dall'Italia centro-settentrionale si spingerà fino alle Fiandre e alle città della lega anseatica. Alla ripresa dei commerci mediterranei verso l'Oriente bizantino e islamico farà riscontro la nascita di un altro mercato che dal Baltico arrivava fino a Novgorod e di qui fino a Mosca e a Kiev, seguendo il corso dei grandi fiumi russi. Dopo secoli di gestazione l'ancor giovane Europa s'impegnerà in uno sviluppo economico destinato a durare a lungo; e le sue potenze, provvisoriamente unite sotto il vessillo di Cristo, daranno inizio alla controffensiva contro l'Islam e i principati arabi del Vicino Oriente e della penisola iberica.

2

La storia dell'Europa nascente è una storia di progressiva espansione (anche se non sono mancati periodi di stasi e di ripiegamento), che ne ha allargato i confini terrestri come quelli marittimi. In una fase iniziale essa ha dovuto subire la minaccia incombente dapprima di Normanni e di Ungari, e più tardi la spinta offensiva dei Mongoli. Ma insediandosi in Britannia a metà del secolo XI, invadendo la parte settentrionale della Gallia e impegnandosi in una guerra secolare con i sovrani francesi, poi creando un proprio regno nella lontana Sicilia, i Normanni finirono per integrarsi anch'essi nello spazio geopolitico europeo, per adottare strutture sociali simili, ancorché non sempre identiche, a quelle degli abitanti dell'area carolingia. In quanto agli Ungari, la loro avanzata si arrestò di fronte alla resistenza dei principati germanici, finché la conversione di re Stefano alla fede cristiana e il processo di latinizzazione della loro cultura non diedero vita, nella prima metà del secolo XI, a una monarchia sul modello dell'Occidente europeo. L'Europa nascente estendeva così i propri confini territoriali da una parte con le conquiste di nuovi territori, dall'altra esercitando un'attrazione sempre maggiore sui popoli circostanti, a est come a nord, nella pianura pannonica come nelle isole britanniche e in Scandinavia, integrandoli progressivamente in un sistema di scambi commerciali ma anche culturali.

Nei primi tre secoli dopo il Mille, intorno all'originario nucleo carolingio si era così costituito un complesso di unità politiche per lo più recalcitranti ad accettare l'autorità imperiale, se non addirittura indipendenti da questa. Esse presentavano molte affinità: la struttura feudale, il particolarismo del potere, la coesistenza di regni e principati in concorrenza tra loro, la giuridicizzazione dei rapporti politici all'insegna della rinascita del diritto romano, la ripresa del commercio e delle attività artigianali, la nascita di luoghi di scambio interregionale come le grandi fiere, infine una religione comune con un'organizzazione parallela a quella a quella temporale, la quale faceva capo ai vescovi e, in ultima analisi, al papato di Roma. Questo complesso non possedeva un'unità politica se non formale, e neppure un centro permanente di gravità. Al contrario, al suo interno cominciava a delinearsi una dicotomia tra l'asse costituito dal centro tedesco e dalla penisola italiana, dove una pluralità di principati e di città governate dalla borghesia capitalistica cercava di affermare e mantenere la propria indipendenza dall'impero come dai signori feudali, e le regioni più periferiche in cui il processo di unificazione metteva capo alla nascita di signorie su base dinastica pre- o proto-nazionali; nello stesso periodo cominciava a delinearsi il carattere originale del cammino inglese. Ma gli elementi di affinità prevalevano pur sempre sulle differenze. L'Europa si estendeva ormai dalla penisola scandinava alla Sicilia, dall'Inghilterra alla Francia, a gran parte della Germania (dove a nord i Cavalieri Teutonici avevano conquistato la Pomerania e la Prussia), dall'Ungheria alla Polonia. La frontiera terrestre dell'Europa si era ormai spostata dalla linea Reno-Danubio, che aveva segnato il confine dell'espansione romana, ben oltre l'Elba, fino alla Vistola; e verso sud-ovest era ormai iniziata, dalla Navarra alla Catalogna, la *reconquista* della penisola iberica.

Più complicati erano i confini marittimi. A nord si era formato un altro mare "chiuso", dove accanto alle città anseatiche erano presenti le nuove monarchie scandinave, per larga parte di origine vichinga. Il Mediterraneo non era più né bizantino né arabo, e non divenne mai normanno; Venezia, Genova, Pisa controllavano in larga misura il traffico commerciale con il mondo musulmano, e stabilivano fondaci nei porti orientali. Ma il Mediterraneo rimaneva, politicamente e culturalmente, uno spartiacque tra mondi differenti, anche se i loro rapporti economici si erano infittiti: l'epoca delle Crociate si era conclusa senza vincitori né vinti; ne aveva fatto le spese soprattutto l'impero bizantino, sostituito per oltre mezzo secolo da un effimero impero "latino", mentre si affacciava all'orizzonte la minaccia dei Turchi Ottomani. E neppure diventò un luogo di "incontro" tra la civiltà europea e quella islamica. Questo si era realizzato piuttosto dove il conflitto era stato più diretto, nella penisola iberica, cioè dove i diversi regni cristiani si contrapponevano al califfato di Córdoba. Dalla penisola iberica, e dal Marocco, arrivarono nella nascente Europa le traduzioni arabe di testi filosofici e scientifici greci, che ritradotti a loro volta avrebbero costituito la base della cultura scolastica impartita nelle università di Francia e d'Inghilterra.

3

Per i secoli successivi, a partire dal Tre-Quattrocento, i confini terrestri dell'Europa hanno registrato sì mutamenti, ma di portata minore rispetto all'epoca precedente. È proseguita l'espansione verso est, coinvolgendo i popoli slavi che avevano gradualmente occupato, durante il tramonto dell'impero romano, i territori lasciati liberi da quelli germanici. In queste regioni erano ormai nate monarchie nazionali, anche se il potere del sovrano era fortemente condizionato dalla feudalità: città come Buda, Praga, Cracovia si erano stabilmente inserite nel circuito dell'economia come della cultura europea. Verso la fine del secolo XIV l'unione tra Polonia e Lituania, sotto la dinastia degli Jagelloni, assicurerà la difesa dei confini orientali rispetto alla pressione delle altre popolazioni slave, oltre a costituire una barriera nei confronti dell'avanzata dei Cavalieri Teutonici. Più a sud, sulle sponde orientali dell'Adriatico, l'influenza di Venezia aveva favorito la nascita di principati locali che proteggevano le sue rotte commerciali dalle incursioni bizantine e arabe. Il processo di espansione incontrava però dei limiti difficili da superare. Nella parte settentrionale dell'Europa l'insediamento vichingo (più esattamente variago) di Novgorod – sorto nel secolo IX – era diventato il punto di partenza di una via commerciale che, seguendo il corso del Dnieper, conduceva fino al Mar Nero, assicurando in tal modo il collegamento con la capitale dell'impero bizantino. E tra Kiev e Mosca si formava il principato di Rus', il nucleo del futuro impero russo. In Crimea e nelle regioni circostanti si era insediata una popolazione mongola, che aveva dato luogo a quattro formazioni politiche, i khanati. Mentre una parte del mondo slavo s'integrava nella costruzione dell'Europa, le città di origine vichinga e il principato di Rus' gravitavano su Costantinopoli: la conversione al Cristianesimo, ad opera di Vladimiro il Santo, si era fondata sull'ortodossia bizantina, non sul cattolicesimo romano. Sotto il profilo religioso come sul versante politico-commerciale il mondo slavo guardava, e guarderà a lungo, all'impero d'Oriente, non all'Europa centro-occidentale.

Questa tendenza si consoliderà con l'ascesa del potere centrale (in netta antitesi con il prevalere della nobiltà feudale nei regni viciniori) nel principato di Rus', che verso la fine del secolo XV assoggettava Novgorod e poneva fine al khanato dell'Orda d'Oro. All'espansione territoriale farà riscontro l'instaurazione di un regime assoluto, che celebrerà i suoi fasti, il secolo dopo, sotto Ivan IV il Terribile. Nel frattempo, però, l'avanzata dei Turchi Ottomani aveva posto fine alla lunga stagione dell'impero d'Oriente, le cui fondamenta erano state irrimediabilmente minate dal mezzo secolo di impero "latino". L'asse tra il mondo russo e Costantinopoli perdeva così uno dei suoi poli. Il nuovo impero russo, privo del suo centro tradizionale di riferimento, poteva presentarsi come l'erede – politico e religioso – di quello bizantino, e guardare a Mosca come alla "terza Roma".

Il processo di unificazione della Russia era avvenuto, all'incirca, nello stesso arco temporale del crollo dell'impero bizantino e dell'ascesa della potenza ottomana. Per secoli le flotte bizantine avevano impedito che il Mediterraneo diventasse un dominio esclusivamente arabo; a partire dal Mille erano poi subentrate in questa funzione le città marinare, in particolare Genova e Venezia, ma anche il regno normanno di Sicilia. Le Crociate erano state rese possibili, tra l'altro, dalla maggiore presenza europea nei mari del Mediterraneo centro-orientale. Se i sovrani arabi erano riusciti a difendere i luoghi santi della cristianità dalle ripetute spedizioni degli eserciti europei, conservandone alla fine il possesso, ai margini dei loro domini premevano in misura crescente le armate ottomane, che partendo dall'Anatolia avevano conquistato Macedonia, Tracia, Bulgaria, Kosovo, e circondato Costantinopoli. Nel 1453, al momento della caduta dell'antica capitale imperiale, la potenza ottomana si estendeva ormai a gran parte dei Balcani, fino ai confini dell'Ungheria e della Polonia. Nasceva un nuovo impero, il quale si poneva al di fuori e in conflitto con l'Europa cristiana, nonostante periodi di pace e anche temporanee alleanze con alcuni stati europei, e i cui eserciti riprendevano la spinta espansiva che era stata, secoli prima, propria degli Arabi.

Ai confini dell'Europa si erano così costituite, nel secolo XV, due realtà politiche estranee ad essa, che coprivano entrambe un vasto territorio, e che erano dotate di una forte potenza militare. Questa estraneità aveva una radice profonda, culturale e soprattutto religiosa. Nei primi secoli dell'èra cristiana la nuova fede si era diffusa in forme differenti, come dottrina e come organizzazione. La divergenza aveva avuto origine dall'interpretazione della natura – umana o divina, o duplice – di Cristo, e dal dibattito sul rapporto delle tre "persone" della trinità. Il Concilio di Nicea del 325 aveva definito la questione attribuendo a Gesù sia la natura divina (in quanto persona della Trinità) sia quella di uomo, e condannando come eresia la dottrina di Ario, che gli negava la prima; gran parte delle chiese orientali aveva aderito all'arianesimo, e i popoli barbari avevano abbracciato la fede cristiana in questa versione, per convertirsi soltanto in un secondo tempo all'interpretazione sancita a Nicea. Qualche secolo più tardi il dibattito sull'iconoclastia approfondì la divergenza, e la chiesa di Roma venne sempre più differenziandosi dal cesaropapismo bizantino. A partire da allora Cristianesimo greco e Cristianesimo romano procedettero per strade separate. Ancor più radicale era la contrapposizione rispetto all'Islam, che non distingueva tra religione e politica, e in cui la figura del califfo rappresentava al tempo stesso il vertice temporale e quello spirituale. L'impero turco ereditava questo principio, riprendendo in forma più radicale la politica di diffusione coercitiva della religione islamica.

Veniva perciò meno, per l'Europa del Quattro-Cinquecento, la possibilità di un allargamento verso est; al massimo, le monarchie orientali e la repubblica veneta potevano contenere la tendenza espansiva dell'impero ottomano. La vittoria conseguita dalla flotta cristiana a Lepanto nel 1571 ebbe un risultato momentaneo, e non riuscì a compensare le conquiste territoriali che nella prima metà del secolo XVI esso aveva ottenuto sotto Solimano, giunto fino alle porte di Vienna. Anche la frontiera meridionale si era stabilizzata: decresceva l'importanza delle città marinare italiane, e la penisola diventava sempre più terra di conquista per le monarchie d'oltralpe, o quanto meno un'area marginale della geopolitica europea. Al principio dello stesso secolo, però, si apriva una nuova frontiera, non terrestre ma marittima. Quelle che per l'antichità erano state le "colonne d'Ercole" diventavano la via di accesso a un nuovo mondo, che nel volgere di un paio di secoli sarebbe entrato stabilmente nell'orbita europea. Eliminata la presenza araba nella penisola iberica, le flotte portoghesi e spagnole aprivano nuove rotte verso l'Oriente, e stabilivano possedimenti in un continente fin allora sconosciuto, importandone i tesori e determinando una rivoluzione nei prezzi delle merci. Al declino delle città situate sulle coste del Mediterraneo faceva riscontro lo sviluppo di altre città, di altri paesi affacciati sull'oceano: dapprima Portogallo e Spagna, poi Paesi Bassi, Inghilterra, Francia. Il *mare nostrum* dell'Europa era ormai diventato l'Atlantico, non più il "mare di mezzo" dell'antichità – e tale rimarrà per mezzo millennio.

4

Tra Cinquecento e Novecento sono così sorte, fuori di quello che geograficamente viene designato come il continente (o sub-continente) europeo, altre Europe, che in parte riproducevano le caratteristiche politiche e culturali dei paesi che avevano presieduto alla loro fondazione: l'Europa latina dei *conquistadores*, i quali avevano depredato le ricchezze del Sud-America sterminando o riducendo in schiavitù le popolazioni indigene; l'Europa dei coloni olandesi, francesi e inglesi, spesso rifugio di minoranze religiose perseguitate; più tardi l'Europa australe, nata dai discendenti dei forzati britannici. Se la bolla di Alessandro VI aveva favorito la spartizione del continente sud-americano tra Portoghesi e Spagnoli, il Nord-America fu per due secoli teatro dello scontro tra Francia e Inghilterra, e i loro conflitti furono esportati sul suolo americano. La rivoluzione delle colonie inglesi non rappresentò tuttavia una rottura con la madrepatria: se gli scrittori nord-americani facevano a gara nel proclamare la superiorità morale degli Stati Uniti sulla vecchia Europa, fornendo una piattaforma ideologica alla politica isolazionistica, la solidarietà anglosassone fu decisiva nel duplice conflitto mondiale del Novecento, e ancora all'epoca della "guerra fredda".

Ben diversamente si è configurato il rapporto tra l'Europa e i due imperi sorti, a metà dello scorso millennio, sui suoi confini orientali. A partire dal Seicento, con le riforme introdotte da Pietro il Grande, la Russia avviò un processo di modernizzazione, ispirandosi a modelli europei. Ma questo processo fu tutt'altro che lineare, né riuscì a incidere stabilmente sulla struttura sociale del paese, dove la grande proprietà fondiaria, il predominio dell'aristocrazia di corte e la servitù della gleba sopravvissero fino a tutto il secolo XIX. Pur inserendosi nel gioco delle grandi potenze europee, prendendo parte alle guerre di successione settecentesche e ricavandone un cospicuo vantaggio territoriale, ergendosi a garante della Santa Alleanza, impegnandosi a difesa degli stati balcanici nei confronti del dominio turco, l'impero russo mantenne nei confronti dell'Europa un rapporto ambivalente, di imitazione e di competizione. La tradizione cesaropapista fu di ostacolo ai tentativi di separazione tra potere politico e potere religioso, e costituì al tempo stesso il baluardo dell'autocrazia zarista. Le idee illuministiche, per quanto accolte e incoraggiate soprattutto da Caterina II, non furono il punto di partenza di una laicizzazione dello stato, meno che mai di una riforma della società in senso laico. Tra lo sviluppo in senso liberale dei regimi politici in occidente e l'autocrazia zarista permase una netta divaricazione; e la rivoluzione sovietica si risolse, con Stalin, in una forma ammodernata di potere assoluto esercitato dispoticamente.

Ancor più estraneo al mondo europeo, e soprattutto alla sua cultura, è stato l'impero ottomano, che tra Cinque e Seicento raggiunse la sua massima espansione, completando la conquista della penisola balcanica, assoggettando gran parte dell'Ungheria, spingendosi nel Vicino Oriente fino a Bagdad e al Golfo Persico, affermando il proprio dominio sulle coste africane del Mediterraneo fino all'Algeria. Soltanto Vienna e gli Asburgo riuscirono a resistere agli assalti di Solimano e poi all'assedio del 1683; e il fallimento di questo tentativo contribuì in larga misura al rafforzamento degli Asburgo e al ruolo che essi avrebbero avuto, fin dopo Napoleone, sulla scena politica europea. Dopo di allora la spinta offensiva dell'impero ottomano si esaurì, anche a causa dell'inferiorità della sua tecnologia militare, e i tentativi di modernizzazione intrapresi nel secolo XVIII non ebbero esito. Il contrasto tra la Sublime Porta e le rivendicazioni di autonomia dei popoli balcanici, cui pure era stata concessa l'autonomia religiosa e, in parte, amministrativa, costrinsero l'impero ottomano ad assumere un atteggiamento difensivo soprattutto nei confronti della politica interventista del più potente impero russo.

Entrambi gli imperi si estendevano ben al di là dell'Europa intesa in senso geografico. Il territorio asiatico dell'impero russo prevaleva per estensione su quello europeo – e ciò varrà anche per l'Unione Sovietica. Lungi dall'essere il confine tra due mondi, la catena degli Urali costituì soltanto una linea di separazione interna tra una parte dell'impero ormai colonizzata e una parte in via di colonizzazione. In quanto all'impero ottomano, l'insieme dei territori asiatici e africani superava in misura rilevante, anche dopo la conquista dei Balcani, quella dei paesi europei sottomessi. L'uno e l'altro, è vero, s'inserirono nel gioco delle potenze europee, ricavandone vantaggi in termini di alleanze e di allargamento del proprio dominio. Ma la loro cultura era nell'un caso quella della "Santa Russia", legata all'eredità bizantina e all'esaltazione della "terza Roma", nell'altro quella di una religione estranea alla tradizione cristiana e ad essa ostile, che riprendeva la politica di conversione e di sottomissione inaugurata un millennio prima dagli invasori arabi. La modernizzazione dell'impero russo si coniugò con la rivendicazione di una cultura autoctona diversa da quella europea, che si richiamava piuttosto all'eredità di Bisanzio, mentre la riforma dell'impero ottomano incontrò la resistenza insormontabile delle *élites* religiose tradizionali.

Né si può dire che la situazione sia mutata in maniera sostanziale nel corso del Novecento. Dopo il 1917 il nuovo stato sovietico si è sempre più contrapposto ai regimi "capitalistici" europei, più ancora che all'espansione della Germania nazista, traendone – come già faceva l'impero russo – vantaggi territoriali, come in Polonia, e all'indomani del '45 circondandosi di una cerchia di paesi satelliti. Il sogno di una rivoluzione mondiale del proletariato ha ceduto il posto alla concezione del socialismo "in un solo paese", che poteva agevolmente richiamarsi al nazionalismo della Russia zarista. La tradizione religiosa ortodossa è stata soffocata ma anche, durante la guerra, risuscitata come sostegno ideologico della resistenza all'invasore tedesco. Più incisivo è stato lo sforzo di modernizzazione in senso europeo della Turchia kemalista, che ha dato vita a uno stato laico respingendo la tradizione islamica; ma a distanza di quasi un secolo il fondo tradizionale è riemerso, e con esso la pretesa di fondare la legislazione statale sulla legge sacra. Al pari del dispotismo russo, erede del cesaropapismo bizantino, l'integralismo religioso segna tuttora la distanza profonda sia tra Turchia europeizzata e Turchia tradizionale, sia tra la Turchia e il mondo europeo.

5

Finora si è parlato dei confini esterni dell'Europa e dei mutamenti che hanno subito nel corso dei secoli; ma a questi si affiancano altri confini ad essa interni. Si tratta, ovviamente, di confini più o meno stabili tra regni, principati, stati, i quali sono mutati nel tempo producendo la nascita o la scomparsa di formazioni politiche, nonché il mutamento del loro territorio e della loro popolazione. Ma non sono questi i confini che ci interessano. E neppure appaiono particolarmente rilevanti i confini etnico-linguistici, in parte riconducibili alle diverse ondate migratorie dall'est e dal nord, che diedero vita a quelli che sono stati chiamati i regni romano-barbarici. Altri, invece, sembrano rivestire una maggiore portata.

Il primo confine, che già presuppone l'ampliamento dell'originario nucleo carolingio e la formazione di regni nazionali (o quanto meno pluriregionali) nell'Occidente europeo, è quello che risale alla divisione tra l'area dello sviluppo cittadino a partire dal Mille e le aree circostanti, dove l'urbanizzazione e lo sviluppo economico costituiscono fenomeni posteriori. Si tratta di una regione che va da sud a nord, dall'Italia centro-settentrionale alle Fiandre, percorrendo la fascia renana, e che si prolunga nell'Inghilterra sud-orientale e, con la lega anseatica, sulle coste baltiche. Essa ha avuto la propria base nel commercio e nella produzione artigianale che si sviluppò all'interno delle mura cittadine, sorretta da corporazioni di mestiere che assicuravano la qualità delle merci e la formazione dei lavoranti. Luoghi di scambio furono soprattutto le città marinare e i fondaci da esse costituiti nei porti stranieri, ma anche le grandi fiere annuali dello Champagne o di Lione. In questa regione si sono sviluppati i traffici con l'Oriente mediterraneo, da cui si dipartiva la "via della seta", o con la Rus' di Mosca e di Kiev, e più tardi con le nuove terre d'oltreoceano; da essa venivano le risorse finanziarie di cui principati e stati avevano bisogno per condurre le loro guerre; da essa, in particolare dall'Inghilterra, prenderà le mosse, secoli dopo, il processo di industrializzazione. Ancora nel Novecento, all'indomani del secondo conflitto mondiale, dagli stati che coprono questa regione è venuta la spinta per la formazione della CECA, la Comunità europea del carbone e dell'acciaio. E per mezzo secolo Francia, Germania e Italia hanno costituito la struttura portante di quella che oggi è l'Unione europea.

Fenomeni economici e fenomeni religiosi sono strettamente legati, come già sosteneva Max Weber; e ciò vale in maniera particolare per la storia europea. Un altro confine interno, anzi una vera e propria spaccatura si è avuta con la Riforma protestante e la divisione dell'Europa in due campi contrapposti, dando luogo a una serie di guerre civili fondate su motivazioni religiose. I secoli del Medioevo avevano anch'essi conosciuto forme differenti di fede cristiana, conflitti tra sostenitori del "credo" definito a Nicea e dell'eresia ariana; ma questi conflitti si erano risolti in prevalenza con la riconversione dei sovrani dei popoli barbari invasori al cattolicesimo romano, e sul loro esempio con l'adesione dell'intero popolo a questa scelta. Così il papato aveva evangelizzato questi popoli, era penetrato con Bonifacio nelle isole britanniche, si era messo a capo delle Crociate, mentre il mondo slavo, gravitando su Bisanzio, aveva adottato la versione "ortodossa" della fede cristiana. Con la Riforma, invece, la divisione penetrava all'interno dei singoli paesi: la Germania si divideva tra principi cattolici e principi luterani, e nei cantoni svizzeri fiorivano riformatori e chiese riformate in contrasto tra loro, mentre in Francia un forte partito ugonotto sfidava il potere sovrano. Ci vorrà più di secolo, fino alla pace di Westfalia, perché la carta geografica delle confessioni religiose si stabilizzi, in base al principio della scelta del sovrano e dell'obbedienza dell'intera popolazione alla sua scelta. La Francia usciva dalle guerre di religione rimanendo (almeno formalmente) cattolica; e il cattolicesimo controriformistico prevaleva in Italia e in Spagna sulle simpatie protestanti di alcune minoranze intellettuali, che venivano represse dall'Inquisizione, ma anche nella lontana Polonia; la Germania rimaneva divisa in due campi, ma la pacificazione era sancita dalla volontà dei principi; il luteranesimo diventava chiesa di stato in Scandinavia; le sette e le piccole chiese che reclamavano una riforma più radicale erano perseguitate, e i loro seguaci costretti a emigrare nelle colonie nord-americane. L'Inghilterra aveva scelto una strada a sé, quella di una chiesa nazionale che conservava l'impianto dottrinale cattolico, ma sotto il governo diretto del sovrano e non più del papato.

Un terzo confine è quello tra i paesi nei quali il potere monarchico si era affermato nel corso del Medioevo, dando poi luogo, tra Sei e Settecento, a uno stato nazionale, e quelli in cui la presenza di poteri con pretese universali ne aveva impedito il processo di formazione. Mentre a est come a ovest le monarchie erano riuscite a sconfiggere la nobiltà di origine feudale, o per lo meno ad associarla al potere, nella fascia centrale del continente europeo, dalla Prussia alla penisola italiana, il processo di accentramento aveva trovato un ostacolo duraturo nell'impero asburgico o nel papato, e più spesso nella loro alleanza. Quando, dopo la rivoluzione francese, la coincidenza tra lo stato e la nazione si presentò come l'obiettivo naturale della politica, e ogni nazionalità – poco importa quanto reale o "inventata" – rivendicò la propria autonomia, i nuovi stati emergenti sconvolsero l'assetto definito all'indomani della caduta di Napoleone: un nuovo impero si affermò nel cuore del continente, e anche la penisola italiana si unificò politicamente dopo secoli di aspirazioni frustrate. La divisione tra vecchi e nuovi stati nazionali fu resa più profonda dal fatto che, mentre i primi avevano trovato potuto fondare colonie in altri continenti, i secondi non ebbero più a disposizione territori in cui espandersi se non sul suolo europeo. Se la rivoluzione francese aveva proclamato il carattere "sacro" della nazione in armi, i nuovi stati nazionali praticarono una politica aggressiva per procurarsi quello spazio vitale che ritenevano loro diritto: non potendo trovarlo in Africa o in Asia, lo cercarono nel cuore stesso dell'Europa, con le conseguenze che ci sono ben note.

Questi (e altri) confini che contrassegnano nei secoli la storia europea hanno ormai perduto oggi d'importanza. Le identità nazionali si sono affievolite, e l'appartenenza religiosa appare anch'essa, in una società secolarizzata, un vincolo piuttosto debole. Se si vogliono cercare linee divisorie nell'Europa del tardo Novecento, esse sono da ricondursi piuttosto al diverso esito del processo di realizzazione del *welfare state*, con le garanzie che questo ha offerto e offre ai propri cittadini. Un'ampia parte del continente – l'Europa del Centro-Nord, inclusa la Francia – è riuscita a equilibrare il sostegno fornito agli individui con una politica fiscale che ha consentito la redistribuzione del reddito tra i diversi strati della società. Nell'Europa mediterranea, invece, la debolezza della struttura statale, congiunta alla resistenza delle classi più ricche, lo ha impedito e lo impedisce tuttora. A est, dalla Polonia alla penisola balcanica, il *welfare state* è ancora un miraggio, e il livello economico non permette a tutt'oggi l'adozione di efficaci politiche redistributive. In questo senso si può parlare di Europe diverse; ma i confini tra l'una e l'altra si sono fatti ormai fluidi, e il mondo europeo si presenta come un grande mercato, internamente squilibrato, nel quale molte aziende migrano verso i paesi orientali, mentre la manodopera, e in particolare quella qualificata, punta a trasferirsi nel Centro-Nord.

Non soltanto i confini interni, ma anche i confini con il mondo circostante si sono progressivamente relativizzati. Se il rapporto dell'Europa con la Russia e la Turchia appare per certi versi di estraneità, per altri di possibile convergenza, i mari hanno acquistato un nuovo ruolo, per un verso di luogo d'incontro, per l'altro verso di frontiera non soltanto fisica ma politico-culturale. Questo ruolo, però, si è venuto configurando in maniera differente, se non antitetica, nel caso dell'Atlantico e del Mediterraneo. Nella prima metà del secolo scorso, dalla "dottrina Wilson" al piano Marshall, i legami tra le due sponde dell'Atlantico si erano rinsaldati, e la solidarietà anglosassone si era estesa alla parte occidentale del continente. La difesa della democrazia liberale e di un'economia fondata sul libero scambio, minacciate prima dalla Germania hitleriana e poi dall'Unione Sovietica, sembrava averli resi irreversibili. E infatti, nonostante che i suoi obiettivi primari fossero di carattere politico-militari, il Patto Atlantico è stato per decenni ben più che una semplice alleanza tra le potenze delle due sponde. Oggi la situazione è mutata considerevolmente: lo stesso processo di unificazione europea ha fatto sì che emergessero divergenze sia di interessi che di impostazione politica. Da parte sua il Mediterraneo è ritornato ad essere, come nel VII-VIII secolo e poi nel Quattro-Cinquecento, il confine tra Europa e un mondo islamico diviso tra aspirazioni di rinnovamento e derive integralistiche, diventando così una frontiera tra popoli di diversa tradizione e di difficile integrazione reciproca. Il processo di relativizzazione dei confini, se per un verso li ha resi molto più permeabili che in passato, favorendo inarrestabili flussi migratori – a distanza di secoli la Sicilia è ritornata a essere la porta d'Europa – appare ben lungi dal fare di questo mare e delle sue coste un luogo d'incontro tra civiltà.

Bibliografia

Abulafia, D 2011, *The Great Sea: a Human History of the Mediterranean*, Oxford University Press, Oxford.
Anderson, BR 1983, *Imagined Communities: reflections on the origin and spread of nationalism*, Verso, London.
Braudel, F 1966, *La Méditerranée et le monde méditerranéen à l'époque de Philippe II*, 2nd edn, Colin, Paris.
Brown, P 1995, *The Rise of Western Christendom*, Oxford University Press, Oxford.
Dawson, C 1956, *The Making of Europe. An Introduction to the History of European Unity*, Meridian, New York.
Febvre, L 1999, *L'Europe. Genèse d'une civilisation*, Perrin, Paris.
Fischer, J 1957, *Oriens-Occidens-Europa. Begriff und Gedanke „Europa" in der späten Antike und im Frühen Mittelalter*, Steiner, Wiesbaden.
Galasso, G 2001, *Storia d'Europa*, Laterza, Roma-Bari.
Geary, PJ 2002, *The Myth of Nations. The Medieval Origins of Europe*, Princeton University Press, Princeton.
Groh, D 1961, *Russland und das Selbstverständnis Europas. Ein Beitrag zur europäischen Geistesgeschichte*, H. Luchterhand, Neuwied.
Lewis, B 1993, *Islam and the West*, Oxford University Press, New York.
Osterhammel,J 1998, *Die Entzauberung Asiens. Europa und die asiatischen Reichen im 18. Jahrhundert*, C.H. Beck, München.
Pomian, K 1990, *L'Europe et ses nations*, Gallimard, Paris.
Pirenne, H 1937, *Mahomet et Charlemagne*, Alcan & Nouvelle Société d'éditions, Paris-Bruxelles.
Rossi, P 2007, *L'identità dell'Europa*, Il Mulino, Bologna.
Tilly, C 1975, *The Formation of National States in Western Europe*, Princeton University Press, Princeton.
Weber, M 1923, *Wirtschaftsgeschichte. Abriß der universalen Sozial- und Wirtschaftsgeschichte*, Duncker & Humblot, München.

Pietro Rossi
Foreword

1

Like the other "regions" of the globe where the human species has settled, Europe, being occupied by what – with an equivocal but irreplaceable term – we call "civilisations", has its boundaries: boundaries in time and boundaries in space. With the difference that the boundaries in time are only boundaries *a quo*, since it is clearly impossible to know if and when the often proclaimed *finis Europae* will occur, whereas the boundaries in space are more definable, being determined by the limits of the expansion of European civilisation to the north and south, and to the east and west; and they include both terrestrial and maritime boundaries.

These two kinds of boundary, though theoretically distinct, are interconnected, and to some extent condition each other. This was particularly true of the beginnings of Europe as a historical and cultural construct. Greco-Roman antiquity knew the term "Europa", which it used both to designate the mythical maiden whom Zeus seized and carried through the air to Crete, and to denote one of the three parts of the earth, the other two being Asia and Libya (that is, what would later be called Africa). But that Europe was very different, in position and extent, from the geographical space that we indicate with the same term today; to the ancient Greeks it comprised Greece itself, together with the countries to the north – those that lie along the shores of the Pontus Euxinus, as far as the present-day Don, and later perhaps as far as the Volga. The fact is, at that time Europe simply did not exist. Antiquity's centre of gravity was the Mediterranean and the regions around it; its cities formed on the coasts of that sea (or on the banks of rivers near it), and the sea was also the principal vehicle of trade and cultural exchange, and the theatre of wars – those between the Greek colonies or between Athens and the Persian empire, and later the crucial showdown between Roman and Carthaginian power. It is true that its territorial extent later went beyond the Alps, as far as Britannia, and southwards towards the African deserts, and that its south-eastern boundary would always remain fluid; but the metropolises of antiquity – from Athens to Alexandria, from Rome to Carthage, and later Constantinople – stood either directly on *mare nostrum* or near to it. Cities like Trier and Cologne, however, were situated on the edge of the empire; they were points of contact with peoples extraneous to that world and that civilisation; and many other cities were essentially colonies created to guard the empire's *limes*.

As Marc Bloch wrote in 1935, "Europe arose when the Roman empire crumbled". But perhaps the relation of contemporaneity that this formula suggests is misleading, for although the collapse of the empire was indeed a pre-condition for the birth of Europe, a *conditio sine qua non*, it was not its immediate antecedent. Late antiquity's centre of gravity long remained in the Mediterranean; after the barbarian invasions and the division of the empire between West and East, the Byzantine fleets guaranteed trade between the different provinces and the defence of their coasts. Another even more important condition was necessary for the birth of Europe: political and economic separation between the northern and southern coastal regions of the Mediterranean. This occurred several centuries later, at the end of the seventh century and the beginning of the eighth, when Islamic armies from the Arabian peninsula invaded and permanently occupied the countries of North Africa, penetrating into the heart of the Iberian peninsula. A well-known book which has often been contested but never confuted in its central thesis, Henri Pirenne's *Mahomet et Charlemagne* (published posthumously in 1937), stressed the pluri-continental nature of the Roman empire, which "knows neither Asia, nor Africa, nor Europe", and which survived migratory waves of new peoples from the northern forests and the Steppes in the east for centuries. What made possible the formation of the first nucleus of Europe – a distinct Europe in competition with the Byzantine empire, namely the Holy Roman Empire – was the loss of the northern coasts of Africa, which eliminated the Mediterranean's traditional function as an area of intercommunication and trade. A new religion, different from the ancient cults, though, like them, founded on a monotheism of Jewish origin, now opposed Christianity, demanding and enforcing adherence to the new faith.

The fact that the Carolingian empire, in an ambiguous relationship with the papacy, was the nucleus of Europe, does not mean that Europe already existed. What existed – as Pirenne pointed out, and as Lucien Febvre and many others have since repeated – was a continental area, increasingly isolated from the eastern Mediterranean trade routes controlled by Constantinople; in this area the pre-Roman substratum had merged with colonies of Roman origin and invaders of German extraction, creating a mixture held together by common allegiance to the Christian religion. It was still part of "Romania", a region with unclear geographical boundaries, particularly to the east and south, which had formed politically at the expense of previous invaders – the Saxons to the east, and the Lombards in the Italian peninsula. Its basis was a dynasty which had developed in the shadow of the Merovingian dynasty; its consecration was an act of great symbolic value: the assumption of the imperial crown, blessed by the papacy. Most of what would in later centuries constitute Europe remained outside this nucleus; indeed, on Charlemagne's death the nucleus itself fragmented, and the imperial crown passed from one Germanic dynasty to another, without implying actual power; the alliance with the papacy would also have its fluctuations.

From the eighth to the tenth centuries it is possible to speak not of Europe, but of a *respublica Christiana* in which the papacy's emergence as a political power compensates, or attempts to compensate, for the fragmentation of power characteristic of feudal society. The relationships of dominion and subjection take on a personal character in the absence of institutions; they become relationships between lord and feoffee, between major and minor vassals, or between landowners and serfs. Only at the beginning of the second millennium did the re-emergence of cities and their calls for autonomy initiate a process of political reorganisation which would lead to the formation of an urban area stretching from central and northern Italy to Flanders and the cities of the Hanseatic League. The resumption of Mediterranean trade with the Byzantine and Islamic east was accompanied by the creation of another market ranging from the Baltic to Novgorod, and on to Moscow and Kiev, along the courses of the great Russian rivers. After centuries of gestation the young Europe enjoyed an economic development which proved to be long-lasting; and its powers, temporarily united under the standard of Christ, began a counter-offensive against Islam and the Arabian principates of the Near East and the Iberian peninsula.

2

The history of the nascent Europe is one of progressive expansion (though not without intervals of stagnation and regression), which increased its terrestrial and maritime boundaries. During an initial phrase it had to face first the major threat of the Normans and Ungars and then the offensive pressure of the Mongols. But by settling in Britannia in the mid-eleventh century, invading the northern part of Gaul and engaging in centuries-long war with the French sovereigns, and then creating a kingdom of their own in distant Sicily, the Normans gradually became integrated into European geopolitical space, and adopted social structures similar, though not always identical, to those of the inhabitants of the Carolingian area. As for the Ungars, their advance was blocked by the resistance of the German principates, until King Stephen's conversion to the Christian faith and the progressive Latinisation of their culture gave rise, in the first half of the eleventh century, to a monarchy on the model of those of the European West. The nascent Europe thus extended its territorial boundaries partly by conquering new territories and partly by exerting an ever greater attraction on neighbouring peoples to the east and north, on the Pannonian plain and in the British Isles and Scandinavia, integrating them progressively into a system of commercial, but also cultural, exchanges.

Thus in the first three centuries of the second millennium a complex of political units, most of which were reluctant to accept imperial authority, or even independent of it, had formed around the original Carolingian nucleus. These units had many things in common: their feudal structure, the particularism of power, the coexistence of rival kingdoms and principates, the juridicisation of political relationships with a renascence of Roman law, the revival of trade and artisanal activities, the rise of places of interregional trade such as the great fairs, and lastly a common religion with an organisation parallel to that of the temporal powers, overseen by bishops, and ultimately by the papacy in Rome. This complex had no more than a formal political unity and lacked any permanent centre of gravity. Indeed, within it a dichotomy began to form between the axis comprising the German centre and the Italian peninsula, where a multiplicity of principates and cities governed by the capitalist bourgeoisie tried to assert and maintain their independence from the empire, in the manner of feudal lords, and the more peripheral regions, where the process of unification was fomented by the rise of dynastically based pre- or proto-national seignories; during this period, too, the distinctive nature of the English development began to emerge. But the elements of affinity remained stronger than the differences. Europe now stretched from the Scandinavian peninsula to Sicily, from England to France and most of Germany (in the northern part of which the Teutonic Knights had conquered Pomerania and Prussia), and from Hungary to Poland. By now the terrestrial boundary of Europe had shifted from the Rhine-Danube line, which had marked the limit of Roman expansion, well beyond the Elbe, to the Vistula; and in the south, from Navarre to Catalonia, the reconquest of the Iberian peninsula had begun.

The maritime boundaries were more complicated. In the north another "closed" sea had formed, the domain of the Hanseatic cities and the new Scandinavian monarchies, mainly of Viking origin. The Mediterranean was now no longer Byzantine nor Arabian, and never became Norman; Venice, Genoa and Pisa had predominant control of trade with the Muslim world, and established depots in eastern ports. But the Mediterranean remained politically and culturally a watershed between different worlds, though economic relations between those worlds had intensified: the age of the Crusades had ended without victors or vanquished; the Byzantine empire suffered most, for it was supplanted for more than half a century by an ephemeral "Latin" empire, while the threat of the Ottoman Turks appeared on the horizon. Nor did the Mediterranean become a "meeting place" between the European and Islamic civilisations. This had occurred, rather, where the conflict had been more direct – in the Iberian peninsula, where the different Christian kingdoms had opposed the caliphate of Córdoba. It was from the peninsula, and from Morocco, that Arabic translations of Greek philosophical and scientific texts arrived in the nascent Europe, where, after being translated a second time, they would form the basis of the scholastic culture taught in the universities of France and England.

3

In the following centuries, from the fourteenth and fifteenth centuries onwards, there were some changes to the terrestrial boundaries of Europe, but less significant ones than in the preceding period. Eastward expansion continued, embracing the Slavic peoples which had progressively occupied the territories left vacant by the Germanic peoples with the decline of the Roman empire. National monarchies had emerged in these regions, though the sovereign's power was strongly conditioned by feudality: cities such as Buda, Prague and Kraków had permanently established themselves within the circuit of the European economy and culture. In the late fourteenth century, union between Poland and Lithuania, under the Jagiellonian dynasty, strengthened the defence of the eastern boundaries against pressure from other Slavic populations, as well as forming a barrier against the advance of the Teutonic Knights. Further south, on the eastern shores of the Adriatic, the influence of Venice had favoured the rise of local principates which protected her trade routes from Byzantine and Arab incursions. However, the process of expansion encountered some obstacles which were hard to surmount. In northern Europe the Viking (or to be more precise, Variangian) settlement of Novgorod, founded in the ninth century, had become the starting point of a trade route which ran south along the course of the Dnieper to the Black Sea, providing a link with the capital of the Byzantine empire. Between Kiev and Moscow the principate of Rus', the nucleus of the future Russian empire, was developing. In Crimea and the surrounding regions a Mongol population had settled, giving rise to four political units, the Khanates. While part of the Slavic world merged with the growing Europe, the cities of Viking origin and the principate of Rus' gravitated towards Constantinople; their conversion to Christianity under Vladimir the Great had been based on Byzantine Orthodoxy, not Roman Catholicism. From a religious point of view and on the political and commercial level the Slavic world looked towards the empire of the East rather than central and western Europe, and would long continue to do so.

This tendency was consolidated by the rise of a central power (in contrast to the predominance of a feudal nobility in neighbouring regions) in the principate of Rus', which towards the end of the fifteenth century subjugated Novgorod and put an end to the Khanate of the Golden Horde. This territorial expansion was accompanied by the emergence of an absolute regime, which would reach its apogee in the next century under Ivan IV the Terrible. In the meantime, however, the advance of the Ottoman Turks had ended the long existence of the eastern empire, whose foundations had been irremediably weakened by half a century of "Latin" empire. Thus the axis between the Russian world and Constantinople lost one of its poles. The new Russian empire, bereft of its traditional point of reference, was able to present itself as the political and religious heir to the Byzantine empire, and look upon Moscow as the "third Rome".

The unification of Russia had come about during roughly the same period as the collapse of the Byzantine empire and the rise of Ottoman power. For centuries the Byzantine fleets had prevented the Mediterranean from becoming an exclusively Arab domain; later, from the beginning of the second millennium, this role had been taken over by the maritime cities, notably Genoa and Venice, and the Norman kingdom of Sicily. Increased European influence over the central and eastern Mediterranean was one of the factos that had made the Crusades possible. Although the Arab sovereigns had succeeded in defending the sacred sites of Christianity against repeated expeditions by European armies, and maintained possession of them to the end, the margins of their dominions were increasingly under threat from Ottoman forces, which, starting out from Anatolia, had conquered Macedonia, Thrace, Bulgaria and Kosovo, and surrounded Constantinople. In 1453, at the time of the fall of the ancient imperial capital, Ottoman power extended over most of the Balkans, as far as the boundaries of Hungary and Poland. A new empire was rising, which stood outside and in conflict with Christian Europe, despite intervals of peace and even temporary alliances with some European states; and its armies were regaining the expansionary momentum that the Arabs had possessed centuries earlier.

Thus in the fifteenth century two political entities extraneous to Europe had formed on its boundaries, each covering a large territory and endowed with strong military power. This extraneousness had deep cultural, and especially religious, roots. In the early centuries of the Christian era the new faith had spread in differing forms, both as a doctrine and as an organisation. The divergence hinged on the interpretation of the nature of Christ – human, divine, or dual – and in the debate on the relationship between the three "persons" of the Trinity. The Council of Nicea of 325 had ruled on the question, attributing to Jesus both a divine nature (as one person of the Trinity) and a human one, and condemning as heresy the doctrine of Arius, who denied him the former; most of the eastern churches had favoured Arianism, and the barbarian peoples had embraced the Christian faith in this version, only later converting to the interpretation approved in Nicea. Several centuries later the debate on iconoclasm deepened the split, and the church of Rome increasingly distanced itself from Byzantine Caesaropapism. Thereafter Greek Christianity and Roman Christianity moved along different routes. Even more marked was opposition to Islam, which did not distinguish between religion and politics, and regarded the figure of the caliph as both a temporal and a spiritual leader. The Turkish empire inherited this principle, adopting the Islamic religion's policy of coercive diffusion in an even more radical form.

Thus in the fifteenth and sixteenth centuries Europe had no possibility of eastward expansion; the most the eastern monarchies and the Venetian republic could do was contain the expansionist tendency of the Ottoman empire. The victory of the Christian fleet at Lepanto in 1571 had only a temporary effect, and could not compensate for the territorial conquests that empire had made in the first half of the sixteenth century under Suleiman, who had advanced right up to the gates of Vienna. The southern frontier, too, had stabilised: the importance of Italy's maritime cities diminished, and the peninsula became increasingly a land of conquest for monarchies north of the Alps, or at least a marginal area of European geopolitics. At the beginning of the same century, however, a new frontier opened up – this time not a terrestrial but a maritime one. What antiquity had known as the "pillars of Hercules" became the gateway to a new world, which over the next two centuries would be taken permanently into the European orbit. Now that the Arab presence in the Iberian peninsula had been eliminated, the Portuguese and Spanish fleets opened up new routes towards the east, and established settlements in a previously unknown continent, importing its treasures and causing a revolution in the price of goods. The decline of the coastal cities of the Mediterranean was matched by the rise of other cities in other countries that looked towards the ocean: first Portugal and Spain, then the Low Countries, Britain, France. The Atlantic, rather than antiquity's "middle sea", was now Europe's *mare nostrum*, and would remain so for half a millennium.

4

Thus other Europes formed, in the period from the sixteenth and to the twentieth centuries, outside what is geographically defined as the European continent (or subcontinent) – Europes which partly replicated the political and cultural characteristics of the countries that had presided over their foundation: the Latin Europe of the *conquistadores*, who had plundered the riches of South America, exterminating or enslaving the indigenous populations; the Europe of Dutch, French and English colonists, often a refuge for persecuted religious minorities; and later Austral Europe, born from the descendants of transported Britons. While Alexander VI's bull had favoured the partition of the South American continent between the Portuguese and the Spanish, North America was for two centuries a theatre of struggle between France and Britain, whose conflicts were exported on to American soil. The revolution of the British colonies did not, however, constitute a break with the mother country: although North American writers vied with another in proclaiming the moral superiority of the United States over old Europe, providing an ideological platform for isolationist politics, Anglo-Saxon solidarity proved crucial in the two world wars of the twentieth century, and again during the "Cold War".

The relationship between Europe and the two empires which arose on its eastern boundaries in the middle of the last millennium took a very different course. In the seventeenth century, with the reforms introduced by Peter the Great, Russia began a process of modernisation, inspired by European models. But this process was far from linear, nor did it leave a lasting mark on the social structure of the country, where landed property, the dominance of court aristocracy, and serfdom survived until the end of the nineteenth century. Although the Russian empire joined in the game of the great European powers, participating in the eighteenth-century wars of succession and making significant territorial gains as a result, setting itself up as the guarantor of the Holy Alliance, and acting in defence of the Balkan states against Turkish dominion, it had an ambivalent relationship – part imitation and part competition – with Europe. The Caesaropapist tradition was an obstacle to attempts at separating political and religious power, and at the same time represented the mainstay of Tsarist autocracy. The ideas of the Enlightenment, though welcomed and encouraged by Catherine II in particular, did not lead to the state being secularised, much less to society being reformed in a secular sense. There remained a clear distinction between the liberalising development of political regimes in the west and Tsarist autocracy; and the Soviet revolution developed, under Stalin, into a modernised form of despotically exercised absolute power.

Even more alien to the European world, and particularly to its culture, was the Ottoman Empire, which reached its widest extent in the sixteenth and seventeenth centuries, completing the conquest of the Balkan peninsula, subjugating most of Hungary, advancing in the Near East as far as Baghdad and the Persian Gulf, and asserting its dominion over the African coasts of the Mediterranean as far as Algeria. Only Vienna and the Habsburgs held out against Suleiman's attacks and the later siege of 1683; and the failure of this attempt played a significant part in strengthening the Habsburgs and the role they would have, until after the time of Napoleon, on the European political scene. After that, the offensive impetus of the Ottoman Empire diminished, partly because of the inferiority of its military technology, and eighteenth-century attempts at modernisation came to nothing. The conflict between the Sublime Porte and the claims to autonomy of the Balkan peoples, who had been granted religious and, to some extent, administrative autonomy, compelled the Ottoman Empire to take a defensive attitude, particularly in the face of the interventionist policies of the more powerful Russian Empire.

Both empires extended far beyond Europe in geographical terms. The Asiatic territory of the Russian empire was larger in extent than that of Europe – and this would be true of the Soviet Union too. Far from being the boundary between two worlds, the chain of the Urals constituted only an internal line of separation between one part of the empire that had already been colonised and another part that was still being colonised. As for the Ottoman empire, the sum of its Asian and African territories was significantly larger, even after the conquest of the Balkans, than that of the European countries it had subjugated. Both empires, it is true, joined in the game of the European powers, deriving advantages from it in terms of alliances and an increase in the extent of their dominions. But their culture was in the one case that of "Holy Russia", linked to the Byzantine heritage and the exaltation of the "third Rome", in the other that of a religion extraneous and hostile to the Christian tradition which revived the policy of conversion and subjection adopted by the Arab invaders a millennium earlier. The modernisation of the Russian empire was linked to the assertion of an autochthonous culture distinct from that of Europe and inspired rather by the heritage of Byzantium, while the reform of the Ottoman empire came up against the insurmountable resistance of traditional religious elites.

Nor can the situation be said to have changed significantly in the twentieth century. After 1917 the new Soviet state was increasingly hostile to "capitalist" European regimes, even more than to the expansion of Nazi Germany, drawing territorial advantage from it – for example in Poland – as the Russian empire had done before it, and surrounding itself with a circle of satellite countries after 1945. The dream of a worldwide revolution of the proletariat gave way to the concept of socialism "in one country", reminiscent of the nationalism of Tsarist Russia. The Orthodox religious tradition was suffocated, but also, during the war, revived as ideological support to resistance against the German invader. More effective were the attempts at European-style modernisation in Kemalist Turkey, which created a secular state, rejecting the Islamic tradition; but almost a century later the traditional base has re-emerged, and with it the aspiration to found state legislation on holy law. Like Russian despotism, religious integralism is a legacy of Byzantine Caesaropapism, and it is still a mark of the deep divide between Europeanised Turkey and traditional Turkey, and between Turkey and the European world.

5

Thus far we have considered Europe's external boundaries and the changes they have undergone through the centuries; but there are also other boundaries within Europe. These, of course, are the more or less permanent boundaries between kingdoms, principates and states, which have changed over time, leading to the creation or disappearance of political entities, and changes in their territories and populations. These, however, are not the boundaries that concern us here. Nor do the ethnic and religious boundaries, partly resulting from successive waves of migration from the east and north, which gave rise to what have been called the Romano-barbarian kingdoms, seem particularly important. But there are others which do seem more significant.

The first boundary, which already presupposes the expansion of the original Carolingian nucleus and the formation of national (or at least multiregional) kingdoms in the European west, is the one that derives from the distinction between the area where urban development took place at the beginning of the second millennium and the surrounding areas, where urbanisation and economic development are later phenomena. The area of early urban development runs from south to north – from central and northern Italy to Flanders, along the Rhine valley, continuing into south-eastern England and, with the Hanseatic League, along the Baltic coast. Its basis was trade and artisanal work carried on within the city walls, supported by guilds which guaranteed the quality of goods and the training of workers. The main trading posts were the maritime cities and the depots they established in foreign ports, and the great annual fairs in Champagne and Lyon. This region developed trade with the eastern Mediterranean, where the "Silk Road" began, and with the Rus' of Moscow and Kiev, and later with the new countries on the other side of the ocean; this region produced the financial resources that principates and states needed in order to fight their wars; this region, and especially England, would a few centuries later be the birthplace of industrialisation. Even in the twentieth century, after the Second World War, it was the states of this region that provided the impetus for the formation of the CECA, the European Coal and Steel Community. And for half a century France, Germany and Italy formed the central core of what is today the European Union.

Economic phenomena and religious phenomena, as Max Weber pointed out, are intimately linked, and that is particularly true of European history. Another internal boundary, indeed a split, was created by the Protestant Reformation and the division of Europe into two opposing camps, which led to a series of civil wars based on religious motivations. The centuries of the Middle Ages, too, had known different forms of Christian faith, conflicts between supporters of the "creed" laid down at Nicea and those of the Arian heresy; but those conflicts had usually been resolved by the sovereigns of invading barbarian peoples converting to Roman Catholicism, and their peoples following their example. By this means the papacy had evangelised those populations; it had penetrated into the British Isles under Boniface, and had led the Crusades, while the Slavic world, gravitating towards Byzantium, had adopted the "orthodox" version of the Christian faith. With the Reformation, however, the split appeared within individual countries: Germany was divided between Catholic and Lutheran princes, and in the Swiss cantons reformers and reformed churches flourished in conflict with one another, while in France a strong Huguenot party challenged the sovereign power. It would be more than a century before, with the Peace of Westphalia, the map of religious confessions was stabilised, on the basis of the principle of the sovereign's choice and his people's obedience to that choice. France emerged from the war of religion still (at least nominally) Catholic; and in Italy and Spain Counter-Reformation Catholicism prevailed over the Protestant sympathies of some intellectual minorities, which were repressed by the Inquisition; Catholicism also prevailed in distant Poland; Germany remained divided between two camps, but peace was guaranteed by the princes' will; Lutheranism became the state church in Scandinavia; sects and small churches that called for more radical reform were persecuted, and their followers forced to migrate to the North American colonies. England had chosen a path of its own, that of a national church which preserved the Catholic doctrinal framework, but under the direct government of the sovereign, no longer that of the papacy.

A third boundary is that between countries where monarchic power had emerged during the Middle Ages, later giving rise, in the seventeenth and eighteenth centuries, to a national state, and those where the presence of powers with universal claims had prevented the development of monarchic rule. In the east and west monarchies had succeeded in defeating the nobility of feudal origin, or at least in incorporating it into their dominions, but in the central area of the European continent, from Prussia to the Italian peninsula, the process of centralisation had encountered a lasting obstacle in the form of the Habsburg empire and the papacy, indeed most often in an alliance between them. When, after the French revolution, the convergence between state and nation was presented as the main natural objective of politics, and each nationality – no matter how real or "invented" – claimed its own autonomy, the new emerging states overthrew the order established after the fall of Napoleon; a new empire arose in the heart of the continent, and the Italian peninsula was unified politically after centuries of frustrated aspirations. The division between old and new nation states was deepened by the fact that, while the former had been able to found colonies in other continents, the latter had no territories into which they could expand, except on European soil. Whereas the French revolution had proclaimed the "sacred" nature of the nation under arms, the new nation states practised an aggressive policy in order to acquire that *Lebensraum* which they considered their right: not being able to find it in Africa or Asia, they sought it in the heart of Europe, with consequences that are well known to us.

These (and other) boundaries which characterise European history through the centuries have now lost much of their importance. National identities have faded, and religious allegiance too seems a weak bond in a secularised society. If any dividing lines do exist in late twentieth-century Europe, they are traceable rather to differing outcomes of the implementation of the welfare state, with the guarantees that this has offered, and continues to offer, to its citizens. Much of the continent – central and northern Europe, including France – has succeeded in balancing the support given to individuals with a fiscal policy that has made it possible to redistribute income among the various layers of society. In Mediterranean Europe, however, the weakness of the state structure, added to the resistance of the wealthier classes, has prevented this, and continues to do so. In the east, from Poland to the Balkan peninsula, the welfare state is still a mirage, and the economic level makes it impossible even today to adopt effective policies of redistribution. In this sense it is possible to speak of different Europes; but the boundaries between one and the other have become fluid, and the European world today is like a large, internally unbalanced market, where many firms migrate towards the eastern countries, while workers, particularly qualified ones, aspire to move to the centre and north.

Not only the internal boundaries but also those with the surrounding world have been increasingly relativised. While Europe's relationship with Russia and Turkey seems one of extraneity in some respects and possible convergence in others, the seas have acquired a new role – on the one hand as a meeting place, on the other as a physical, political and cultural frontier. This role, however, has developed in a different, indeed antithetical manner in the cases of the Atlantic and the Mediterranean. In the first half of the last century, from the "Wilson doctrine" to the Marshall Plan, ties between the two shores of the Atlantic strengthened, and Anglo-Saxon solidarity extended to the western part of the continent. The defence of liberal democracy and of an economy based on free trade, values which were threatened first by Hitlerian Germany and later by the Soviet Union, seemed to have made these ties irreversible. Indeed the Atlantic Pact, though its primary objectives were political and military, was for decades far more than a mere alliance between the powers on the two sides of the ocean. Today the situation is very different: the process of European unification has highlighted differences both in interests and in political attitudes. The Mediterranean, for its part, has again become, as it was in the seventh and eighth centuries, and again in the fifteenth and sixteenth, the boundary between Europe and an Islamic world torn between aspirations to renewal and integralist tendencies. The increasing relativisation of boundaries may have made them much more permeable than in the past, fomenting unstoppable streams of migration – after many centuries, Sicily has once again become the gateway to Europe – but it seems far from making this sea and its coasts a meeting place between civilisations.

Translated from the Italian by Jonathan Hunt

Bibliography

Abulafia, D 2011, *The Great Sea: a Human History of the Mediterranean*, Oxford University Press, Oxford.
Anderson, BR 1983, *Imagined Communities: reflections on the origin and spread of nationalism*, Verso, London.
Braudel, F 1966, *La Méditerranée et le monde méditerranéen à l'époque de Philippe II*, 2nd edn, Colin, Paris.
Brown, P 1995, *The Rise of Western Christendom*, Oxford University Press, Oxford.
Dawson, C 1956, *The Making of Europe. An Introduction to the History of European Unity*, Meridian, New York.
Febvre, L 1999, *L'Europe. Genèse d'une civilisation*, Perrin, Paris.
Fischer, J 1957, *Oriens-Occidens-Europa. Begriff und Gedanke „Europa" in der späten Antike und im Frühen Mittelalter*, Steiner, Wiesbaden.
Galasso, G 2001, *Storia d'Europa*, Bari, Roma.
Geary, PJ 2002, *The Myth of Nations. The Medieval Origins of Europe*, Princeton University Press, Princeton.
Groh, D 1961, *Russland und das Selbstverständnis Europas. Ein Beitrag zur europäischen Geistesgeschichte*, H. Luchterhand, Neuwied.
Lewis, B 1993, *Islam and the West*, Oxford University Press, New York.
Osterhammel, J 1998, *Die Entzauberung Asiens. Europa und die asiatischen Reichen im 18. Jahrhundert*, C.H. Beck, München.
Pirenne, H 1937, *Mahomet et Charlemagne*, Alcan & Nouvelle Société d'éditions, Paris-Bruxelles.
Pomian, K 1990, *L'Europe et ses nations*, Gallimard, Paris.
Rossi, P 2007, *L'identità dell'Europa*, Il Mulino, Bologna.
Tilly, C 1975, *The Formation of National States in Western Europe*, Princeton University Press, Princeton.
Weber, M 1923, *Wirtschaftsgeschichte. Abriß der universalen Sozial- und Wirtschaftsgeschichte*, Duncker & Humblot, München.

Arnaldo Marcone
Il Mediterraneo da "mare nostrum" a frontiera tra civiltà

1 Il mare e l'impero

Roma arrivò a conquistare il predominio sul Mediterraneo in un arco di tempo sorprendentemente limitato. La vittoriosa guerra con Cartagine nella seconda metà del III secolo a.C. le garantì il controllo del Tirreno centrale con l'acquisizione di Sicilia, Sardegna e Corsica. Nello stesso tempo anche l'Adriatico divenne oggetto dell'interesse di Roma a espandere il proprio dominio: le dinamiche politiche si correlano e si intrecciano sempre più strettamente con quelle economiche. All'inizio del II secolo Roma era ormai diventata una grande potenza mediterranea, ponendosi sullo stesso piano dei regni ellenistici più potenti – Egitto, Siria e Macedonia. Ebbe allora inizio una lunga serie di conflitti alla fine dei quali, nell'arco di pochi decenni, Roma avrebbe assunto un controllo territoriale senza precedenti nell'antichità. Già nel 146 a.C., con la distruzione di Cartagine, il suo predominio sul Mediterraneo poteva dirsi acquisito. Esso fu completato nei decenni successivi con le guerre vittoriose contro Giugurta nell'Africa nord-occidentale e contro Mitridate in Asia minore; infine anche l'Egitto, rimasto almeno formalmente indipendente, fu nel 30 a.C. incorporato nell'impero.

L'unificazione del Mediterraneo da parte di Roma determinò la nascita di un impero che, se politicamente (e militarmente) aveva come base la potenza romana, era però culturalmente e anche linguisticamente greco-romano. Fin dall'epoca della seconda guerra punica, venuta a contatto con il mondo greco per il tramite delle colonie fondate nell'Italia meridionale e in Sicilia, la cultura romana aveva trovato in esso i propri modelli: la città di contadini – fondata, secondo la tradizione, dai "gemelli" allattati dalla lupa – cominciò ad arricchirsi di edifici templari costruiti sull'esempio delle metropoli della Magna Grecia. Lo stesso *pantheon* romano riproduceva del resto, mutando i nomi delle divinità, quello greco. Già nel corso del III secolo a.C., e in misura crescente in quello successivo, si sviluppò una letteratura latina di stampo ellenizzante, ed ebbe inizio, non senza forti resistenze, l'importazione della filosofia greca.

L'impero fondato da Augusto si esprimeva indifferentemente nelle due lingue divenute dominanti, il greco e il latino. Bilingue, redatto in greco e in latino, è anche il testo ufficiale più famoso, le *Res Gestae* di Augusto. E nel quadro di tale "condominio" culturale la posizione dei Greci, i quali con Alessandro avevano imposto la propria lingua in un'area vastissima, si mantenne culturalmente egemonica. Lo stesso "mito" fondativo di Roma si collegava a un evento della storia greca arcaica, la guerra di Troia, anche se l'origine della stirpe romana era indicata non in una città ellenica, bensì nella città antagonista della Grecia. Ai Romani i Greci avevano fornito i modelli politico-costituzionali e la relativa riflessione teorica. E a Roma la filosofia e la medicina continuarono a essere insegnate in greco: ancora l'imperatore Marco Aurelio annoterà i suoi pensieri in greco, non già in latino. La frontiera linguistica passava per il territorio dell'Illirico: di qui si parlava il latino, di là il greco.

Proprio dal controllo sul Mediterraneo Roma sviluppò una concezione ecumenica del proprio impero. Già Cicerone aveva dichiarato che nessun senatore poteva ormai permettersi d'ignorare la conformazione e la consistenza dei territori dell'impero e progetterà – avendo ascoltato Posidonio a Rodi – un'opera geografica, che però non realizzerà mai. Una sintetica presentazione della concezione ecumenica dell'impero romano ci è stata però fornita da Augusto nelle *Res Gestae*, che costituiscono al tempo stesso un testamento politico e un resoconto puntuale del suo operato. Colpisce in esso il rilievo dato alla definizione di uno spazio geografico ormai concluso rispetto al quale Roma si trova a detenere un dominio assoluto e che deve governare. Le *Res Gestae* rappresentano la legittimazione di questa vocazione, come emerge già nella formula di apertura in cui si può leggere una sintesi di una filosofia imperialistica: "gli atti con cui (Augusto) sottomise il mondo al dominio del popolo romano". In due capitoli specifici (il 26 e il 27) vengono ricordati, secondo un ordine logico e geografico, la pacificazione delle province confinanti (Gallia e Germania), il controllo strategico delle regioni alpine, le spedizioni navali nell'Oceano settentrionale o quelle terrestri in Etiopia e in Arabia; e inoltre le annessioni territoriali o i protettorati realizzati in Oriente, i rapporti diplomatici con nemici tradizionali come i Parti, i Pannoni e i Daci; infine le legazioni di popoli lontani come gli Indiani; quindi il popolamento delle diverse regioni attraverso lo stabilimento di colonie di veterani.

La pace imperiale celebrata da Augusto pose in essere le condizioni indispensabili di una crescita economica complessiva, anche se accertare il carattere e le dimensioni di questa crescita appare oggi problematico. In ogni modo, già al tempo di Cesare e di Augusto la popolazione di Roma, se non toccò il milione di abitanti, vi si accostava certamente, ponendo gravissimi problemi di sostentamento di una plebe urbana che era stata coinvolta nelle guerre civili tra Mario e Silla, e poi in quelle dei due triumvirati. In epoca imperiale questo sviluppo proseguì, e così crebbe pure la necessità di un regolare approvvigionamento. Esso fu reso possibile dal trasferimento di risorse provenienti dalle campagne verso la capitale e verso le altre grandi città dell'impero, alle quali occorreva assicurare le risorse necessarie – come del resto occorreva assicurare quelle per l'esercito, in larga misura schierato lungo frontiere e in regioni lontane tra loro, ma lontane anche dai luoghi di produzione dei cereali e delle altre derrate alimentari. La mobilitazione e la distribuzione delle risorse è un fattore decisivo per il successo del governo romano: la questione era saperle indirizzare e gestire tempestivamente là dove potevano realmente servire. Uno degli esiti più importanti di questo sforzo organizzativo fu la crescente monetarizzazione dell'economia, alla quale si accompagnò lo sviluppo di regole comuni di diritto commerciale e di comuni sistemi metrologici.

L'impero offrì all'economia una infrastruttura di collegamenti e di trasporti creata, nel corso dei secoli, dall'amministrazione pubblica. Questa infrastruttura era rappresentata nella penisola italiana dalla rete delle vie consolari che portavano persone e merci alla capitale, e che assicuravano contemporaneamente la trasmissione degli ordini e il mantenimento delle legioni al di là delle Alpi. Fuori dei confini della penisola – dove le strade consolari non esistevano ancora – e ovviamente correlata con tale rete, vi erano le rotte marine che collegavano il centro dell'impero con le periferie. Le loro direttrici principali interessavano la parte occidentale e quella orientale dell'impero, nonché le coste settentrionali dell'Africa. Le grandi navi onerarie trasportavano soprattutto cereali dalla Sicilia e dall'Africa settentrionale e olio dalla Spagna meridionale. Ma l'instradamento di queste merci seguiva anche il dislocamento delle legioni nelle varie aree del Mediterraneo. E presto iniziò il commercio di spezie e di prodotti di lusso che arrivavano ad Alessandria dall'Oriente e di qui erano avviati per mare verso Roma. Il rapido intensificarsi di queste relazioni commerciali, in primo luogo con l'Africa settentrionale e quindi con tutto il Mediterraneo implicò l'ampliamento delle strutture portuali in Italia e anche la creazione di nuove strutture. Al porto di Ostia si affiancò nel II secolo a.C. quello di Pozzuoli nel golfo di Napoli e quindi, nella prima età imperiale, quello di Porto, nei pressi della foce del Tevere cui era collegato mediante un canale.

Nei secoli della costruzione dell'impero i Romani lasciarono a mercanti specializzati (in primo luogo greci e siriaci, eredi degli antichi Fenici) le attività propriamente commerciali, e si concentrarono sull'esportazione del loro modello di città, della legislazione e dell'amministrazione, ma anche dello stile di vita cittadino. In un certo senso si può dire che Roma abbia fondato sempre la stessa città, in quanto riprodusse in ogni angolo dell'impero la medesima tipologia urbana. Sulle coste, ma anche all'interno delle province, nacquero città nuove, o mutarono fisionomia altre preesistenti, con caratteristiche che ripetevano quelle della stessa Roma: ne sono esempi significativi Cartagine, portata a nuova vita dopo che fu elevata da Augusto al rango di capitale della provincia dell'Africa proconsolare, e Nicopoli in Epiro, la città voluta da Augusto per celebrare la vittoria di Azio del 31 a.C. Un discorso analogo vale per Nîmes e Béziers nella Gallia Narbonense, per Marsiglia e per molte altre città ancora. Queste città rimanevano organismi di autogoverno con un loro mercato, che facevano circolare il *surplus* della produzione, ma soprattutto con un'aristocrazia impegnata ad arricchire la città con opere pubbliche che testimoniavano della sua importanza e del suo livello di vita.

In presenza di un organismo politico unitario, capace di sviluppare forme avanzate di integrazione economica e di razionalizzazione del sistema tributario – non si deve sottovalutare l'importanza dei censimenti – poterono così instaurarsi, anche per esigenze fiscali, rapporti commerciali a lunga distanza. Indubbiamente alcuni prodotti venivano scambiati direttamente tra produttori e consumatori sul mercato locale, oppure arrivavano direttamente dal luogo di produzione a quello di consumo. Ma ciò avveniva nel quadro, almeno potenziale, di un mercato complesso ed esteso che abbracciava l'intera area mediterranea, e nel quale i centri urbani avevano un ruolo decisivo. Probabilmente non è casuale che un provvedimento tanto discusso dalla storiografia moderna, vale a dire la concessione da parte di Caracalla della cittadinanza romana a tutti o quasi gli abitanti dell'Impero – la cosiddetta *constitutio Antoniniana* del 212 o 213 d.C. – non abbia trovato eco in quella antica, fatto salvo uno scarno passo di Cassio Dione. Agli occhi dei contemporanei esso appariva probabilmente come l'esito scontato di un processo plurisecolare, come il semplice riconoscimento di una realtà di fatto.

Del resto, già verso la metà del I secolo d.C. Seneca – richiamandosi a riflessioni che già erano state, tra gli altri, di Aristotele, di Eratostene, di Posidonio e infine di Strabone – pensava al mare che divide la Spagna dall'India come a un tratto di mare che poteva essere attraversato da una nave addirittura in pochissimi giorni. Nella premessa alle *Naturales Questiones* egli si chiedeva: "quanto è grande la distanza tra le estreme coste della Spagna e gli Indiani? uno spazio di pochissimi giorni, se un vento favorevole sospinge la nave". Dunque il Mediterraneo era, ai suoi occhi, luogo propizio per il rapido transito di uomini e di merci. E nel coro della *Medea* sempre Seneca evocava la spedizione alla ricerca del vello d'oro, e quindi gli esiti benefici della navigazione che hanno reso accessibile il mondo. Un secolo dopo, nell'orazione celebrativa di Roma, Elio Aristide presenterà il Mediterraneo come disteso intorno a Roma, definita come "il grande emporio del mondo, il mercato di tutti i prodotti della terra". A quell'epoca il Mediterraneo era veramente diventato il *mare nostrum* dell'impero, e Roma ne costituiva il centro, assicurando l'unità delle sue sponde.

2 La minaccia ai confini e gli inizi della crisi

L'esistenza di questo complesso organismo politico e della sua economia era assicurata da confini lontani, i quali erano il risultato dell'espansione militare del I secolo a.C. e delle colonie cui questa aveva dato luogo. Dopo la distruzione di Cartagine e l'assorbimento delle colonie puniche fondate sulla costa africana e nella penisola iberica le rive meridionali del Mediterraneo non costituivano più un problema militare di rilievo: l'impero si estendeva verso il Medio Atlante, fin nel cuore del Marocco, dove era stata fondata una città come Volubilis (nei pressi dell'odierna Meknès). Le catene montane e, al di là di queste, la vastità del deserto offrivano un retroterra sicuro anche alla Libia, che non richiedeva quindi una particolare protezione. In quanto alla Nubia, essa costituiva non un pericolo ma piuttosto un'area di collegamento con le rotte carovaniere dell'Africa sub-sahariana e con le correnti di traffico dell'Oceano Indiano. Ben diversa era la situazione sul continente europeo, soprattutto nella sua parte occidentale. Cesare aveva conquistato l'intera Gallia sottomettendo i Celti, in parte anche sterminandoli, e si era poi spinto fino in Britannia. In entrambe le regioni si avviò, nei secoli dell'impero, un processo di crescente romanizzazione che mise capo alla fondazione di centri urbani fiorenti anche a grande distanza dal Mediterraneo. Ma questo processo ebbe anche dei limiti. Mentre sulle rive occidentali del Mar Nero – antica area di colonizzazione greca – Roma sottomise i Geti e incluse nel proprio impero la Dacia, il tentativo di Augusto di penetrare in Germania andò incontro a un clamoroso insuccesso. Nel 9 d.C. Arminio sterminò, nella selva di Teutoburgo, le legioni comandate da Publio Quintilio Varo; e nessuno degli imperatori successivi ebbe il coraggio di ripetere l'impresa fallita.

Dopo di allora i confini settentrionali dell'impero si stabilizzarono lungo la linea segnata da due grandi fiumi, il Reno a ovest e il Danubio a sud-est, con qualche parziale ma limitato sconfinamento. Non mancarono, nei primi due secoli dell'impero, spedizioni di carattere sia difensivo che offensivo, soprattutto ai confini tra la Gallia e la Germania, oppure nelle regioni transalpine della Rezia e della Pannonia; parimenti, la conquista della Britannia non fu mai completata, ma si arresterà al Vallo di Adriano, che separava l'Inghilterra dalla Scozia. Anche l'Oriente fu teatro di ribellioni e di conflitti, come la rivolta della Giudea conclusa con la distruzione di Gerusalemme da parte dell'imperatore Tito e le due sanguinose guerre contro i Parti, la prima sotto Traiano e la seconda sotto Settimio Severo. Alla fine, però, un altro fiume, l'Eufrate, servì a delimitare l'area di influenza romana e ad assicurare condizioni di pace durevoli nelle regioni a ovest del suo corso. In Occidente come in Oriente l'impero si impegnò nello sforzo di fortificare le frontiere, costruendo un sistema di strade a scopo militare e creando un'area (il *limes*) che consentisse una difesa elastica e che favoriva, al tempo stesso, gli scambi di prodotti con le popolazioni confinanti. Alle legioni, formate soprattutto di elementi italici, si affiancarono corpi ausiliari reclutati nelle province i quali le coadiuvavano nella sorveglianza delle frontiere.

In questo modo il processo di urbanizzazione non soltanto si estese, ma assunse una fisionomia parzialmente nuova. Fin allora le grandi città del mondo antico erano state erano state tutte città costiere o prossime al mare – così la stessa Roma, legata a Ostia per via fluviale; ora sorgevano invece nuove città, spesso collocate lungo grandi fiumi, ma di natura prettamente continentale. Ciò comportava un lento ma sostanziale cambiamento della natura stessa dell'impero: alla fine del II secolo d.C. esso non era più un organismo politico gravitante in modo esclusivo sul Mediterraneo, ma – ferma restando la funzione economica di quest'ultimo – si era trasformato in un impero mediterraneo/continentale, che aveva pure altri centri di gravità, tutti al di là delle Alpi oppure, in Oriente, lontani dal mare.

La potenza militare di Roma era riuscita a impedire che questa trasformazione mettesse in crisi la struttura dell'impero – e ciò anche per il susseguirsi, dopo il governo della *gens* Giulio-Claudia, di due altre dinastie imperiali che permisero la pacifica trasmissione del potere, quella Flavia nella seconda metà del I secolo e quella Antonina nei primi decenni del successivo. Ma l'edificio politico creato da Augusto, e varie volte riformato nel corso del tempo, pagò ad essa un prezzo: quello dell'ingerenza crescente delle legioni nell'elezione degli imperatori, quale si era manifestato per la prima volta già nel 69, alla morte di Nerone. Gli eserciti che difendevano le province avevano come destinatari della loro fedeltà i propri generali, che si trasformarono perciò in figure carismatiche; e la competizione per la dignità imperiale sfociò spesso in guerre civili, anche se spesso di breve durata. Il potere centrale, con il senato e la classe senatoria esautorati, non era in grado di controllare un impero che si era esteso e che, estendendosi, stava cambiando la propria natura. E le legioni, coinvolte in queste lotte, furono sempre meno impegnate nel compito di difesa delle frontiere.

Alla crisi politica si accompagnò la crisi demografica, che ebbe inizio con la cosiddetta "peste antonina" (probabilmente un'epidemia di vaiolo), scoppiata verso il 170/180 d.C., nella seconda parte del regno di Marco Aurelio. La diminuzione della popolazione ebbe conseguenze diverse nelle varie regioni; ma provocò una generale riduzione della manodopera disponibile e, di conseguenza, un aumento della sua capacità contrattuale. Ciò suscitò nei proprietari la ricerca di forme di costrizione extra-economica per trattenere al lavoro gli agricoltori rimasti. La piccola proprietà contadina, che aveva fornito in passato anche le leve dell'esercito, lasciò sempre più posto al latifondo e ai vincoli che esso comportava: le varie tipologie di lavoro non libero furono unificate in una sola categoria, quella dei coloni legati alla terra. Le tensioni sociali, che pur non erano mancate nei primi due secoli dell'impero (ma già in età repubblicana), diventarono sempre più forti, determinando un calo della produzione e degli scambi commerciali, e quindi anche un decremento delle entrate fiscali. Ciò avvenne in coincidenza con la crescente burocratizzazione della "macchina" statale e con l'aumento dei costi di mantenimento delle legioni che dovevano difendere le frontiere.

Anche la geografia economica dell'impero andò radicalmente cambiando; e ciò riguardò in primo luogo la situazione della penisola italiana. Nei secoli precedenti le sue regioni meridionali avevano avuto, tutto sommato, un ruolo di secondo piano nel rifornimento alimentare di Roma. A partire dal IV secolo, invece, l'Italia meridionale diventerà un'area di interesse primario perché su di essa ricadeva ora, in prima istanza, il compito di provvedere al rifornimento alimentare della città. Anche la Sicilia fu inserita tra le regioni dette "suburbicarie", sulle quali gravava in prima istanza questo onere, il che implicava la creazione di un rapporto istituzionale con le esigenze della capitale. L'instabilità del controllo imperiale sull'Africa valorizzava l'importanza di quest'isola come produttrice di grano. Ciò spiega l'interesse che per la Sicilia manifestarono i grandi proprietari, i gestori del patrimonio imperiale e i rappresentanti del potere centrale. Ma così iniziava anche il declino della circolazione di uomini e di merci nel Mediterraneo.

La minaccia ai confini si andava intanto aggravando rapidamente. Soprattutto dopo il 235, quando si estinse la dinastia dei Severi, la frontiera che separava la Gallia e le altre province transalpine dalle popolazioni germaniche divenne sempre più permeabile: all'invasione degli Alemanni si susseguirono quelle di Vandali, di Svevi, di Franchi, di Goti, di Sassoni, e via dicendo. L'intera parte orientale dell'Europa era in movimento sotto la spinta di altri popoli più lontani, i quali premevano alle spalle degli invasori, dando luogo a una *Völkerwanderung* globale che coinvolgeva gran parte del continente eurasiatico. Né la situazione nell'area sud-orientale era più rassicurante: nel 227 il regno partico soccombette ai Persiani Sasanidi i quali avevano adottato come religione ufficiale lo Zoroastrismo, e l'impero si trovò a dover affrontare un avversario ben più forte del precedente. Alla fine del III secolo Diocleziano corse ai ripari riorganizzando la struttura statale sulla base di una tetrarchia che comprendeva due "Augusti" e altrettanti "Cesari", i quali dovevano governare separatamente la parte orientale e quella occidentale dell'impero. A partire da allora il Mediterraneo cominciò a perdere la propria funzione strategica, e insieme a questa anche la propria unità.

3 Oriente e Occidente: due destini separati

La crisi che mise a dura prova la sopravvivenza stessa dell'impero nel corso del III secolo sembrò superata grazie alla capacità riformatrice di Diocleziano e poi di Costantino. Tuttavia la riorganizzazione della struttura statale produsse esiti che avrebbero avuto conseguenze rilevanti sulla stessa unità del Mediterraneo. In primo luogo Roma cessò di essere il luogo di residenza dell'imperatore e si crearono più capitali che furono spostate altrove, secondo una logica di crescente distinzione tra Oriente e Occidente. Veniva meno anche la posizione privilegiata dell'Italia, dal punto di vista fiscale, rispetto alle altre province. Con Costantino si realizzò un evento fondamentale: la creazione nel 330 di una nuova capitale sul Bosforo che da lui prese nome, Costantinopoli. Gran parte del grano egiziano fu indirizzato verso questa città, e quindi i rifornimenti granari di Roma dipesero sempre più dall'Africa e dalla Sicilia.

La fondazione di Costantinopoli avviò un processo di differenziazione anche culturale tra la parte orientale dell'impero, di lingua prevalentemente greca, e quella occidentale, dove prevaleva invece la lingua latina. Il fatto che la nuova capitale esercitasse in modo continuativo il ruolo di città egemone sulla parte orientale dell'impero conferì all'apparato di governo che vi operava un carattere marcatamente distintivo rispetto a quello delle *regiae urbes* in Occidente. Non si trattò soltanto della creazione di un nuovo ceto dirigente socialmente più aperto, ma soprattutto del fatto che la costante presenza dell'imperatore, a partire dal regno di Arcadio, assicurò alla città un ruolo politico esclusivo rispetto agli altri centri che componevano il pur ricco mosaico dell'urbanesimo dell'Oriente mediterraneo. Alessandria, Antiochia, Berito, Gaza, Cesarea in Palestina, Edessa, Efeso, Atene, Tessalonica mantenevano il loro prestigioso apparato monumentale e una vita intellettuale intensa, a volte anche più fervida di quella della capitale; ma a Costantinopoli si prendevano le decisioni che contavano davvero. Inoltre, il servizio nel palazzo imperiale portò, tra la fine del IV e il V secolo, alla nascita di un ceto di dignitari che acquisì una condizione sociale sempre più elevata in virtù non della propria origine, ma semplicemente della familiarità con il sovrano.

Questa peculiarità di Costantinopoli come centro di potere fu importante anche nel rapporto tra i barbari e l'impero all'indomani della morte nel 395 di Teodosio I, che di fatto attribuì ai figli Onorio e Arcadio il governo rispettivamente dell'Occidente e dell'Oriente. La possibilità che l'impero rimanesse unito, per quanto diviso nelle sedi di governo, si sarebbe rivelata rapidamente irrealistica. Nel giro di pochi decenni le due parti dell'Impero conobbero uno sviluppo politico e sociale molto diverso, che contribuì ad allontanarle sempre di più l'una dall'altra.

Del resto, già all'epoca di Diocleziano e di Costantino la minaccia barbarica si poneva con urgenza assai maggiore in Occidente che non in Oriente. Lo sfondamento della frontiera renana da parte dei barbari nell'inverno 406-407 sembrò l'inizio della fine dell'Occidente romano. Il sacco di Roma del 410, da parte di Alarico, per quanto di breve durata e non particolarmente distruttivo, rappresentò un trauma terribile perché era la prima volta, dopo otto secoli, che Roma veniva, sia pure temporaneamente, conquistata dallo straniero. Ma mezzo secolo dopo il sacco alariciano, alla morte di Valentiniano III i Vandali di Genserico, dopo essersi impadroniti dell'Africa settentrionale, saccheggiarono Roma una seconda volta, e ben più brutalmente. Non soltanto la penisola italiana, ma tutta l'area circostante il Tirreno fu investita dalle armate dei popoli barbari. Alla fine del V secolo la sua carta geografica si presentava ormai del tutto mutata. I Visigoti si erano impadroniti dell'Aquitania e di qui erano transitati in Spagna, spingendo i Vandali nell'Africa nord-occidentale, nelle regioni che avevano fatto parte dell'antico dominio punico; i Franchi e i Burgundi erano penetrati nella Gallia, dove si insedieranno stabilmente dando luogo a due centri di aggregazione politica; i Goti dell'est, cioè gli Ostrogoti, avevano occupato gran parte dell'Italia centro-settentrionale, e ad essi faranno più tardi seguito, nel 568, i Longobardi. I regni che essi fondarono furono però relativamente poco distruttivi di quel che rimaneva dell'ordinamento romano e della struttura sociale su cui questo si reggeva. Ciò vale specialmente per il regno goto instaurato in Italia tra la fine del V e l'inizio del VI secolo, che rappresentò un tentativo – seppure non riuscito – di coesistenza e di collaborazione tra gli invasori e la burocrazia di origine romana.

Nella parte orientale dell'impero, al contrario, il V secolo rappresentò tutto sommato un'età di non devastante conflittualità militare. La guerra contro i grandi nemici dell'impero d'Oriente, i Sasanidi, si accese soltanto per brevissimi periodi, nel 421-422 e nel 440. La Grecia, la Macedonia, la Tracia, perfino la parte meridionale della Dacia rimasero sotto il dominio imperiale; e così pure avvenne per Creta e Cipro, nonché per l'Egitto. Decisivo fu, a questo proposito, il controllo del mare da parte della flotta bizantina, il quale si estese al di là della parte orientale del Mediterraneo per comprendere le grandi isole tirreniche. Verso la metà del VI secolo, sotto il lungo regno di Giustiniano, Belisario sconfisse infatti i Vandali – l'unico tra i popoli barbari che disponesse di una flotta consistente – e riconquistò la Sicilia, cercando poi vanamente di sottrarre la penisola italiana al dominio dei Goti. La controffensiva bizantina dovette infatti arrestarsi di fronte alla resistenza delle nuove strutture politiche che si erano dati, o si stavano dando, i vari regni barbarici. La supremazia navale non riuscì a tradursi, come l'impero d'Oriente si proponeva, nella riconquista né dell'Italia né, tanto meno, della parte occidentale del Mediterraneo.

Anche l'impero d'Oriente, infatti, era ben lontano dall'essere uno stato "forte", capace di imporre un proprio sistema fiscale. È vero che per qualche decennio, fin verso la metà del V secolo, esso aveva finanziato in diverse occasioni le guerre in Occidente, ma proprio queste iniziative finirono per provocare uno squilibrio delle spese militari nel bilancio statale. Ancora nel VI secolo si registra, per altro, il mancato riconoscimento della nuova situazione politica da parte dei sovrani bizantini, i quali continuavano infatti a considerare l'unità politica del Mediterraneo come un elemento essenziale della stessa idea di impero. Il progetto di Giustiniano inteso a sottrarre l'Italia al dominio goto portò soltanto a un conflitto che sarebbe durato diciotto anni, senza conseguire lo scopo. Alla fine il risultato della "riconquista" dell'Occidente si limitò a una parte limitata della penisola italiana e a una parte ancor più ridotta della Spagna. Dopo la sconfitta dei Vandali la flotta bizantina rimase padrona dei mari; ma le regioni costiere erano definitivamente perdute anche per l'impero d'Oriente.

Nel corso dei secoli la burocrazia imperiale aveva sempre più perduto d'importanza, mentre era cresciuto il ruolo dei grandi proprietari che appaiono condividere responsabilità pubbliche con caratteristiche che rendono difficile distinguere le funzioni pubbliche da quelle private. D'altra parte i regni barbarici dell'Occidente non avevano più bisogno di forme di approvvigionamento sottoposte all'autorità statale, come era avvenuto per Roma e come richiedeva ancora la nuova capitale d'Oriente; anche la produzione agricola e quella artigianale subirono un netto declino. Erano venute meno le condizioni indispensabili per l'esistenza di un mercato sorretto dal commercio a lunga distanza di grandi quantità di prodotti, e l'economia si andava ormai localizzando. Quelli che sopravvivevano erano gli scambi a livello locale o regionale, nonché il limitato traffico di beni di lusso richiesti dall'aristocrazia militare dei nuovi regni. Il commercio internazionale si ridusse fino a cessare quasi del tutto nel secolo VIII, in netto contrasto con l'aumento di scambi che si andava registrando nel Mare del Nord.

Tra V e VI secolo il Mediterraneo aveva cessato per sempre di essere il *mare nostrum* dell'impero, anche perché quest'ultimo non esisteva più, o esisteva soltanto per la parte orientale. Politicamente esso era ormai spaccato in due; economicamente aveva perduto il ruolo che aveva avuto nell'antichità. Ci vorranno molti secoli – anzi, quasi mezzo millennio – prima che le navi delle città e dei regni dell'Occidente europeo ritornino a solcarlo, recando merci in Oriente ma soprattutto importandone, e trasportando le armate dei Crociati verso i luoghi santi della religione cristiana; ma allora la potenza di Costantinopoli era anch'essa al tramonto, e la flotta bizantina aveva da tempo perduto il controllo del mare.

4 Le sponde contrapposte

Un'altra e più profonda rottura si profilava all'orizzonte. Nella prima metà del VII secolo una nuova religione si affacciava sul Mediterraneo, in competizione tutt'altro che pacifica con la religione cristiana che era uscita vincitrice, tre secoli prima, dallo scontro con l'autorità imperiale. Tra il Cristianesimo e l'Islam vi erano tratti comuni tutt'altro che secondari. Entrambi poggiavano sulla fede in un unico Dio, anche se il monoteismo islamico si rivelò subito ben più radicale di quello cristiano; entrambi erano "religioni del Libro", si fondavano cioè su un testo sacro che si riteneva contenesse la parola stessa di Dio; entrambi si richiamavano a una medesima tradizione profetica, quella dei profeti dell'Antico Testamento – e l'Islam si spingeva fino ad annoverare Gesù nella serie dei profeti culminata in Maometto. Ma della comune origine ebraica essi avevano ereditato un elemento che li avrebbe resi nemici mortali: l'esclusivismo della propria fede, e quindi l'intolleranza verso la fede altrui.

I guerrieri arabi che si spinsero, dopo la morte di Maometto, alla conquista del mondo e alla conversione (o alla sottomissione) dei suoi abitanti erano combattenti per la fede, e sulla fede poggiava la loro organizzazione politica. La loro avanzata fu dirompente: sconfitto nel 634 l'imperatore Eraclio nei pressi di Gerusalemme, in pochi anni si impadronirono della Palestina e della Siria verso nord, dell'Egitto e delle coste libiche verso ovest. E nei decenni successivi si spinsero fino alla Mesopotamia e alla Persia, poi fino all'Asia centrale, ai confini con l'India e con la Cina; contemporaneamente conquistarono pure le coste occidentali dell'Africa. L'impero d'Oriente resistette, ma dopo aver perduto Cipro, Creta e le isole dell'Egeo fu sconfitto anche sul mare. In breve tempo gli Arabi avevano conquistato regioni strategicamente importanti sia per il gettito fiscale che per il potenziale di reclutamento, e avevano anche costruito una propria flotta in grado di respingere le iniziative della flotta bizantina.

Così il Mediterraneo orientale, per secoli solcato dalle flotte romane e poi da quella bizantina, passò gradualmente sotto il controllo arabo; o per lo meno ebbe termine il predominio bizantino sul mare. I nuovi invasori si impegnarono a creare una flotta in grado di competere con quella di Costantinopoli; e nelle nuovi basi navali nella Palestina vennero impiegati anche costruttori di navi provenienti dalla Persia e dall'Iraq. A questo scopo gli Arabi si avvalsero in larga misura della manodopera siriana ed egiziana (soprattutto dei Copti dell'Egitto), che fino ad alcuni anni prima avevano invece costruito navi e equipaggi per il loro nemico. La mancanza di illustrazioni preecedenti al XIV secolo non consente di avere informazioni sicure sulle caratteristiche delle prime navi di guerra arabe, ma è lecito presumere che i loro tentativi abbiano tratto ispirazione dalla preesistente tradizione marittima mediterranea. Data una nomenclatura nautica largamente comune, e i rapporti che intercorsero almeno sul terreno tencologico, le navi bizantine e quelle arabe condividevano molti aspetti anche per quanto riguarda la tattica e l'organizzazione generale delle flotte; le traduzioni dei manuali militari bizantini, per esempio, erano disponibili agli ammiragli arabi.

Dopo aver occupato Cipro nel 649 ed aver saccheggiato Rodi, Creta e la Sicilia, la giovane marina araba inflisse una sconfitta decisiva ai Bizantini condotti dall'imperatore Costante II in persona nella battaglia di Phoenix del 655. A partire dal califfato di Muawiyah (661–680) le incursioni degli Arabi si intensificarono, ed erano perfino in corso i preparativi per un grande assalto alla stessa Costantinopoli. Ma la superstite potenza marittima dell'impero riuscì a impedirne la caduta. Nel corso del primo assedio arabo di Costantinopoli (674-678) la flotta bizantina risultò infatti decisiva nel garantire la sopravvivenza dell'Impero: le flotte arabe furono sconfitte grazie all'impiego di una nuova e distruttiva arma segreta di nuova invenzione, il "fuoco greco". L'avanzata islamica in Asia minore e nell'Egeo fu arrestata, e tra i due imperi fu firmata una tregua di trent'anni. Ma la presenza araba era destinata a farsi sentire con crescente intensità aumentando le difficoltà delle relazioni tra l'impero e gli altri paesi che si affacciavano sul Mediterraneo. Nel 711, completato l'assoggettamento dell'Africa settentrionale, le armate arabe attraversarono lo stretto di Gibilterra e passarono per la prima volta sul continente europeo: nel giro di pochi anni quasi tutta la Spagna cadde sotto il controllo arabo, e vi rimarrà a lungo.

Il Mediterraneo era ormai spaccato in due, su una base non più longitudinale – come nel caso della separazione tra l'impero d'Oriente e quello di Occidente – ma latitudinale. A nord, sulle coste di quella che diventerà l'Europa, i regni di origine barbarica che avevano soppiantato il dominio romano cercavano di darsi una struttura organizzativa, fondata sulla collaborazione ma anche sulla rivalità tra il potere dei principi e dei loro feudatari e l'apparato di governo della Chiesa. Lo sforzo arabo di penetrare al di là dei Pirenei s'infranse contro la resistenza dei Franchi, vittoriosi nel 732 a Poitiers. In quanto alla penisola italiana, essa divenne un campo di battaglia non tanto tra le armate arabe e le milizie cristiane, quanto tra l'impero d'Oriente e i diversi popoli barbari che vi giunsero a ondate successive. Se alcune regioni e soprattutto le isole rimasero sotto il controllo più o meno stretto di Bisanzio, nel resto della penisola al dominio goto succedette quello longobardo, che s'insediò sia al centro della pianura padana sia tra la Campania e la Puglia; poi arrivarono i Franchi in soccorso del papato; infine, un paio di secoli dopo, la parte meridionale e la Sicilia caddero sotto il dominio di un popolo nuovo, i Normanni, gli "uomini del Nord". Il paese che era stato il centro dell'impero si era ormai trasformato in terreno di conquista. E quello che restava della sua antica centralità era il papato, costretto però a muoversi rincorrendo sempre nuove alleanze, in un ambiguo rapporto di forza con il suo protettore, l'impero franco del quale consacrerà la nascita nella notte di Natale dell'800.

Le sponde meridionali del Mediterraneo furono invece monopolio arabo. Ma, come il Mediterraneo aveva perduto il suo ruolo politicamente ed economicamente centrale, così l'Africa del Nord ormai arabizzata non ebbe una posizione prevalente nella politica del califfato islamico. In realtà, la sua occupazione – e, in generale, la spinta araba verso occidente – rappresentò soltanto una delle direzioni dell'espansione dell'Islam, e neppure la più importante. A differenza della cultura greco-romana, per la quale il Mediterraneo fu sempre il centro dell'*ecuméne*, la cultura araba ha avvertito la posizione della terra dell'Islam come mediana, quasi interposta, tra il Mediterraneo e l'Oceano indiano o, se si vuole, tra il "mare dei Romani" e il "mare dei Persiani" oppure "il mare dei Cinesi". Il centro di gravità del mondo arabo si trovava infatti nella regione degli istmi, tra il Golfo Persico, il Vicino Oriente, il mar Nero e il mar Caspio, e dunque al punto di incontro tra due grandi aree geografiche: quella dell'Oceano indiano – collegata da un lato alle coste dell'Africa orientale, dall'altro ai mari della Cina – e quella mediterranea.

Non si trattava però soltanto di una spaccatura politica, e neppure politico-economica. A trasformarla in uno scontro di civiltà fu la sua radice religiosa, l'incontro e il conflitto tra due religioni "universali" che esigevano entrambe la conversione alla fede dei dominatori, poco importa se frutto di un'adesione spontanea o di un'imposizione più o meno coercitiva. L'antichità mediterranea aveva conosciuto una molteplicità di culti, locali e non soltanto locali; il suo *pantheon* era aperto all'ingresso di nuove divinità. Il culto dell'imperatore, che il potere politico aveva richiesto a partire da Augusto, e l'apoteosi dell'imperatore defunto non avevano alcun carattere di esclusività; erano, tutto sommato, il simbolo dell'appartenenza a un unico organismo politico. E proprio su questo punto si era consumata la rottura tra il Cristianesimo, erede del monoteismo ebraico, e la cultura greco-romana, che ebbe una parte importante nel processo di indebolimento e di disgregazione culturale dell'impero. Gli Arabi condividevano con i Cristiani la fede in unico dio, ma lo raffiguravano richiamandosi a due differenti tradizioni: l'unico dio aveva nomi diversi ed era concepito in maniera diversa, e i credenti di entrambe le religioni guardavano con avversione ai fedeli dell'altra, considerati come "infedeli". La guerra tra gli eredi dell'impero, o di ciò che di esso rimaneva, e gli adoratori di Allah si trasformava inevitabilmente in una "guerra santa" tra gli abitanti delle due rive del Mediterraneo.

Per molti secoli, a partire dalla fine del secolo VII, l'impero d'Oriente e i regni barbarici dell'Occidente si scontrarono con il califfato islamico, in una guerra di conquista e di riconquista che divenne appunto scontro di civiltà. E il Mediterraneo ne diventò il teatro, o almeno il teatro principale, anche quando al dominio arabo si sostituì una nuova potenza, quella dei Turchi Ottomani, che a metà Quattrocento assediarono e conquistarono Costantinopoli, facendone la capitale di un nuovo impero islamico. Ciò non impedì che tra le due sponde si istituissero relazioni commerciali e anche alleanze politiche, come nel caso dei traffici tra le città marinare italiane e i terminali arabi della via delle Indie, e molto più tardi in quello del tentativo francese (fin dalla spedizione di Napoleone in Egitto) di colonizzare l'Africa settentrionale. Guerre e traffici si alternarono; ma il Mediterraneo era ormai diventato – e lo è tuttora – la frontiera dell'Europa con un altro mondo, con una civiltà diversa. Ma questa è un'altra storia.

Bibliografia

Abulafia, D 2011, *The Great Sea: A Human History of the Mediterranean*, Oxford University Press, Oxford.
Alföldy, G 1989, *Die Krise des römischen Reiches. Ausgewählte Beiträge*, Steiner, Stuttgart.
Arena, P (ed.), Augustus, 2014, *Res Gestae: i miei atti*, Edipuglia, Bari.
Brogiolo, GP & Ward-Perkins, B (eds) 1999, *The Idea and Ideal of the Town between Late Antiquity and the early Middle Ages,* Brill, Leiden.
Brown, P 2012, *Through the Eye of a Needle: Wealth, the Fall of Rome, and the Making of Christianity in the West, 350-550 AD*, Princeton University Press, Princeton.
Cameron, A 2012, *The Mediterranean World in Late Antiquity AD 395-700*, 2nd edn, Routledge, London.
Carlà, F & Marcone, A 2011, *Economia e finanza a Roma*, Il Mulino, Bologna.
Christie, N 2006, *From Constantine to Charlemagne: An Archaeology of Italy, AD 300–800*, Ashgate, Farnham.
Delogu, P 2010, *Le origini del Medioevo. Studi sul settimo secolo*, Jouvence, Rome.
Evans, EC (ed.) 2012, *Byzantium and Islam: Age of Transition, 7th-9th Century*, Metropolitan Museum, New York.
Fisher, G 2011, *Between Empires: Arabs, Romans, and Sasanians in Late Antiquity*, Oxford University Press, Oxford.
Giardina, A (ed.) 1986, *Società romana e Impero Tardoantico*, Laterza, Bari.
Henning, J (ed.) 2007, *Post-Roman Towns, Trade and Settlement in Europe and Byzantium*, W. de Gruyter, Berlin.
Hodges, R & Bowden, W (eds) 1998, The Sixth Century: Production, Distribution and Demand, Brill, Leiden.
Lombard, M 1971, *L'Islam dans sa première grandeur: VIIIe-XIe siècle*, Flammarion, Paris.
MacMullen, R 1976, *Roman Governments' Response to Crisis: A. D. 235-337*, Yale University Press, New Haven.
Mathisen, R & Schanzer, D (eds) 2011, *Romans, Barbarians and the Transformation of the Roman World*, Ashgate, Farnham.
McCormick, M 2001, *Origins of the European Economy: Communications and Commerce, 300-900*, Cambridge University Press, Cambridge.
Nicolet, C 1988, *L'inventaire du monde*, Fayard, Paris.

Pirenne, H 1937, *Mahomet et Charlemagne*, Félix Alcan, Paris.
Sarris, P 2006, *Economy and Society in the Age of Justinian*, Cambridge University Press, Cambridge.
Veyne, P 2005, *L'Empire gréco-romain*, Éditions du Seuil, Paris.
Ward-Perkins, B 2005, *The Fall of Rome and the End of Civilization*, Oxford University Press, Oxford.
Wickham, C 2005, *Framing the Early Middle Ages. Europe and the Mediterranean, 400-800*, Oxford University Press, Oxford.

Arnaldo Marcone
The Mediterranean from "Mare Nostrum" to Frontier between Civilisations

1 The Sea and the Empire

Rome achieved dominance over the Mediterranean in a surprisingly short time. The victorious war against Carthage in the second half of the third century BC gave it control of the central part of the Tyrrhenian Sea, with the acquisition of Sicily, Sardinia and Corsica. At the same time the Adriatic, too, became an object of Rome's interest in expanding its dominion: political considerations were increasingly correlated and interwoven with economic ones. By the beginning of the second century Rome had become a major Mediterranean power, on a par with the most powerful Hellenistic kingdoms, Egypt, Syria and Macedonia. A long series of conflicts ensued, by the end of which, only a few decades later, Rome held a territorial control without precedent in the ancient world. As early as 146 BC, with the destruction of Carthage, its dominance over the Mediterranean was established. It was completed in the following decades with victorious wars against Jugurtha in north-west Africa and Mithridates in Asia Minor; finally, Egypt, which had remained at least formally independent, was incorporated into the empire in 30 BC.

Rome's unification of the Mediterranean determined the birth of an empire which, though politically (and militarily) based on Roman power, was culturally, and also linguistically, Graeco-Roman. From the time of the Second Punic War, having come into contact with the Greek world through colonies in southern Italy and Sicily, Roman culture had found its exemplars in that world: the peasants' town – founded, according to tradition, by "twins" suckled by a she-wolf – began to fill with temple buildings modelled on those of the cities of Magna Graecia. Indeed, the Roman pantheon itself reproduced the Greek one, changing the names of the deities. Already in the third century BC, and in increasing measure in the next century, a Hellenising Latin literature developed, and, despite some resistance, the importation of Greek philosophy began.

The empire founded by Augustus expressed itself in the two now dominant languages, Greek and Latin, interchangeably. Its most famous official document, Augustus's *Res Gestae*, was produced in a bilingual edition, with Greek and Latin texts. And within this cultural "condominium", the position of the Greeks, who had imposed their language over a vast area through Alexander, was still culturally hegemonic. Rome's founding legend itself was linked to an event in archaic

Greek history, the Trojan War, though the origin of the Roman ruling line was traced back not to a Hellenic city, but to the one that been Greece's antagonist. The Greeks had provided the Romans with political and constitutional models and with the relevant theoretical literature. The Romans continued to study philosophy and medicine in Greek: the emperor Marcus Aurelius still wrote down his thoughts in Greek, not Latin. The linguistic frontier passed through the territory of Illyria, Latin being spoken on one side, Greek on the other.

Rome's control of the Mediterranean gave it an ecumenical conception of its empire. Cicero had declared that no senator could now afford to ignore the conformation and extent of the territories of the empire, and he later planned – after studying under Posidonius in Rhodes – a geographical work, though he never actually wrote it. However, a succinct presentation of the economic conception of the Roman empire has been provided by Augustus in the *Res Gestae*, a political testament and at the same time a detailed account of his achievements. The striking feature of this work is the emphasis it places on defining a now completed geographical space over which Rome finds itself holding absolute dominion and which it has to govern. The *Res Gestae* is the legitimisation of this vocation, as emerges already in the opening formula, where one can read the synthesis of an imperialist philosophy: "the acts by which (Augustus) subjected the world to the dominion of the Roman people". Two specific chapters (26 and 27) describe, in logical and geographical order, the pacification of the neighbouring provinces (Gaul and Germany), the acquisition of strategic control over the Alpine regions, the sending of naval expeditions into the northern Ocean and terrestrial ones into Ethiopia and Arabia; then territorial annexations and the creation of protectorates in the East, and diplomatic contacts with traditional enemies such as the Parthians, Pannonians and Dacians; lastly, legations from distant peoples such as the Indians; and the population of the various regions by founding colonies of veterans.

The imperial peace celebrated by Augustus created the conditions indispensable for general economic growth, though it is difficult now to estimate the nature and extent of that growth. At any rate, by the time of Caesar and Augustus the population of Rome, if it had not yet reached a million, was already close to that figure, and this posed serious problems for the maintenance of an urban populace which had been involved in the civil wars between Marius and Sulla, and then in those of the two triumvirates. That maintenance was achieved by transferring resources from the countryside to the capital and to the other big cities of the empire, which had to be supplied with the necessary resources – as did the army, which was mainly deployed along frontiers and in regions not only distant from each other, but also distant from the areas where cereals and other foodstuffs were produced. The mobilisation and distribution of resources is a crucial factor in the success of Roman government: the key was transporting them to, and distributing them in, areas where they were really needed. One of the most important results of this organisational effort was the increasing monetarisation of the economy, together with the development of common rules of commercial law and common systems of measurement.

The empire provided the economy with an infrastructure of connections and transportation created by the public administration over the centuries. In the Italian peninsula the infrastructure consisted of a network of consular roads which conveyed people and goods to the capital and at the same time made it possible to send orders to, and maintain, the legions on the other side of the Alps. Outside the peninsula – where consular roads did not yet exist – and linked to that network, were the sea routes that connected the centre of the empire with the peripheries. Their chief destinations were the western and eastern parts of the empire, and the northern coasts of Africa. The big cargo ships mainly transported cereals from Sicily and northern Africa and oil from southern Spain. But the routing of these goods also followed the deployment of the legions in the various parts of the Mediterranean. Soon, too, the trade in spices and luxury products began: arriving in Alexandria from the East, they were transported from there to Rome by sea. The rapid intensification of these commercial interchanges, first with north Africa and later with the whole Mediterranean, led to the expansion of existing harbours in Italy and the creation of new ones. The harbour of Ostia was supplemented in the second century BC by that of Puteoli in the Bay of Naples and later, in the imperial age, by that of Portus, near the mouth of the Tiber, to which it was linked by a canal.

During the centuries when the empire was being built, the Romans left the specifically commercial activities to specialised merchants (notably Greeks and Syrians, heirs of the ancient Phoenicians), and concentrated on exporting their models of the city, legislation and administration, but also of the urban lifestyle. In a sense it is true to say that Rome founded the same city over and over again, for it reproduced the same urban typology in every corner of the empire. On the coasts, but also in inland areas of the provinces, new cities were founded, or other pre-existent ones changed their physiognomy, with characteristics which repeated those of Rome itself; significant examples are Carthage, raised to new life after promotion by Augustus to the rank of capital of the province of proconsular Africa, and Nicopolis in Epirus, the city founded by Augustus to commemorate his victory at Antium in 31 BC. Much the same happened in Nîmes and Béziers in Gallia Narbonensis, Marseilles and many other cities. These cities remained self-governing organisms with a market, which allowed the surplus of production to circulate, and above all with an aristocracy committed to enriching the city with public works which testified to its importance and standard of living.

With the existence of a unitary political organism, capable of developing advanced forms of economic integration and rationalising the tax system – we should not underestimate the importance of censuses – it was possible to establish, partly for fiscal reasons, long-distance commercial relationships. Some products were undoubtedly exchanged directly between producers and consumers on the local market, or travelled straight from the place of production to that of consumption. But this happened within the at least potential context of a complex, extensive market which embraced the entire Mediterranean area, and in which urban centres played a major part. It is probably no coincidence that a measure widely discussed by modern historians, Caracalla's grant of Roman citizenship to almost all the inhabitants of the Empire – the so-called *constitutio Antoniniana* of 212 or 213 AD – is never mentioned by ancient historians, except for a passing allusion by Cassius Dio. In the eyes of contemporaries it probably seemed like the obvious culmination of a process that had been going on for centuries, the mere acknowledgement of a matter of fact.

Indeed, even earlier than this, in the mid-first century AD, Seneca – drawing on the work of Aristotle, Eratosthenes, Posidonius, Strabo and others – thought of the sea that separates Spain from India as a stretch of water that could be covered by a ship in a few days. In the foreword to his *Naturales Questiones* he wondered: "how great is the distance between the furthest coasts of Spain and the Indians? A space of a few days, if a favourable wind drives the ship". So the Mediterranean was, in his eyes, a favourable place for the rapid transit of men and goods. And in the chorus of the *Medea* Seneca evoked the expedition in search of the Golden Fleece, and therefore the benefits of the navigation which had made the world accessible. A century later, in his oration in praise of Rome, Aelius Aristides would describe the Mediterranean as surrounding Rome, which he called "the great emporium of the world, the market of all the products of the earth". By that time the Mediterranean really had become the *mare nostrum* of the empire, and Rome formed its centre, guaranteeing the unity of its shores.

2 The Threat to the Borders and the Beginnings of the Crisis

The existence of this complex political organism and of its economy was guaranteed by distant borders, which were the result of the military expansion of the first century BC and the resulting colonies. After the destruction of Carthage and the absorption of the Punic colonies founded on the African coast and in the Iberian peninsula, the southern coasts of the Mediterranean no longer constituted a significant military problem: the empire extended towards the Middle Atlas, in the heart of Morocco, where the city of Volubilis (near modern Meknès) was founded. The mountain chains, and beyond them the vastness of the desert, offered a secure hinterland to Libya too, which therefore required no special protection. As for Nubia, it represented not a danger but rather an area of connection with the caravan routes of sub-Saharan Africa and with the flows of trade in the Indian Ocean. The situation in Europe, especially in its western part, was very different. Caesar had conquered the whole of Gaul, subjugating the Celts and in part exterminating them, and then had advanced into Britannia. This initiated a process of growing Romanisation in both regions during the centuries of the empire, based on the foundation of flourishing urban centres, often far away from the Mediterranean. But this process also had limitations. While on the western shores of the Black Sea – an ancient area of Greek colonisation – Rome subjugated the Getae and included Dacia in its empire, Augustus's attempt to penetrate into Germany ended in abject failure. In 9 AD Arminius wiped out the legions commanded by Publius Quintilius Varo in the Teutoberg forest; and no later emperor dared to repeat the failed enterprise.

From that time onwards the northern boundaries of the empire stabilised along the line marked by two great rivers, the Rhine in the west and the Danube in the south-east, with a few partial but limited encroachments beyond them. There were plenty of expeditions, both defensive and offensive, in the first two centuries of the empire, especially along the borders between Gaul and Germany, and in the transalpine regions of Raetia and Pannonia; similarly, the conquest of Britannia was never completed, but stopped at Hadrian's Wall, which separated England from Scotland. The East, too, was the theatre of rebellions and conflicts, such as the revolt of Judaea, which ended in the destruction of Jerusalem by the emperor Titus, and two bloody wars against the Parthians, the first under Trajan and the second under Septimius Severus. Eventually, however, another river, the Euphrates, served to delimit the Roman area of influence and guarantee lasting conditions of peace in the regions west of its course. In the West and the East the empire set about fortifying the frontiers, building a system of roads for military purposes and creating an area (the *limes*) which made flexible defence possible and at the same time encouraged trading products with neighbouring peoples. The legions, made up mainly of Italic troops, were supported by auxiliary bodies recruited in the provinces which helped them guard the frontiers.

In this way the process of urbanisation not only spread, but to some extent changed in nature. Hitherto, the major cities of the ancient world had all been situated on the coast or close to the sea – like Rome itself, linked to Ostia by its river; now, however, new cities arose, often situated on large rivers but decidedly continental in nature. This led to a gradual but significant change in the very nature of the empire: by the end of the second century AD it was no longer a political organism centred exclusively on the Mediterranean, but – despite the continuing economic importance of that sea – had been transformed into a Mediterranean/continental empire, with other additional centres, all beyond the Alps or, in the East, far from the sea.

Rome's military power had managed to prevent this transformation from undermining the structure of the empire, partly because of the succession, after the rule of the Julio-Claudian *gens*, of two other imperial dynasties which made the peaceful transmission of power possible – the Flavian dynasty in the second half of the first century and the Antonine in the early decades of the following century. But the political edifice erected by Augustus, and several times reformed in the course of time, paid a price for this: that of increasing interference by the legions in the election of emperors, a phenomenon which had occurred for the first time in 69, after the death of Nero. The armies that defended the provinces owed their loyalty to their generals, who thus became charismatic figures; and competition for imperial rank often led to civil wars, though these were often short. The central authority, now that the senate and the senatorial class had been disempowered, was unable to control an empire which was expanding, and changing in nature as it did so. And the legions, being involved in these struggles, were less and less engaged in the task of defending the frontiers.

The political crisis was accompanied by a demographic crisis, which began with the so-called "Antonine plague" (probably an epidemic of smallpox), which broke out around 170-180 AD, in the latter part of the reign of Marcus Aurelius. The decline in the population had different effects in the various regions; but it caused a general decrease in the available workforce, and a corresponding increase in its bargaining power. This prompted landowners to seek forms of extra-economic constraint to keep the remaining farmers at work. The peasant smallholding, which in the past had also supplied the recruitment needs of the army, was increasingly replaced by the latifundium and the bonds that it entailed: the various kinds of unfree labour were brought together into a single category, that of colonists tied to the land. Social tensions, which had not been absent even in the first two centuries of the empire (or indeed in the republican age before that), grew in strength, causing a fall in production and trade, and therefore a decrease in fiscal revenue. This development coincided with a growing bureaucratisation of the state "machinery" and a rise in the costs of maintaining the legions that had to defend the frontiers.

The economic geography of the empire was changing radically too; and this primarily concerned the situation in the Italian peninsula. In the preceding centuries its southern regions had played, all things considered, a minor role in supplying Rome with food. From the fourth century onwards, however, southern Italy would become an area of major interest, because it now bore the main burden of supplying the city with food. Sicily, too, was included among the so-called *regiones suburbicariae*, which had primary responsibility for this task, and this entailed the creation of an official relationship with the capital's needs. The instability of imperial control increased the island's importance as a producer of wheat. This explains the interest shown in Sicily by the great landowners, the controllers of imperial finances and the representatives of central power. But it also marked the beginning of a decline in the circulation of people and goods in the Mediterranean.

The threat to the borders, meanwhile, was growing rapidly. Especially after 235, when the dynasty of the Severi died out, the frontier separating Gaul and the other transalpine provinces from the German populations became more and more permeable: an invasion by the Alemanni was followed by others by the Vandals, the Suebi, the Franks, the Goths, the Saxons, and many more. The entire eastern part of Europe was shifting under the impetus of more distant peoples, who put pressure on the invaders from behind, giving rise to a global *Völkerwanderung* which affected most of the Eurasian continent. Nor was the situation in the south-eastern area any more reassuring: in 227 the Parthian kingdom succumbed to the Persian Sasanids, who had adopted Zoroastrianism as their official religion, and the empire was confronted by an enemy far stronger than its predecessor. At the end of the third century Diocletian sought to remedy the situation by reorganising the state structure on the basis of a tetrarchy comprising two "Augustuses" and two "Caesars", who were to govern the eastern and western parts of the empire separately. From this time onwards the Mediterranean began to lose its strategic function, and along with that its unity.

3 East and West: Two Separate Destinies

The crisis that threatened the very survival of the empire in the third century seemed to have been overcome thanks to the reforming abilities of Diocletian and later of Constantine. Nevertheless, the reorganisation of the state structure produced results that would have important consequences for the unity of the Mediterranean. In the first place, Rome ceased to be the place of residence of the emperor and several capitals were created elsewhere, according to a logic of a growing distinction between East and West. Moreover, Italy lost its privileged fiscal position compared to other provinces. Under Constantine a major event occurred: the founding in 330 of a new capital on the Bosphorus named after him:

Constantinople. Most of the wheat produced in Egypt was now sent to that city, so Rome was increasingly dependent on Africa and Sicily for its food supplies.

The foundation of Constantinople also initiated a process of cultural differentiation between the predominantly Greek-speaking eastern part of the empire and the western part, where Latin was prevalent. The fact that the new capital now exercised permanent hegemony over the eastern part of the empire gave the governmental apparatus that operated there a markedly different character from that of the *regiae urbes* in the West. The difference was partly due to the emergence of a new ruling class which was more open from a social point of view, but the most important factor was that the constant presence of the emperor, from the time of Arcadius onwards, gave the city an exclusive political role with respect to the other centres which made up the rich mosaic of the urbanism of the eastern Mediterranean. Alexandria, Antioch, Berytus, Gaza, Caesarea in Palestine, Edessa, Ephesus, Athens and Thessalonica maintained their prestigious monumental apparatus, as well as an intense intellectual life – sometimes more intense, indeed, than that of the capital; but it was in Constantinople that the decisions that really mattered were taken. Moreover, service in the imperial palace led, in the late fourth and the fifth centuries, to the emergence of a class of dignitaries who acquired higher social status not because of their origins but simply because of their familiarity with the sovereign.

This peculiarity of Constantinople as a centre of power was also important in the relationship between the barbarians and the empire after the death of Theodosius I in 295, which in effect gave his sons Honorius and Arcadius sovereignty over the West and East respectively. Hopes of the empire remaining united, though divided in its seats of government, would soon prove unrealistic. In the space of a few decades, the two parts of the empire underwent very different political and social developments, which helped to move them even further apart.

Moreover, even in the time of Diocletian and Constantine the barbarian threat was much stronger in the West than in the East. The crossing of the Rhine frontier by the barbarians in the winter of 406-407 seemed like the beginning of the end of the Roman west. The sack of Rome in 410 by Alaric, though short-lived and not particularly destructive, came as a terrible shock because it was the first time in eight centuries that Rome had been, albeit temporarily, taken by foreigners. But half a century after Alaric's incursion, on the death of Valentinian III the Vandals led by Genseric, after seizing control of northern Africa, sacked Rome for the second time, and much more brutally. Not only the Italian peninsula but the whole area around the Tyrrhenian was attacked by the armies of the barbarian peoples. By the end of the fifth century the map of Italy looked completely different. The Visigoths had taken Aquitania and from there had crossed over into Spain, driving the Vandals into north-west Africa, into regions that had formed part of the ancient Punic dominion; the Franks and the Burgundians had penetrated into Gaul, where they settled permanently, creating two places of political aggregation; the Goths of the east, or Ostrogoths, had occupied most of central northern Italy, and were later, in 568, followed by the Lombards. The kingdoms that they founded, however, destroyed relatively little of the Roman order and of the social structure on which it had rested. That is especially true of the Gothic kingdom which was established in Italy in the later fifth and early sixth centuries, an attempt – albeit an unsuccessful one – at achieving coexistence and cooperation between the invaders and the bureaucracy of Roman origin.

In the eastern part of the empire, by contrast, the fifth century was for the most part a time of relatively undestructive military conflict. The war against the great enemies of the eastern empire, the Sasanids, flared up only for very short periods, in 421-422 and 440. Greece, Macedonia, Thrace, and even the southern part of Dacia, remained under imperial rule; and the same was true of Crete and Cyprus, as well as Egypt. A decisive factor in all this was the Byzantine fleet's control of the sea, which extended beyond the eastern part of the Mediterranean to include the large islands in the Tyrrhenian. In the mid-sixth century, during the long reign of Justinian, Belisarius defeated the Vandals – the only barbarian people that had a sizeable fleet – and reconquered Sicily, before trying in vain to win the Italian peninsula back from the Goths' control. The counter-offensive of the Byzantine fleet was checked by the resistance of the new political structures that the various barbarian kingdoms had created or were creating. Naval supremacy did not lead, as the Eastern empire had hoped it would, to reconquest of Italy and the western Mediterranean.

For the Eastern empire, too, was far from being a "strong" state capable of imposing its own fiscal system. It is true that for a few decades, until the mid-fifth century, it had financed wars in the West on various occasions, but these initiatives eventually caused an imbalance of military expenditure in the state finances. Even as late as the sixth century the new political situation had still not been understood by the Byzantine sovereigns, who continued to consider the political unity of the Mediterranean an essential element in the idea of empire. Justinian's plan to recover Italy from Gothic rule led only to a conflict which would last eighteen years, without achieving its aim. In the end the "reconquest" of the West was limited to a small part of the Italian peninsula and an even smaller part of Spain. After the defeat of the Vandals the Byzantine fleet remained mistress of the seas; but the coastal regions were lost to the Eastern empire as well.

Over the centuries the importance of the imperial bureaucracy had progressively diminished, while an increasingly significant role had been played by the great landowners, who appear to share public responsibilities with characteristics which make it difficult to distinguish public functions from private ones. Moreover, the barbarian kingdoms of the West no longer needed forms of provisioning that were subject to state authority, as had been the case with Rome and as the new Eastern capital still required; as a result, both agricultural and artisanal production went into steep decline. The conditions no longer existed where a market could be supported by long-distance trading of large quantities of products, and the economy was becoming localised. What remained was commercial exchange at a local or regional level, and the limited trade in luxury goods required by the military aristocracies of the new kingdoms. International commerce diminished and almost completely ceased in the eighth century, in stark contrast with the growing trade in the North Sea.

In the fifth and sixth centuries the Mediterranean had ceased to be the *mare nostrum* of the empire, chiefly because that empire no longer existed, or existed only in its eastern part. Politically the sea was now split in two; economically it had lost the role it had occupied in antiquity. It would be many centuries – indeed, almost half a millennium – before the ships of the cities and kingdoms of Western Europe would sail it again, carrying goods to the East but especially importing them, and transporting the Crusader armies towards the holy places of the Christian religion; but by then the power of Constantinople was itself on the wane, and the Byzantine fleet had long since lost control of the sea.

4 The Opposite Shores

Another, deeper breach was on the horizon. In the first half of the seventh century a new religion was appearing on the Mediterranean, in far from peaceful competition with the Christian religion which had emerged victorious three centuries before from its confrontation with imperial authority. Christianity and Islam had certain important features in common. Both were based on faith in one God, though Islamic monotheism immediately proved far more radical than its Christian equivalent; both were "religions of the Book" – that is, they were based on a sacred text which was held to contain the very word of God; both drew on the same prophetic tradition, that of the Old Testament prophets – and Islam even included Jesus in the series of prophets that culminated in Mohammed. But they had also inherited from their common Jewish origin an element that would make them mortal enemies: exclusivism in their faith, and therefore intolerance towards the faiths of others.

The Arab warriors who set out after the death of Mohammed to conquer the world and convert (or subjugate) its inhabitants were soldiers of the faith, and the faith was the basis of their political organisation. Their advance was extraordinarily rapid: after defeating the emperor Heraclius near Jerusalem in 634, in a few years they conquered Palestine and Syria to the north, and Egypt and the Libyan coasts towards the west. In the ensuing decades they penetrated as far as Mesopotamia and Persia, then central Asia, and the borders with India and China; at the same time they also overran the western coasts of north Africa. The Eastern empire held out, but after losing Cyprus, Crete and the islands of the Aegean it was defeated at sea. In a short time the Arabs had conquered regions that were strategically important both for their fiscal yield and for their recruitment potential, and they had built a fleet capable of repelling the attacks of the Byzantine fleet.

Thus the eastern Mediterranean, for centuries sailed by the Roman and later the Byzantine fleets, gradually came under Arab control; or at any rate, Byzantium's dominance of the sea came to an end. The new invaders set about creating a fleet that could compete with that of Constantinople; and in their new naval bases in Palestine even craftsmen from Persia and Iraq were employed in building ships. For this purpose the Arabs drew to a large extent on the Syrian and Egyptian workforces (especially the Copts of Egypt), which until a few years before had built ships and provided crews for their enemy. Since the earliest illustrations we have date from the fourteenth century, it is impossible to be sure what the first Arab warships looked like, but it is reasonable to assume that their designs were inspired by the existing Mediterranean maritime tradition. Given their broadly similar nautical terminology, and the links that existed between them, at least in the technological field, the Byzantine and Arab fleets also shared many aspects of tactics and general organisation; translations of Byzantine military manuals, for example, were available to the Arab admirals.

After occupying Cyprus in 649 and sacking Rhodes, Crete and Sicily, the new Arab navy inflicted a decisive defeat on the Byzantines led by the emperor Constans II in person at the battle of Phoenix in 655. From the time of the caliphate of Muawiyah (661–680) the Arabs' incursions intensified, and preparations were being made for a major assault on Constantinople itself. But the empire's remaining maritime forces succeeded in preventing its fall. During the first Arab siege of Constantinople (674–678) the Byzantine fleet played a crucial part in guaranteeing the survival of the empire: the Arab fleets were defeated thanks to the use of a new, destructive secret weapon, "Greek fire". The Islamic advance in Asia Minor and the Aegean was stopped, and a thirty years' truce between the two empires was signed. But the Arabs were destined to make their presence felt with growing intensity, increasing the difficulty of relations between the empire and the other countries with coasts on the Mediterranean. In 711, having completed the subjugation of northern Africa, the Arab armies crossed the Straits of Gibraltar and landed on the European continent for the first time; within a few years almost the whole of Spain had fallen under the control of the Arabs, and would remain subject to them for a long time.

By now the Mediterranean was split in two, no longer longitudinally – as in the separation between the Eastern empire and the Western – but latitudinally. To the north, on the coasts of what would become Europe, the kingdoms of barbarian origin that had supplanted Roman rule tried to create an organsational structure for themselves, based on cooperation, but also rivalry, between the power of the princes and their feudal lords on the one hand and the Church's apparatus of government on the other. Arab attempts to penetrate beyond the Pyrenees were thwarted by the resistance of the Franks, who were victorious at Poitiers in 732. As for the Italian peninsula, it became a field of battle not so much between Arab armies and Christian militias as between the Eastern empire and the various barbarian peoples that arrived in successive waves. While some regions, particularly the islands, remained under the generally firm control of Byzantium, in the rest of the peninsula Gothic rule was followed by that of the Lombards, who settled both in the middle of the Po plain and in Campania and Puglia; then came the Franks, in support of the papacy; and finally, two centuries later, the southern part of Italy, together with Sicily, came under the power of a new people, the Normans, or "men of the North". The country that had been the centre of the empire had become a land of conquest. All that remained of its former centrality was the papacy, which, however, was forced to pursue a succession of new alliances, in an ambiguous power relationship with its protector, the Frankish empire, whose birth it would consecrate on Christmas Night, 800.

The southern shores of the Mediterranean, on the other hand, were an Arab monopoly. But just as the Mediterranean had lost its politically and economically central role, so the now Arabised north Africa did not occupy a pre-eminent place in the politics of the Islamic caliphate. In reality, its occupation – and in general the Arab drive towards the west – was only one of the directions of the expansion of Islam, and not the most important. Unlike Greco-Roman culture, for which the Mediterranean was always the centre of the inhabited world, Arab culture saw the position of the land of Islam as a median one, midway between the Mediterranean and the Indian Ocean, or between the "sea of the Romans" and the "sea of the Persians" or the "sea of the Chinese". The hub of the Arab world lay in the region of isthmuses, between the Persian Gulf, the Near East, the Black Sea and the Caspian Sea, and so at the meeting point between two great geographic areas: the Indian Ocean – linked on one side with the coasts of East Africa, and on the other with the seas of China – and the Mediterranean.

This was not, however, a purely political, or even politico-economical division. What made it a clash of civilisations was its religious basis, the meeting and conflict between two "universal" religions, both of which demanded conversion to the rulers' faith, whether by spontaneous adhesion or by varying degrees of coercion. Mediterranean antiquity had known a multiplicity of cults, some local and some not local; its pantheon was open to the admission of new deities. The cult of the emperor, which the political power had imposed since the time of Augustus, and the apotheosis of the emperor on his death, had no characteristics of exclusivity; they were, rather, a symbol of membership of a single political organism. This point had been the source of the breach between Christianity – the heir of Jewish monotheism – and Greco-Roman culture, which played an important part in the weakening and cultural dissolution of the empire. Both Arabs and Christians believed in one god, but they represented him with reference to two different traditions: the one god had different names and was conceived of in a different way, and the believers of each religion looked those of the other with aversion, regarding them as "unbelievers". The war between the heirs to the empire, or what remained of it, and the worshippers of Allah inevitably became a "holy war" between the inhabitants of the two shores of the Mediterranean.

For many centuries, from the end of the seventh century onwards, the Eastern empire and the barbarian kingdoms of the West clashed with the Islamic caliphate, in a war of conquest and reconquest which indeed became a clash of civilisations. And the Mediterranean became its theatre, or at least its main theatre, even when Arab dominance was replaced by a new power, that of the Ottoman Turks, who in the mid-fourteenth century besieged and took Constantinople, making it the capital of a new Islamic empire. This did not prevent the development of commercial relations and even political alliances between the two shores, as in trade between Italian coastal cities and the Arab terminals of the road to the Indies, and much later the French effort (starting with Napoleon's expedition to Egypt) to colonise north Africa. Wars alternated with trade; but by now the Mediterranean had become – as it still is – Europe's frontier with another world, a different civilisation. But that is another story.

Translated from the Italian by Jonathan Hunt

Bibliography

Abulafia, D 2011, *The Great Sea: A Human History of the Mediterranean*, Oxford University Press, Oxford.
Alföldy, G 1989, *Die Krise des römischen Reiches. Ausgewählte Beiträge*, Steiner, Stuttgart.
Augustus, 2014, *Res Gestae: i miei atti*, ed P Arena, Edipuglia, Bari.
Brogiolo, GP & Ward-Perkins, B (eds) 1999, *The Idea and Ideal of the Town between Late Antiquity and the early Middle Ages*, Brill, Leiden.

Brown, P 2012, *Through the Eye of a Needle: Wealth, the Fall of Rome, and the Making of Christianity in the West, 350-550 AD*, Princeton University Press, Princeton.
Cameron, A 2012, *The Mediterranean World in Late Antiquity AD 395-700*, 2nd edn, Routledge, London.
Carlà, F & Marcone, A 2011, *Economia e finanza a Roma*, Il Mulino, Bologna.
Christie, N 2006, *From Constantine to Charlemagne: An Archaeology of Italy, AD 300–800*, Ashgate, Farnham.
Delogu, P 2010, *Le origini del Medioevo. Studi sul settimo secolo*, Jouvence, Rome.
Evans, EC (ed.) 2012, *Byzantium and Islam: Age of Transition, 7th-9th Century*, Metropolitan Museum, New York.
Fisher, G 2011, *Between Empires: Arabs, Romans, and Sasanians in Late Antiquity*, Oxford University Press, Oxford.
Giardina, A (ed.) 1986, *Società romana e Impero Tardoantico*, Laterza, Bari.
Henning, J (ed.) 2007, *Post-Roman Towns, Trade and Settlement in Europe and Byzantium*, W. de Gruyter, Berlin.
Hodges, R & Bowden, W (eds) 1998, The Sixth Century: Production, Distribution and Demand, Brill, Leiden.
Lombard, M 1971, *L'Islam dans sa première grandeur: VIIIe-XIe siècle*, Flammarion, Paris.
MacMullen, R 1976, *Roman Governments' Response to Crisis: A. D. 235-337*, Yale University Press, New Haven.
Mahisen, R & Schanzer, D (eds) 2011, *Romans, Barbarians and the Transformation of the Roman World*, Ashgate, Farnham.
McCormick, M 2001, *Origins of the European Economy: Communications and Commerce, 300-900*, Cambridge University Press, Cambridge.
Nicolet, C 1988, *L'inventaire du monde*, Fayard, Paris.
Pirenne, H 1937, *Mahomet et Charlemagne*, Félix Alcan, Paris.
Sarris, P 2006, *Economy and Society in the Age of Justinian*, Cambridge University Press, Cambridge.
Veyne, P 2005, *L'Empire gréco-romain*, Éditions du Seuil, Paris.
Ward-Perkins, B 2005, *The Fall of Rome and the End of Civilization*, Oxford University Press, Oxford.
Wickham, C 2005, *Framing the Early Middle Ages. Europe and the Mediterranean, 400-800*, Oxford University Press, Oxford.

Franco Cardini
L'Europa e l'Islam: incontri e scontri

1 La nascita dell'Islam e la rottura dell'unità mediterranea

La nuova fede religiosa nata nella penisola arabica nella prima metà del VII secolo, l'Islam, conobbe una rapida e quasi esplosiva espansione già all'indomani della morte del suo fondatore, Muhammad, nel 632. Essa modificò profondamente il volto del mondo afro-asiatico-mediterraneo. Nel giro di circa un quarto di secolo l'impero persiano fu assimilato e quello bizantino costretto a ridefinire la sua politica. Gli Arabi portatori della nuova fede occuparono le coste e parte dell'entroterra dell'Asia minore, della Siria, dell'Egitto, e l'intera Africa settentrionale, che erano le aree di reclutamento delle marinerie dell'impero romano d'Oriente. La loro conversione all'Islam si spiega anche perché si trattava di genti cristiane, ma in massima parte "eretiche" – soprattutto monofisitiche – che dato il loro credo le autorità imperiali di Costantinopoli facevano oggetto di tassazioni, di deportazioni e di altre misure repressive, mentre i nuovi arrivati permisero loro di seguire liberamente il proprio culto in quanto *ahl al-Kitab*, "popoli del Libro", partecipi di una sia pur imperfetta forma di rivelazione e perciò non obbligati a convertirsi. La potenza marinara bizantina ne uscì compromessa al punto da dover spartire con i potentati musulmani la propria talassocrazia mediterranea: d'altronde, il tempestivo insorgere di discordie, scismi e guerre intestine all'interno dell'Islam impedì la trasformazione del Mediterraneo in un "lago musulmano".

In realtà, il Mediterraneo aveva da tempo cessato di essere il *mare nostrum* dell'antichità, e il luogo dell'indiscusso dominio imperiale. Già la divisione dell'impero introdotta da Diocleziano aveva avuto su di esso pesanti conseguenze: la parte occidentale, più esposta alle invasioni dei popoli germanici, e diventata terra d'insediamento dei Goti sia nella penisola italiana che in quella iberica, perdette il controllo delle rotte marittime tra Gallia, Spagna e coste africane, mentre la flotta bizantina riuscì a mantenere a lungo quello del Mediterraneo orientale, almeno fino alla linea Sicilia-Sardegna. Cominciò in tal modo a delinearsi una spaccatura del Mediterraneo in due bacini distinti non soltanto geograficamente ma anche politicamente (e militarmente). Con l'espansione dell'Islam il bacino orientale divenne terreno di scontro tra l'impero d'Oriente e le nuove potenze islamiche, mentre il bacino occidentale rimase a lungo dominio di quest'ultime e delle scorrerie corsare. A partire da allora il Mediterraneo perdette la propria unità, e quello che era stato il baricentro dell'antichità, dei suoi commerci e della sua cultura, si trasformò in una frontiera, per quanto mutevole nel corso dei secoli.

Per molto tempo si è sostenuto, in base alla tesi di Henri Pirenne, che il repentino insorgere della potenza navale musulmana abbia comportato la rottura dell'unità mediterranea che fin lì aveva consentito il mantenimento delle strutture economiche e dell'omogeneità culturale dei popoli che si affacciavano sul mare: ciò avrebbe determinato un ripiegamento della vecchia *pars Occidentis* dell'impero su se stessa, con l'aggravarsi dei processi di recessione in atto e la sua progressiva ruralizzazione. In altri termini, i caratteri di quello che per definizione indichiamo come "Medioevo" si sarebbero presentati tra VII e VIII secolo, con l'affermarsi dell'egemonia musulmana nel Mediterraneo. In realtà, la crisi economica del VI-VII secolo, che proseguì sia pure con alterne vicende e momenti di ripresa fino al X, era il risultato di un processo lento e profondo. E proprio questo sfondo ci aiuta a comprendere anche il mutamento di ruolo subito dal Mediterraneo, nelle sue relazioni con le vicende politico-economiche delle regioni che si affacciavano su di esso.

2 La spinta islamica verso occidente

Con l'avvento al potere nel *dar al-Islam* dei califfi umayyadi (661-750) la corte di Damasco – città di solide tradizioni culturali greche – andò sempre più somigliando al modello di quella romano-orientale di Costantinopoli. Si andarono creando un'arte e una letteratura musulmana molto vicine alle tradizioni eclettiche della cultura bizantina, il che comportò un certo permissivismo nelle cose relative alla fede. Sotto gli umayyadi l'Islam si diffuse in Oriente fino all'Indo Kush e al corso dell'Amu Daryah, quindi agli odierni Afghanistan e Uzbekistan.

Dopo aver conquistato la Siria e la Palestina, gli Arabi sottomisero l'antica provincia romana d'Africa (*Ifriqiya*), comprendente la Tripolitania, la Tunisia e l'Algeria attuali, che era stata invasa nel 647; ma solo dal 663 la resistenza romano-orientale e soprattutto berbera cominciò a cedere. Ormai, una volta padroni delle coste meridionali e orientali del Mediterraneo, gli Arabi e i loro correligionari arabizzati potevano impegnarsi nella conquista delle acque e dei litorali che si trovavano al di là di esse.

Nel mondo visigoto di Spagna ci si era allarmati per tempo dinanzi alle notizie dell'avanzata araba lungo le coste dell'Africa settentrionale. Durante il concilio di Toledo del 694 il re Egica aveva lanciato l'allarme. Si andava spargendo la voce che gli Ebrei, esasperati a causa delle misure vessatorie assunte nei loro confronti, si apprestassero a dare man forte ai "nuovi barbari" che stavano avanzando dall'Oriente; imperversava intanto la guerra civile per la successione all'ultimo re di Toledo; e sembra che uno dei contendenti, Achila, rifugiatosi in Marocco, si rivolgesse per aiuto ai *Mauri* (così detti in quanto provenienti dall'antica Mauretania, che per gli Arabi era *al-Maghreb*, l'"Occidente"), cioè ai Berberi islamizzati alla testa dei quali c'era una non numerosa aristocrazia araba. Erano appunto questi *Mauri* che la successiva epica iberico-latina avrebbe chiamato *los Moros*; ma essi sarebbero stati conosciuti anche come *saraceni* o *agareni*, dai nomi biblici della moglie e della concubina di Abramo.

Fu probabilmente alla fine del luglio del 711 che una grossa flotta musulmana prese terra nella baia di Algesiras, che già l'anno prima era stata razziata. Entro il 720 anche la Catalogna e la Settimania, vale a dire tutti i territori della monarchia visigota a sud e a nord dei Pirenei, erano occupate, anche se tra le asperità dei Pirenei e dei Cantabrici sopravvivevano dei focolai di resistenza cristiana. Dalla Spagna alla Gallia meridionale, dove i Franchi nominalmente dominavano dall'inizio del VI secolo ma le istituzioni erano fragili e le strutture sociali labili, il passo poteva esser breve. Dopo aver occupato Narbona nel 718, gli Arabi si presentarono dinanzi a Tolosa nel 721 e conquistarono Nîmes e Carcassonne nel 725. Ormai, l'intera Provenza col bacino del Rodano era teatro delle loro gesta. Secondo una tradizione radicata, un *raid* musulmano – con ogni probabilità diretto a Tours, dove nel santuario di San Martino era custodito un ingente tesoro – venne fermato a Poitiers dal "Maestro di Palazzo" del regno merovingio d'Austrasia, Carlo Martello: ma la battaglia, combattuta nel 732 o nel 733, è in sé meno importante del mito cui ha dato origine. Ne è prova il fatto che, anche dopo quell'episodio, gli attacchi dei "mori" alle città gallo-meridionali continuarono. Le scorrerie arabo-berbere provocarono diverse reazioni nel mondo franco, proprio a partire dalle continue campagne di Carlo Martello: ma il doppio gioco e il tradimento imperavano, per cui è impossibile parlare di vere e proprie spedizioni "dei Franchi contro l'Islam".

Al pericolo costituito dai "mori" di Spagna, che a loro volta non riuscivano ad esprimere una compagine unitaria, la dinastia dei discendenti di Carlo Martello – che si era sostituita a quella dei Merovingi – doveva la sua fama e la sua gloria. Ma il rischio di un'invasione islamica proveniente dai Pirenei era, tra VIII e IX secolo, in pratica nullo. Al contrario, era stato semmai re Carlo, nipote del Maestro di Palazzo, a tentare nel 776 d'inserirsi nelle lotte fra i piccoli emirati aragonesi. Quell'impresa si era però conclusa male, ma era destinata a entrare nella leggenda: appartiene ad essa il celebre episodio dell'imboscata di Roncisvalle, durante la quale sarebbe caduto un collaboratore e parente di Carlo, il *comes* Rolando, che avrebbe dato luogo alla più tarda, celebre *Chanson de Roland*, uno dei testi epici fondamentali del Medioevo. In realtà, i guerrieri franchi vennero battuti in quell'occasione non già da Musulmani, bensì da montanari baschi cristiani, ostili alla marcia di un esercito straniero attraverso le loro terre.

Carlo riuscì a organizzare a sud dei Pirenei una marca di confine, la marca di Catalogna, con il ruolo di testa di ponte per una possibile espansione nella penisola iberica: grazie ad essa l'intera area pirenaica passava sotto il controllo franco. Nel terzo decennio del secolo VIII la spinta dell'Islam – esteso ormai dall'Indo all'Atlantico, dal Caucaso al Corno d'Africa – dava segni di stanchezza, aggravati dalla fine della dinastia umayyade, sconfitta e travolta de quella rivale degli abbasidi, di origine arabo-persiana, che spostò da Damasco a Baghdad, e quindi sensibilmente ad est, il centro dell'impero musulmano.

Fu il primo califfo abbaside, al-Mansur, a fondare sul fiume Tigri Baghdad, la nuova capitale: il baricentro della nuova dinastia si spostava nell'area mesopotamico-iranica. Ciò sottintendeva un programma di asiatizzazione del califfato, con l'abbandono del modello culturale bizantino seguito dagli Umayyadi e il crescente disinteresse per un'espansione verso quell'Occidente che senza dubbio appariva povero, incolto, barbarico. Veniva così a indebolirsi la pressione musulmana sulla parte occidentale del Mediterraneo, anche se un membro della famiglia califfale decaduta riuscì a raggiungere la penisola iberica e a fondarvi in Córdoba un emirato (dall'arabo *amir*, "principe") che riuscì gradualmente a imporre la propria egemonia sulla penisola iberica e sul Maghreb, tanto che nel 929 l'emiro Abd ar-Rahman poté a sua volta assumere il titolo di califfo.

La più potente fra le dinastie che si affermarono nel Maghreb fu quella degli Aghlabiti di Kairuan: in teoria un governatorato per conto degli Abbasidi, di fatto autonoma e a capo di un territorio che copriva, dai primi del IX secolo, l'attuale Tunisia e l'Algeria orientale. Tra le principali imprese della dinastia aghlabita vi fu la conquista della Sicilia. L'invasione partì nell'827 dall'emirato di Tunisi, ma solo ai primi del secolo successivo i Musulmani completarono la conquista: se Palermo era già presa nell'831, Siracusa non cadde che nell'878. Nell'829 essi assalirono il porto di Roma, *Centumcellae*, e da questo le bande di predatori colpirono la Tuscia, la Maremma, la Sabina, giungendo fino a saccheggiare le basiliche suburbane di San Paolo e di San Pietro.

Le scorrerie nell'Italia meridionale e poi anche lungo le coste tirreniche si susseguirono tra il secolo IX e l'inizio dell'XI. Di solito l'obiettivo degli incursori era la razzìa rapida, il prelievo di gente prevalentemente giovane con cui alimentare il commercio degli schiavi, l'occasionale imposizione di tributi e di riscatti; più di rado il *raid* aveva come esito l'impianto di un "nido" corsaro, cioè di una piccola colonia commerciale-militare. Talvolta si trattò però anche di insediamenti duraturi, come nel caso delle isole mediterranee di Creta, Malta, Sicilia e dell'arcipelago delle Baleari, tutte conquistate nel corso dei secoli IX-X e mantenute più o meno a lungo.

Intanto, nel corso del X secolo l'emiro Abd ar-Rahman III, che aveva guidato la dinastia neo-umayyade di Córdoba al massimo splendore, era riuscito a estendere il suo potere anche su parte del Maghreb occidentale. La penisola iberica si presentava, con le sue comunità urbane dinamiche alla ricerca di intense relazioni commerciali con i paesi sotto controllo musulmano, di modo che in questa circolazione anche il mondo occidentale diventava partecipe dei ricercati prodotti d'Oriente. Le città della penisola iberica ebbero intorno al Mille rapporti diversi con il mare: da Barcellona a Siviglia fino alla costa atlantica i centri urbani svolsero ruoli diversi nel risveglio del commercio occidentale. Córdoba, la capitale del califfato neo-umayyade iberico, superava nel secolo X tutte le altre città della penisola, ed era collegata ad esse da una rete di strade con un rapido sistema di corrieri appositamente addestrati.

Nel califfato umayyade Arabi e Berberi non si erano però mai propriamente fusi tra loro: la fiera aristocrazia di colore che si consideravano i soli autentici eredi del Profeta disprezzava i *parvenus* africani. Tuttavia era ben presto prevalsa una moderata integrazione con i discendenti dei Latini, dei Celti e dei Germani: la vera distinzione qualificante restava quella tra i Musulmani discendenti dei conquistatori, gli abitanti locali guadagnati in tempi diversi alla fede coranica (i *muwalladun*) e i Cristiani rimasti fedeli alla loro religione ma arabizzati nella lingua e nei costumi, per quanto sovente non dimentichi del latino o meglio dell'idioma volgare che da esso si era sviluppato (i *musta'riba*, che gli occidentali conoscono meglio con il termine di "mozarabi").

3 La circolazione delle merci e delle culture

L'importanza assunta dal commercio arabo nel Mediterraneo risulta in primo luogo dalla diffusione delle monete musulmane, che ben presto affiancarono e in molte aree soppiantarono l'egemonia del *denarius* aureo bizantino, il celebre "iperpero" o "bisante". A somiglianza del *denarius*, il *dinar* arabo pesava 4,25 grammi d'oro: ma più diffuso di esso era il quarto di *dinar*, il *ruba'i*, che s'impose rapidamente non solo in Sicilia ma anche nell'Italia meridionale, dove assunse il nome di *tari* ("fresco", ossia moneta appena coniata), e dove Amalfitani e Salernitani ne producevano imitazioni. Le specie monetarie argentee erano essenzialmente rappresentate dal *dirahm* (il nome, passato attraverso il persiano, deriva dal greco "dracma") di grammi 2,90 e dalla piccola *kharruba* di 2 decigrammi. Anche nella lontana Rus', tra il Dnieper e il Don, circolava la moneta araba: meno l'aurea, molto però quella argentea. Attraverso il mondo musulmano giungevano in Europa le merci preziose provenienti dall'Africa e soprattutto, lungo la via delle spezie e la via della seta, dal continente asiatico. L'Europa del tempo, invece, non possedeva né produceva merci d'esportazione verso il mondo bizantino o quello arabo-berbero musulmano: se le aristocrazie del tempo volevano importare qualcosa da quelle aree (e si trattava sempre di merci lussuose e costose), dovevano pagare in oro, un metallo che, salvo in casi eccezionali, né le monarchie romano-barbariche prima, né l'impero carolingio e i regni posteriori si sognavano di coniare. La disponibilità aurea del mondo occidentale si assottigliò pertanto paurosamente, e la bilancia commerciale dell'Occidente nei confronti dell'Oriente rimase a lungo passiva; soltanto nel corso dell'XI secolo qualcosa cominciò a cambiare al riguardo.

Il commercio arabo-musulmano tra IX e X secolo era d'altronde, per queste ragioni, poco interessato all'Europa occidentale. Tuttavia c'era una merce apprezzata dagli Arabi e prodotta dai "Franchi" (in tal modo, *faranj*, erano chiamati tutti gli Europei occidentali, mentre i Greco-bizantini erano detti *rumi*, "romani"). Tale merce era il ferro, sia in lingotti sia in oggetti forgiati, anzitutto armi – di cui il mondo orientale era invece carente. Le "spade franche", prodotte soprattutto nella Germania sud-occidentale e nell'Italia settentrionale, erano ambite per le doti di solidità e di bellezza delle loro lame paragonabili solo al *gauhar*, l'acciaio bianco yemenita, o al *pulad*, l'acciaio azzurro indiano. Tuttavia spesso le spade venivano acquistate, ma poi lavorate di nuovo, passate attraverso le forge specializzate musulmane, magari ageminate con tecniche raffinatissime, come nel caso delle spade e degli acciai "di Damasco" o "di Toledo". Un'altra merce proveniente dal "paese dei franchi" o dal mondo bizantino era il legname, essenziale per i cantieri musulmani piuttosto a corto di alberi di alto fusto. Dalla medesima area provenivano all'Islam cera, miele, pellicce, canapa e soprattutto la pregiatissima ambra che dava il suo nome al fascio viario – prevalentemente marittimo e fluviale – dal Baltico al Bosforo.

Se il mondo islamico si presentò al proscenio del secondo millennio della nostra era molto frazionato sotto il profilo politico, straordinario fu invece il suo ruolo di mediazione, di originale rielaborazione e di sintesi sotto il profilo scientifico e culturale. "Cercate la scienza dovunque si trovi, fino in Cina": questa sarebbe stata una raccomandazione del Profeta ai suoi fedeli. La straordinaria capacità dei Musulmani di metabolizzare le culture con le quali erano venuti in contatto dall'Arabia al bacino dell'Indo e oltre, e dal Caucaso al Corno d'Africa e alle colonne d'Ercole, permise loro di sviluppare tra VII e XVI secolo una civiltà straordinariamente flessibile e multiforme, che entrò in vario modo in relazione con quelle circostanti. Ciò vale soprattutto per quella "latina", la quale contrasse nei confronti dell'Islam uno straordinario debito di riconoscenza. Per il suo tramite essa poté rientrare in contatto non soltanto con il patrimonio filosofico-scientifico ellenistico, ma anche con molti tesori delle culture persiana, indiana e cinese, fino ad allora estranei al mondo mediterraneo. Non si deve pensare soltanto ai tre califfati di Baghdad, di Córdoba e del Cairo, centri prestigiosi di studio con le loro "madrase" e le loro immense biblioteche; esistevano anche molti principati musulmani i quali, pur prestando formale ossequio a uno di essi, vivevano in maniera autonoma, ed erano a loro volta promotori e protettori di centri di elaborazione culturale, da Bukhara e Samarcanda fino a Kairuan e a Marrakesh.

La personalità di maggior rilievo nel mondo culturale musulmano di questo tempo è soprattutto il filosofo e medico Abu 'Ali al-Husayn Ibn Sina, che gli occidentali conoscono con il nome di Avicenna, il cui pensiero si radicava nella teologia per espandersi però verso la matematica, la geometria, le scienze naturali, la musica, l'astronomia. La sua opera più nota – in realtà un manuale di medicina, conosciuto col nome greco di *Kanon* – divenne nella sua versione latina il libro di testo delle scuole mediche europee fino al Settecento. Del resto, la letteratura musulmana di questo periodo fu soprattutto scientifica: trattati di storia, di geografia, di astronomia, di medicina, di architettura, ne sono gli esempi più importanti. I geografi arabi del X-XI secolo conoscevano bene la terra e viaggiavano dalla Cina al Circolo polare e all'Africa equatoriale trascrivendo le loro osservazioni in testi che restano classici nella storia delle esplorazioni. In generale, la cultura scientifica musulmana rielaborò il sapere greco antico aggiungendovi i portati di quelli persiano, indiano e cinese: tra i suoi protagonisti furono Geber (Giabir ibn Hayyan), fondatore dell'alchimia; il matematico al-Kawarizmi, da cui l'Occidente ha tratto la parola "algoritmo", nel senso di operazione aritmetica; e il filosofo al-Farabi. A questa letteratura scientifica si accompagnava una costellazione di opere poetiche e narrative, spesso a carattere popolare. Il fattore unificante della lingua araba – al tempo stesso idioma religioso-teologico, giuridico, politico e scientifico (i fedeli potevano leggere e recitare il *Corano* soltanto nella sua "lingua sacra") – ebbe al riguardo un'importanza fondamentale.

Attraverso questa circolazione di studiosi e di testi fu possibile per l'Occidente europeo attingere a patrimoni che erano andati perduti nel corso dell'alto Medioevo. È l'inizio di un processo che culminerà nei secoli XII e XIII, ma che ha le sue origini già nel X secolo, e che ebbe come epicentri le città della penisola Iberica. In arabo erano stati tradotti i tesori della sapienza degli antichi Greci; e, per quanto essi fossero accessibili anche attraverso versioni dal greco – per le quali però al momento erano a disposizione opportunità ben minori – le versioni latine dall'arabo si rivelavano di gran lunga preferibili sia per l'eccellenza dei commenti che traduttori e studiosi arabi avevano redatto, sia per l'abbondanza degli studi da essi intrapresi, sia infine perché ci si andava accorgendo che attraverso l'arabo l'Occidente poteva accedere pure al sapere e ad alcune tecnologie proprie anche di paesi più lontani, dalla Persia all'India e alla stessa Cina.

Sul piano della diffusione del sapere scientifico veicolato nel mondo musulmano attraverso la lingua del Libro sacro, la penisola iberica aveva procurato uno splendido avvio grazie a un precursore: Gerberto d'Aurillac, che giovanissimo aveva viaggiato in Catalogna e appreso fra il 967 e il 970 i rudimenti di aritmetica e di astronomia arabe e forse anche greche. Divenuto in seguito capo della scuola episcopale di Reims e quindi abate di Bobbio, Gerberto poté diffondere le sue conoscenze, in attesa di ascendere al soglio pontificio col nome di Silvestro II. Egli operò infatti una sintesi geniale delle teorie di Aristotele con quelle mediche di Ippocrate. L'Aristotele che egli conobbe e approfondì era tuttavia misto di elementi neoplatonici: tale fu in effetti l'Aristotele che giunse in Occidente prima della "rivoluzione scolastica" del secolo XIII e che influenzò profondamente la stessa filosofia cristiana.

Man mano che le condizioni di vita in Europa miglioravano, cresceva anche la capacità di ricezione di tale patrimonio culturale, al pari della curiosità per la religione islamica. Nel Duecento i tempi erano ormai maturi perché una delle personalità più autorevoli della Chiesa del tempo, Pietro il Venerabile abate di Cluny, si facesse protagonista di una straordinaria iniziativa che avesse come centro Toledo, da poco più di mezzo secolo restituita alla Cristianità, e quale garante il suo arcivescovo, Raimondo di Sauvêtat. Da tale iniziativa nacque l'attività di un'*équipe* che, con la consulenza di Musulmani e di Ebrei, provvide a una prima traduzione del *Corano* che porta il nome di Roberto di Ketton nel Rutlandshire: per quanto piuttosto confusa, lacunosa e incompleta, essa rimase fondamentale per i quattro secoli successivi. La fatica del gruppo coordinato dal Venerabile non si fermò al *Corano*, ma si estese ad altri gruppi operanti, oltre che in Spagna, anche nella penisola inglese e nell'Italia meridionale. I testi islamici redatti in versione latina a cura di traduttori come Giovanni di Siviglia, Domenico Gundisalvi, Ermanno il Dalmata, Platone di Tivoli, Gerardo di Cremona, e quelli islamologici redatti sulla base di quel rinnovato approccio rimasero a lungo la base della conoscenza dell'Islam di cui l'Europa medievale poteva disporre.

4 La ripresa delle città e degli scambi commerciali con l'Oriente

Alcuni storici hanno usato il concetto di "rivoluzione commerciale" per indicare il complesso di fatti economici, sociali, tecnologici che hanno accompagnato la diminuita importanza dell'agricoltura come fattore trainante dell'economia, e l'affermarsi di attività diverse: il commercio, l'artigianato su scala manifatturiera, gli strumenti di cambio e di credito. La città è naturalmente il luogo privilegiato nel quale avviene questo mutamento, del quale essa è in parte causa e al tempo stesso effetto. Ma, beninteso, la città non basta a spiegare il mutamento, così come i miglioramenti climatici e l'esplosione demografica successivi al secolo X non possono esserne ritenute i soli fattori remoti. In tutti questi elementi possiamo scorgere componenti del nuovo tipo di economia, di dinamica sociale, di ripartizione della proprietà e del lavoro che si era affermata già a partire dai secoli XI-XII, e che divenne evidente in tutta la sua pienezza nel Duecento.

In alcune città marinare italiche attività economica e autonomia politica datavano già dall'Alto Medioevo. In questi centri – ai quali se ne aggiungeranno poi alcuni provenzali, come Marsiglia, o catalani come Barcellona – si sviluppano, in complesso rapporto con l'antica aristocrazia urbana o quella di origine basso-feudale inurbata da poco, nuovi ceti dediti ad attività mercantili e armatoriali. Ad essi si deve l'affermarsi di un nuovo, più audace modo di fare affari: quello di riunirsi in "compagnie", "commende", *societates*, mettendo in comune capitali e accettando certi rischi allo scopo di realizzare precisi guadagni. Poiché i grandi commerci si svolgevano per vie marittime, essi avevano bisogno di navi e di naviganti; ed ecco che le città marittime si riempirono di cantieri con i relativi lavoratori addetti e di marinai. Fu questa una rivoluzione economica e in parte sociale. Non ancora tecnologica, però, in quanto l'accresciuta mobilità marittima non condusse a sostanziali modifiche nei tipi di naviglio, che continuarono a rispondere alle condizioni di navigazione nel Mediterraneo.

Intorno al Mille alcune città italo-bizantine affacciate sul mare avevano già raggiunto livelli di vita e capacità commerciali assai elevate. Dal principio del secolo IX Amalfi, Napoli e Salerno battevano una moneta propria, che derivava dal tarì arabo, segno che l'Islam, e non soltanto Bisanzio, costituiva la loro area privilegiata di scambio. Doveva però essere Venezia a spiccare il volo, riuscendo a intrecciare interessi fondiari e commerciali con attività agricole e finanziarie in un impero marittimo di grande portata. Le città italo-meridionali, inquadrate precocemente nel regno normanno, non smisero di esercitare funzioni commerciali, ma non poterono mai svilupparle di pari passo con quelle politiche.

Resa sicura la navigazione in Adriatico tra il IX e il X secolo, all'inizio del Duecento la rete di interessi commerciali dei Veneziani si estendeva tra Costantinopoli, la costa siro- palestinese, l'Africa settentrionale e la Sicilia. Nonostante i reiterati divieti imperiali e papali, Venezia vendeva agli Arabi generi proibiti come il legname, il ferro e gli schiavi provenienti soprattutto dall'Istria, dalla Slovenia e dalla Croazia. Contemporaneamente, altre città marittime italiane stavano sviluppando una loro politica autonoma: tra queste emersero presto Genova e Pisa.

Furono dunque queste tre città a imporre, in concomitanza con la prima crociata, dei veri e propri itinerari che si snodavano sull'asse est-ovest e viceversa, e che univa i loro porti a Costantinopoli e alle colonie mercantili che le tre città avevano fondato tanto nell'impero bizantino quanto sulla costa siro-palestinese. I conflitti che scaturirono tra loro nei secoli XII-XIII ebbero sovente origine da tensioni nate oltremare. Ad esempio, l'inimicizia tra Genova e Pisa cominciò quando si trattò di stabilire quale tra la due città avrebbe dovuto stabilire la propria egemonia sulle grandi isole di Corsica e di Sardegna; e continuò poi sia a Costantinopoli, sia ad Acri e a Tiro (i due maggiori porti del regno crociato), dove i "quartieri" veneziano, pisano e genovese erano contigui.

Queste colonie commerciali delle città italiche sorgevano in quartieri urbani ben distinti dagli altri, addirittura dotati di loro fortificazioni, e prospicienti il mare: disponevano pertanto d'infrastrutture portuali, avevano fondachi e arsenali ed erano popolate da cittadini della madrepatria i quali passavano parte dell'anno su una sponda e parte sull'altra del Mediterraneo. Esse erano empori di straordinaria importanza, dove giungevano le merci dalle grandi città mercantili dell'entroterra come Damasco e Aleppo e addirittura da più lontano, attraverso la via della seta. Da lì partivano verso l'Europa i preziosi carichi di spezie indispensabili alla medicina, all'alimentazione, alla conservazione dei cibi, ma soprattutto all'attività manifatturiera e anche all'arte (per esempio le materie coloranti, le quali servivano tanto a tingere le stoffe tessute in Occidente quanto alla pittura e alla vetreria); ma da lì arrivavano i panni di lana e le tele di canapa, i prodotti alimentari, il legname da costruzione, i pani di metallo greggio e le armi ch'erano tutti prodotti occidentali sempre più richiesti in Oriente e sempre meglio pagati, per quanto i papi cercassero con ogni mezzo di fermare la vendita di armi ai Saraceni. In questo modo, nel corso del Duecento, la bilancia commerciale (fin allora favorevole all'Oriente) s'invertì, e grazie all'afflusso di oro nelle casse dei mercanti latini l'Europa poté accedere alla coniazione della moneta d'oro, che dal IV al XIII secolo era stato privilegio praticamente esclusivo dei Bizantini e di alcuni potentati musulmani.

Se Venezia, con la quarta crociata, riaffermava il controllo su Costantinopoli, Pisani e Genovesi puntarono immediatamente sui porti egiziani di Alessandria e Damietta, dove fondarono colonie commerciali. Genova cercò poi di estendere i suoi interessi oltre il Bosforo, nei porti del Mar Nero, dai quali si commerciava l'allume, a contatto con i Tartari dell'orda d'Oro e con i principati russi, in modo da sfruttare le correnti mercantili che attraverso il Volga e il Don provenivano dal Baltico, e che approdavano ai porti della Crimea e al rifornimento di grano ucraino per l'Occidente.

5 La controffensiva cristiana

Nel corso del secolo XI l'Europa occidentale – la cui identità era rappresentata essenzialmente dal rapporto con la disciplina, la liturgia e la lingua comune della Chiesa latina – presentò un deciso incremento demografico che ben presto si tradusse in ripresa economica in virtù dell'espansione delle colture, in sviluppo delle reti viarie, in dilatazione dei centri urbani e quindi in numerose iniziative commerciali e militari per mare e per terra. Andava profilandosi, dalla Spagna alla Sicilia alla Terrasanta, una dinamica spesso aggressiva delle genti cristiano-occidentali, che alcuni studiosi hanno interpretato come una "risposta" all'espansione musulmana dei secoli VII-X.

Il complesso fronte delle lotte cristiano-musulmane nel Mediterraneo – che tuttavia si accompagnava, non si sostituiva agli scambi commerciali – si andò spostando nel quadrante di nord-ovest, dove protagonista era l'emiro di Denia e delle Baleari, il cui epiteto onorifico musulmano era al-Mujahid ("il Combattente del *jihad*"), graziosamente corretto dai cronisti latinofoni in "Musettus". Nel 1005, mentre i Pisani erano impegnati a dar man forte ai Cristiani di Calabria contro i musulmani, al-Mujahid assalì Pisa e ne incendiò una parte. Nel medesimo anno 1016, fatidico per Salerno e per tutto il Meridione peninsulare, Musettus dava l'assalto alla città di Luni in Garfagnana, e la distruggeva costringendo gli abitanti a fuggire per le montagna apuane. Ma tempestiva giungeva la risposta congiunta di Genovesi e Pisani, che sconfiggerano la compagine degli assalitori e obbligavano il capo-predone a rientrare nel suo covo in Sardegna.

Più tardi si sarebbe profilato il vero e proprio contrattacco. Mentre fra Aragona e Castiglia si profilavano i primi segni delle vittoriose offensive cristiane nei confronti degli emirati arabo-berbero-iberici, i Pisani assalivano nel 1063 il porto di Palermo e nel 1087 quello tunisino di al-Mahdiya, a fianco dei Genovesi e anche degli Amalfitani. Da allora prese l'avvio la controffensiva delle due città tirreniche che per quasi tre secoli si sarebbero contese l'egemonia del Mediterraneo centro-occidentale e, più tardi, dopo la prima crociata, anche del litorale siro-palestinese.

A quel periodo risale l'arrivo in forze dei Normanni nel Meridione peninsulare d'Italia. Inserendosi come mercenari nel complesso scenario politico della regione, essi si impossessarono in pochi decenni della regione. Fra il 1061 e il 1094 Ruggero detto "il Granconte", fratello di Roberto il Guiscardo, condusse a termine la conquista della Sicilia. All'atto della conquista l'isola era abitata quasi totalmente da Arabo-berberi e da indigeni di origine greco-latina islamizzati; soltanto a Palermo e in alcune ristrette aree nord-orientali vi erano comunità greco-cristiane di una certa consistenza. Durante la campagna militare Ruggero aveva assicurato a tutti libertà di culto, reclutando nel proprio esercito anche molti musulmani. Al tempo stesso egli lavorò a un ripopolamento di Cristiani latini e, quando si sentì più sicuro, mutò il suo atteggiamento nei confronti dei Musulmani rendendolo più severo. Comunque, per tutto il periodo del regno normanno e anche oltre funzionari arabi continuarono a lavorare nel *diwan*, l'ufficio addetto all'organizzazione tributaria.

Anche sul fronte spagnolo le cose andavano mutando. Quando nel 996-997 il califfo cordobano al-Mansur diede l'assalto alla città di Compostela, egli compì un gesto dimostrativo di straordinario valore simbolico. Alla tomba dell'apostolo di Compostela stava convenendo un numero di anno in anno crescente di pellegrini dalle regioni poste al di là dei Pirenei: la notizia della profanazione del santuario, lungi dal seminare paura e sconcerto, fu perciò seme d'indignazione, e la causa dell'apostolo Giacomo diventava quella della Cristianità intera. Il pellegrinaggio alla tomba dell'Apostolo assunse ben presto anche un ruolo guerriero. Si diceva che durante la battaglia di Clavijo dell'844 l'Apostolo fosse apparso in una veste abbagliante, montato su un candido destriero, e avesse guidato i Cristiani all'assalto contro i nemici. Visioni di questo genere facevano parte di una sacralizzazione del conflitto che si può facilmente collegare alla propaganda ecclesiastica, ma che si radicava in una sensibilità collettiva eccitata, in una disposizione nuova al combattimento e al martirio.

Dopo la liquidazione del califfato di Córdoba, la Spagna musulmana era divisa tra i vari *reinos de taifas*. La situazione rimase per un certo periodo in uno stato d'instabile equilibrio perché anche i regni cristiani erano percorsi da rivalità e da inimicizie. Le cose cambiarono verso il 1055, quando Ferdinando I – dal 1037 acclamato re di Castiglia e di León – fu in grado di scatenare un'offensiva che mise in suo potere la bassa valle del Duero. Frattanto il fronte aragonese rischiava il tracollo per la morte del re Ramiro I durante l'assedio alla fortezza saracena di Graus. Poiché l'infante Sancho era ancora minorenne, spettò a papa Alessandro II prendere l'iniziativa che condusse alla conquista della piazzaforte di Barbastro, non lungi da Saragozza, con una spedizione che si avvalse del contributo di molti cavalieri francesi. Al movimento del pellegrinaggio a Santiago partecipavano parecchi aristocratici, dal momento che per i figli cadetti della nobiltà non si prevedevano assegnazioni ereditarie, ed essi avevano quindi soltanto la scelta fra carriera ecclesiastica o avventura guerriera.

La scomparsa di Ferdinando I nel 1065 provocò una nuova battuta d'arresto. Oltre le colonne d'Ercole si era affermato il potere della confraternita degli al-Murabitun, "uomini dei *ribat*" (da cui "Almoravidi"), gli austeri abitanti dei conventi-fortezze oltre il deserto, sulle rive del Senegal e del Niger, che si erano quindi impadronitisi di Marocco e Algeria. Lo scontro avvenne nel 1086 presso la Guadiana, a Zallaqa (oggi Sagrajas), e fu una grave sconfitta per i Cristiani. Lo stesso re Alfonso si salvò a stento, con poche centinaia di cavalieri, riparando a

Coria. Yusuf obbligò i *reyes de taifas* a sottomettersi alla sua autorità: chi cercò di resistere, naturalmente alleandosi con i Castigliani, fu inesorabilmente piegato. Toledo restava ai Cristiani, ma a sud del Tago non rimaneva più nulla dei tentativi di conquista degli anni precedenti.

Tuttavia il potere almoravide andò presto deteriorandosi a causa della riscossa militare dei regni cristiani di Spagna (soprattutto di quello d'Aragona), ma anche per l'affermarsi di una corrente mistico-teologica sviluppatasi nel Maghreb a partire dal secondo quarto del secolo XII. Gli *al-Muwahiddun*, i "fedeli dell'unità divina", o Almohad, erano sorti come movimento politico-religioso a carattere rigoristico guidato dal *mahdi* Muhammad ibn Tumart, insorto contro le concessioni all'antropomorfismo letterale del Corano in qualche modo accettate dai teologi almoravidi. Nel 1162 un'armata almohade sbarcò nella penisola iberica, dove il collasso degli Almoravidi aveva ricondotto l'Islam locale a una nuova frammentazione, e occupò Siviglia mentre i Castigliani approfittavano della situazione per impadronirsi della ricca Almeria e i Portoghesi di Lisbona.

Il potere almohade fu molto più restrittivo di quello almoravide: furono perseguitati e costretti all'esilio o al confino anche i due maggiori pensatori del tempo, l'ebreo Moshe ben Maimun (Maimonide) e il musulmano Ibn Rush (Averroè). Maimonide finì in Egitto dove sarebbe divenuto nel 1172 *naghid*, cioè capo della locale comunità ebraica, e quindi medico del sultano Saladino e dei suoi successori. Ma l'intolleranza almohade terminò presto: la dinastia berbera permise l'impiantarsi in Marocco di culti simili a quelli dei santi cristiani, mentre una rinnovata libertà di ricerca dava luogo al fiorire di pensatori come Ibn Tufayl e – dopo i primi sospetti nei suoi confronti – Averroè. Anche l'economia conobbe un forte rilancio in virtù di un massiccio impegno nel miglioramento delle opere d'irrigazione, mentre nel commercio si stipularono alleanze con le città italiane.

La nuova crociata predicata da Innocenzo III, alla quale presero parte i re Alfonso di Castiglia e Pietro d'Aragona, si concluse nel 1212 con la vittoria di Las Navas de Tolosa, che apriva ai Cristiani le porte della regione dell'Andalusia e preludeva alla caduta della stessa capitale del califfato almohade, Córdoba, che venne conquistata nel 1236 dal re Ferdinando III il Santo. Nel 1260 gran parte della conquista cristiana della penisola iberica poteva dirsi compiuta: mentre il regno del Portogallo (nato da una contea castigliana e riconosciuto dal papa nel 1179) tendeva a colonizzare la parte sud-occidentale della penisola, la zona del cosiddetto Algarve, entrando perciò in conflitto con la Castiglia, il regno castigliano si impadroniva dell'area a sud del Guadalquivir, escluso il piccolo emirato di Granada, che sarebbe rimasto musulmano fino al 1492.

Dal punto di vista della qualità della vita la cosiddetta *reconquista* cristiana non segnò l'avvio di una stagione positiva per la Spagna. Nei circa cinque secoli del loro dominio in terra iberica i Musulmani avevano fatto un giardino di terre per loro natura desertiche, come l'arido altopiano della Meseta: vi avevano condotto le acque per mezzo di ardite opere di irrigazione, vi avevano avviato colture di cereali, canna da zucchero, agrumi. Nelle popolose città da essi governate vivevano in pace e in armonia anche le comunità cristiane "mozarabiche" (che usavano correntemente l'arabo nella loro liturgia) e quelle ebraiche, e si era sviluppato un ceto urbano di mercanti e di artigiani. Tra il XI e il XV secolo le guerre si alternarono a lunghi periodi di pace: tanto nei regni cristiani quanto negli emirati musulmani si stabiliva un clima di distensione e di tolleranza reciproca tra comunità cristiane, musulmane ed ebraiche: nulla sarebbe più errato che leggere crociate e guerre iberiche medievali come "guerre di religione". Ma i sovrani di Castiglia, che si appoggiavano su un'aristocrazia feudale di cavalieri i cui interessi economici si legavano con la più primitiva economia pastorale, non avevano alcun interesse a mantenere questi livelli di vita. Non incoraggiarono quindi né l'agricoltura né l'artigianato né il commercio, perseguitando Musulmani ed Ebrei che ne costituivano il nerbo. La Castiglia si avviò a divenire una terra desolata di poveri pastori, di agricoltori miserabili e di un ceto nobiliare privo di mezzi, caratterizzato da un genere di vita ispirato ai valori guerrieri e a una religiosità sentita anzitutto come lotta contro gli "infedeli".

6 Le Crociate e il Mediterraneo orientale

Potrà a questo punto sembrare strano che, pur accennandone qua e là, non si sia ancora affrontato il tema delle Crociate, che ancor oggi riempie di sé i libri di storia del mondo mediterraneo. Tale scelta è dipesa dalla volontà di sottolineare lo stretto collegamento esistente tra le "imprese d'oltremare" (e tutto il contesto economico, commerciale, culturale e politico-diplomatico che le accompagnò) e quelle che si erano già profilate prima del loro avvio nella penisola iberica e nel Mediterraneo centrale, nel Meridione peninsulare italico e in Sicilia.

Nel corso del secolo XI una tribù originariamente turkmena – appartenente cioè a un ramo specifico delle etnie turco-mongole – che noi denominiamo "selgiuchide" dal nome di un loro *khan* chiamato Selgiuq, convertita all'Islam da pochi decenni, giunse dalle steppe dell'Asia centrale a rafforzare con la sua fede e la sua forza militare (essi erano cavalieri e arcieri formidabili) il pericolante potere del califfo abbaside di Baghdad. Non solo rapidamente islamizzati, ma anche iranizzati nella lingua e nei costumi (il persiano fu loro sempre più familiare di quanto non fosse l'arabo), i Turchi selgiuchidi fondarono così un impero politico-militare che dall'Anatolia si estendeva alla Persia centrale. Essi erano divenuti famosi di colpo quando, nel 1071, avevano battuto clamorosamente l'esercito bizantino nella battaglia di Manzikert fondando in Anatolia il sultanato che fu detto "di Rum" (dal nome arabo con cui si indicava la "nuova Roma", Costantinopoli) con capitale nella città di Iconio.

Questa situazione dette luogo a una serie di spedizioni guerriere che la storiografia occidentale ha chiamato "crociate", anche se il termine sarebbe rientrato abbastanza tardi nel lessico delle lingue europee. L'abitudine a contare sette o otto o nove spedizioni crociate è stata per molto tempo privilegiata; ma le spedizioni incoraggiate e addirittura legittimate o bandite direttamente dalla Chiesa, che avevano come scopo iniziale la conquista (e quindi il mantenimento o la riconquista) di Gerusalemme e dei "luoghi santi" cristiani, durarono molto più a lungo, giungendo fino al Settecento. Esse interessarono non soltanto l'area siro-palestinese, bensì anche quella iberica e quella anatolica, e furono utilizzate, grazie a una serie di accorgimenti giuridici, contro obiettivi diversi da quelli musulmani, come ad esempio eretici o nemici politici del papato. Per apprezzare il fenomeno ci si deve perciò riferire non tanto a singole "crociate" quanto a un complesso "movimento crociato", che determinò nuove formazioni politico-istituzionali nonché conseguenze fiscali e finanziarie, e che produsse una propria cultura giuridica e una propria letteratura.

L'Islam del secolo XI non aveva familiarità con il mondo latino ed euro-occidentale. I Musulmani presero quindi a prestito la parola greca con la quale nella cultura bizantina s'indicavano gli europei d'Occidente (*Phrankoi*, dal latino *franci*) e la rese con l'arabo *faranj*. Nel 1097-98 un grande eterogeneo esercito di *faranj*, il cui nerbo era costituito dai temibili cavalieri pesantemente armati, accompagnati da una turba di pellegrini, fece la comparsa nella penisola anatolica, l'attraversò e seguendo la costa siriaca giunse fino a Gerusalemme, conquistandola il 15 luglio 1099 con un sanguinoso assalto. Muovendo da lì, e aiutati dai marinai dei centri costieri italici, quei guerrieri – tra i quali v'erano alcuni nobili signori che avevano già partecipato a spedizioni contro i Musulmani nella penisola iberica e in Sicilia – intrapresero una serie di campagne militari che in alcuni decenni li condussero a conquistare un'area corrispondente grosso modo a quella oggi occupata dall'attuale stato d'Israele, dal Libano e da parte della Siria e della Giordania.

Per governare questa regione, inquadrata nelle istituzioni della Chiesa romana, si dette vita a un "regno franco di Gerusalemme" organizzato come una monarchia feudale – con alcuni principati vassalli: la contea di Edessa, il principato di Antiochia, il principato di Tripoli, le contee di Giaffa, di Ascalona e dell'Oltregiordano. Esso sopravvisse circa due secoli anche in virtù dell'apporto di gruppi di guerrieri che accettarono di rimanere in Terrasanta e di difenderla costituendo dei veri e propri ordini religioso-militari come i cavalieri di San Giovanni, i Templari, i cavalieri di San Lazzaro, più tardi i cavalieri di santa Maria dei Teutoni. I *faranj* insediati nel Vicino Oriente riuscirono progressivamente a conquistare l'intera costa del Mar di Levante, dal Golfo di Alessandretta fino all'istmo di Suez; frattanto si organizzavano spedizioni nell'entroterra, in modo da sottomettere i principali centri di Galilea, Samaria e Giudea. Verso la fine del primo quarto del secolo XII l'intera regione dal Tauro al Sinai e dalla costa del Mediterraneo al Giordano, con un'*enclave* a est rappresentata dall'area attorno alla fortezza di Kerak, era ormai presidiata dai Franchi, anche se le strade restavano insicure e la guerriglia musulmana era endemica.

Nel frattempo il mondo musulmano si stava riavendo dalla sorpresa e si andava riorganizzando. La riscossa partì dalle città siro-mesopotamiche settentrionali, Aleppo e Mosul, governate nel nome del califfo di Baghdad e del suo consigliere-protettore selgiuchide, il sultano, da una dinastia di *atabeg* (in turco "padre dei capi", cioè governatore generale) fondata da Imad ad-Din Zenqi. Egli ambiva a unificare sotto il suo potere tutti gli emirati della regione tra il Mar di Levante e l'Eufrate; inoltre, musulmano sunnita intransigente, guardava con ostilità al califfato sciita del Cairo. La definitiva caduta nel 1146 in mani turche della città armena di Edessa (oggi Urfa in Turchia), dal 1097 una contea crociata, costituì un segnale d'allarme. Contro il crescente potere *dell'atabeg* si organizzò in Europa una grande spedizione (poi detta "seconda crociata") che partì nel 1147 al comando di Luigi VII re di Francia e di Corrado III re di Germania, ma che fallì anche in quanto i suoi capi non conoscevano la situazione vicino-orientale e si gettarono sulla ricca città di Damasco, il cui emiro arabo era l'unico vero avversario di Zenqi e avrebbe potuto essere un loro alleato prezioso. Il fallimento di quella spedizione causò in Europa una lunga scia di recriminazioni e d'inimicizie che impedirono per più di quarant'anni qualsiasi aiuto ai re crociati di Gerusalemme.

L'*atabeg* di Aleppo e Mosul si comportava ormai come un principe indipendente sebbene, sotto il profilo formale, fosse funzionario del sultano selgiuchide. Alla sua morte il suo dominio fu diviso tra i figli e perse in parte di potenza; ascese al potere Yusuf ibn Ayyub, che nella storia musulmana è conosciuto come al-Malik an-Nasir Salah ad-Din ("il Sovrano Vittorioso, Integrità della Fede") e in quella occidentale come "il Saladino". Il califfo egiziano al-Adid nominò il Saladino suo *vizir* ma, nel 1171, fu da questi deposto: con lui terminò l'esperimento califfale sciita e l'Egitto ritornò all'ortodossia sunnita. Il paese fu affidato al governo del Saladino, che si affrancò in tal modo dal servizio agli *atabeg* turco-siriaci, assumendo il titolo di sultano e dando avvio a una dinastia che, dal suo nome di famiglia, fu detta "ayyubide".

Il nuovo sultanato del Saladino era distinto in due grandi territori: l'Egitto e la Siria con capitale Damasco, a sua volta da lui sottomessa. In questo modo egli chiudeva il regno crociato di Gerusalemme da nord e da sud-ovest. Tuttavia non attaccò subito i *faranj*, con molti dei quali mantenne anzi amichevoli rapporti. Ma non esitò più all'indomani della morte del giovane re Baldovino IV (il "Re lebbroso"), anche perché gli atti di violenza e di rapina compiuti dall'audace ma violento signore crociato dell'Oltregiordano, Rinaldo di Chatillon, richiedevano una risposta esemplare. L'esercito di Rinaldo fu sconfitto dal Saladino nel luglio 1187; poche settimane più tardi egli entrava pacificamente in Gerusalemme sgombrata dai Crociati. Il regno di Gerusalemme trasferì la sua capitale ad Acri e per tutto il secolo, fino al 1291, rimase padrone della costa.

In seguito alla conquista musulmana di Gerusalemme fu bandita in Europa una nuova spedizione (rimasta famosa con il nome di "terza crociata"), che fu guidata dai più prestigiosi sovrani del tempo: l'imperatore Federico I, il re di Francia Filippo II Augusto, il re d'Inghilterra Riccardo Cuor di Leone. Tuttavia Federico morì durante il viaggio, il re di Francia rientrò presto in Europa, e il Saladino firmò con quello d'Inghilterra una pace che riconosceva come Gerusalemme fosse ormai tornata in mano musulmana e come i "Franchi" fossero attestati sul litorale. Ma il sultano morì nel 1193, dividendo tra i suoi figli il sultanato. Da allora due distinte dinastie dette "ayyubidi", ostili tra loro, regnarono rispettivamente a Damasco e al Cairo. La dinastia ayyudide d'Egitto visse negli ultimi tempi quasi prigioniera di onnipotenti primi ministri (i *vizir*) e di truppe mercenarie di origine servile (conosciute quindi col nome di "mamelucchi" dall'arabo *mamluk*, "schiavo"). E furono i sultani di stirpe mamelucca a sostenere l'ondata mongola dei successori di Genghiz Khan che aveva sommerso il califfato abbaside di Baghdad e quindi a riprendere l'offensiva contro le città e le fortezze costiere siro-libanesi, cancellando completamente nel 1291 il vecchio regno franco di Gerusalemme, mentre gli ordini religioso-militari si rifugiarono nelle isole, i Templari a Cipro e i cavalieri di San Giovanni a Rodi.

Dopo la caduta di San Giovanni d'Acri nel 1291, il periodo delle Crociate in Terrasanta sembrava chiuso. Ma l'insorgere di una lunga fase di crisi nel secondo quarto del Trecento, caratterizzato da una drammatica catena di carestie e di epidemie e dal disagio socio-economico che colpì l'intera Europa, fu accompagnato da un quasi simultaneo frammentarsi tanto dell'impero dell'impero bizantino quanto dai khanati tartari nati dalle conquiste di Genghiz Khan. Ciò ebbe come effetto la mobilitazione di altri gruppi nomadici turco-mongoli, tra i quali uno, quello guidato dalla stirpe degli Ottomani, arrivò nel corso del secolo a insediarsi nella penisola anatolica, battendo o fagocitando altri gruppi vicini e minacciando l'impero di Costantinopoli ormai ridotto a poco più della capitale.

Alla fine del Trecento il vecchio e desueto ideale della crociata contro gli infedeli in Oriente rinacque con un nuovo, diverso obiettivo: ormai non si trattava ovviamente più di riconquistare la Terrasanta, bensì di difendere la Cristianità da una minaccia che si presentava come formidabile. I sultani ottomani, accampati nelle loro ricche capitali di Bursa in Asia e di Adrianopoli (o Edirne) nella penisola balcanica, cingevano ormai Costantinopoli di un assedio minaccioso. I *basileis* bizantini, invocando contro di loro la solidarietà e il soccorso dei fratelli in Cristo latini, potevano offrire in cambio soltanto la cultura degli intellettuali greci che sempre più numerosi riparavano in Occidente con i loro preziosi carichi di manoscritti – e questo fenomeno è una delle basi della rivoluzione culturale umanistica – e la fine dello scisma tra Chiesa latina e Chiesa greca che si era avviato nel 1054, e che difatti si chiuse con una solenne dichiarazione congiunta durante il concilio di Firenze, nel 1441. La crociata di liberazione che i principi occidentali avrebbero dovuto attuare si risolse in una maldestra spedizione che nel 1444 s'infranse con la disastrosa sconfitta presso Varna sul Mar Nero; nove anni dopo, nel 1453, il giovane sultano Mehmed II occupò Costantinopoli non senza il dissimulato appoggio di potenze cristiane come Firenze e Venezia, desiderose di far buoni affari con i nuovi padroni del Mediterraneo orientale. Una nuova spedizione crociata nel 1456 ebbe il risultato di fermare gli Ottomani sotto Belgrado; ma l'impresa guerriera che papa Pio II auspicava non si realizzò mai.

La lotta tra Cristiani e Musulmani poteva così procedere sotto il segno di una vistosa asimmetria: l'Islam ottomano avanzava sommergendo parte della penisola balcano-danubiana e strappando a Venezia anche alcune isole greche (ma la Serenissima avrebbe guadagnato alla fine del secolo l'isola di Cipro, lasciatale in eredità dall'ultima regina della stirpe crociata dei Lusignano); entro il primo ventennio del secolo successivo i sultani di Costantinopoli (ormai detta Istanbul) avrebbero affermato il loro dominio anche sull'Egitto e su tutta l'Africa settentrionale. Frattanto, però, nella penisola iberica l'ultimo emirato arabo-berbero restato indipendente – quello di Granada – cadeva nelle mani dei re cattolici, Ferdinando d'Aragona e Isabella di Castiglia, nello stesso fatidico anno della scoperta del Nuovo Mondo. Vittorioso a oriente, l'Islam mediterraneo retrocedeva ad occidente e si barricava sulle coste meridionali, in Africa. Intanto i mercati mediterranei continuavano a essere attivi nonostante il disturbo arrecato dalle incursioni corsare (dei barbareschi musulmani, ma anche di Catalani, Genovesi e cavalieri di Rodi): la guerra non impediva né gli scambi commerciali, né i ricchi affari nei quali entravano ormai sempre più i Portoghesi, l'Etiopia e l'India. Sarà la scoperta del Nuovo Mondo, con la conquista di nuove terre e di nuovi correnti di traffico, a cambiare la situazione e i rapporti di forza. Il mondo, ormai, era divenuto più grande; e il Mediterraneo – ridotto al ruolo di frontiera tra società e culture differenti – non ne costituiva più il centro.

Bibliografia

Bresc, H 2001, *Europa y el Islam en la Edad Media*, Critica, Barcelona.
Cardini, F 1999, *Europa e Islam. Storia di un malinteso*, Laterza, Roma-Bari.
Fletcher, R 1993, *Moorish Spain*, University of California Press, Berkeley.
Goitein, SD 1966, *Studies in Islamic History and Institutions*, E.J. Brill, Leiden.
Holt, PM & Lambton, AKS & Lewis, B (eds) 1970, *The Cambridge History of Islam*, Cambridge University Press, Cambridge.
Humphreys, S 1977, *From Saladin to the Mongols: The Ayyubids of Damascus, 1193-1260*, State University of New York Press, Albany, NY.
Provençal, EL & Balbás, LT (1976), *España musulmana (711-1031). La Conquista, el Emirato, el Califato*, in *Historia de España*, dir. por RM Pidal, Espasa Calpe, Madrid.
Nicolle, D 2003, *Warriors and their Weapons around the Time of the Crusades: Relationships between Byzantium, the West, and the Islamic World*, Ashgate/Variorum, Aldershot.
Riley-Smith, J 2009, *Storia delle Crociate*, Mondadori, Milan.
Watt, WM 1972, *The Influence of Islam on Medieval Europe*, Edinburgh University Press, Edinburgh.

Franco Cardini
Europe and Islam: Encounters and Confrontations

1 The Birth of Islam and the Break-up of Mediterranean Unity

The new religious faith of Islam, which originated in the Arabian peninsula in the early seventh century, spread rapidly after the death of its founder, Mohammed, in 632. It completely transformed the Asian and African areas of the Mediterranean. Within a quarter of a century it had absorbed the Persian empire and compelled the Byzantine empire to change its policies. The Arabs who brought the new faith occupied the coasts and some of the inland parts of Asia Minor, Syria, Egypt, and northern Africa, which were the recruitment areas for the fleets of the Eastern Roman Empire. The conversion of their populations to Islam can be partly explained by the fact that although they were Christian, they were mostly "heretics" – particularly Monophysites – whom the imperial authorities of Constantinople had subjected to harsh taxation, deportation and other repressive measures because of their beliefs; the incoming Arabs, by contrast, allowed them to pursue their religion freely, on the principle that they were *ahl al-Kitab*, "peoples of the Book", who had received a form of revelation, albeit an imperfect one, and so did not need to convert. This development seriously impaired the maritime power of Byzantium. It now had to share its command of the sea with the Muslim potentates, though the emergence of discord, schisms and internecine wars within Islam prevented the Mediterranean coming entirely under Muslim control.

In reality, the Mediterranean had long since ceased to be the *mare nostrum* of antiquity, an area under indisputed imperial control. Diocletian's partition of the empire had already had a significant impact: the western empire, more vulnerable to incursions by Germanic peoples such as the Goths, who had settled in Italy and in the Iberian peninsula, lost control of the sea routes between Gaul, Spain and the African coasts; Byzantium, on the other hand, managed to keep control of the eastern Mediterranean, at least as far as the line marked by Sicily and Sardinia. So the Mediterranean was split into two basins which were quite distinct from each other, not only geographically but also politically and militarily. As Islam spread, the eastern basin became a scene of conflict between the Eastern Empire and the new Islamic powers; the western basin, however, long remained an area of Muslim control and corsair activity. The Mediterranean had lost its unity, and what had once been the hub of the ancient world, its trade and its culture, became a frontier, albeit one that changed over the centuries.

Scholarly consensus used to favour Henri Pirenne's theory that the sudden rise of Muslim naval power caused a breakdown of the Mediterranean unity which had previously preserved the economic structures and cultural homogeneity of the peoples that lived on its coasts; this, it was believed, caused the old *pars Occidentis* of the empire to turn in on itself, intensifying the existing processes of recession and ruralisation. In other words, the characteristics of what we call the "Middle Ages" first appeared in the seventh and eighth centuries, when the Muslims gained control over the Mediterranean. In reality, the economic crisis of the sixth and seventh centuries, which was to continue, with fluctuations and periodic revivals, until the tenth century, were the result of a slow underlying process. This background helps us understand the change that took place in the Mediterranean's role, in relation to the political and economic development of the regions along its coasts.

2 The Islamic Push towards the West

After the Umayyad caliphs had come to power in *dar al-Islam* (661-750), the court of Damascus, a city with strong Greek cultural traditions, came increasingly to resemble the eastern Romanised court of Constantinople. A Muslim kind of art and literature were being created which had affinities with the eclectic traditions of Byzantine culture, and this led to a certain permissiveness in religious matters. Under the Umayyads, Islam spread eastwards as far as the Hindu Kush and the River Amu Darya – in other words, as far as modern Afghanistan and Uzbekistan.

After conquering Syria and Palestine, the Arabs moved further west towards the ancient Roman province of Africa (*Ifriqiya*), comprising modern Tripolitania, Tunisia and Algeria; the first invasion took place in 647, but it was not until 663 that eastern Roman, and especially Berber, resistance finally crumbled. At this point, having established control of the southern and eastern coasts of the Mediterranean, the Arabs and their Arabised co-religionists turned their attention to conquering the sea itself and the coasts that lay beyond it.

In Visigoth Spain, concern had soon spread at the news of the Arab advance along the coasts of northern Africa. King Egica sounded the alarm at the Council of Toledo in 694. It was rumoured that the Jews, resentful of the oppressive measures taken against them, were preparing to go over to the "new barbarians" who were advancing from the east; meanwhile a civil war was being fought over the succession to the last king of Toledo; and apparently one of the contenders,

Achila, who had taken refuge in Morocco, appealed for help to the Mauri (so called because they originated from ancient *Mauretania*, which to the Arabs was *al-Maghreb*, the "West"), Islamised Berbers led by a small Arab aristocracy. These Mauri would later be known in Spanish epic as *los Moros*; they would also be called *Saraceni*, or *Agareni*, from the biblical names of Abraham's wife and concubine.

It was probably late July 711 when a large Muslim fleet landed in the Bay of Algeciras, which had been raided the previous year. By 720 the Arabs had occupied Catalonia and Septimania – the entire territory of the Visigoth monarchy both south and north of the Pyrenees – though a few pockets of Christian resistance survived in the more difficult terrain of the Pyrenees and the Cantabrician Mountains. From Spain the Arabs moved on to southern Gaul, where the Franks had been in nominal control since the early sixth century, but political institutions were fragile and social structures weak. After occupying Narbonne in 718, the Arabs besieged Toulouse in 721 and took Nîmes and Carcassonne in 725. By now the whole of Provence and the Rhone basin was within their reach. Tradition has it that a Muslim expedition – probably heading for Tours, where a hoard of treasure was kept in the shrine of Saint Martin – was stopped at Poitiers by Charles Martel, the *Maître de Palais* of the Merovingian kingdom of Austrasia; but the battle itself, fought in 732 or 733, was less significant than the legend to which it gave rise; indeed, the "Moors" continued their raids on the cities of southern Gaul even after this battle. The Arab and Berber incursions prompted various responses in the Frankish world, notably constant campaigns by Charles Martel; but duplicity and betrayal were rife, and these activities can hardly be described as expeditions of "the Franks against Islam".

The danger posed by the "Moors" of Spain, who also found it impossible to present a unified front, conferred lasting fame on Charles Martel's dynasty, which had supplanted that of the Merovingians. But the risk of an Islamic invasion from the Pyrenees was virtually non-existent in the eighth and ninth centuries. On the contrary, the most significant invasion was made in the opposite direction, by King Charles, the *Maître de Palais's* nephew, when he attempted to intervene in the conflicts between the small Aragonese emirates in 776. That enterprise failed, but was destined to go down in legend: it was the setting for the famous episode of the ambush at Roncesvalles, when an ally and relative of Charles, the *comes* Roland, was killed; this was to be the subject of the later *Chanson de Roland*, one of the most important epic poems of the Middle Ages. In reality, however, the warriors who defeated the Franks on that occasion were not Muslims, but Christian Basque mountain dwellers who objected to a foreign army marching across their land.

Charles succeeded in creating a marchland, Catalonia, south of the Pyrenees, as a bridgehead for possible expansion into the Iberian peninsula; and this led to the whole area of the Pyrenees coming under Frankish control. In the third decade of the eighth century, however, the advance of Islam – whose reach now extended from the Indus to the Atlantic, and from the Caucasus to the Horn of Africa – was beginning to lose impetus, especially after the Umayyad dynasty had been defeated and overthrown by the rival Abbasid dynasty, of Arabo-Persian origin. This change shifted the hub of the Muslim empire much further east, from Damascus to Baghdad.

The first Abbasid caliph, al-Mansur, founded a new capital, Baghdad, on the River Tigris: the centre of the new dynasty moved to the area of Mesopotamia and Iran. This was part of a programme of Asianising the caliphate and abandoning the Byzantine model followed by the Umayyads and any great interest in expansion towards the West, which must now have appeared poor, uncultured and barbaric. As a result, Muslim pressure on the western Mediterranean eased. However, a member of the deposed caliphal family managed to reach the Iberian peninsula and founded there, in Córdoba, an emirate (from the Arabic *amir*, "prince") which gradually gained control of the Iberian peninsula and the Maghreb.

The most powerful of the dynasties that established themselves in the Maghreb was that of the Aghlabids of Kairuan: in theory they were governing on behalf of the Abbasids, but in fact they were autonomous and controlled a territory which, by the early ninth century, covered what is now Tunisia and eastern Algeria. One of the Aghlabid dynasty's most important achievements was the conquest of Sicily. They first invaded in 827 from the emirate of Tunis, but did not complete the conquest until the beginning of the next century; although Palermo was taken as early as 831, Syracuse did not fall until 878. In 829 they attacked the port of Rome, *Centumcellae*, and from there bands of marauders struck at Tuscia, the Maremma and Sabina, even sacking the suburban basilicas of St Paul and St Peter.

The attacks on southern Italy and later right along the Tyrrhenian coast continued from the ninth century to the early eleventh century. Usually the attackers made quick raids, capturing mainly young people to sell as slaves, and occasionally exacting tributes and ransoms; more rarely a raid would result in the founding of a corsair "nest" – a small trading and military colony. Sometimes more lasting settlements were created, as on the Mediterranean islands of Crete, Malta and Sicily and the Balearic archipelago, all of which were conquered in the ninth and tenth centuries and held for a relatively long period.

Meanwhile, in the tenth century the emir Abd ar-Rahman III, who had brought the neo-Umayyad dynasty of Córdoba to the height of its splendour, had succeeded in extending his realm to part of western Maghreb. The next step was the entire Iberian peninsula, with its dynamic urban communities in search of close commercial relations with the countries under Muslim control, so that through this circulation the western world came to share in the sought-after products of the Orient. The individual cities of the Iberian peninsula had different relationships with the sea: from Barcelona to Seville and the Atlantic coast the urban centre played varying roles in the revival of western trade. Córdoba surpassed all the other cities of the peninsula in the tenth century, and was linked to them by a network of roads with a rapid system of specially trained couriers.

The Arabs and Berbers had never really mixed in the Umayyad caliphate; the proud aristocracy of the former, who considered themselves the only true heirs of the Prophet, despised the African *parvenus*. By contrast, there had been some degree of integration with the descendants of the Latins, Celts and Germans. The most important distinction, however, was still that between Muslim descendants of the conquerors, local inhabitants who had converted to Islam at various times (the *muwalladun*), and Christians who had remained faithful to their religion but had adopted Arabic language and customs. Still, many of these Christians had not forgotten Latin, or at least the vernacular that had developed from it – the *musta'riba*, better known to westerners as "Mozarabic".

3 The Circulation of Merchandise and Cultures

The important part played by Arab trade in the Mediterranean is clear from the spread of Muslim coins, which were soon used alongside, and in many areas instead of, the Byzantine gold *denarius*, the well-known "hyperperon" or "besant". Like the *denarius*, the Arab *dinar* weighed 4.25 grammes of gold: more common, however, was the quarter *dinar* – the *ruba'i* – which was soon adopted not only in Sicily but also in southern Italy, where it was called *tari* ("fresh" or newly minted coin), and the Amalfitani and Salernitani made copies of it. The main silver coins were the *dirahm* (the name, assimilated via Persian, is derived from the Greek "drachma"), weighing 2.90 grammes, and the small *kharruba*, weighing 2 decigrammes. Arab coins even circulated in distant Rus', between the Dnieper and the Don; in this case the gold ones were less common, but silver coins abounded. It was via the Muslim world that expensive products reached Europe from Africa and especially Asia, along the Spice Road and the Silk Road. By contrast, Europe neither possessed nor produced any goods that were exportable to the Byzantine or Arab and Berber Muslim areas during this period; if European aristocrats wanted to import anything from those areas – and what they wanted were always luxury goods – they had to pay in gold, a metal which, with rare exceptions, had never been coined by the Romano-barbarian monarchies, the Carolingian empire or any later kingdoms. So gold became very scarce in the western world, and the West's balance of trade with the East remained negative for a long time; not until the eleventh century was there any sign of change.

At any rate, Muslim Arab traders had comparatively little interest in western Europe in the ninth and tenth centuries, for the reasons that have just been explained. Nevertheless, there was one commodity that was appreciated by the Arabs and produced by the "Franks" (*farany*: such was their name for the western Europeans; the Byzantine Greeks they called *rumi*, "Romans"). That commodity was iron, both in ingots and in the form of forged objects, notably weapons, of which there was a shortage in the east. "Frankish swords", mainly produced in south-western Germany and northern Italy, were much admired for the strength and beauty of their blades, which were matched only by *gauhar*, Yemeni white steel, or *pulad*, Indian blue steel. However, after being bought, the swords were often remodelled in specialised Muslim forges, sometimes being damascened with highly sophisticated techniques to produce "Damascus" or "Toledo" swords and steel. The "country of the Franks" and Byzantium also supplied wood, which was urgently needed by Muslim dockyards, tall trees being more scarce in the east. They also provided Islam with wax, honey, furs, flax, and particularly amber, which gave its name to the mainly maritime and fluvial trade route from the Baltic to the Bosphorus.

Although the Islamic world was still politically very fragmented at the beginning of the second millennium of our era, it played a vital role as a mediator and synthesiser of science and culture. "Search for science where it can be found, as far as China", the Prophet is said to have urged his followers. The Muslims had an extraordinary capacity for metabolising the cultures that they had come into contact with, from Arabia to the Indus basin and beyond, and from the Caucasus to the Horn of Africa and the Pillars of Hercules. This enabled them to develop, from the seventh to the sixteenth century, an extraordinarily flexible and variegated civilisation, which interacted with the surrounding cultures in different ways. Particularly important were their links with "Latin" civilisation, which owed Islam a great debt. Islam not only put western Europe in touch with its Hellenistic philosophical and scientific heritage, but also introduced it to many treasures of the Persian, Indian and Chinese cultures previously unknown in the Mediterranean. The three caliphates of Baghdad, Córdoba and Cairo had prestigious research centres with "madrasas" and huge libraries; and many smaller Muslim principates, such as Bukhara, Samarkand, Kairuan and Marrakesh, which remained largely independent while paying formal obedience to one of these caliphates, also played an important part in the preservation and transmission of culture.

The leading figure in Muslim culture during this period is the philosopher and doctor Abu 'Ali al-Husayn Ibn Sina, known to westerners as Avicenna, whose work was rooted in theology but spread to take in mathematics, geometry, the natural sciences, music and astronomy. His best-known work – a medical handbook, known by the Greek name *Kanon* – was to remain, in Latin translation, the standard textbook for European medical schools until the eighteenth century. Most Muslim literature, in fact, was scientific during this period, its most important products being treatises on history, geography, astronomy, medicine and architecture. The Arab geographers of the tenth and eleventh centuries knew a lot about the world and travelled from China to the Polar Circle and equatorial Africa, recording their observations in texts which are still classics of the history of exploration. In general, Muslim science was based on ancient Greek science, which it supplemented with elements from the Persian, Indian and Chinese traditions: its leading exponents included Geber (Giabir ibn Hayyan), the founder of alchemy; the mathematician al-Kawarizmi, from whom the West has taken the word "algorithm", in the sense of an arithmetical procedure; and the philosopher al-Farabi. This scientific literature was accompanied by a wide range of poetic and narrative works, often of a popular nature. The unifying factor of Arabic – a religious, juridical, political and scientific language (believers could read and recite the *Koran* only in its "sacred language") – was crucial in this respect.

This circulation of scholars and texts gave western Europe access to legacies that had been lost during the early Middle Ages. The process would reach its peak in the twelfth and thirteenth centuries, but its origins lay in the tenth century, when its main centres were the cities of the Iberian peninsula. The ancient Greek texts had been translated into Arabic; and although they were also accessible through versions translated directly from Greek – which, however, were far less numerous at this time – Latin translations from Arabic proved far more popular. This was partly because of the excellent commentaries provided by the Arab translators and scholars, and the treatises on the Greek works that they themselves composed. But there was also, in general, a growing awareness that Arabic could give western Europe access to the science, and sometimes the technology, of more remote countries, from Persia to India and even China.

An important impulse to the spread of scientific knowledge conveyed by the Muslim world through Arabic was provided in the Iberian peninsula by Gerbert d'Aurillac, who travelled in Catalonia as a young man in the period 967-970, learning the rudiments of Arab, and perhaps also Greek, arithmetic and astronomy. Later he became head of the episcopal school of Reims and then abbot of Bobbio, and was able to pass on his knowledge, until he ascended the papal throne as

Silvester II. He made an ingenious blend of Aristotle's ideas with Hippocrates' medical theories. The Aristotle that he knew and studied was, however, mingled with neo-Platonic elements: this was the form in which Aristotle reached the West before the "scholastic revolution" of the thirteenth century, leaving a profound imprint on Christian philosophy.

The steady improvement in the standard of living in Europe enhanced the reception of this cultural heritage, and stimulated curiosity about Islam as a religion. In the thirteenth century one of the leading figures in the church, Peter the Venerable, abbot of Cluny, launched a remarkable initiative in Toledo – which had been restored to Christendom just over half a century earlier – with the support of the archbishop of Toledo, Raymond de Sauvêtat. Under their guidance, a team was formed which, with expert advice from Muslims and Jews, produced the first translation of the *Koran*, which bears the name of Robert of Ketton; though incomplete, and marred by distortions and omissions, this remained the standard translation for the next four centuries. The work of Peter the Venerable's team was not limited to the *Koran*, and it was supplemented by the work of other groups based not only in Spain but in England and southern Italy. Latin translations of Islamic texts by such men as John of Seville, Dominicus Gundissalinus, Herman of Carinthia, Plato Tiburtinus and Gerard of Cremona, and the studies of Islam inspired by them, long remained the basis for the knowledge of that religion in medieval Europe.

4 The Revival of the Cities and of Trade with the Orient

Some historians have used the term "commercial revolution" to denote the combination of economic, social and technological developments which arose from the decrease in the importance of agriculture as a driving factor in the economy, and the rise of other activities – trade, craftsmanship on an industrial scale, and the instruments of exchange and credit. The city was the main site of this change, and was both cause and effect of it. But the rise of cities alone is not a sufficient explanation of the change, just as the changes in climate and the demographic explosion after the tenth century cannot be considered its only remote factors. All these developments are part of the new kind of economy, social dynamic and division of property and labour which had emerged in the eleventh and twelfth centuries and became fully evident in the thirteenth century.

Some Italian maritime cities had had their own economic activity and political autonomy since the early Middle Ages. In these cities – and later in some

Provençal cities too, such as Marseille, or in Catalan cities such as Barcelona – new classes emerged, which specialised in trade and shipbuilding, in a complex relationship with the old urban aristocracy and the newly urbanised aristocracy of late feudal origin. These classes promoted a new, bolder way of doing business, which consisted of forming "companies", *commende, societates*, pooling their capital and accepting a certain degree of risk in exchange for the prospect of making profits. Since large-scale trade was conducted by sea, these companies needed ships and crews; so the maritime cities acquired docks manned by specialised workers and sailors. This was an economic revolution, and in a sense a social one too. But it was not yet a technological revolution, for increased maritime mobility did not lead to any significant changes in ship design, which continued to be based on the needs of sailing in the Mediterranean.

Around the year 1000 some Italian and Byzantine coastal cities had already achieved a high standard of living and trading capacity. From the beginning of the ninth century Amalfi, Naples and Salerno had their own coinage, derived from the Arab *tarì*, a sign that Islam, not Byzantium, was their chief area of trade. But the city that really expanded dramatically was Venice, which successfully combined property and trading interests with agricultural and financial activities in an extensive maritime empire. The southern Italian cities, which were soon absorbed into the Norman kingdom, continued to engage in trade, but were never able to develop it alongside political interests.

Navigation in the Adriatic had been safe since the ninth and tenth centuries, and in the early thirteenth century the Venetians' network of trade contacts ranged from Constantinople to the Syrian and Palestinian coasts, north Africa and Sicily. Despite repeated imperial and papal prohibitions, Venice sold the Arabs forbidden wares such as wood, iron and slaves – the latter mainly from Istria, Slovenia and Croatia. At the same time, other Italian maritime cities were developing policies of their own, chief among them Genoa and Pisa.

These three cities, and the First Crusade, imposed strict trade routes, which ran from east to west and vice versa, and which linked their ports to Constantinople and the trading colonies which the three cities had founded in the Byzantine empire and along the Syrian and Palestinian coasts. The conflicts that broke out between these cities in the twelfth and thirteenth centuries often arose from tensions that had originated overseas. For example, hostilities between Genoa and Pisa began when there was a dispute about the control of the large islands of Corsica and Sardinia; and it continued both in Constantinople and in Acre and Tyre, the two biggest ports of the Crusader kingdom, where the Venetian, Pisan and Genoese "quarters" were adjacent to each other.

These commercial colonies of the Italian cities formed in urban districts distinct from the others, defended by their own fortifications and overlooking the sea; they possessed harbour infrastructures, had *fondachi* and arsenals, and were populated by citizens of the parent city who spent part of the year on one shore of the Mediterranean and part on the other. They were commercial emporia of exceptional importance, which imported goods from big inland mercantile cities such as Damascus and Aleppo and from even further afield, via the Silk Road. From these sources they shipped to Europe precious cargoes of spices indispensable to medicine, nutrition, food conservation, and particularly manufacturing, but also art (as in the case of dyes, which were used both for dying woven materials and for painting and glass); and they sent eastwards western products such as woollen cloths and hempen cloth, foodstuffs, building timber, metal ingots and weapons, all increasingly in demand in the east, where they fetched increasingly high prices, though the popes used every means at their disposal to stop the sale of arms to the Saracens. As a result, the balance of trade, hitherto favourable to the east, swung towards the west in the thirteenth century, and thanks to the inflow of gold into the coffers of Latin merchants, Europe was able to mint gold coins, previously, from the fourth to the thirteenth century, almost the exclusive preserve of the Byzantines and a few Muslim potentates.

While Venice, through the Fourth Crusade, regained control over Constantinople, the Pisans and Genoese concentrated on the Egyptian ports of Alexandria and Damietta, where they founded trading colonies. Genoa later tried to extend its commercial interests beyond the Bosphorus, to the ports of the Black Sea – from where alum was imported – establishing contacts with the Tartars of the Golden Horde and with the Russian principates, to exploit the trade routes that ran south down the Volga and Don from the Baltic to the ports of the Crimea, and the supply of Ukrainian corn to the West.

5 The Christian Counter-Offensive

During the eleventh century western Europe – whose identity was rooted in its links with the discipline, liturgy and language of the Latin Church – underwent a significant rise in population, which soon had its effects: there was an economic revival thanks to increased agricultural production, road systems were extended, towns grew larger and many commercial and military initiatives were launched by land and sea. From Spain to Sicily and the Holy Land, the Christian peoples of the west adopted a more aggressive approach, which some scholars have seen as a "reaction" to Muslim from the sixth to the tenth centuries.

The complex area of Christian-Muslim conflicts in the Mediterranean – which accompanied commercial exchanges and did not replace them – gradually moved towards the north-west, where the dominant figure was the emir of Denia and the Balearics, whose honorific Muslim title was al-Mujahid ("the fighter of the *jihad*"), elegantly turned by Latin chroniclers into "Musettus". In 1005, while the Pisans were supporting the Christians of Calabria against the Muslims, al-Mujahid attacked Pisa and burned part of it down. In 1016, a fateful year for Salerno and the whole of southern Italy, Musettus attacked the town of Luni in Garfagnana and destroyed it, forcing the inhabitants to flee across the Apuan mountains. But the Genoese and Pisans swiftly made a combined response, routing the raiders' army and compelling their leader to return to his base in Sardinia.

Later came a full-scale counter-offensive. While in Aragon and Castile there were the first signs of victorious Christian offensives against the Arab-Berber emirates of Iberia, the Pisans, supported by the Genoese and the Amalfitani, attacked first the port of Palermo in 1063, then the Tunisian port of al-Mahdiya in 1087. This was the start of a long counter-offensive by Pisa and Genoa, which for almost three centuries would compete for control over the central and western Mediterranean, and later, after the First Crusade, of the Syrian and Palestinian coasts.

During this period the Normans arrived in force in the southern part of the Italian peninsula. Having first entered the region's complex political scenario as mercenaries, within a few decades they had taken possession of the whole region. In 1061-1094 Roger "The Great Count", brother of Robert Guiscard, completed the conquest of Sicily. At the time of the conquest the island was almost totally inhabited by Arab Berbers and by Islamised indigenous peoples of Graeco-Latin origin; only in Palermo and in some restricted north-eastern areas were there Christian Greek communities of any size. During his military campaign Roger had allowed complete freedom of religion, recruiting many Muslims into his own army. At the same time he encouraged repopulation by Latin Christians, and when he felt more secure, he changed his attitude towards the Muslims, becoming more restrictive. Nevertheless, throughout the period of the Norman kingdom and beyond, Arab functionaries continued to work in the *diwan*, the office responsible for the tax system.

In Spain, too, things were changing. The Córdoban caliph al-Mansur's assault on the city of Compostela in 996-997 was an act of great symbolic significance. Every year more and more pilgrims came from the regions on the other side of the Pyrenees to visit the tomb of the Apostle of Compostela; so the news of the shrine's profanation, far from spreading fear and dismay, was greeted with indignation, and the cause of James the Apostle became that of all Christendom. The pilgrimage to the Apostle's tomb soon took on military significance. The Apostle was said to have appeared at the battle of Clavijo in 844 in a shining costume, mounted on a white steed, and to have led the Christian attack on the enemy. The story is part of a sacralisation of the conflict which it is easy to attribute to ecclesiastical propaganda, but which was rooted in a heightened collective sensibility, a new preparedness for combat and martyrdom.

After the collapse of the caliphate of Córdoba, Muslim Spain was divided up between the various *reyes de taifas*. For a while there was a state of uneasy equilibrium, because the Christian kingdoms too were divided by mutual rivalry. A change came in 1055, when Ferdinand I – who had been acclaimed king of Castile and León in 1037 –launched an offensive which brought the Douro Valley under his control. Meanwhile the situation in Aragon became precarious after King Ramiro I was killed while besieging the Saracen fortress of Graus. Since Infante Sancho was still a minor, it was left to Pope Alexander II to bring about the taking of Barbastro, near Zaragoza, through an expedition which included a number of French knights. Many Christian noblemen were accustomed to go as pilgrims to Santiago, since cadet sons of the nobility inherited no land, so that their only choice was between an ecclesiastical career and military adventure.

The death of Ferdinand I in 1065 was a new setback. On the other side of the Pillars of Hercules power was now in the hands of the confraternity of the al-Murabitun, "men of the *ribats*" (hence the modern term "Almoravids"), the austere inhabitants of the fortress-monasteries across the desert on the banks of the Senegal and the Niger, who had seized control of Morocco and Algeria. The decisive battle took place in 1086 near the Guadiana, at Zallaqa (now Sagrajas), and it resulted in a serious defeat for the Christians. King Alfonso himself barely escaped, with a few hundred knights, taking refuge in Coria. Yusuf forced the *reyes de taifas* to submit to his authority; anyone who tried to resist by forming an alliance with the Castilians was ruthlessly crushed. Toledo remained in Christian hands, but south of the Tago all the land gained in the preceding years was lost.

However, the Almoravids soon began to lose their hold on power. One reason for this was a military revival of the Christian kings of Spain, notably the king of Aragon. Another was the rise of a mystic movement which emerged in the Maghreb in the second quarter of the twelfth century. The *al-Muwahiddun*, "believers in the unity of God", or Almohads, had begun as a strict religious group led by the *mahdi* Muhammad Ibn Tumart, who had objected to Almoravid theologians' concessions to the literal anthropomorphism of the *Koran*. In 1162 an Almohad army disembarked in the Iberian peninsula, where the collapse of the Almoravids had led to a new fragmentation of local Islam, and occupied Seville. Meanwhile, the Castilians took advantage of the situation to seize control of rich Almeria and the Portuguese took Lisbon.

Almohad rule was much more restrictive than that of the Almoravids: the two greatest thinkers of the time, the Jew Moshe ben Maimun (Maimonides) and the Muslim Ibn Rush (Averroes) were persecuted and forced into exile or isolation.

Maimonides ended up in Egypt, where in 1172 he would become *naghid* – leader of the local Jewish community – and later physician to the sultan Saladin and his successors. But Almohad intolerance did not last long; the Berber dynasty allowed cults similar to those of the Christian saints to spread in Morocco, and a new liberalisation of research allowed thinkers such as Ibn Tufayl and – after some initial suspicion – Averroes to flourish. The economy, too, underwent a strong revival thanks to a large-scale improvement of irrigation works, while trading alliances were formed with the Italian cities.

The new Crusade launched by Innocent III, and involving kings Alfonso of Castile and Peter of Aragon, ended in 1212 with victory at Las Navas de Tolosa, which opened the harbours of the region of Andalusia to the Christians and presaged the fall of Córdoba, capital of the Almohad caliphate, which was conquered in 1236 by King Ferdinand III "el Santo". By 1260 the Christian conquest of the Iberian peninsula was virtually complete. The Kingdom of Portugal (created out of a Castilian county, and recognised by the Pope in 1179) colonised the south-eastern part of the peninsula, the so-called Algarve, which brought it into conflict with Castile; meanwhile Castile itself conquered the whole area south of the Guadalquivir, except for the small emirate of Granada, which would remain Muslim until 1492.

As far as living conditions were concerned, the Christian *reconquista* did not bring a better season for Spain. In the approximately five centuries of their rule, the Muslims had made fertile land out of desert areas, such as the arid plateau of the Meseta, where they had brought water by means of large-scale irrigation works, and begun growing cereals, sugar cane and citrus fruits. In the populous cities that they governed, "Mozarabic" Christian communities (which regularly used Arabic in their liturgy) and Jewish communities lived peacefully together, and an urban class of merchants and artisans had been created. From the eleventh century to the fifteenth century wars alternated with long periods of peace. Both the Christian kingdoms and the Muslim emirates were characterised by détente and mutual tolerance between Christian, Muslim and Jewish communities; so that it would be quite wrong to describe the medieval Spanish Crusades and wars as "wars of religion". But the rulers of Castile, who relied for support on a feudal aristocracy of knights whose economic interests were linked to a more primitive pastoral economy, had no interest in maintaining these standards of living. So they did not encourage agriculture, crafts or trade; on the contrary, they persecuted the Muslims and Jews who were the chief support of those activities. Castile became a desolate land of poor herdsmen and growers and an indigent aristocracy, whose lives revolved around military values and a religiosity mainly seen as a struggle against "unbelievers".

6 The Crusades and the Eastern Mediterranean

It may seem strange that, despite occasional references above, we have not yet specifically discussed the theme of the Crusades, which continues to fill histories of the Mediterranean even today. This was a conscious decision, arising from a desire to stress the close link that existed between these "overseas enterprises" (as well as the whole economic, commercial, cultural, political and diplomatic context that accompanied them) and events that had occurred in the Iberian peninsula and the central Mediterranean, in southern peninsular Italy and in Sicily, before the Crusades began.

The tribe that we now call "Seljukid", from the name of one of its *khans*, Seljuq, was of Turkmen origin; that is, it belonged to a particular branch of the Turko-Mongol ethnic group. In the eleventh century, having converted to Islam a few decades earlier, the Seljukids came from the steppes of central Asia to support, with their faith and military prowess (they were expert horsemen and archers), the tottering regime of the Abbasid caliph of Baghdad. They adopted Persian customs, and their preferred language was always Persian rather than Arabic. This was the beginning of a dominion which stretched from Anatolia to central Persia. They became famous when they unexpectedly defeated the Byzantine army at the Battle of Manzikert in 1071, founding in Anatolia the sultanate of Rum (from the Arabic name for the "new Rome", Constantinople), whose capital was the city of Iconium.

This situation gave rise to a series of military expeditions which western historiography has called "Crusades", though the term did not actually enter the vocabulary of the European languages until much later. Historians used to speak of seven or eight or nine Crusader expeditions, but in fact the expeditions encouraged and actually legitimised or launched directly by the Church with the purpose of the conquest (and subsequently the holding or reconquest) of Jerusalem and the Christian "holy places", went on for much longer, continuing into the eighteenth century. They took place not only in Syria and Palestine, but also in Iberia and Anatolia, and legal quibbles were exploited to deploy them against non-Muslim targets too, such as heretics or political enemies of the papacy. It is more appropriate, therefore, to speak not of individual "Crusades" but of a complex "Crusader movement", which created new political formations as well as having fiscal and financial consequences, and gave rise to a whole new legal tradition and literature.

Since tenth-century Islam was not familiar with the Latin world of western Europe, in referring to western Europeans the Muslims borrowed the term current in Byzantine Greek, *Phrankoi*, from Latin *Franci*, and adapted it into Arabic *faranj*. In 1097-98 a large, heterogeneous army of *faranj*, consisting of a core of heavily armed knights accompanied by a host of pilgrims, who included noblemen who had previously fought against the Muslims in the Iberian peninsula and Sicily, arrived in the Anatolian peninsula, marched across it and continued down the Syrian coast to Jerusalem, taking the city on 15 July 1099 after a bloody assault. From there, with the help of ships from the Italian coastal cities, these soldiers conducted a series of military campaigns, and within a few decades had conquered an area roughly corresponding to present-day Israel, Lebanon and parts of Syria and Jordan.

The region was subsumed into the institutions of the Roman Church, and for the purposes of government a "Frankish Kingdom of Jerusalem" was created. It was organised like a feudal monarchy, with some vassal principates – the county of Edessa, the principate of Antioch, the principate of Tripoli and the counties of Jaffa, Ashkalon and Outre-Jourdain. The kingdom lasted for about two centuries, largely thanks to groups of soldiers who agreed to remain in the Holy Land and defend it, forming religious military orders such as the Knights of St John, the Templars, the Knights of St Lazarus, and later the Knights of Saint Mary of the Teutons. The *faranj* gradually succeeded in conquering the whole coast of the Levantine Sea, from the Gulf of Alexandria to the isthmus of Suez; meanwhile expeditions went further inland to subdue the main towns of Galilee, Samaria and Judaea. By the end of the first quarter of the twelfth century the whole region from the Taurus to Sinai and from the coast of the Mediterranean to the Jordan, with an *enclave* to the east around the fortress of Kerak, was under Frankish control, though the roads remained dangerous and Muslim raids were endemic.

Meanwhile, the Muslim world was recovering from the surprise and reorganising. The counter-offensive began from the northern Syrian-Mesopotamian cities, Aleppo and Mosul, which were governed on behalf of the caliph of Baghdad and his Seljukid counsellor-protector, the sultan, by an *atabeg* dynasty (*atabeg* is a Turkish word meaning "father of the chiefs", i.e. governor general) founded by Imad ad-Din Zenqi. The latter planned to gain control of all the emirates of the region between the Sea of Levant and the Euphrates; being a strict Sunnite, he was hostile to the Shiite caliphate of Cairo. The Armenian city of Edessa (now Urfa in Turkey), a Crusader county since 1097, was taken by the Turks in 1146. A great expedition against the growing power of the *atabeg*, later known as the "Second Crusade", was organised in Europe, and set out in 1147 under the command of the King of France, Louis VII, and the King of Germany, Conrad III. However, the expedition failed, partly because its leaders, who were unfamiliar with political relationships in the Near East, attacked the wealthy city of Damascus, whose Arab emir was Zenqi's only real adversary and could have been an invaluable ally to them. The failure of this expedition led to a long series of recriminations and hostilities which meant that no help was given to the Crusader kings of Jerusalem for more than forty years.

By now the *atabeg* of Aleppo and Mosul, though technically only a functionary of the Seljukid sultan, was acting like an independent prince. On his death his dominion was divided up between his sons, and was consequently to some extent weakened; power passed to Yusuf ibn Ayyub, known in Muslim history as al-Malik an-Nasir Salah ad-Din ("the Victorious Sovereign, Integrity of Faith") and in western history as "Saladin". The Egyptian caliph al-Adid appointed Saladin his *vizir*, but in 1171 was deposed by him; this marked the end of the Shiite caliphal experiment, and Egypt returned to Sunnite orthodoxy. The country was governed by Saladin, who thus broke away from service to the Turko-Syrian *atabegs*, assuming the title of sultan and founding the dynasty known as "Ayyubid", from his family name.

Saladin's new sultanate was split between two large territories, Egypt and Syria, whose capital, Damascus, he had also taken. This enabled him to cut off the Crusader kingdom of Jerusalem both from the north and from the southwest. Nevertheless, he did not immediately attack the *faranj*; on the contrary, he remained on friendly terms with many of them. This changed, however, after the death of the young king Baldwin IV, the "Leper King", because the acts of violence and rapine carried out by the bold but violent Crusader lord of Outre-Jourdain, Raynald of Châtillon, demanded an exemplary response. Saladin defeated Raynald's army in 1187, and a few weeks later peacefully entered Jerusalem, from which the Crusaders had fled. The kingdom of Jerusalem transferred its capital to Acre, and maintained control of the coast for a hundred years, until 1291.

When the Muslims took Jerusalem, a new expedition, now known as the "Third Crusade", was launched in Europe; it was led by the most powerful sovereigns of the day, the Holy Roman Emperor, Frederick I, the King of France, Philip II Augustus, and the King of England, Richard the Lionheart. However, Frederick died during the journey, the King of France soon returned to Europe, and Saladin signed a peace treaty with the King of England under which it was recognised that Jerusalem had returned into Muslim hands and that the "Franks" controlled the coast. However, the sultan died in 1193, whereupon the sultanate was split between his sons. From that time onwards, two distinct and mutually hostile Ayyubid dynasties ruled in Damascus and in Cairo. The Ayyubid dynasty of Egypt came to be dominated by powerful prime ministers (the *vizirs*) and mercenary troops of servile origin, hence their name "Mamelukes" from Arabic *mamluk*, "slave". The sultans of Mameluke descent withstood the Mongol incursions of the successors of Genghis Khan, who had overthrown the Abbasid caliphate of Baghdad. Then they resumed the offensive against the coastal cities and fortresses of Syria and Lebanon, eliminating the old Frankish kingdom of Jerusalem in 1291. The religious military Orders took refuge on the islands – the Templars on Cyprus and the Knights of St John on Rhodes.

After the fall of St John of Acre in 1291, the period of Crusades in the Holy Land seemed over. But in the second quarter of the fourteenth century there was a long period of instability, with a series of famines and epidemics and accompanying socio-economic unrest all over Europe. During the same period the Byzantine Empire and the Tartar khanates that had resulted from the conquests of Genghis Khan broke up. The effect of this was to mobilise other nomadic Turko-Mongol groups, one of which, led by the Ottoman family, settled in the Anatolian peninsula, defeating or absorbing other nearby groups and threatening the empire of Constantinople, whose dominion by now comprised little more than the capital itself.

In the late fourteenth century the old ideal of the Crusade against unbelievers in the East was revived with a new, different purpose – not to reconquer the Holy Land, but to defend Christendom against what appeared to be a formidable threat. The Ottoman sultans, based in their flourishing capitals, Bursa in Asia and Adrianopolis (or Edirne) in the Balkan peninsula, now encircled Constantinople ominously. The Byzantine *basileis* called on their Latin brothers in Christ for support and assistance. They had little to offer in exchange. One thing they *could* offer was the erudition of Greek intellectuals, who fled to the West in ever greater numbers with their precious collections of manuscripts, which provided an important impulse to the cultural revolution of humanism. Another was the end of the schism between the Latin Church and the Greek Church, which dated back to 1054; this was terminated with a solemn joint declaration at the Council of Florence in 1441. However, the Crusade of liberation which the western princes were supposed to implement was badly organised and ended in disastrous defeat at Varna, on the Black Sea, in 1444; nine years later, in 1453, the young sultan Mehmed II took Constantinople, with tacit support from Christian cities such as Florence and Venice, which were keen to do business with the new masters of the eastern Mediterranean. A new Crusader expedition in 1456 succeeded in stopping the Ottomans south of Belgrade; but the military enterprise desired by Pope Pius II never materialised.

The struggle between Christians and Muslims proceeded asymmetrically: the Ottomans advanced, conquering part of the Balkan-Danubian peninsula and wresting some Greek islands away from Venice; though at the end of the century the Serenissima gained the island of Cyprus, a bequest from the last queen of the Crusader family of the Lusignans. By 1520 the sultans of Constantinople (now Istanbul) would take control over Egypt and the whole of north Africa. In the Iberian peninsula, by contrast, the last independent Arab-Berber emirate that had remained independent, Granada, fell into the hands of the Catholic sovereigns, Ferdinand of Aragon and Isabel of Castile, in the same year when the the New World was discovered. Though victorious in the east, in the west Islam was retreating to the coasts of north Africa. In the meantime, Mediterranean trade continued to thrive, despite disruption from piracy by the Barbary Muslims, the Catalans, the Genoese and the Knights of Rhodes; war did not prevent trade or the other profitable businesses in which the Portuguese, Ethiopia and India were increasingly involved. What changed the situation and the balance of power was the discovery of the New World, which opened up new lands and new trade routes. The world was bigger now, and the Mediterranean, now only a frontier between different societies and cultures, was no longer its centre.

Translated from the Italian by Jonathan Hunt

Bibliography

Bresc, H 2001, *Europa y el Islam en la Edad Media*, Critica, Barcelona.
Cardini, F 1999, *Europa e Islam. Storia di un malinteso*, Laterza, Rome & Bari.
Fletcher, R 1993, *Moorish Spain*, University of California Press, Berkeley.
Goitein, SD 1966, *Studies in Islamic History and Institutions*, E.J. Brill, Leiden.
Holt, PM & Lambton, AKS & Lewis, B (eds) 1970, *The Cambridge History of Islam*, Cambridge University Press, Cambridge.
Humphreys, S 1977, *From Saladin to the Mongols: The Ayyubids of Damascus, 1193-1260*, State University of New York Press, Albany, NY.
Provençal, EL & Balbás, LT (1976), *España musulmana (711-1031). La Conquista, el Emirato, el Califato*, in *Historia de España*, ed RM Pidal, Espasa Calpe, Madrid.
Nicolle, D 2003, *Warriors and their Weapons around the Time of the Crusades: Relationships between Byzantium, the West, and the Islamic World*, Ashgate/Variorum, Aldershot.
Riley-Smith, J 2009, *Storia delle Crociate*, Mondadori, Milan.
Watt, WM 1972, *The Influence of Islam on Medieval Europe*, Edinburgh University Press, Edinburgh.

Bo Stråth
The Conquest of the North

1 The Vikings and the Concept of Periphery

The idea of a Northern periphery from the perspective of the civil world, which understood itself not only as civilised but also as the centre of the world, emerged through the term *ultima Thule*, used for probably the first time by Pytheas from Massalia (Marseilles), who in the 320s BCE explored Britain and maybe also visited the Orkney and Shetland islands, perhaps even Scandinavia. He was searching for the origin of tin and amber. His utmost Thule has, rightly or wrongly, been identified as Scandinavia. Thule became a mythical word conceptualising the unknown North, known but at the same time as a *terra incognita*. Goethe contributed to the myth with his ballad "The King in Thule" set to music by Franz Schubert.

The Roman historian Tacitus in *Germania* (98 CE), an ethnological study of the Germanic tribes, which he contrasted with the moral decadence in Rome, referred to the *sviones*, who have been identified as a people north of the Gothes in today's Sweden, around Uppsala. Iordanis, the Roman-Gothic sixth-century historian, argued in his 12-volume *Getica* that the Gothes came from Scandinavia. Gradually, over almost a millennium, the ancient imagery emerged of a Northern periphery inhabited by tribes with names.

During the reconstruction of what was understood as the civilised world after the fall of the Roman Empire, the Roman *limes* moved under Charlemagne northward but did not reach the areas around the Baltic. This area became a target of exploration and religious, political and economic control from the reconstructed dual Roman centre of power. The Emperor looked for raw materials, and the Pope for new proselytes and taxpayers.

However, before the conquest *of* the North there was the conquest of Europe *by* the North. In the Carolingian time, from the end of the eighth until the mid-eleventh century, the Vikings, seafaring peoples from what today is Scandinavia, raided, traded, explored and settled in wide areas of Europe, Asia, and the North Atlantic islands. Their wooden longships with wide, shallow-draft hulls allowed for navigation in rough seas as well as shallow river waters. Their light weight enabled them to be hauled over portages. On the versatile ships with their snake-headed stems they sailed from the Baltic on the Russian lake and river system to Volga and down to the Caspian Sea. There is archaeological evidence that Vikings reached Baghdad. The south-westbound pillage and trade expeditions took them from the North Sea via the Bay of Biscay and Gibraltar into the Mediterranean, as far as to Constantinople and further through the Bosphorus into the Black Sea. They visited the kingdom of Nekor in today's Morocco. They travelled as far west as Iceland, Greenland and Newfoundland. They founded independent settlements in Shetland, Orkney, Faroe, Iceland and Greenland. The Danish King established a North Sea realm including today's Denmark, South Sweden and large parts of England; the Danelaw.

Looting and piracy went hand in hand with trade and commerce with tar, furs and slaves. The Vikings were both mercenaries and settlers. They had a military organisation based on their ships, the *ledung*, and a political organisation which loosely divided them into connected and competing chieftains which, towards the end of the ninth century, merged into proto-kingdoms. In cultural terms they had an alphabet, *runor*, written in stone and wood. The written language was for obvious reasons laconic.

The borders once set by the Romans were no longer valid. Charlemagne's reconstruction of the Empire operated with other borders, which the Vikings circumvented rather than confronted. The polytheist Vikings discovered two monotheist religions but rather than converting to them they found the Christian churches and monasteries a suitable target for looting and enrichment.

However, their contact with other cultures was not only a matter of violent confrontation but also of various degrees of merger. In the eleventh century, towards the end of the proper Viking era, the powers of the southern part of the Apennine peninsula hired Norman mercenaries, descendants of the Vikings, who under Roger I defeated the Muslims on Sicily and established a kingdom there in 1091. The Norman descendants of the Vikings came to Sicily from the peninsula named after them in today's France, Normandy, which they had conquered in the tenth century when the peninsula was a Gallo-Roman rest of the Merovingians. From Normandy, the Viking descendants under William the Conqueror invaded England in 1066. Via the Normans, the Vikings merged with the old Carolingian and Anglo-Saxon political cultures, the latter of which in turn, through the Danelaw, had already merged with the Vikings to a considerable extent. William the Conqueror short-circuited the expansion of the Vikings.

In the turbulent time between 300 and 600 years after the fall of the Roman Empire, the Great Migrations and the German invasions, it is not clear what was central and what was peripheral. Only from the past perspective of the Roman Empire might one talk about Northern Europe as a periphery and about the Vikings as conquerors from the North in the wake of the barbarians who, before the Vikings, had invaded the ancient world and destroyed its culture. From the perspective of the Vikings, one might talk about an expansive Scandinavian centre that permeated the European continent, which was conceptualised in terms of Christianity, and on its outskirts Islam, rather than as Europe. The old

Roman *limes* was relativised as a cultural borderline. In commercial and military terms, the dynamics came considerably from the North; in religious terms, from the South.

The Vikings should be connected to the theory of the Belgian Medievalist Henri Pirenne. In his famous essay *Mohammed and Charlemagne* (1937) Pirenne argued that the continuity of Roman civilisation in transalpine (northern) Europe after the fall of Rome was not the basis on which Charlemagne built his empire. The real change in Europe came from the rise of Islam, not barbarian invasions. His conclusion was that without Islam, there had probably been no Charlemagne's Empire. Charlemagne without Muhammad was inconceivable. The Vikings were warriors who could ravage and devastate but they were not state builders or a hearth of culture and ideological power, and therefore they did not constitute a serious threat to Charlemagne. The exceptional case was the Danelaw and the Danish British realm in the tenth and early eleventh century.

2 The Continental Counter Movement: Christian Mission and Commerce

Missionary expeditions to the North since the early ninth century were mainly unsuccessful. Only after 1000 did the sociopolitical organisation of Christianity begin to achieve durable success in the North, at about the same time as the chieftains of the Viking era began to merge into larger kingdoms in Scandinavian competition between what began to be conceptualised as Denmark, Sweden and Norway. The kingdoms assimilated Christendom and made it the legitimising state religion. Monarchy and monotheism reinforced each other. Sweden conquered today's Finland through missionary expeditions. Feudal forms of political organisation were also incorporated: more in Denmark and Sweden, less in Norway. However, the low density of population, in comparison with the rest of the continent, with large forests and also mountains in Norway made feudal control problematic and the degree of feudalism less pronounced than in continental Europe. However, by the thirteenth century the direction of the cultural, religious and political impact was quite obviously northbound, in contrast with the Viking era. Continental influences permeated the North. This trend was reinforced through commerce, in particular the Hanseatic League, a commercial and military confederation of merchant guilds and their market towns dominating trade along the Baltic and North Sea coasts from the thirteenth century until the culmination of its power in the early sixteenth century. The League was created to protect economic interests and develop legal privileges in the cities and countries which the merchants visited, where they developed the rights to use their own laws of government and commerce.

The spread of German cultural and economic activity around the Baltic began in the twelfth century. *Plattdeutsch*, Lübeck artwork, and commercial families formed a tightly spun web. The German influence was also felt politically as the Teutonic Knights extended their influence across the Baltic region. Danish expansion plans in the same direction in the beginning of the thirteenth century were effectively stopped with the battle of Bornhoved in 1227. Albrecht of Mecklenburg became King of Sweden in the second half of the fourteenth century and brought with him a considerable retinue of mercenaries and administrators. That is as far as Germanisation went. Albrecht's administration encountered resistance from the aristocracy, the church and the peasants: in other words, from all centres of power. Queen Margrethe of Denmark exploited this resistance and organised it politically and militarily. Albrecht's German forces were defeated on the battlefield in 1389 and the King was forced to withdraw home to Mecklenburg. From Rostock and Wismar a trade boycott was mounted against the Nordic nations, and pirate and freebooter activity was supported in the Baltic. German pirates occupied Stockholm and raided the Swedish and Finnish coasts, lending their support to the Hansa in the Baltic in a conflict that had a clear German–Nordic dimension. The Kalmar Union of 1397 between Sweden (of which Finland was an integral part), Denmark, and Norway can be seen as a political counterblow aimed at the Hanseatic "colonialism" in the north. This union, which lasted until 1521, was the political response of the Nordic powers to the German infiltration in culture, language, economics, administration and politics. The idea of "German" and "Nordic" as elements of the *same* Germanic culture was transformed into a conflict between German and Nordic cultures. There thus developed a line in the southern Baltic that marked the division between north and south, confronting the Hanseatic idea of the Baltic as a seamless web of commerce.

Strong political, economic and cultural forces acted upon the Nordic–German dividing line. The Nordic front in particular was not especially solid since the Kalmar Union was full of conflicts between potentates and was characterised by economic interests in ever-shifting constellations. There was no real question of an early form of German and Nordic national feelings that stood against each other. In parts of Sweden there soon developed dissatisfaction with the union's policy against the Hansa, which disrupted important commercial interests such as iron exports. The banner of rebellion was hoisted by Engelbrekt. The Hansa therefore not only had a unifying effect, but also a disrupting one. The same forces that drove the Nordic kingdoms together in a union also drove them apart.

The search for a new ideology after the end of the Cold War led to a different history. The imagery of a peaceful Baltic and a seamless web of trade organised by the Hansa fit well with the neoliberal language of the end of history and globalisation, with the market as a special fetish. However, against the neoliberal idealised view of the Baltic as a borderless region woven together through culture and commerce, one must juxtapose the image of a warlike Baltic, notorious for military conflicts, plundering and piracy, a *mare bellicus* as it were. Of course, this is not to say that the view in the 1990s was completely false and that a different, more "truthful" one should be set up to replace it. We are dealing here with different descriptions of reality. Both images contain elements that have a basis in the sources. The Baltic was a sea that bridged and dissolved boundaries as well as a sea inviting conflicts about boundaries.

The idealised view of the Baltic as a borderless, rich and communicative body of water can be traced back even further than the Hansa. The same is also true for the opposite view of the warlike Baltic region, criss-crossed by dynastic, religious and economic ambitions. The extensive body of historical writing on the Vikings has taken the Baltic as an important field of study, and the Viking era can, in many ways, be seen as a preliminary stage of the Hanseatic epoch. It is especially in reference to the Hansa that there has emerged an idealised image of the Vikings as a people engaged in peaceful commerce as opposed to the conventional warlike view. It is debatable to what extent the Vikings' expansion across Europe should be seen as a consequence of peaceful trade or systematic plundering, but it is clear in any case that the idealised image is much too simple for both the Viking era and for the Hansa. This is an image that reflects the mood that prevailed when the image was recreated around 1990, not the time it is intended to describe.

The European trans-oceanic, political and military expansion that began in the 1490s directed commercial interests more and more towards the Atlantic. This marked the end of the Baltic's golden age as the region lost importance in relative terms and Baltic trading became increasingly peripheral. But if Germany's economic and political penetration of the Baltic region to the north became less significant, its cultural and administrative influence continued: the introduction of Protestantism to the Nordic countries and the translation of the New Testament into the Scandinavian and Finnish languages were, of course, inspired by Luther; Gustav Vasa brought in German assistants to Sweden to structure and develop a centralised state administration; and political reforms were introduced on the Saxon model. Laurentius Andrae, Olaus Petri, Conrad von Pyhy and Georg Norman are some of the figures who personify this process of Germanisation. A parallel development occurred in Denmark. In this sense, we can speak of a significant continuity in German permeation after the formal dissolution of the Hansa. We can also speak of a network that linked the Baltic region together, although here it is important that we do not regard the content of these network relationships in purely idealistic terms, but also consider their political power context. German political and administrative support in the construction of Swedish and Danish central power entailed a significant amount of exploitation in the context of centre–periphery relations.

There developed, superimposed on this German network across the Nordic countries, a new dividing line in the Baltic. The old division between the Nordic region and the Hansa was replaced by a new one between Sweden and Denmark. The power struggle over the control of the Baltic shifted from being a German-Nordic affair to an intra-Nordic affair, in keeping with the Baltic region's increasing commercial marginalisation. The region was therefore still marked by a dividing line, albeit of a different appearance and content, and in this, as well as in the presence of the interwoven networks, there was a clear element of continuity.

Before 1500 it is difficult to discern a clear boundary between continental Europe and the North. It was much more a matter of a boundary zone where the Baltic increasingly emerged as both a demarcation and as a communicative bridge for the conveyance of political, economic and religious power. Today's Russia, Finland and Baltic states were ever more exposed to these influences and seen as a part of Northern Europe. The Catholic mission – Orthodox in Russia – together with commerce and warfare can be seen as the Europeanisation of the North and a blurring of this boundary zone.

The sixteenth century brought a counter movement to this trend. Protestantism and the consolidation of monarchical state power in Scandinavia reinforced each other in a confrontation of Catholicism and Hanseatic commercial power. The demarcation between the North and continental Europe became in a certain sense more distinct; however, in another sense, not so. The boundary remained, in many respects, a vague zone. Protestantism, for example, joined the territories to the North and South of the Baltic, the Scandinavian- and Finnish-speaking cultures with the German-speaking, and the consolidation and centralisation of monarchical state power resulted in two competing Scandinavian conglomerate states with land beyond the Fenno-Scandinavian peninsula in today's Baltic states and Germany: Denmark-Norway and Sweden. Schleswig-Holstein was not understood as German in the meaning these names would come to have in the nineteenth-century nationalism. They were simply two duchies under the Danish crown where a large part of the population happened to be German. Sweden built, through conquest of the Eastern shores of the Baltic, a zone that prevented Russian access to the sea.

3 The Military Construction of the North

The Thirty Years War threw Denmark and Sweden into the centre stage of the European war theatre. Their plundering and looting armies certainly, like the Vikings, came from the North, which, however, represented more of a continuum than a boundary to continental Europe. The outcome of the war was that Sweden came out as superior to Denmark and made the Baltic a *mare nostrum*. The conflict between the two powers continued, however, after the Peace of Westphalia in 1648 and through the next 167 years until the Congress of Vienna in 1815, involving them in shifting coalitions with and against Britain and the continental powers of France, Prussia and Russia.

The Great Nordic War (1700–1721) was a conflict in which a coalition led by Russia confronted the Swedish supremacy in the Baltic. The continued military coalitions and the cabinet wars in the eighteenth century involved the Scandinavian powers in a European network of military relationships in flux, transcending the Baltic as a border and connecting them to, rather than demarcating them, from continental Europe. However, the struggle between the Swedish and the Russian realms during the first two decades of the eighteenth century was decisive for a new understanding of the border. Charles XII's seemingly planless wandering campaign deep into Russia overstretched the Swedish communication lines. The Swedish monarch was in this respect a forerunner of Napoleon and Hitler. With Peter I came the end to the Baltic as a Swedish *mare nostrum* and the sea again became a dividing line. Until then, for some two hundred years, Russia, together with Denmark, had been the sworn hereditary enemy of Sweden with frequent wars and shifting border lines. The three powers struggled about the power over the Baltic region. They were seen as and identified themselves as North European powers on the European periphery confronting each other in a contentious game of power and borders in the North. After Russia's definite triumph over Sweden around 1720, the empire emerged ever more as the dominating power. The neighbours west and south of the Baltic began to see Russia as the threat in the east. The enlightenment philosophers did the rest to demarcate Russia as an East European power with a certain contempt for its degree of modernity and civilisation, as Larry Wolff has demonstrated. Russia was no longer Northern Europe. However, it is important not to see the division between Eastern and Western Europe through the filter of Stalin and the Cold War. Russia was a leading member of the European concert after 1815 and far from peripheric, although after 1830 in the public opinion it became increasingly a representative of the reaction as opposed to the counter-image of the liberal Britain, underpinning the view of the enlightenment philosophers and playing down the role of enlightened monarchs like Catherine II and Alexander I and the liberal reforms of Alexander II.

In cultural terms, the enlightenment philosophy spread from its French, British, German, Italian and Dutch centres to the universities in Northern Europe, involving them in an emerging European *république des lettres* that transcended the old religious Catholic–Protestant division. The North was certainly more taking than giving in this spread of the enlightenment thought, but, as was the case with the Nordic involvement in the European military conflicts, it was more a matter of a continuum with than a separation from continental Europe. The enlightenment discourse meant the development of a dividing line between Eastern and Western Europe, where Russia began to be seen as an East rather than North European power and Northern Europe as part of Western Europe.

The industrial revolution reinforced this trend, but before that the French revolution and the Napoleonic wars, which heavily involved the Nordic countries in the European turbulence and rapidly shifting borderlines, shook up the borderlines between the Nordic countries under new connections to the continental powers. The British naval bombardment of Copenhagen in 1807 threw Denmark from its status as neutral into the Napoleonic camp, whereas Sweden under its new crown prince, Napoleon's field marshal Jean Baptiste Bernadotte, placed its stakes on the coalition against France in a deal with the Russian Tsar in 1812. Sweden was allowed to conquer Norway from Denmark in return for siding with the coalition and confirmed the Russian conquest of Finland as a service in return in the deal with the Tsar. Finland became, in the new mental map, more of an Eastern connection whereas the United Kingdoms of Sweden-Norway (in plural as opposed to the British UK) and Denmark consolidated their new power relationships under de-escalation of their martial heritage supported by an emerging Panscandinavianist ideology. The spread of nationalism in Europe after 1815 worked in Northern Europe to unify rather than divide. The issue at stake was the role of Finland. The language of *Nordism* emphasised Finland as a part of a Nordic unification, challenging the Russian conquest. Scandinavianism emphasised the unification between the three Scandinavian countries of Sweden, Norway and Denmark. In Finland, the main trend was the forward-looking recognition of the new status as a Grand Duchy under the Russian Tsar with the possibility of a state-building of its own rather than the backward-looking Nordic unity under Swedish supremacy.

4 Nationalism and the Construction of the North in Science and Art

The languages of Scandinavianism and Nordism from the 1830s to the 1860s created a certain demarcation from continental Europe. They were part of the broader European nationalist rhetoric in the wake of the French revolution with a growing emphasis on ethnicity and cultural community as the basis of political unification. Nationalism created new kinds of boundaries in Europe and the North was in this respect part of a broader European pattern. Scandinavianism and Nordism went hand in hand with Danish, Norwegian and Swedish nationalism under mutual reinforcement. Nationalism in general, and Scandinavianism and Pangermanism in particular, underpinned ideas of a larger Germanic community in the North with a potential boundary conflict between the Nordics and the Germanics about their separation or amalgamation.

In the construction of a fictive German nation at the beginning of the nineteenth century, the creation had to be legitimised by giving it an origin. The nation builders directed the searchlight towards the North when they, under demarcation to the French, tried to show that Germany was different. They were looking for an alternative to the French derivation of origin from the Roman Empire and Catholicism. The Old Norse mythology and the Icelandic sagas fit like a hand in a glove. German philologists, archaeologists and antiquarians began, with diligence and industry, to elaborate the Old Norse material from language and literature in their efforts to find the German in the Nordic mirror. Ernst Moritz Arndt, Johann Gottlieb Fichte and Henrich Steffens imagined a merger of the German and Nordic peoples on the basis of a reanimation of Tacitus' rejuvenating thought about the noble Nordic distinctive character, to be used anew. Arndt developed the idea of the Nordic origin in a Great-German direction. In a turbulent time in the search for new meaning and new communities, the things that in posterity would be split up in democratic, patriotic, nationalistic and anti-Semitic thoughts and tendencies were mixed. It was all still a web of trends in which one could not yet see to where the Nordic and the German tendencies would carry and what development that direction would take. Nationalism stood for freedom and democracy and few considered anti-Semitism to be anything remarkable. The Nordic folk songs and ballads provoked German fervour and feelings of the light of morning. The study by the Grimm brothers of these ballads and the Icelandic sagas was the beginning of the modern German philology. The Nordic was a more original and genuine prototype of the German *Deutschtum* they tried to define and demarcate.

The sciences and arts created, from the early nineteenth century onwards, an image of *Norden* and its Germanic peoples as an emotional community. German scholars in the search for the origin of a German nation partly found what they were looking for in the North and built an idealising xeno-stereotype. Nordic scholars developed an auto-stereotype influenced by the image of the North outlined in Germany. Xeno- and auto-stereotypes reinforced each other in the drafting of a shared Germanic-Nordic space, a fixing of a mental boundary and imagery which in the 1930s would be a goldmine for Nazi ideologists in the search for origin and historical legitimacy as well as for a greater Germany.

The Nordic became for many an integrated part of the German. Comparative historical linguistics became a playground for Nordic thought during Romanticism. With scientific pretensions, languages in the distant past began to be related to ancient tribes and migrations in a pursuit which step by step defined its goal: the Indo-European original home. The language was seen as indistinguishable from the history of the peoples. The enlightenment philosophy had undermined the Biblical story of the creation. Comparative historical linguistics and text-critical philology were aimed at an alternative development narrative, which was on safe ground and verified by the sources. The task was to identify the primitive peoples and tribes and their origins. The German origin was in Asia. Jacob Grimm talked about Indo-German languages, which later were conceptualised as Indo-European. With his outline of the conformity to law by the sound development of the consonants and vowels, under observation of the differences and similarities between different languages, he paved the way for the comparative etymology, the teaching of the original meaning of the words.

The Grimm brothers connected the etymology to ethnology in a powerful language creating the image of the Nordic and the German. The Scandinavian linguists and historians were inclined to draw a sharp border between Scandinavia and the Germans in the South, whereas their German fellows included Scandinavia in a greater German people, among the Saxons, Bavarians, Franks and other peoples. The different views in this respect animated the debate between Scandinavian and German scholars at the same time as they cooperated around a shared theme.

The claim for scientific precision thus underpinned the image of the Nordic woven together into a historical narrative which varied as to the location of the borderline: was the Nordic part of a greater German culture or a special entity separate from it? Comparative ethnohistory developed a method based on the combination of linguistic analysis and investigation of literary sources. The Eddic saga and other Icelandic and Old Norse texts became important historical sources in the debate in the 1820s and 1830s on the question of from where the Æsir god Odin and his people had immigrated. Only somewhat later, with the breakthrough of the source-critical thoughts by Leopold von Ranke and others, did the role of the mythology in the derivation of the Nordic origin decline.

However, the myths survived with the help of other academic disciplines. The archaeologists continued, with other methods, the retrieval of the Old Norse with questions about when and from where the immigration had occurred. The question dealt with whether the original Indo-European home had been at the Caspian Sea or even further eastwards, or in the Baltics or even South Scandinavia. The longer the debate continued, the closer this original home moved to Southern Scandinavia.

Henry Wheaton was an American diplomat and expert on international law; he is less known for his extensive historical work. As an ambassador to Denmark he published *History of the Northmen, or Danes and Normans, from the Earliest Times to the Conquest of England* (1831) which brought him recognition in the Nordic countries and made him a member of the Scandinavian and Icelandic historical societies. He also wrote *Scandinavia, Ancient and Modern; being a History of Denmark, Sweden and Norway* (1841). His aim was obviously the search for a position for the USA as an equal player in the global community of the time by giving it a story of origins:

> Even to us [in America]... the literature of the North must have its interests, since we deduce our origin, our language, and our laws, from the Scandinavian and Teutonic races. The filiation of languages is not only a curious subject of philosophical inquiry, but an acquaintance with it is absolutely essential to a perfect knowledge of the structure of our own language, derived as it is from the mingled streams of all Northern dialects, and enriched with the addition of copious supplies from classic sources. (Obregón)

During the second half of the nineteenth century, a displacement occurred in the scientific ideologisation of the culture from the human sciences, operating with idealism and culturalism as key concepts, towards natural sciences, operating with materialism and naturalism as explanatory factors. The increasing role of the natural sciences followed economic, social, and political changes in the wake of the spread of industrial capitalism, a spread which led to a growing role for the natural sciences in the universities. Of course, Darwin's evolution theory also played a role.

In the wake of the growing role of natural sciences in the public debate, the Germans were increasingly described as a race; a group of humans with specific physical and distinctive mental characteristics given by nature. The anthropologists took over the concept of the Indo-German from the philologists and the linguists, creating an image of an ancient master race which, with a civilising mission in its self-esteem similar to the colonial powers of the time, fought against dark-skinned underpeople. The Indo German/Indo European concept was linked to the concepts of the Nordic race or Arians – the origin of whom was initially sought in Asia, but concurrently with the progress of anthropology was displaced towards Europe and finally Northern Europe. The physical anthropology confirmed the narrative by means of skull measurements, and with the division of humans into races as the method.

The debate on the location and the borders of the Indo Europeans welded together the imagery of a distinctive people in the North even if the borderline was disputed and therefore floating. It was clear, however, that it was a matter of a historically existing people and that their original home was not a biblical paradise but an earthly reality of great importance for humankind. The scholars, of course, did not realise what explosive power their search for borders by means of language and skulls, and imageries of races, contained. The mix became really shattering when the Indo-European language family began to connote an imagined Arian race group and the Arian original home was placed in Northern Europe. One should not, however, become anachronistic and attribute to the scholars the responsibility for the political abuse of the theories a few generations later. One should rather reflect on the time-boundedness and limitation of the academically established theories, whether in the name of truth or not.

The mutually reinforcing dynamics between auto- and xeno-stereotypes in Germany and *Norden* since the early nineteenth century accelerated after the German unification in 1871, resulting in a tectonic shift of the power relationships and the boundary imageries in Europe, which also impacted Northern Europe. In the conservative Sweden, Germany emerged ever more as a political, cultural and intellectual point of reference after the earlier attachment to France by the Bernadotte dynasty.

Finland was drawn into the geopolitical conflict about naval power in the Baltic between the Russian and the German empires in the 1890s and, a couple of decades later, the German orientation of the conservatives and the Soviet orientation of the left after the Russian revolution led to the bloody civil war in 1918.

In the more liberal Norway, the German point of reference was less distinct. The considerable opposition against the union with Sweden was also an argument for a demarcation to the German ideal of the conservative Sweden, and gave priority to an orientation towards Britain, also because of greater commercial interests there.

In Denmark, the national liberal conflict after 1848 about the duchies of Schleswig and Holstein relativised the German attraction. After the Prussian-Austrian attack on Denmark and the loss of Schleswig and Holstein in 1864, and after the German show of strength in 1871, the government ultimately developed a neutrality policy with a German bias, which occasionally provoked protests and expressions of popular anti-German feelings.

The proclamation of the German empire triggered different reactions in the North, but in the long run Germany became a point of reference that was difficult to ignore. The strong German orientation blurred the Nordic boundary with continental Europe in the North, and in Germany the imagery of a racial community extended the imagery of the Germanic beyond the boundary of Northern Europe.

5 Neutrality and Welfare in the Construction of the North

The conservative orientation towards Germany in *Norden* was contested and challenged from the left even if the German social democrats became a different kind of point of reference for the socialists in the North than that of the conservatives. When the idealisation of the Arian original home escalated in shrill overtones, the demarcation grew in the North to the Nordic hero myth in the South, but considerable opinions remained and during World War II the resistance movement was not so massive and fully heroic as in the story that was told after 1945. Before that, World War I had already imposed a certain demarcation onto Germany through the joint decision of the Scandinavian governments on neutrality during the war which was manifested in a meeting between the three kings.

For a short period after World War I, political dynamics were generated much more from utopias produced by the Russian Revolution and the collapse of three Empires than from history. Utopia was projected into the future rather than derived from the past, and the idea that history had a direction resembled the ideas of 1789, but seen from a new perspective. The new outline of the future incorporated international co-operation and peace, guaranteed by free and independent nations and the League of Nations. The Scandinavian demarcation from continental Europe, manifested through the neutrality politics during the war, shifted towards a cautious opening towards Europe and the League. The boundary between the North and Europe lost importance. The Scandinavian Social Democrats, who now emerged for the first time as a serious alternative for government, were very active in the development of this optimistic scenario, and were active players on this European/international scene. The expectations invested in the League of Nations by the Scandinavian Social Democrats and Liberals were considerable. Finland was still mainly occupied by the demarcation to the Soviet Union and by coming to terms with the domestic social and political boundaries in the wake of the civil war.

From the perspective of the Swedish Social Democrats, the League of Nations should be an organisation with full powers to guarantee the observance of international law with a bridge rather than demarcation to Europe. This attempt to fill the national trope with international content was invalidated by developments in world politics. The 1930s smothered any expectations of a peaceful world, as Scandinavia's geographical location in the intersection between Germany and the Soviet Union began to look increasingly ominous. In this context of uncertainty, the building of a mental demarcation to this threatening development began. National consolidation and Nordic co-operation once more became the theme as it was during World War I. It was a reaction in a Social Democratic version of a national, romantic construction of identity founded upon imageries of free peasants, Protestantism, political progress – that is, social democracy – and a history of popular and patriotic warrior kings fighting for the defence of the distinctive Danish, Norwegian and Swedish character. The contrast with continental Catholic culture, clericalism, conservatism and capitalism was increasingly emphasised as the dreams of the League of Nations faded away.

Arthur Engberg, one of the most pre-eminent spokesmen for international co-operation within the framework of the League of Nations in the 1920s, became possibly the most ardent builder of a barrier against Catholicism in the 1930s. Drawing on the national romantic narration and the great power trope of power and poverty, he warned in numerous articles against the spread of an expansive Catholic church unconstrained by any form of political control. In a Lutheran state church under political, that is, social democratic, control he saw a guarantee against the Catholic "lust for power" and the instrument to make "the nation invulnerable to the weapons of papism". In a parliamentary debate in 1930, Engberg, who was to become Social Democratic Minister for Church and Education a few years later, built a wall between the Swedish/Lutheran "Us" and the Catholic "Other": "I prefer an iron-like closed Swedish state church system on the pattern we have, to the order of things we would experience if Catholicism were allowed to throw its weight about in our country."

It is difficult to explain why Catholicism was wheeled out as a threat in this development. As a threat, Catholicism cannot have been more than a creation of the imagination. However, as a rhetorical referent to emphasise Swedishness, and as a linguistic tool in the political struggle over religious and cultural power, the Catholic threat was effective. Dangerous Catholicism was set off against Swedish cultural heritage, guaranteed by Social Democratic politics.

Although Social Democratic leaders in the interwar period such as Hjalmar Branting, Richard Sandler and Arthur Engberg in Sweden or Halvdan Koht in Norway, were, *per se*, Europe-oriented in their cultural view – and several of them spoke English, German and French fluently (Engberg was also skilled in Latin and Greek) – the image of a Catholic threat activated in the 1930s contained obvious elements of xenophobia *vis-à-vis* continental Europe. The growing military threat to the east and south of the Baltic closed down the openness towards the continent and reinforced the demarcation from World War I in religious and cultural terms. The new demarcation in the 1930s left remaining effects, which are still visible in the EU policies of the Scandinavian countries, although less so Finland.

The Cold War rather reinforced the boundary with the continent. The fact that only Sweden and Finland pursued neutrality politics, whereas Denmark and Norway joined NATO, should not be misunderstood as a continental European orientation in West Scandinavia. The orientation was towards the USA, which rather underlined the continued demarcation of continental Europe. Although the EC/EU membership of Denmark (1973), Finland (1995) and Sweden (1995) in a formal sense has changed this situation, the two Scandinavian countries prefer to define themselves as a periphery within the union, and Norway defines itself as a periphery without the union.

Bibliography

Arvidsson, S 2009, Germania. "Noen hovedlinjer i forskningen om fortidens germanere" in *Jakten på Germania. Fra nordnsvermeri till SS-arkeologi*, eds T Emberland & J Sem Fure, Humanist Forlag, Oslo.

Chibnall, M 2000, *The Normans*, Blackwell, Oxford.

Dolliner, P 1964, *La Hanse (XIIe-XVIIe siècles)*, Aubier, Paris.

Kabell, A 1961, "Über die nordische Philologie und die germanische Altertumskunde" Inaugural lecture for the Chair of Nordic Philology and Ancient Germanic History and Culture in the Faculty of Philosophy at the Ludwig-Maximilians-Universität, Munich.

Nilsson, K 2012, *Baltic-Finns and Scandinavians. Comparative-Historical Linguistics and the Early History of the Nordic Region*. PhD Dissertation, Lund University.

Obregón, L 2014, "Normative Histories of the World Written in the Long European Century" in *Europe 1815-1914: Creating Community and Ordering the World*, eds M Koskenniemi & B Stråth, Helsinki University, Helsinki.

Sawyer, P 1972, *Age of the Vikings*, Palgrave, London.

Sørensen, Ø & Stråth, B (eds) 1995, *The Cultural Construction of Norden*, Scandinavian University Press, Oslo.

Stråth, B 1997, "Scandinavian Identity: a Mythical Reality", in *European Identities: Cultural Diversity and Integration since 1700*, ed N Sörensen, Odense University Press.

Stråth, B 2000, "Poverty, Neutrality and Welfare: Three Key Concepts in the Modern Foundation Myth of Sweden", in *Myth and Memory in the Construction of Community, Historical Patterns in Europe and Beyond*, ed B Stråth, PIE-Peter Lang, Brussels.

Stråth, B 2011, "Nordic Foundation Myths after 1945 in a European Context" in *Narratives of the Second World War. National Historiographies Revisited*, eds H Stenius, M Österberg, J Östling, Nordic Academic Press, Lund.

Wolff, L 1994, *Inventing Eastern Europe: The Map of Civilisation on the Mind of the Enlightenment*, Stanford University Press, Stanford.

Manfred Hildermeier
Die Ausdehnung nach Osten

Grenze ist bekanntlich nicht gleich Grenze. Der Begriff ist zwar nicht vieldeutig, umfasst aber auch in seiner historischen Verwendung mehrere Inhalte. Im landläufigen Sinn meint er jene Linie, die ein privates oder staatliches Territorium von einem anderen trennt. Solche Grenzen hingen mit tatsächlicher oder reklamierter Herrschaft zusammen und waren in der Regel durch Tradition oder verbrieftes Recht begründet. Auch wenn sie entlang natürlicher Barrieren wie Flüssen oder Bergrücken verliefen, bildeten sie keine wirklichen Hindernisse, die ihnen zu längerer Dauer verholfen hätten. Im Gegenteil, die Grenzen kleinerer und mittlerer Herrschaften waren oft kurzlebig, weil sie auf dynastischen Ansprüchen oder auf kriegerischer Eroberung beruhten. Staatengrenzen hatten meist länger Bestand, haben sich aber auch erst in dem Maße wirklich verfestigt, in dem militärische Gewalt als Mittel ihrer Verschiebung ausschied. Es liegt auf der Hand, dass solche staatsrechtlich-territorialen Grenzen zwar auch gemeint sind, wenn vom Prozess der Ausdehnung Europas nach Osten die Rede ist, aber nicht primär. Sie bilden ihn eher ab, als dass sie ihn ausmachen.

Grenze kann aber auch auf größere Räume bezogen werden. Die Ebene, die dann angesprochen ist, lässt sich schon nicht mehr so exakt angeben wie bei der herrschafts- bzw. staatsterritorialen Definition, zumal über die Jahrhunderte durchaus verschiedene Dimensionen relevant werden. Handelsbeziehungen und allgemein zwischenstaatliche Verbindungen können ein ebenso sinnvolles Merkmal von Zugehörigkeit und Differenz sein wie eine gemeinsame Religion, die Teilhabe an übergreifenden geistigen Bewegungen – Wissenschaft, Architektur und Kunst eingeschlossen – oder die Ausbreitung wesentlicher, den Alltag und die Lebensweise prägender Errungenschaften der materiellen Kultur. Im Idealfall kommen die Dimensionen solcher Vernetzung zusammen. Die Linie ihrer Kongruenz bildet gleichsam die Außengrenze jenes Raums, der verbindet und einen gemeinsamen Namen trägt, z. B. von Europa – oder aus russischer Sicht: „Westeuropa".

Eine Grenze in diesem Sinn besitzt einen eigenartigen ‚epistemischen' Status. Sie ist einerseits real, andererseits und überwiegend aber *mental*, weil die Kriterien der Dazugehörigkeit schwanken. Nicht nur verändern sich die Selbst- und Fremdzuschreibung von Herrschern, Staaten und nationalen Eliten. Auch die Dimensionen selber, von Wirtschaftsbeziehungen bis zu Weltanschauungen, verlieren oder gewinnen an Bedeutung, in der Realität ebenso wie in der Wahrnehmung. Dabei mag offen bleiben, was Ursache und was Wirkung war. Wer an der Peripherie Europas sichtbar wurde, konnte bald dazu gehören, *auch* weil er sich dort *sah*. Die geistige Karte der Akteure war oft wichtiger als die tatsächliche Verfassung ihrer Länder.

Von selbst versteht sich, dass der geistig-kulturelle „Horizont", der damit angesprochen ist, durch geographische Nähe oder Ferne stark geprägt werden konnte. Historisch war dies nur anfänglich und teilweise als natürliche Gegebenheit wirksam. Als langfristig wichtiger erwies sich die Möglichkeit, den Raum zu überwinden. Auch mühevolle wochenlange Überlandreisen, die aber stattfanden und häufiger wurden, von Hansekoggen oder später der Eisenbahn nicht zu reden, ließen die Ferne schrumpfen. Dadurch verschwanden zwar keine Grenzen, aber sie wurden gleichsam in einen zunehmend größeren Zusammenhang integriert. Ein Geflecht aus Beziehungen verschiedenster Art: wirtschaftlicher, politischer und dynastischer ebenso wie in wachsendem Maße kulturell-weltanschaulicher und partiell auch religiöser, überwölbte die staatlich-territorialen Trennlinien. So gesehen, kann das Vordringen „Europas" nach Osten auch als Beleg für eine inhärente Dynamik zu verstärkter Interaktion und Verschränkung, zu Verdichtung und Vernetzung gelesen werden. Nichts spricht dafür, dass dabei andere Triebkräfte am Werk gewesen wären als in anderen Regionen auch.

1 Die deutsche Ostsiedlung und die Entstehung „Neueuropas"

Solche Einordnung der Grenzverschiebung nach Osten in *allgemein*europäische Prozesse gilt inzwischen auch für einen Vorgang, der über viele Jahrzehnte vorwiegend unter ideologischen Vorzeichen diskutiert wurde – die deutsche Ostsiedlung. Was im 12. Jahrhundert einsetzte und im 13. Jahrhundert in vollem Gange war, erweist sich in zweierlei Hinsicht als weniger spezifisch und auch als weniger spektakulär, als eine in die Vergangenheit zurückgespiegelte „nationalimperialistische" Deutung implizit unterstellt. Zum einen wanderten nicht so viele Menschen in die Gebiete jenseits von Elbe und Saale, dass man von einer wirklichen Massenbewegung sprechen könnte. Für das erste Jahrhundert hat man 200 000 Siedler angenommen, für den Hauptstrom des folgenden Jahrhunderts ca. das Doppelte. Aufs Jahr umgerechnet ergibt sich daraus eine Migration von jeweils wenigen Tausend Familien. Zum anderen war dies kein zentral gesteuerter Vorgang. Seine wichtigsten Akteure waren im Gegenteil regionale Landesherren, in deren Auftrag Lokatoren Siedler anwarben. Aus guten Gründen liegt es nahe, ihn in die breitere Migrationsbewegung insgesamt einzuordnen, die vom Bevölkerungswachstum Nordwesteuropas ausgelöst wurde und gleichsam für einen ‚Druckausgleich' in relativ leeren Räumen sorgte.

Zugleich markiert das Ergebnis ein epochales Geschehen und das bedeutendste dieser Art im beginnenden späten Mittelalter für unseren Kontext: den Landesausbau in der *Germania Slavica,* vor allem in Brandenburg, Sachsen und Schlesien, der aufgrund dieser Migration ein großes Stück vorankam. Nicht nur zahlreiche Dörfer, auch viele Städte entstanden neu. Die Grenze Mitteleuropas, wenn man den deutschen Raum als seinen Kern betrachten will, wanderte an die Oder. In der vergleichenden Geschichtsbetrachtung, die historische Räume voneinander abzugrenzen und sowohl strukturell als auch durch charakteristische Entwicklungen zu identifizieren suchte, sind die Begriffe *Alteuropa* und *Neueuropa* weitgehend unbestritten. Alteuropa meint dabei im Kern das Territorium des Frankenreichs, dessen Nordgrenze zugleich in etwa dem römischen Limes entsprach, also jenes Territorium, in dem es zur Verschmelzung von antikem Erbe und neuer germanischer Herrschafts- und Sozialverfassung kam. Neueuropa heißen die Regionen nordöstlich davon, die in den folgenden Jahrhunderten unterworfen, erschlossen und besiedelt wurden. Die Grenze des deutsch dominierten neueuropäischen Raumes war zu Beginn des späten Mittelalters an die Oder gewandert.

Hier aber blieb sie im Großen und Ganzen auch stehen. Jenseits eines nicht allzu breiten Landstreifens östlich des Flusses und mit Ausnahme Pommerns begann in Gestalt des Königreichs Polen nicht nur ein anderes Herrschaftsgebiet, sondern auch der Siedlungsraum einer anderen *natio*. Überzeugend hat man argumentiert, dass die tiefere Ursache für diese Demarkation im vielbeschworenen Akt von Gnesen zu suchen sei (W. Conze). Denn als sich Otto III. und Bolesław Chrobry im Jahre 1000 hier trafen, erkannte der deutsche Kaiser den polnischen Herrscher nicht nur als *cooperator regni* an, sondern begründete an diesem Ort auch ein eigenständiges Bistum, das dem römischen Papst *direkt* unterstand. Beiden Entscheidungen kann man fraglos säkulare Bedeutung zubilligen. Die weltliche schuf – wie umstritten ihre genaue Bedeutung bald auch sein mochte – die Voraussetzung für die Entstehung eines separaten Herrschaftsgebildes, das *außerhalb* des Heiligen Römischen Reiches blieb. Und die religiös-kirchenpolitische brach mit der bisherigen, auf Otto I. zurückgehenden Politik , das Erzbistum Magdeburg (gegr. 968) mit der Mission des Nordostens zu betrauen, d. h. ihm die jenseits von Elbe und Saale neu gegründeten Bistümer zu unterstellen.

Stattdessen legte der Akt von Gnesen die weitere Festigung des lateinischen Christentums, zu dem Bolesławs Vater Mieszko I. 966 übergetreten war, in die Hände einer *autochthonen,* nur Rom untergeordneten Keimzelle. Katholizismus und nationaler Staat konnten sich in einer Symbiose entfalten, die bis in die Gegenwart anhält. Polen wurde zum paradigmatischen Fall jener Fusion von lateinischem Christentum und nationaler Staatsbildung (im vormodernen Sinn) auf der Grundlage der Übernahme essentieller Merkmale der Herrschafts- und

Sozialverfassung des Frankenreichs, die man zum kennzeichnenden Merkmal *Neu*europas erklärt hat (K. Zernack). Komplementär bedeutete dies auch: Hinter der Oder endete im Inland – d. h. von den Randgebieten an der Ostsee abgesehen – der deutsche Herrschafts-, Siedlungs- und Kulturraum endgültig und begann ein ethnisch, sprachlich und kulturell anders geprägter, der sich aber selbstverständlich immer in Europa sah.

2 Ostmitteleuropa und die Verbreitung des römischen Christentums

Wie genau und nach welchen Kriterien er abzugrenzen sei, darüber ist intensiv diskutiert worden. Kaum zufällig erlebte diese Debatte in der Zwischenkriegszeit des 20. Jahrhunderts ihren Höhepunkt. Denn sie verband sich weltanschaulich aufs engste mit der Neuordnung der politischen Landkarte, die nach dem Ersten Weltkrieg in Versailles und den anderen Pariser Vororten vorgenommen worden war. Nicht zuletzt polnische Historiker bemühten sich darum, auch historisch zu begründen, dass ihr wiedergeborener Staat schon immer *in* Europa und nicht an dessen Rand gelegen habe. Osteuropa sei nicht als einheitlicher Raum zu betrachten, wie die gemeinsame Grenze zwischen dem Deutschen Reich und dem Zarenreich nahezulegen schien, die faktisch seit 1795 (vom kurzlebigen Marionettenstaat Napoleons, dem Großherzogtum Warschau 1807-1814, abgesehen) bestanden hatte. Vielmehr bilde er, zusammen vor allem mit der Tschechoslowakei eine eigene Region, die mit dem eigentlichen Osteuropa wenig, aber mit der Mitte Europas viel zu tun habe. Als charakteristische, definitorische Merkmale dieses Raums wurden vor allem die genannten gesehen: die Ähnlichkeit der herrschaftlichen und sozialen Grundstrukturen zu denen Alteuropas (vom Lehenswesen bis zum Ständestaat), die Übernahme des weströmischen Christentums sowie, nicht zuletzt, die Teilhabe an allen bedeutenden kulturell-geistigen Entwicklungen Mitteleuropas, von der Renaissance und der Reformation bis zur Aufklärung. Wenn sich Polen und die Tschechoslowakei auf diese Weise zum östlichen Teil *Mittel*europas rechneten (dem sich auch Ungarn anschloss, um der Zurechnung zum Balkan zu entgehen), war komplementär deutlich, was man *nicht* sein wollte: Teil des ‚ferneren' Osteuropa, das im wesentlichen auf Russland bzw. aktuell die Sowjetunion schrumpfte. Oskar Halecki, mit dessen Namen sich dieses Konzept einer großräumlichen Gliederung Europas in besonderem Maße verband, hat denn auch keinen Zweifel an dieser ‚geopolitischen' und weltanschaulichen Stoßrichtung seiner historischen Geographie gelassen. Das neue

Polen sollte und wollte in Geschichte und Gegenwart zentral und europäisch, nicht marginal und halbasiatisch sein.

Nicht ganz so klar war allerdings, wo dieses „Ostmitteleuropa", das an der polnischen Westgrenze begann, im Osten enden sollte. Eine Linie im staatsrechtlichen Sinn lässt sich nicht benennen. Vielmehr versiegte Ostmitteleuropa gleichsam in einem Streifen, der vom litauischen Kerngebiet im Norden über die weißrussischen Pripjetsümpfe und Wolhynien hinunter nach Podolien reichte. Im wesentlichen deckte sich dieser Grenzsaum mit jenen ‚Randmarken', die in der polnischen Republik der Zwischenkriegszeit als *kresy* bezeichnet wurden. Symptom ihres Übergangscharakters war aus geografischer Sicht der Beginn der riesigen osteuropäischen Tiefebene, der man in aller Regel (allerdings mit sehr unterschiedlicher Gewichtung) auch eine staats- und gesellschaftsprägende, mithin historische Bedeutung zuerkannt hat. Wichtiger aber war – zumal in unserem Kontext – eine häufige Überschneidung von Staat und ethnischer Nation, der eine parallele Inkongruenz von Staat und Religion entsprach. Anders gesagt: In diesem Grenzstreifen durchdrangen sich verschiedene *nationes*: Litauer, westslavische Polen, ostslavische Weißrussen und Ukrainer sowie nicht zuletzt Juden; zugleich prallten ihre Religionen samt der von ihr stark geprägten kulturellen Traditionen und Lebensformen aufeinander: Katholizismus, Orthodoxie und Judentum.

Wer diesen Charakter der Grenze Ostmitteleuropas erklären will, muss abermals weit in die Geschichte zurückgehen. Er muss sich daran erinnern, dass Litauen im 13. und 14. Jahrhundert zu einer Großmacht aufstieg. Fürst Mindaugas und seine Nachfolger schufen eines jener Riesenreiche, die man als vormoderne Überschichtungsstaaten bezeichnet hat. Primär auf militärische Überlegenheit gestützt, eroberten sie in relativ kurzer Zeit ausgedehnte Territorien und versammelten die dort ansässigen, angesichts der Größe dieser Gebiete recht unterschiedlichen Völkerschaften unter ihrer Herrschaft. Eine Fehde innerhalb der herrschenden Dynastie veranlasste einen der Prätendenten nun, sich nach Hilfe und Stärkung umzusehen. Zusätzlichen Anlass dürfte der wachsende Druck zur Christianisierung gegeben haben, da Litauen der einzige, noch heidnische Staat dieser Region war. Jogaila hätte die Option gehabt, sich nach Osten zu wenden und das Angebot einer dynastischen Verbindung mit dem Moskauer Großfürsten (Dmitrij Donskoj) anzunehmen. Er tat aber das Gegenteil, erklärte dem polnischen Adel, der sich um eine Nachfolge des 1382 verstorbenen Königs Ludwig I. (von Anjou, zugleich ungarischer Herrscher) bemühte, sein Interesse, heiratete 1386 Ludwigs Tochter Jadwiga und trat als Preis dafür zum Katholizismus über. So wurde der litauische Großfürst als Władysław II. Jagiełło nicht nur zum Ahnherrn einer neuen polnischen Königsdynastie, die den Thron für beinahe zwei Jahrhunderte behaupten konnte. Zugleich brachte er sein Reich in eine Personalunion mit dem polnischen Königreich ein und legte den Grundstein für die Verschmelzung beider in der Realunion von Lublin (1569) zur polnisch-litauischen „Adelsrepublik" (1572-1795). In langfristiger Perspektive offenbart sich diese Entscheidung Jogailas als ein ähnlich säkularer, ja „millenarer" Akt wie die Herrscherbegegnung von Gnesen: Sie schob das weströmische Christentum und die eng damit verbundene polnische Kultur insgesamt weit nach Osten vor. Das litauische Kernland wurde nach und nach katholisch. In den eroberten Gebieten Weiß- und Kleinrusslands behauptete sich der orthodoxe Glauben zwar; aber er wurde durch die Union von Brest 1596 als „griechisch-katholisch" in die weströmische Hierarchie eingegliedert und sah sich permanenter, offener oder latenter Mission ausgesetzt. Vor allem die Ukraine avancierte zu einem Kontaktraum zwischen lateinischer und orthodoxer Kultur (und hat in dieser Funktion nach ihrem Anschluss an das Zarenreich 1654 eine wichtige Vermittlerrolle in der Genese der Reformen Peters des Großen gespielt).

3 Die Ostsee-Region und der Aufstieg des Deutschen Ordens

Anders verlief die Entwicklung in der kontinentalen Randzone der Ostsee. Hier erstreckte sich über lange Jahrhunderte gleichsam eine ‚Zunge' deutscher Kultur, die erst spät zunächst von der russischen, dann in der zweiten Hälfte des 19. Jahrhunderts von den jeweiligen autochthonen nationalen Kulturen herausgefordert wurde. Die Wurzeln auch dieser Sonderentwicklung reichen ins frühe Spätmittelalter zurück. Sie verbanden sich aber weniger mit der ‚Sickerwanderung' nach Osten, die gleichsam nur nachfolgte. Entscheidend war vielmehr die kriegerische Missionstätigkeit des Deutschen Ordens, den der polnische Herzog Konrad von Masowien 1225/26 zur Unterwerfung der heidnischen Prussen zu Hilfe rief. Die Kreuzritter nahmen das Angebot angesichts zunehmender Probleme in Palästina gern an, ließen sich Privilegien von Papst und Kaiser ausstellen und eroberten „Preußen" im Laufe des nächsten halben Jahrhunderts (endgültig 1283). In der Folgezeit errichteten sie hier nicht nur einen eigenen Staat, in dem sie, vergleichbar mit Fürstbischöfen, als weltliche Obrigkeit herrschten. Darüberhinaus blieb ihr Territorium außerhalb des Reiches, ein Umstand, der ihre Handlungsmöglichkeiten erheblich stärkte. Schon deshalb traf die Fusion des Deutschen Ordens mit dem Schwertbrüderorden, der das nördlich angrenzende Livland – in der historischen, auch Kurland und Teile Estlands umfassenden Bedeutung – unterworfen und die dortigen heidnischen Stämme christianisiert hatte, auf keinen Widerstand. Faktisch war damit ein selbständiges, von der Weichselmündung bis an den finnischen Meerbusen reichendes Territorium entstanden, dessen Herrenschicht ebenso wie das Bürgertum in den entstehenden Städten, von Königsberg bis Reval, deutsch war und dessen Kultur, einschließlich der Rechts- und Sozialordnung, ebenfalls aus dem deutschen Raum importiert worden war.

In dem Maße, in dem dieser Ordensstaat seine ursprüngliche Zweckbestimmung einbüßte, verwandelte er sich in ein normales, weltliches Machtgebilde, das mit äußeren und zunehmend auch mit inneren Feinden zu kämpfen hatte. Zum wichtigsten äußeren Rivalen wurde der polnische Herrscher, der seit der zweiten Hälfte des 13. Jahrhunderts auch wieder über ein vereintes Reich verfügte und seit 1386 noch die Ressourcen Litauens in Anspruch nehmen konnte. Zum hauptsächlichen inneren Opponenten wuchsen die Stände, d. h. die Repräsentation der adeligen Grundherren heran, zumal sie sich mit den wenigen, aber wirtschaftlich starken Städten zusammenschlossen. Als dieser „Preußische Bund" seiner Obrigkeit, i. e. dem Ordensmeister und seinen Komturen, auch noch den Gehorsam aufkündigte und sich dem polnischen König unterstellte, war das Schicksal des Ordensstaates besiegelt. Der ersten – in national aufgeheizten Zeiten symbolisch stark befrachteten – Niederlage bei Tannenberg 1410 folgten nach der Jahrhundertmitte in einem mehrjährigen zerstörerischen Krieg weitere. Am Ende stand 1466 ein Friede (von Thorn), der das Land teilte: in ein westliches Gebiet um Danzig einschließlich des Bistums Ermland, des Kulmer Landes und der Handelsstädte Elbing und Thorn, das als Westpreußen dem polnischen König unterstellt wurde; und das restliche Gebiet mit Königsberg als Zentrum, das als Ostpreußen beim Orden blieb (auch wenn es sich der Oberhoheit des Königs unterwerfen musste). Eben dieses Territorium wurde in ein weltliches Herzogtum umgewandelt, als der letzte Hochmeister, Albrecht von Hohenzollern, 1525 zum Luthertum übertrat. Es blieb dabei ein polnisches Lehen, zugleich aber verband es sich eng mit dem Hauptterritorium der Hohenzollern – Brandenburg. Während das „königliche" Preußen trotz formaler Sonderrechte immer stärker in den polnischen Staat integriert wurde, blieb im „herzoglichen" die rein deutsche Prägung erhalten.

Ein wiederum anderes Schicksal ereilte Livland. Weiter im Nordosten gelegen, weckte es nicht nur die Begehrlichkeit seines unmittlbaren Nachbarn Polen-Litauen. Darüber hinaus geriet es in den Horizont jener Mächte, die sich hier anschickten, Hegemonialreiche aufzubauen. Im Norden begann Schweden, auf die ihm gegenüberliegende Seite der bald als *mare nostrum* reklamierten Ostsee auszugreifen; im Osten unternahm Ivan IV. (der Schreckliche) den ersten Versuch, seinem souveränen, aus der „Sammlung der russischen Erde" seit Beginn des 14. Jahrhunderts hervorgegangenen Gesamtstaat Zugang zu einem eisfreien Hafen zu verschaffen. Allen drei Nachbarn kam dabei der Zerfall der Ordensherrschaft entgegen, zumal diese sich auch noch in zunehmende Konflikte mit immediaten

Bistümern (Ösel-Wieck, Dorpat, Riga) und den wirtschaftlich starken Städten (vor allem Riga und Reval) verstrickten. In Livland entstand jenes ‚Machtvakuum', das in vormoderner Zeit wohl ausnahmslos einen Sog zu seiner Aufhebung durch äußere Intervention auslöste. Als Ivan 1558 seine Truppen in Bewegung setzte, begann er nicht nur einen 25-jährigen verheerenden Krieg, der sein Land an den Rand des Abgrunds brachte. Er lud die genannten Mächte auch nachgerade dazu ein, ebenfalls einzugreifen. Im Angesicht der russischen Bedrohung unterwarf sich der ‚estnische' Norden um Reval Schweden, während sich der größere Landesteil, das livländische Kernland im Süden, Polen-Litauen anschloss. So scheiterte der russische Zar auf der ganzen Linie; er musste die eroberten Gebiete wieder räumen und einen Frieden unterschreiben, der ihm soeben das Gesicht zu wahren half.

In der *longue durée* allerdings entpuppt sich der Livlandkrieg als ‚prophetischer' Vorschein auf die Zukunft. Noch wurde keine Grenze verschoben; das lateinische Christentum – der Protestantismus dabei eingeschlossen –, das im konservativ-eurozentrischen Diskurs des 20. Jahrhunderts zum Abendland verklärt wurde, endete nach wie vor im Osten der polnisch-litauischen Adelsrepublik. Aber indem Ivan IV. seinen Expansionsdrang nur wenige Jahre nach der Unterwerfung des Chanats von Kazan' im Osten nicht nach Süden gegen die Krim-Tataren richtete, sondern nach Nordwesten, nahm er einen Kampf auf, der das gesamte 17. Jahrhundert prägen sollte. Hauptgegner wurden das schwedische Großreich im Norden und das polnisch-litauische im Westen, dessen Niederringung auch zunehmende Konflikte mit dem Osmanischen Reich und seinen krimtatarischen Vasallen im Süden nach sich zog. Damit wandte der russische Staat, der 1547 zum Zarenreich geworden war, sein Gesicht nach jahrhundertelanger Unterbrechung durch das mongolisch-tatarische „Joch" (das keines war) wieder Europa zu. Dass es nach außen hin ein kriegerisches war und Ivans Herrschaft in der entstehenden europäischen Publizistik bald zum Schreckbild wurde, war nur die eine Seite dieser Neuausrichtung. Die andere bestand im wachsenden Interesse an Errungenschaften der „westeuropäischen" – wie man aus russischer Perspektive fortan sagte – Technik, Wissenschaft und materiellen Kultur: von Kanonen über den Buchdruck bis zu frühen medizinischen Kenntnissen und Praktiken.

4 Der russische Drang nach Westen

Zugleich rückte das russische Reich auch aus westlicher Sicht näher. Schon Kaiser Maxilian hatte 1516/17 und 1526/27 seinen Gesandten Sigismund von Herberstein zu Vasilij III. geschickt, um ihn für ein Bündnis zu gewinnen; Herbersteins Reisebeschreibung begründete die europäische Russlandkunde und diente mehr als ein Jahrhundert lang als hauptsächliche Informationsquelle über ein Land, das fremd und irritierend, verschlossen und wenig einladend erschien – und dennoch immer deutlicher am eigenen Horizont sichtbar wurde. Gewiss trugen der Aufstieg des Osmanischen Reichs und die Furcht vor einer Islamisierung Europas maßgeblich dazu bei, dass die christlichen Staaten des Westens auch nach Bundesgenossen im Osten suchten. Aber die Aufmerksamkeit füreinander nahm auch unabhängig davon zu. Neue Gesandtschaften lieferten neue Schilderungen von Land und Leuten, die zwar weiterhin zu manchem überheblichen Kopfschütteln Anlass gaben, aber auch die Kenntnis vertieften. Kaum zufällig im Umfeld der Belagerung Wiens trat das Zarenreich schließlich auch der „Heiligen Liga" gegen die Türken bei (1686). Kurz, wenn man – aus der Vogelperspektive eines Milleniums – eine Epoche benennen möchte, in dem Europa als Kulturraum auch über die Grenze dessen, was im 20. Jahrhundert Ostmitteleuropa genannt wurde, hinauswuchs, dann war es das 17. Jahrhundert, vor allem dessen zweite Hälfte, die dabei frühe Kontakte aus der Zeit Ivans IV. wiederaufnahm.

Diese kulturräumliche Erweiterung verband sich paradoxerweise mit einer Westverschiebung der *russischen* Grenze. Das Zarenreich wuchs gleichsam nach Europa hinein und zerdrückte jenen Staat, der dazwischen lag: die polnisch-litauische Adelsrepublik. „Außenpolitisch" war das 17. Jahrhundert aus russischer Sicht vor allem durch *einen* Vorgang geprägt – den Konflikt mit Polen-Litauen, an dessen Ende eine säkulare ‚Wachablösung' in der Hegemonialstellung über Osteuropa stand. Dieses Ergebnis wurde zwar erst zu Beginn des 18. Jahrhunderts sichtbar. Aber Peter I. erntete damit, was sich ein Dreivierteljahrhundert vorbereitet hatte.

Dabei sah es zu Beginn des 17. Jahrhunderts wahrlich nicht nach einer solchen Wende aus. Im Gegenteil, das Zarenreich versank in Adelsfehden, die dem Aussterben der Rjuriken-Dynastie mit dem kinderlosen Tod von Ivans schwachsinnigem Sohn Fedor 1598 gefolgt waren. Polen nutzte das Chaos zur Intervention, erreichte aber das Gegenteil von Gefügigkeit – eine ‚proto-nationale' Sammlungsbewegung, die seine Besatzungstruppen vertrieb und 1613 in Gestalt der Romanovs eine neue Herrscherdynastie installierte. Es folgten einige Jahrzehnte des Wiederaufbaus, in denen das Land an den äußeren Grenzen nur eines brauchte – Ruhe. Im Frieden von Stolbovo einigte man sich 1617 mit Schweden, das die Moskauer Schwäche ebenfalls genutzt hatte, um von Livland aus nach Osten auf Pskov vorzustoßen; Konzessionen waren nötig, aber Gustav II. Adolf begnügte sich im wesentlichen mit Ingermanland (dem Gebiet um das Delta der Neva). Ein Jahr später kam in Deulino auch eine Vereinbarung mit Polen zustande, die dem Zarenreich den Verzicht auf die stets umstrittene Festung und Stadt Smolensk abverlangte; aber sie trug ihm die faktische Anerkennung des neuen Zaren Michail samt dem förmlichen Ende des Krieges ein.

Doch Moskau sann auf Vergeltung und nutzte in den folgenden Jahrzehnten jede Schwäche des Nachbarn, um ihm – bald weit über verlorenes Terrain hinaus – Gebiete abzujagen. Der Einmarsch nach dem Tod des polnischen Königs Sigismund III. 1632 erwies sich noch als Fehlschlag; zwei Jahre später musste sich Russland im Frieden von Poljanovka (1634) wieder weitgehend auf die Grenzen von Deulino zurückziehen; Smolensk blieb polnisch-litauisch. Eine neue Chance brachten erst wachsende Probleme der Adelsrepublik im weiten Niemandsland des Südostens. Ob man sie als Folgen einer „imperialen Überdehnung" bezeichnen will, mag offen bleiben. In jedem Fall entglitten die Kosaken, die hier die Grenze gegen das Osmanische Reich sichern sollten, der Warschauer Kontrolle. Weil sich erheblicher sozialer Sprengstoff angesammelt hatte, sagten sie sich 1648 von Polen-Litauen los und flüchteten sich angesichts eines letztlich übermächtigen Gegners 1654 unter den Schutz des Moskauer Zaren. Russland ergriff diese Chance, wohlwissend, dass damit ein abermaliger Konflikt mit der Adelsrepublik unausweichlich wurde.

Letztlich trog das Gefühl nicht, trotz mancher innerer Probleme eine erhebliche Stärke (jedenfalls im Vergleich zu den ersten Jahrzehnten der neuen Ära) wiedergewonnen zu haben. Zwar erwies sich der Krieg als lang und erschöpfend. Zwar griff, kaum überraschend, nach anfänglichen Erfolgen Russlands auch Schweden in den Konflikt ein, der sich nun zum „Ersten Nordischen Krieg" (1655-1661) ausweitete. Zwar schlugen sich die Erzfeinde im Süden, die Krimtataren, umgehend auf die Seite Polen-Litauens. Aber am Ende erreichte das Zarenreich in Andrusovo 1667 einen Waffenstillstand, der seine Grenzen so weit nach Westen vorschob wie nie zuvor: Der gesamte breite Streifen von Smolensk über Černigov bis Kiev wurde russisch. Polen musste die östliche (linksufrige) Ukraine räumen; der untere Dnepr wurde zum Grenzfluss, wobei Kiev, das auf der ‚falschen' Seite lag, ebenfalls dem zarischen Territorium zugeschlagen wurde. Solch enormen Gewinn konnte das Moskauer Reich auch im förmlichen „Ewigen Frieden" von 1686 verteidigen, zumal Polen-Litauen in diesen Jahren, auf dem Höhepunkt des ‚christlichen' Abwehrkampfes gegen den Islam, alle Kräfte auf seinen Hauptfeind im Südosten konzentrierte und zu Konzessionen bereit war. Russland zahlte ja seinen „Preis" und trat der Abwehrfront, wie erwähnt, zeitgleich bei.

In der Perspektive des russischen ‚Drangs nach Westen' markiert das neue, 18. Jahrhundert keine Zäsur. Vielmehr zeigt sich eine bemerkenswerte Analogie zu der inzwischen akzeptierten These, dass das vielzitierte „Fenster nach Europa" schon geöffnet war, das Peter der Große 1700 mit ganzer Kraft aufstieß. Als der russische Zar den entscheidenden Sieg im Großen Nordischen Krieg (1700-1721) errang und Karl XII. von Schweden bei Poltava 1709 vernichtend schlug, da fiel ihm auch die Adelsrepublik gleichsam in den Schoß. Denn sein Triumph half dem zuvor von Karl entthronten polnischen König, August II. (dem Starken), zwar wieder auf die Beine. Aber der wiedereingesetzte Monarch empfing sein Reich aus russischer Hand. Faktisch hatte Polen-Litauen, das noch ein Jahrhundert zuvor den Kreml besetzt und umgekehrt den russichen Thron beansprucht hatte, seine Souveränität verloren. Fortan marschierten zarische Truppen nach Belieben aus und ein. Nach dem Tod Augusts 1733 verabredeten sie sich dabei mit preußischen, die von der anderen Seite her eindrangen, um ihren gemeinsamen Kandidaten (August III.) zu installieren.

Dreißig Jahre später wiederholte Katharina die Große dieses Spiel, als sie ihren einstigen Favoriten und polnischen Gesandten am St.Petersburger Hof zum neuen König machte (Stanislaus August Poniatowski). Ihm mutete sie als Strafe für unerwartete Unbotmäßigkeit auch den erheblichen Gebietsverlust zu, den schon die erste Teilung Polens 1772 mit sich brachte. Obwohl Friedrich II. von Preußen (der sich die lebenswichtige Landbrücke zwischen Pommern und Ostpreußen einverleibte) allem Anschein nach die treibende Kraft dieser Amputation war, ließ sie sich doch nicht lange bitten, ebenfalls zuzugreifen. Zwanzig Jahre später hatte sich die politische Situation nicht nur in Polen, sondern in ganz Europa fundamental verändert. Während die erste Teilung Polens gleichsam noch Teil absolutistischer (machiavellistischer) Kabinettspolitik war, stand die zweite im Kontext der Französischen Revolution und des Abwehrkampfes der *Anciens régimes*. Deshalb übernahm Katharina nun die Iniative. Die neuerliche Teilung (1793) beließ der Adelsrepublik nur noch ein Restterritorium, das zu wirklicher Rekonvaleszenz nicht ausgereicht hätte. Ihr vollständiges Ende in der dritten Teilung (1795) folgte mit erheblicher Zwangsläufigkeit. Die Amputation wurde zur Vivisektion. Zum ersten Mal in der neueren Geschichte Europas verschwand ein Staat von der politischen Landkarte, der hundert Jahre zuvor noch eine Großmacht und sogar die Hegemonialmacht in Osteuropa gewesen war. Die Folgen ließen sich an eben dieser Karte besonders klar ablesen: Preußen und Russland, die beiden Parvenüs des 18. Jahrhunderts, hatten plötzlich eine gemeinsame Grenze. Das hieß umgekehrt aber auch: Russland stand nun nicht mehr nur vor der Tür Europas, sondern im Haus.

Dies war umso eher der Fall, als der Triumph im Großen Nordischen Krieg eine weitere wichtige Folge für Russland hatte. Gleich nach der hastigen Flucht Karls XII. marschierte Peter nach Norden und nahm jenes Land endgültig in Besitz, um dessetwillen der Krieg begonnen worden war: Livland. Er empfing die Huldigung der Ritterschaft und der Städte – und gewährte ihnen ein Privileg (1710), das seinen Namen verdiente. Der russische Zar garantierte darin nichts Geringeres als die Wahrung der gewachsenen adelig-ständischen und der patrizisch-städtischen Selbstverwaltung. Die Urkunde stellte den *status quo ante* zwar nicht wieder her, weil die Oberhoheit selbstredend beim Zaren lag. Aber in ihrem Land erhielten die alten Herren so weitgehende Autonomierechte, wie es sie in keiner anderen Provinz gab. Das hatte seinen guten Grund. Peter, der die westliche Kultur bekanntlich verehrte, wusste, was er am deutsch geprägten Livland hatte: ein Stück Europa im eigenen Reich. Die ritterschaftliche Selbstverwaltung blieb bis zum Beginn des 20. Jahrhunderts im Kern erhalten, und Livland selber, nach der Liquidierung Polens 1795 um Kurland und Litauen erweitert, gehörte bis seinem Untergang zum Zarenreich. Auch diese Grenze führte Russland, in aller Ambivalenz, nahe an Europa heran: Hier brauchte Napoleon im Juni 1812 nur einen Fluss (die Memel/Njemen) zu überqueren, um von Preußen nach Russland zu gelangen.

5 Die Südgrenze und der Streit zwischen Russland und der Türkei

Bleibt ein Blick auf die südlichen Grenzen Russlands und Europas. Hauptgegner des Zaren- und des Habsburger Reichs gleichermaßen war das Osmanische Reich. Über seine Vasallen am Nordrand des Schwarzen Meeres (einschließlich der Krim) war es auch auf der anderen Seite des Schwarzen Meeres präsent. Zwar lag die faktisch herrenlose Steppe lange Zeit zwischen den Krimtataren und dem Moskauer Staat, wo Krieger-Bauern (Kosaken) eine teils sesshafte, teils nicht sesshafte Grenzbevölkerung bildeten. Doch je weiter der zentralrussische Staat in diese „Ukraine" (i. e. Randzone) vordrang, desto schmaler wurde die Pufferzone. Als sich die „linksufrigen" Kosaken 1654 dem Zaren faktisch unterstellten und unter Peter dem Großen ihre relative Unabhängigkeit endgültig einbüßten, endete sein Reich nur noch unweit des Schwarzen Meeres. Schon seit dem ausgehenden 17. Jahrhundert häuften sich daher militärische Konflikte mit dem Osmanischen Reich. Zu Beginn des 18. Jahrhundert scheint es noch eine ungefähre Kräftebalance gegeben zu haben. Peter siegte im zweiten Anlauf auf die Festung Azov (1696), kam dann aber am Pruth 1712 nur mit knapper Not davon. Auch Kriege in den 1730er Jahren erbrachten nicht viel.

Erst unter Katharina schlug das Pendel immer weiter zur Seite des erstarkenden Zarenreichs aus, während das Osmanische Reich an Kraft verlor und jener Abstieg begann, der es schließlich zum „kranken Mann am Bosporus" machte. Als der Sultan 1768 russische Probleme in Polen ausnutzen wollte und einen Krieg vom Zaun brach, hat er sicher nicht damit gerechnet, sechs Jahre später eine Art Diktatfrieden unterzeichnen zu müssen (1774, von Kucuk-Kaynarca). Faktisch hatte die Zarin fortan freie Hand auf der Krim und annektierte diese strategisch zunehmend wichtige Halbinsel 1783. Es folgte ein ‚Revanchekrieg" zwischen beiden Mächten, den Russland definitiv für sich entschied (im Frieden von Jassy 1792). Auch der westliche Teil der Nordküste des Schwarzen Meeres bis zum Dnestr, wo bald Odessa gegründet wurde, gehörte nun zum Zarenreich. Als im folgenden Jahr noch der polnisch-litauische Staat weiter zurückgedrängt und wenig später vollständig liquidiert wurde, kamen die nördlichen Nachbarregionen Podolien und Wolhynien hinzu. Damit ergab sich am Oberlauf des Dnestr auch eine gemeinsame Grenze mit dem Habsburger Reich, dem Galizien zugeschlagen worden war. Mithin stand das Zarenreich am Ende des 18. Jahrhunderts in dieser Region ebenfalls, wie im Norden, nicht mehr am Rand, sondern *in* Europa.

6 Widerspenstiges Polen und unklare Westgrenzen

Im folgenden Jahrhundert bis zum Ersten Weltkrieg hat es an der Westgrenze des russischen Imperiums keine weiteren dauerhaften Grenzverschiebungen von größerem Ausmaß mehr gegeben. Im Süden konnte es das Osmanische Reich noch ein Stück zurückdrängen, vom Dnestr an den Pruth (1812). Im Norden nutzte es die finnisch-schwedische ‚Erbfeindschaft' und das Abkommen mit Napoleon (von Tilsit 1807), um Finnland in Personalunion an sich zu binden; Finnland behielt aber eine weitgehende administrative Autonomie und gehörte nie zum Zarenreich selber.

Nach außen hin anders verhielt es sich mit Polen. Auf dem Wiener Kongress (1814/15) war es als formal selbständiges Königreich wiederhergestellt und ebenfalls ‚nur' in Personalunion an das Zarenreich angeschlossen worden. Nach dem Novemberaufstand in Warschau 1830 fand diese formale Eigenständigkeit durch die Erklärung eines permanenten Ausnahmezustands faktisch ihr Ende, und nach dem zweiten Aufstand von 1863/64 wurde sie auch förmlich kassiert. Selbst der Name verschwand abermals von der Landkarte; aus Polen wurde das „Weichselgouvernement". Im Herzen des katholischen Landes, in Warschau, errichtete man sogar eine orthodoxe Kathedrale. Dennoch blieb Polen Polen. Es sperrte sich ethnisch, sprachlich sowie nicht zuletzt religiös und kulturell in viel stärkerem Maße gegen die russische Oberhoheit und erst recht gegen die Russifizierung, die im Geist des überall in Europa grassierenden Nationalismus vor dem Ersten Weltkrieg auch hier vorangetrieben wurde, als etwa die ehemaligen Ostgebiete der polnisch-litauischen Adelsrepublik, die im Zuge der ersten und zweiten Teilung annektiert worden waren; hartnäckiger auch als die baltischen Gouvernements.

Dennoch: auch wenn man *Staats*grenzen gerade im Westen des russischen Imperiums nicht mit *Kultur*grenzen verwechseln darf, galt doch spätestens seit Ende der Herrschaftszeit Katharinas der Großen, was sie zu Beginn in ihrer berühmten „Großen Instruktion" (1767) geschrieben hatte: „Russland ist eine europäische Macht." Wie weit die geborene deutsche „Duodez"-Prinzessin (von Anhalt-Zerbst) auf diesem Weg gekommen war, zeigte nicht nur ihre erfolgreiche Vermittlung zwischen Preußen und Österreich im Bayrischen Erbfolgekrieg (dessen Beilegung im Teschener Frieden 1779 es garantierte). Vor allem ihr Enkel Alexander I. demonstrierte diese neue Rolle und Bedeutung seines Landes: unglücklich in der Blamage gegen Napoleon bei Austerlitz 1805, triumphal bei der Verfolgung des in Moskau geschlagenen Helden quer durch Mitteleuropa 1813. Als der russische Zar und Kaiser Ende März 1814 über die Champs Elysées paradierte – wurde Katharinas programmatischer Satz für die gesamte europäische Öffentlichkeit so anschaulich wie nie zuvor.

Literatur

Conze, W 1993, *Ostmitteleuropa. Von der Spätantike bis zum 18. Jahrhundert*, Hg. Klaus Zernack, Beck, München.

Hildermeier, M 2006, „Osteuropa als Gegenstand vergleichender Geschichte" in *Transnationale Geschichte. Themen, Tendenzen und Theorien. [Jürgen Kocka zum 65. Geburtstag]*, Hg. G Budde, Vandenhoeck und Ruprecht, Göttingen, S. 117–136.

Hildermeier, M 2013, *Geschichte Russlands. Vom Mittelalter bis zur Oktoberrevolution*, Beck, München.

Jaworski, R, Lübke, C, & Müller, MG 2000, *Eine kleine Geschichte Polens*, Suhrkamp, Frankfurt am Main.

Szücs, J 1990, *Die drei historischen Regionen Europas*, Neue Kritik, Frankfurt am Main.

Wojciechowski, M & Schattkowsky, R (Hg.) 1996, *Historische Grenzlandschaften Ostmitteleuropas im 16. - 20. Jh. : Gesellschaft - Wirtschaft – Politik*, Uniwersytet Mikołaja Kopernika, Toruń.

Zernack, K 1994, *Polen und Rußland: Zwei Wege in der europäischen Geschichte*, Propyläen, Berlin.

Zernack, K (Hg.) 2001, *Preußen - Deutschland - Polen : Aufsätze zur Geschichte der deutsch-polnischen Beziehungen*, Hg. W Fischer & M Müller, Duncker und Humblot, Berlin.

Manfred Hildermeier
The Expansion towards the East

"Boundary" does not always mean the same thing in every context. Although the term is not ambiguous, in its historical usage it encompasses several meanings. In the widely understood sense it means the line that separates a private or state territory from another. Such boundaries were related to actual or claimed dominions and were generally based on tradition or vested right. Even if they went along natural barriers such as rivers or mountain ridges, they did not pose any real hindrances that would have enabled them to be of long duration. On the contrary, the boundaries of small and medium-sized dominions were often short-lived because they were based on dynastic claims or on military conquest. State boundaries were usually more permanent, but they first became really fixed to the extent that military force was no longer accepted as a means to displace them. While it is clear that such territorially defined state boundaries are meant when the process of eastward expansion of Europe is mentioned, these boundaries are not the primary aspect. They depict rather than determine this expansion.

However, boundaries can also delineate larger areas. The level addressed here can no longer be specified as precisely as the dominion or state territory definition, especially since over the centuries different dimensions were relevant. Trade relations and general relations between states can be an equally meaningful feature of belonging and difference as a common religion, participation in overarching intellectual movements – including science, architecture and art – or the dissemination of significant achievements of material culture which profoundly influence everyday life and the lifestyle. Ideally, the dimensions of such interconnectedness converge. The line of their congruence forms the outer boundary of the area that connects and supports a common name, such as "Europe" – or from the Russian perspective – "Western Europe".

A boundary in this sense has a unique "epistemic" status. On the one hand it is real but on the other hand it is primarily *mental*, because the criteria of belonging fluctuate. Not only is the attribution "belonging to one's own group" or "foreign" by rulers, states or national elites variable and subject to change. Even the dimensions themselves – ranging from economic relations to philosophical or religious outlooks and beliefs – lose or gain in significance, in reality as well as in perception. What is cause and what is effect may remain unresolved. Whoever appeared on the Europe's periphery could soon belong to Europe – *just* because he *saw* himself there. The mental map of the players was often more important than the actual condition of their countries.

It is self-evident that the intellectual and cultural "horizon" at issue here could be strongly influenced by geographical proximity or distance. Historically, this was only initially and partially effective as a natural condition. Over the long term, it proved to be more important to *overcome* distance. Moreover, arduous weeks of overland travel, which nevertheless were undertaken and became more frequent, not to mention the Hanseatic cogs or later the railways, could shrink the distance. These did not make the boundaries disappear, but they were integrated into an increasingly larger context. A complex web of relationships developed: economic, political and dynastic and to an increasing degree cultural-ideological and partially also religious relationships, overlapping the state-territorial dividing lines. From this perspective, the advance of "Europe" eastward can also be read as evidence of an inherent dynamism to increased interaction and interrelationships, to compaction and networking. There is no evidence that there were different driving forces at work here than in other regions.

1 German Settlement of the East and the Development of "New Europe"

Such a classification of the shift of boundaries eastward in *general* European processes meanwhile also applies to a process that was discussed over many decades mainly from an ideological perspective – the German eastward expansion. What began in the 12th century and was in full swing in the13th century proves to be in two respects less specific and also less spectacular than a "national imperialist" interpretation applied to the past would implicitly assume. First of all, not as many people migrated to the areas beyond the Elbe and Saale rivers for this to be considered a real mass migration. For the 12th century it has been assumed that there were 200 000 settlers; in the main stream of migration in the following century there were about twice that many. Per year this amounted to a migration of only circa several thousand families. Second, this was not a centrally controlled process. On the contrary, its main actors were regional lords, on whose behalf authorised locators recruited the settlers. For good reasons, this process can be seen in the context of the broader migration movement as a whole, which was triggered by population growth in northwestern Europe and which elicited a "pressure equalization" in comparatively unpopulated areas.

At the same time, for our context the result marked an epochal event and the most important of its kind in the beginning Late Middle Ages: the development of land in the *Germania Slavica*, in particular in Brandenburg, Saxony and Silesia, which due to this migration made great progress. This not only led to the founding of many villages but also of many cities. The boundary of Middle Europe, if one wishes to consider the German area as its core, shifted to the Oder River. In the comparative study of history, which sought to delineate the historical areas from each other and to identify them both structurally and through characteristic developments, the terms *Old Europe* and *New Europe* are largely undisputed. Old Europe is defined basically as the territory of the Frankish Empire, whose northern border was approximately that of the Roman Limes, i.e. the territory where a fusion took place between the heritage of antiquity and the new Germanic socio-political order. The regions northeast of this area were called New Europe, which in the following centuries were conquered, opened up and settled. The boundary of the new German-dominated European area had shifted at the beginning of the Late Middle Ages to the Oder River.

Thereafter, however, the border remained largely static. Beyond a relatively narrow strip of land east of the river and with the exception of Pomerania, not only another dominion began, but also the settlement area of another *natio* in the form of the Kingdom of Poland. It has been convincingly argued that the root cause for this demarcation can be seen in the often cited Act of Gniezno (W. Conze). When Otto III and Bolesław Chrobry met here in 1000 AD, the German emperor not only recognised the Polish sovereign as a *cooperator regni*, but also founded an independent diocese here, which was *directly* subordinate to the Roman Pontiff. Both decisions had a truly historical significance and created the precondition for the emergence of a separate ruling entity that remained *outside* the Holy Roman Empire. And the religious-ecclesiastical politics broke with the previous politics dating back to Otto I to entrust the Archdiocese of Magdeburg (founded in 968) with the mission of the Northeast, i.e. to place the newly founded dioceses beyond the Elbe and Saale Rivers under its authority.

Instead, the Act of Gniezno further strengthened Latin Christianity, to which Bolesław's father Mieszko I had converted in 966 AD, creating an *autochthonous* germ cell that was only subordinate to Rome. Catholicism and the national state were able to develop in a symbiosis that continues to the present day. Poland became the paradigmatic case of that fusion of Latin Christianity and the formation of a nation state (in the pre-modern sense) on the basis of the adoption of essential features of the socio-political order of the Frankish Empire, which has been declared the characterising attribute of *New* Europe (K. Zernack). Conversely, this also meant that beyond the Oder River in the interior – i.e. apart from the outlying areas of the Baltic Sea – German domination and the German settlement and cultural area came to an end, and an ethnically linguistically and culturally different area began, which however always viewed itself to be within Europe.

2 East Central Europe and the Spread of Roman Christianity

Exactly how and by what criteria this area is to be delineated has been the subject of intense discussion. It is no coincidence that this debate reached its zenith in the interwar period of the 20th century. Ideologically, this discussion was closely connected with the rearrangement of the political map which was made after the First World War in Versailles and other Paris suburbs. Polish historians, in particular, attempted to justify also historically that their reborn state had always been located *in* Europe and not on its periphery. According to them, eastern Europe should not be regarded as a single area, as the common border between the German Empire and the Tsarist Empire seemed to suggest, which had existed since 1795 (apart from the short-lived puppet state of Napoleon, the Grand Duchy of Warsaw, between 1807 and 1814). Rather, in their view it constitutes an own region, together in particular with Czechoslovakia, which has little to do with eastern Europe as such but much to do with the centre of Europe. The following features were mentioned especially as characteristic and definitive for this area: the similarity of fundamental hierarchical and social structures to those of Old Europe (from feudalism to an estate-based society), the adoption of western Roman Christianity and, not least, the participation in all major cultural and intellectual developments of central Europe from the Renaissance and the Reformation to the Enlightenment. When Poland and Czechoslovakia considered themselves in this way to be part of the eastern part of *Central* Europe (as did Hungary, to escape being considered part of the Balkans), it was conversely also quite clear what they did *not* want to be: part of the "more distant" eastern Europe, which thus shrank to consist of Russia or the then Soviet Union. Oskar Halecki, whose name is particularly associated with this concept of a macro-regional division of Europe, left no doubt about the "geopolitical" and ideological thrust of his historical geography. In his view the new Poland should be and also sought to be central and European and not marginal and half-Asian, both historically and in the present.

However, it was not quite as clear where this "East Central Europe", which began at the Polish western border, should end in the east. A line in the constitutional sense cannot be named. Rather, East Central Europe gradually faded out in a strip extending from the Lithuanian heartland in the north to the Belarusian Pripet Marshes and Volhynia to Podolia. Essentially, this border seam was congruent with the eastern borderlands, which in the interwar period in the Republic of Poland, were designated as *kresy*. Their transitional nature from a geographic perspective was indicated with the beginning of the enormous East European plain, which has usually been recognised (although with very different emphasis) as having a formative state and societal significance. However, more important – especially in our context – was a frequent overlap between the state and ethnic nation, which corresponded to a parallel incongruence between state and religion. In other words, different *nationes* penetrated this border strip: Lithuanians, West Slavic Poles, East Slavic Belarusians and Ukrainians and last but not least Jews. At the same time their religions clashed and along with this their cultural traditions and ways of life which were strongly impacted by their religions: Catholicism, Orthodoxy and Judaism.

To explain this character of the border of East Central Europe, one must again go far back into history. It must be remembered that Lithuania became a great power in the 13th and 14th centuries. Prince Mindaugas and his successors created an extensive, pre-modern empire. Primarily based on military superiority, they conquered extensive territories in a relatively short time and placed the indigenous population there – in view of the size of the areas quite different tribes – under their dominion. A feud within the ruling dynasty led one of the pretenders to power to look for assistance and reinforcements. Another reason is likely to have been the growing pressure to convert to Christianity, since Lithuania was the only remaining pagan state in the region. Jogaila would have had the option to turn eastward and to accept the offer of a dynastic link with Moscow's Grand Prince (Dmitry Donskoy). But he did the opposite; he declared his interest to the Polish nobility, which sought a successor to the late King Louis I (of Anjou, at the same time ruler of Hungary) who had died in 1382. Jogaila married Louis' daughter Jadwiga in 1386 and as price for this converted to Catholicism. Thus, the Lithuanian Grand Duke as Władysław II Jagiełło not only became the ancestor of a new Polish royal dynasty that would claim the throne for almost two centuries. At the same time he brought his Empire into a personal union with the Kingdom of Poland and laid the cornerstone for the fusion of the two in the Union of Lublin (1569) to form the Polish-Lithuanian Commonwealth (1572-1795). In a long-term perspective, this decision by Jogaila turned out to be a similar secular, indeed "millennium" act like the encounter of the rulers at Gniezno: It pushed Western Roman Christianity and the closely related Polish culture far to the east. The Lithuanian heartland gradually became Catholic. In the conquered areas of White Russia and Little Russia the Orthodox faith retained its status; but through the Union of Brest in 1596 it was included in the West Roman hierarchy as Greek-Catholic and was exposed to a permanent open or latent missionising activity. In particular, the Ukraine became an interface between Latin and Orthodox culture (and in this function, following its annexation to the Tsarist Empire in 1654, played an important mediating role in instigating the reforms of Peter the Great).

3 The Baltic Sea Region and the Rise of the Teutonic Order

The development was different in the continental border zone of the Baltic Sea. A "tongue" of German culture existed here for many centuries, which was challenged only late by the Russian culture, and then in the second half of the 19th century was challenged by the respective autochthonous national cultures. The roots of this special development also date back to the early Late Middle Ages. However, it was connected less with the "step-by-step migration" eastward that was to follow as a result. The decisive factor was rather the bellicose missionising activity of the Teutonic Order, which the Polish Duke Conrad of Masovia in 1225/26 called on to help subdue the pagan Prussians. The Order of Knights gladly accepted the offer in view of increasing problems in Palestine. They arranged to receive privileges from the pope and the emperor and conquered "Prussia" in the course of the next half century (ultimately in 1283). In the following era they not only built a separate state, in which they, comparable with prince-bishops, ruled as secular authority. Moreover, their territory remained outside the Empire, a circumstance which considerably strengthened their options for action. For that reason alone, the fusion of the Teutonic Order with the Livonian Brothers of the Sword, which had conquered Livonia, the area bordering on the north – in the historical sense which also encompassed Courland and parts of Estonia – and had christianised the pagan tribes there, met with no resistance. In fact, an independent territory emerged ranging from the Vistula estuary to the Gulf of Finland, whose ruling class as well as the middle class in the emerging cities from Königsberg (now Kaliningrad) to Reval (now Tallinn) was German and whose culture, including the legal and social order, had likewise been imported from the German area.

To the extent in which this Teutonic Order state lost its original purpose, it turned into a normal, secular power structure that had to struggle with external as well as increasingly with internal enemies. The Polish ruler became the most important external rival; since the second half of the 13th century his empire had once again become united and from 1386 on, he was able to claim the resources of Lithuania. The nobles developed into the main internal adversaries, i.e. the representation of the noble landlords, especially since they merged with the few but economically powerful cities. When this "Prussian Confederation" renounced obedience to the authority of the Teutonic Order, i.e. to the grand master and his knights, and placed itself under the rule of the Polish king, the fate of the Order state was sealed. The first defeat in the Battle of Grunwald (Tannenberg) – in times of nationalist fervour a historical event fraught with symbolism – in 1410 was followed after the middle of the century by subsequent defeats in a devastating war lasting several years. In the end, in 1466 a peace was attained (Second Peace of Thorn) that divided the territory: into a western area around Danzig including the diocese of Warmia, the Kulm region and the commercial cities of Elbing and Thorn, which as West Prussia were subject to the rule of the Polish king, and the remaining area with Königsberg as its centre, which as East Prussia remained under the Order (even if it had to subject to the sovereignty of the king). This territory was transformed into a secular duchy when the last grand master, Albrecht von Hohenzollern, converted to Lutheranism in 1525. It remained a Polish fiefdom, but at the same time it allied itself closely with the main territory of the Hohenzollerns – Brandenburg. While "Royal" Prussia despite formal special rights increasingly became an integral part of Poland, "Ducal" Prussia retained its purely German character.

Yet another fate befell Livonia. Located further to the northeast, it not only aroused the greed of its immediate neighbour Poland-Lithuania. It also appeared on the horizon of those powers that were preparing to establish hegemonic empires. In the north, Sweden began laying claim to land on the opposite side of the Baltic Sea, which it soon called its *mare nostrum*. In the east Ivan IV (the Terrible) undertook his first attempt for his sovereign state, which had emerged since the beginning of the 14th century from the "collection of Russian lands", to gain access to an ice-free port. All three neighbours benefited from the disintegration of the rule of the Teutonic Order, since it was also entangled in the increasing conflicts with exempt dioceses (Ösel-Wiek, Dorpat, Riga) and the economically strong cities (especially Riga and Reval). In Livonia a "power vacuum" arose which in pre-modern times without exception created a pull to resolve it through external intervention. When Ivan set his troops in motion in 1558, he not only began a devastating 25-year war that brought his country to the brink of the abyss. Indeed, he invited the above-mentioned powers to also intervene. In the face of the Russian threat the Estonian northern area around Reval surrendered to Swedish rule, while the greater part of the country, the Livonian heartland in the south, joined Poland-Lithuania. Thus, the Russian Tsar failed all down the line; he had to give up the territories he had conquered and sign a peace treaty to barely save face.

In the *longue durée*, however, the Livonian War turned out to be a "prophetic" vision of the future. Still no border had been redrawn; Latin Christianity – which included Protestantism – which in the conservative -Eurocentric discourse of the 20th century was glorified as the Occident, still ended in the eastern part of the Polish-Lithuanian Commonwealth. However, because Ivan IV – only a few years after conquering the Khanate of Kazan in the east – directed his expansionism not towards the south against the Crimean Tatars but instead towards the northwest, he initiated a struggle that was to characterise the entire 17th century. The main adversaries were the Swedish empire in the north and the Polish-Lithuanian in the west, whose decline also led to increasing conflicts with the Ottoman Empire and its Crimean-Tatar vassals in the south. Thus the Russian state, which in 1547 had become a Tsarist empire, turned its face after centuries of interruption due to the Mongolian-Tatar "yoke" (which was none) once again towards Europe. That this face was outwardly warlike and Ivan's reign soon became a spectre of terror in the emerging European journalism, was only one aspect of this realignment. The other was the growing interest in the achievements of "Western Europe" – the term used from then on from the Russian perspective – technology, science and the material culture: ranging from cannons and the printing press to early medical knowledge and practices.

4 The Russian Drive towards the West

At the same time the Russian Empire moved closer also from a Western perspective. Emperor Maximilian had sent his ambassador Sigismund von Herberstein to Vassily III already in 1516/17 and again in 1526/27 to win his favour for an alliance. Herberstein's notes on the geography, history and customs of Russia contributed greatly to early Western European knowledge of that area and for more than a century served as the main information source about a land that appeared strange and irritating, closed and less than inviting – and nevertheless was becoming increasingly visible on the European horizon. Certainly the rise of the Ottoman Empire and the fear of the Islamisation of Europe contributed significantly to the fact that the Christian states of the West were also looking for allies in the east. But the attention for each other increased independently of this. New envoys provided new descriptions of the land and people, which elicited some incredulous headshaking, but which also contributed to greater knowledge. It is hardly coincidental that in the context of the siege of Vienna, the Tsarist Empire ultimately joined the "Holy League" against the Turks (1686). In short, if one – from the bird's eye view of a millennium – would like to name an epoch in which Europe as cultural area expanded even beyond the boundary of what in the 20th century was called East Central Europe, then it was the 17th century, especially its second half, in which early contacts from the era of Ivan IV were resumed.

This cultural-spatial expansion was paradoxically associated with a westward shift of the *Russian* border. The Tsarist Empire grew so-to-speak into Europe and crushed the state that lay in between: the Polish-Lithuanian Commonwealth. In the 17th century "foreign policy" from a Russian perspective was marked in particular by *one* process – the conflict with Poland-Lithuania, at whose end a secular "changing of the guard"' took place in the hegemonic position over Eastern Europe. This result was not apparent until the beginning of the 18th century. But Peter I reaped the harvest of what had been cultivated during three quarters of a century.

At the beginning of the 17th century, however, such a development seemed inconceivable. On the contrary, the Tsarist Empire sank into feuds among the nobility, which followed the end of the Rurik dynasty with the death in 1598 of Ivan's childless, feeble-minded son Fyodor 1598. Poland took advantage of the chaos to intervene, but attained the opposite of submission – a "proto-national" collective movement, which drove out its occupation troops and in 1613 installed a new ruling dynasty in the shape of the Romanovs. This was followed by several decades of reconstruction, in which the country only needed one thing on its external borders – peace. In the Peace of Stolbova in 1617 an agreement was reached with Sweden, which also had exploited Moscow's weakness to advance from Livonia eastward to Pskov; concessions were necessary, but Gustav II Adolf contented himself essentially with Ingria (the area around the Neva delta). A year later the Truce of Deulino was signed with Poland, stipulating that the Tsarist Empire would relinquish the always disputed fortress and city of Smolensk; but the truce also de facto recognised the new Tsar Michael as well as the formal end of the war.

But Moscow was out for revenge and in subsequent decades exploited every weakness of the neighbour – to recapture lost terrain and to conquer new territory. The invasion after the death of the Polish King Sigismund III in 1632 turned out to be a failure; two years later Russia had to largely withdraw back to the borders of Deulino again in the Peace of Polyanovka (1634); Smolensk remained Polish-Lithuanian. A new opportunity did not present itself until the Commonwealth developed growing problems in the vast no man's land of the southeast. Whether this was due to "imperial overstretch" remains unanswered. In any case, Warsaw lost control over the Cossacks who were supposed to secure the border here against the Ottoman Empire. Because substantial social dynamite had accumulated, the Cossacks renounced fealty to Poland-Lithuania in 1648 and fled from an ultimately superior enemy to the protection of the Muscovite tsar. Russia seized this opportunity, knowing that thus a repeated conflict with the Commonwealth was unavoidable.

Ultimately, this intuition was not deceptive; despite some internal problems, a considerable strength had been recovered (at least in comparison to the first decades of the new era). The war proved to be long and exhaustive. After initial successes by Russia, Sweden also intervened in the conflict, which now escalated to become the "First Northern War" (1655-1661). The archenemies in the south, the Crimean Tatars, immediately sided with Poland-Lithuania. But in Andrusovo in 1667 the Tsarist Empire ultimately achieved a truce, which pushed its boundaries farther west than ever before: The entire broad strip extending from Smolensk and Chernigov to Kiev became Russian. Poland had to vacate the eastern (left-bank) Ukraine; the lower Dnieper became the border river, whereby Kiev, which was situated on the "wrong" side, was also annexed to the Tsarist territory. The Muscovite empire was also able to defend this enormous gain in the formal "Eternal Peace" of 1686, especially since Poland-Lithuania, in these years at the height of its "Christian" defensive struggle against Islam, concentrated all of its forces on its main enemy in the southeast and was ready to make concessions. Russia paid its "price" and joined the defensive front, as was mentioned, at the same time.

In the perspective of the Russian "drive towards the West'" the new 18th century marks no caesura. Rather, a remarkable analogy points to the meanwhile accepted hypothesis that the much cited "window to Europe" that Peter the Great pushed open in 1700 with all his might was actually already open. When the Russian Tsar won the decisive victory in the Great Northern War (1700-1721) and dealt Charles XII of Sweden a devastating defeat at Poltava in 1709, the Commonwealth in essence landed in his lap. His triumph did indeed help the Polish King August II (the Strong), who had previously been dethroned by Charles XII, back onto his feet. But the reinstated monarch received his kingdom from the Russians. Poland-Lithuania, which a century before had occupied the Kremlin and then had claimed the Russian throne, had in fact lost its sovereignty. Henceforth Tsarist troops marched in and out of the country at will. After the death of August in 1733 they struck an agreement with the Prussian troops, who invaded from the other side, in order to install their mutual candidate (August III).

Thirty years later Catherine the Great repeated this game when she installed her former favourite and Polish envoy to the Court of St. Petersburg as new king (Stanislaus Augustus Poniatowski). As punishment for his unexpected insubordination, she also made him accept the considerable loss of territory that had already resulted from the first partition of Poland in 1772. Although Frederick II of Prussia (who incorporated the vital land bridge between Pomerania and East Prussia) apparently was the driving force behind this amputation, she did not need to be persuaded for very long to likewise seize territory. Twenty years later the political situation had changed fundamentally not only in Poland but in the whole of Europe. While the first partition of Poland was so to speak still part of the absolutist (Machiavellian) Cabinet policy, the second partition took place within the context of the French Revolution and the defensive struggle by the *anciens régimes*. That is why Catherine now took the initiative. The new partition (1793) only left the Commonwealth with a territorial remnant, which would not have sufficed for a real recovery. The final end of the Commonwealth inevitably followed with the third partition in 1795. The amputation became a vivisection. For the first time in the modern history of Europe a state that a hundred years before had been a great power and even the hegemonic power in Eastern Europe disappeared from the political map. The consequences could be clearly read on just this map: Prussia and Russia, the two parvenus of the 18th century, suddenly had a common border. Conversely this also meant: Russia no longer just stood at the door of Europe, but inside the house.

This was all the more the case because the triumph in the Great Northern War had another important consequence for Russia. Immediately after the hasty escape of Charles XII, Peter marched northward and finally took possession of that land over which the war had begun: Livonia. He received the homage of the knights and the cities – and granted them a privilege (1710) which was worthy of its name. The Russian Tsar guaranteed nothing less than the preservation of the well-established self-government of the noble and patrician-urban classes. The privilege charter of course did not restore the *status quo ante* because the Tsar retained the sovereignty. But in their country the old lords were granted far-reaching autonomy rights – more than in any other province, and for good reason. Peter, who is known to have revered Western culture, knew what he had with the German-influenced Livonia: a piece of Europe in his own empire. The self-government of the knights remained basically intact until the beginning of the 20th century, and Livonia itself, expanded to include Courland and Lithuania after the liquidation of Poland in 1795, belonged until its downfall to the Tsarist Empire. This border, too, in all ambivalence led Russia close to Europe: Here in June 1812 Napoleon only had to cross one river (the Neman, in German Memel) to get from Prussia to Russia.

5 The Southern Border and the Dispute between Russia and Turkey

What remains is a look at the southern boundaries of Russia and Europe. The main enemy of both the Tsarist and the Habsburg Empires was the Ottoman Empire. Via its vassals on the northern shore of the Black Sea (including the Crimea), it was also present on the other side of the Black Sea. The de facto unclaimed steppe lay for a long time between the Crimean Tatars and the Muscovite state, where warrior-peasants (Cossacks) constituted a partially settled, partially nomadic borderland population. But the further the central Russian state penetrated into this "Ukraine" (i.e. borderland), the narrower the buffer zone became. When "left bank" Cossacks de facto subordinated themselves to the Tsar in 1654 and finally lost their relative independence under Peter the Great, his empire ended not far from the Black Sea. For that reason, ever since the late 17th century, military conflicts with the Ottoman Empire increased. At the beginning of the 18th century there seems to have been a balance of power. In his second attempt, Peter took the fortress of Azov (1696), only to escape narrowly at the Pruth River in 1712. Wars in the 1730s did not achieve much either.

It was not until the reign of Catherine that the pendulum swung ever further to the side of the Tsarist Empire, which was growing in strength. Meanwhile, the Ottoman Empire lost power and began its decline, ultimately becoming the "sick man on the Bosporus". When in 1768 the Sultan wanted to exploit the problems Russia was having in Poland and therefore started a war, he certainly did not expect that he would have to sign a kind of dictated peace treaty six years later (in 1774, the Treaty of Kuchuk Kainarji). In fact, Catherine now had a *carte blanche* in the Crimea and annexed this increasingly important peninsula in 1783. A "revenge" war soon followed between the two powers, which Russia won definitively (in the Treaty of Jassy in 1792). The western part of the northern coast of the Black Sea as far as Dniester River, where Odessa was soon founded, now also belonged to the Tsarist Empire. When in the following year the Polish-Lithuanian state was pushed back further and soon after was completely liquidated, the northern adjacent regions Podolia and Volhynia were added. This resulted in a shared border along the upper reaches of the Dniester River with the Habsburg Empire, of which Galicia soon became part. Thus, at the end of the 18th century in this region just as in the north, the Tsarist Empire was no longer situated at the edge of Europe, but rather *in* Europe.

6 Recalcitrant Poland and Unclear Borders in the West

In the following century up to the First World War there was no longer any extensive shifting of boundaries along the western border of the Russian Empire. In the south it could push back the Ottoman Empire a bit, from the Dniester River to the Pruth River (1812). In the north it took advantage of the Finnish-Swedish enmity and the Treaty of Tilsit in 1807 with Napoleon to bind Finland to it in personal union. Finland, however, maintained substantial administrative autonomy and never belonged to the Tsarist Empire itself.

Outwardly, however, the situation was different with Poland. At the Congress of Vienna (1814/15) it was restored as a formally independent kingdom and likewise was "only'" connected to the Tsarist Empire in personal union. After the November Uprising in Warsaw in 1830, this formal independence de facto came to an end through the declaration of a permanent state of emergency, and after the second uprising in 1863/64 it was definitely quelled. Even the name once again disappeared from the map; Poland became the "Vistula Province." In the heart of the Catholic country, in Warsaw, an Orthodox cathedral was built. But Poland still remained Poland. It shut itself off ethnically, linguistically and not least religiously and culturally against Russian rule and quite particularly against Russification, which in the spirit of nationalism rampant everywhere in Europe before the First World War was intensified also here. Poland shut itself off even more than the former eastern territories of the Polish-Lithuanian Commonwealth, which were annexed in the course of the first and second partition, and also more tenaciously than the Baltic provinces.

Nevertheless, even if state borders in the west of the Russian empire are not to be confused with *cultural* boundaries, at least since the end of the reign of Catherine the Great, what she wrote at the beginning of her famous "Great Instruction" (1767) remained valid: "Russia is a European Power." How far the German-born "duodecimo" princess (of Anhalt-Zerbst) had come is shown not only by her successful mediation between Prussia and Austria in the Bavarian War of Succession. Even more clearly, her grandson Alexander I demonstrated this new role and importance of his country: unfortunate in the disaster against Napoleon at Austerlitz in 1805, triumphant in the pursuit across Central Europe of the hero defeated in Moscow in 1813. When the Russian Tsar paraded down the Champs Elysées at the end of March 1814 – Catherine's programmatic statement became clear to the entire European public as never before.

Translated from the German by Carol Oberschmidt and Thomas Oberschmidt

Bibliography

Conze, W 1993, *Ostmitteleuropa. Von der Spätantike bis zum 18. Jahrhundert*, ed Klaus Zernack, Beck, Munich.

Hildermeier, M 2006, "Osteuropa als Gegenstand vergleichender Geschichte" in *Transnationale Geschichte. Themen, Tendenzen und Theorien. [Jürgen Kocka zum 65. Geburtstag]*, ed G Budde, Vandenhoeck und Ruprecht, Göttingen, pp. 117–136.

Hildermeier, M 2013, *Geschichte Russlands. Vom Mittelalter bis zur Oktoberrevolution*, Beck, Munich.

Jaworski, R, Lübke, C, & Müller, MG 2000, *Eine kleine Geschichte Polens*, Suhrkamp, Frankfurt am Main.

Szücs, J 1990, *Die drei historischen Regionen Europas*, Neue Kritik, Frankfurt am Main.

Wojciechowski, M & Schattkowsky, R (eds) 1996, *Historische Grenzlandschaften Ostmitteleuropas im 16. - 20. Jh. : Gesellschaft - Wirtschaft – Politik*, Uniwersytet Mikołaja Kopernika, Toruń.
Zernack, K 1994, *Polen und Rußland: Zwei Wege in der europäischen Geschichte*, Propyläen, Berlin.
Zernack, K 2001, *Preußen - Deutschland - Polen : Aufsätze zur Geschichte der deutsch-polnischen Beziehungen*, eds W Fischer & M Müller, Duncker und Humblot, Berlin.

Markus Koller
Europa und das Osmanische Reich

1 Entgrenzungsdynamiken im 13. Jahrhundert

In seiner 2009 erschienen „Geschichte des Westens" zitiert Heinrich August Winkler den Wiener Historiker Gerald Stourzh, der sein Verständnis von Europa mit folgenden Worten beschreibt: „Europa ist nicht (allein) der Westen. Der Westen geht über Europa hinaus. Aber: Europa geht auch über den Westen hinaus". Die Kernregion eines historischen Westens sieht Winkler in jenen Teilen des Kontinents, deren geistlicher Mittelpunkt in Rom und deren kulturelle Prägungen vor allem in der christlich-jüdischen Tradition verankert waren. Dieses Europa ging aber im 12. und 13. Jahrhundert endgültig über den Westen im Sinne einer politischen Entgrenzung hinaus und begann seine kulturelle Identität nicht zuletzt in der Begegnung mit dem Islam zu konfigurieren. Eine solche Perspektive stellt insbesondere strukturelle Merkmale und Dynamiken in den Vordergrund, die eine politische Entgrenzung europäischer Geschichte erkennbar werden lassen.

Die islamischen Herrschaftsgebilde auf der iberischen Halbinsel oder die sizilianischen Herrscher verbanden den Kontinent auf vielfältige Weise etwa mit der islamisch geprägten Welt Nordafrikas und die im Gefolge des vierten Kreuzzugs entstandenen lateinischen Herrschaften hatten zu einer, wenngleich temporär und regional stark variierenden, politischen Verflechtung mit bis dahin in unterschiedlichen Graden zum byzantinischen Reich gehörenden Gebieten in Südosteuropa geführt. Aber die Dynamik der Entgrenzung besaß auch eine weit über das rein Politische hinausreichende Dimension, wie sich an den Pilgerfahrten nach Jerusalem oder den Handelsaktivitäten nicht nur norditalienischer Städte wie Pisa, Genua oder Venedig beispielhaft erkennen lässt. Die Politik der Markusrepublik im 13. Jahrhundert deutet eine weitere Komponente europäischer Geschichte an, die Entwicklungen ab dem 14. Jahrhundert zunehmend bestimmen sollte. Durch den Kreuzzug von 1204 begann die Signoria mit dem Aufbau ihrer „Überseebesitzungen" (*stato da mar*) im östlichen Mittelmeer, insbesondere in der Ägäis, wodurch auch Teile des Balkans in ein maritimes Reich eingegliedert wurden. Das lateinische Kaiserreich (1204-1261) unterstand fast durchgehend einer venezianischen Oberherrschaft und ebenso kontrollierte Venedig zahlreiche Häfen in der Levante, die den Zugang zu den Kreuzfahrerstaaten ermöglichten. Diese imperiale Politik am Rialto wies bereits den künftigen Weg politischer und religiöser Entgrenzung im südlichen Europa, der nun zunehmend mit der Herausbildung von Großreichen verbunden war und dessen Dynamiken sich zunächst in zeitgleich ablaufenden Prozessen auf der iberischen und der Balkanhalbinsel beobachten lassen.

2 Strukturelle Merkmale des südosteuropäisch-kleinasiatischen Raumes vom 13. bis zur Mitte des 15 . Jahrhunderts

Mit dem Zerfall des Almohadenreiches, der nach der Niederlage von 1212 gegen eine christliche Kreuzfahrerstreitmacht einsetzte, war einer der letzten Versuche gescheitert, *Al-Andalus* in ein islamisches Reich einzubinden, das die Straße von Gibraltar einschloss. Die anschließende erneute Zersplitterung in kleine Herrschaftsgebilde erleichterte der *Reconquista* das weitere Vordringen, bis schließlich 1291 nur noch das nasridische Granada übriggeblieben war. Dessen Fall 1492 bedeutete das Ende der *Reconquista*, zumindest auf iberischem Boden und die Ausdehnung der katholischen Staatenwelt bis an die Südküste Portugals und des entstehenden Spanien.

Demgegenüber bot sich im südosteuropäisch-anatolischen Raum ein in vielerlei Hinsicht vergleichbares Bild. Der nicht umfänglich erfolgreiche byzantinische Restaurationsversuch von 1261 und die im 14. Jahrhundert im Oströmischen Reich tobenden Bürgerkriege, der etwa zeitgleich zu beobachtende Zerfall des Seldschukenreiches in Anatolien und der Machtverlust der dortigen mongolischen Oberherrn insbesondere in der ersten Hälfte des 14. Jahrhunderts verliehen dem gesamten Raum, wenn auch in regional und zeitlich unterschiedlicher Intensität, ein hohes Maß an politischer Zersplitterung. Unter diesen zahlreichen Herrschaftsgebilden befand sich im nordwestlichen Anatolien das Herrschaftsgebiet eines Osman oder Ataman, wie der Name auch gelesen werden kann. Die auf ihn zurückgehende Dynastie der Osmanen sollte in den folgenden Jahrhunderten weite Gebiete dieses Raumes zusammenführen. Auf den ersten Blick schien es sich dabei zunächst um eine schnelle Expansion gehandelt zu haben. Deren erste Phase fiel in ein Zeitfenster, als sich die katholische Staatenwelt des europäischen Kontinents nicht nur an der südwestlichen Peripherie ausdehnte, sondern auch auf den balkanisch-kleinasiatischen Raum verstärkt auszugreifen begann. Beide Bewegungen berührten sich erstmals im byzantinischen Bürgerkrieg (1341-1354) zwischen Johannes Kantakuzenos und der Partei des Palaiologen Johannes V., in den mit Genua und Venedig zwei um die Vormacht in der Ägäis konkurrierende Mächte verwickelt waren. Ebenso war die (Klein)Staatenwelt des südosteuropäisch-anatolischen Raumes darin involviert. Durch Heiratspolitik sollten die jeweils instabilen Bündnisse abgesichert werden. Johannes Kantakuzenos verheiratete seine Tochter mit Orhan, dem Sohn Osmans, dessen Soldaten wesentlich zum temporären Sieg von Kantakuzenos beitrugen. Das Engagement in den innerbyzantinischen Wirren bildete die Grundlage für die Besetzung der Halbinsel Gallipoli (1354) durch die Kämpfer Orhans; im gleichen Jahr fiel auch Ankara unter deren Kontrolle. In den nächsten Jahrzehnten setzten sich die Entgrenzungsprozesse der katholischen Staatenwelt und des osmanischen Herrschaftsgebietes weiter im südosteuropäisch-balkanischen Raum weiter fort. Die Signoria verstärkte ihre Kontakte zur balkanischen Staatenwelt und die Dynastie der Anjou strebte nach einem größeren Einfluss auf der Balkanhalbinsel. Währenddessen gelang dem Haus Osman die Eroberung von Philippopel/Plovdiv (1363) und Adrianopel/Edirne (1363), das zur Hauptstadt des entstehenden Reiches wurde. 1371 siegten osmanische Heerscharen gegen die vereinigte Streitmacht der serbischen Teilherrschaften an der Marica, die aus der Erbmasse des nach 1355 zerbrochenen nemanjidischen Reiches hervorgegangen waren. 1388 erreichten osmanische Einheiten das Königreich Bosnien und nach der Schlacht auf dem Amselfeld (1389) dehnte das Haus Osman seinen Machtbereich in nördlicher Richtung weiter aus. So fiel 1393 auch die bulgarische Zarenstadt Tărnovo. An der Wende vom 14. zum 15. Jahrhundert erreichte das Ringen um die Vorherrschaft an der südöstlichen Flanke des Kontinents eine neue Dimension, als mit Venedig und dem Osmanischen Reich zwei Hauptakteure in eine existentielle Krise schlitterten. Die Markusrepublik sah sich im Chioggiakrieg (1378-1381) einer Koalition aus Genua, Ungarn, Österreich und italienischen Herrschaften gegenüber, die sie an den Rand des Untergangs brachte. Während die Interessengegensätze der expansiven katholischen Mächte in diesen Kämpfen kulminierten, entluden sich am südöstlichen Ende der europäischen Peripherie die Machtansprüche zweier islamisch geprägter Großreiche um die Vorherrschaft in Anatolien in der Schlacht bei Ankara (1402), in der Bayezid I. (1389-1402) vom mongolischen Eroberer Timur (ca. 1328-1405) vernichtend geschlagen wurde und schließlich in timuridischer Gefangenschaft verstarb. Diese Niederlage stürzte das Osmanische Reich in einen „Bruderkrieg" zwischen den Söhnen Bayezids, aus dem schließlich 1413 Mehmet I. (1413-1421) als Sieger hervorging. Die Wiederherstellung der venezianischen Oberherrschaft über die adriatische Ostküste sowie die Festigung der osmanischen Herrschaft über die bis 1402 eroberten Gebiete standen nun im Vordergrund, so dass das Haus Osman seine expansive Außenpolitik erst wieder ab 1420 in größerem Umfang aufnehmen konnte.

3 Grenzvorstellungen- und Wahrnehmungen im südöstlich-anatolischen Europa

In den kriegerischen Auseinandersetzungen bis zum frühen 15. Jahrhundert gilt es nun aus der zeitgenössischen Binnen- und Außenperspektive Grenzvorstellungen- und Wahrnehmungen zu destillieren, um den vielschichtigen Erfahrungsmustern dieser Zeit zumindest in Ansätzen gerecht zu werden. Die Überlegungen lassen sich mit der Frage beginnen, ob und inwieweit dieser Raum in die ihn umgebende katholische und islamische Welt eingebunden bzw. mit ihr verwoben war. Eine solche Perspektive hat die Forschung bisher meist eingenommen und dabei fast zwangsläufig Südosteuropa und Anatolien als weithin getrennte Raumeinheiten aufgefasst. Strukturgeschichtlich ist mit Blick auf den Betrachtungszeitraum ein solcher Ansatz kritisch zu hinterfragen und auch religiös definierte Kategorien eignen sich dafür nur bedingt.

Zunächst fällt auf, dass der Beginn der osmanischen Expansion in eine Zeit fiel, als durch die „Gefangenschaft der Päpste" in Avignon (1309-1377) und das Große Abendländische Schisma (1378-1417) eine scheinbare politische Schwächung des Heiligen Stuhls zu beobachten war. Dieser stand jedoch eine starke Zentralisierung innerhalb der Kirche gegenüber, die nun umso stärker gegen diejenigen Gruppen im wahrsten Sinn des Wortes zu Felde zog, die aus ihrer Sicht die Kircheneinheit bedrohten. Im Rahmen dieser keineswegs neuen Politik definierte die Kurie eine Reihe vorwiegend innerchristlicher „Feinde", in die im Verlauf des 14. Jahrhunderts die „Türken" aufgenommen wurden. Dazu trug auch erheblich die Kriegspropaganda jener Mächte bei, die am Rande einer sich – im Gegensatz zum 13. Jahrhundert - stärker nach Innen wendenden katholischen Staatenwelt lagen. Der 1387 zum ungarischen König gekrönte Sigismund von Luxemburg führte beispielsweise die expansive Außenpolitik seiner Vorgänger aus dem Haus der Anjou mit südlicher Stoßrichtung weiter fort. Seine Truppen fielen immer wieder in das bosnische Königreich ein, das gleichzeitig im Süden von den Osmanen bedrängt wurde. Sigismund stellte seine Kampagnen als Kreuzzüge dar, die er gegen „Türken, Manichäer und Häretiker [...] und gegen die Schismatiker, die in Bosnien leben" zu führen habe. Er bezog sich dabei auf die Anhänger der von Rom als häretisch angesehenen Bosnischen Kirche, wenngleich im Hintergrund das Streben nach der bosnischen Krone stand. Im südlichen Europa wurde der Kreuzzugsgedanke nur noch dann nach Außen realpolitisch umgesetzt, wenn eine an der Grenze der katholischen Welt liegende Macht ihr Herrschaftsgebiet erweitern wollte. In dieses Bild fügen sich die portugiesischen Einfälle nach Ceuta (1415) und Tanger (1471) ebenso wie der von Ungarn angeführte Kreuzzug des Jahres 1396 ein, der in einer Niederlage gegen osmanische Truppen bei Nicopolis endete. Die Zusammensetzung der Truppen des Sultans zeigt, wie fluide die politische Gemengelage war. Die balkanischen und anatolischen Kleinfürsten wandten weiterhin die bis dahin praktizierten politischen Mechanismen an. Balkanische Adlige holten sich osmanische Truppenhilfe, um in den zahlreichen Fehden ihren jeweiligen Kontrahenten besiegen zu können. Serbische Teilfürstentümer pflegten ebenso wie anatolische *beyliks* die bekannte Heiratspolitik weiterhin, nun eben auch mit dem Hause Osman.

Dennoch lassen sich Konturen von „Grenzerfahrungen" festmachen, wie sie im südosteuropäisch-anatolischen Raum zu beobachten waren. Der orthodoxe Balkanadel wies in vielen Fällen eine zweifache politische Orientierung auf, als sich Familien in zwei Zweige spalteten. Einer setzte sich aus Familienmitgliedern zusammen, die zum Islam übertraten und dem Imperium in hohen Verwaltungs- und Militärpositionen dienten. Der andere Zweig stand in Opposition zu den neuen Oberherren. Beispielsweise kamen aus der albanischen Adelsfamilie der Araniti ein Kommandant der Schweizer Garde unter Julius II. (1503-1513) und ein osmanischer Feldherr. Derartige „Grenzerfahrungen" wurden in das Umfeld des Heiligen Stuhls nun vermehrt von Personen getragen, die aus dem südosteuropäisch-anatolischen und dem iberischen Raum nach Rom und in andere Städte auf der appeninischen Halbinsel kamen. Der Borgia-Papst Calixtus III. (1455-1458), der als Kardinal von Valencia die späte Reconquista unmittelbar miterlebt hatte, gehörte ebenso wie der aus dem Kaiserreich von Trapezunt stammende Kardinal Bessarion zu den berühmtesten Beispielen. Es mag daher auch kein Zufall gewesen sein, dass gerade unter Calixtus III. Begrifflichkeiten insbesondere aus katholischen Gebieten Südosteuropas endgültig aufgegriffen wurden, die zu Synonymen für Grenzvorstellungen geworden sind. Dies gilt vor allem für das Bild der Vormauer, das Dubrovnik 1454 bemühte, als es sich zur Vormauer „unseres Königreiches Dalmatien" stilisierte, um seine Stellung gegenüber anderen christlichen Herrschern zu verteidigen. Es bezog sich aber nicht auf die vorrückenden osmanischen Truppen, die in der zweiten Hälfte des 15. Jahrhunderts Bosnien, die Herzegowina und weite Teile des heutigen Albanien eroberten. Damit bedrohten sie unmittelbar auch Ragusa, das zwar tributpflichtig, aber nicht direkt besetzt war. Eine ähnliche Rhetorik wandte die dalmatinische Küstenstadt auch auf Skanderbeg an, der im albanischen Raum wahrscheinlich aus Blutrache zwischen 1443 und 1468 einen wechselvollen Kampf gegen die Osmanen führte. Der Rat der Stadt bezeichnete Skanderbeg 1452 als „Spiegel und Vorbild aller Christen, der Fürsten und aller Völker". Ähnlich wie Calixtus III. versuchte Pius II. (1458-1464) den Kreuzzugsgedanken wieder politisch umzusetzen, wenngleich der Heilige Stuhl mit solchen Plänen unter den Herrschern des lateinischen Europa kaum Gehör fand. Vor diesem Hintergrund förderte die Kurie das Idealbild eines Grenzkämpfers in der Person des Skanderbeg, der 1457 erstmals in einem päpstlichen Schreiben als „wahrer Athlet und Vorkämpfer des christlichen Namens" angesprochen und dem Renaissance-Europa als Vorbild vor Augen geführt wurde. Ein Jahr später wurde bereits das Bild der „festen Mauer" auf ihn übertragen. Skanderbeg selbst fügte sich bewusst in diese Vorstellungswelt ein und verweist implizit auf das Grenzverständnis, das ganz im Sinne des Kreuzzugsgedankens hinter dieser Rhetorik stand. Er stellte sich als Kämpfer gegen die Feinde des katholischen Christentums dar. Die Idee des „propugnaculum christianitatis" (Vormauer der Christenheit) verbreitete sich über ganz Europa und findet sich bis heute in der Geschichtsvorstellung nicht weniger Nationalstaaten. Die Grenze wurde dadurch auch zu einem virtuellen Raum, und in den zeitgenössischen Konstruktionen von „Grenzhelden" wie Skanderbeg oder der im Grenzraum lebenden Bevölkerung spiegelten sich schließlich die zeitgenössischen Diskurse über Religion, Gesellschaft und Politik wider.

Etwa gleichzeitig bildete sich in der islamisch geprägten Diskurswelt innerhalb des osmanischen Herrschaftsgebietes eine in vielerlei Hinsicht äquivalente Grenzvorstellung aus, deren Genese aufgrund der schwierigen Quellenlage in der Historiographie kontrovers diskutiert wird. Im Zentrum steht die inhaltliche und politische Bedeutung des Begriffs *gaza* (*gazi* als derjenige, der *gaza* praktiziert). Diese Vorstellung fand bis zum Ende des 13. Jahrhunderts im westlichen Anatolien weniger Anwendung für Kämpfe gegen Byzanz als vielmehr gegen die mongolischen Oberherren. Der Terminus erfuhr zu dieser Zeit mehr in den südlichen Fürstentümern wie Aydın oder Menteşe eine Aufladung im Sinne eines antichristlichen Glaubenskampfes, die in Auseinandersetzungen mit Ordensrittern oder Venezianern insbesondere durch Piraterie verstrickt waren. Die verfügbaren Quellen deuten darauf hin, dass sich ab der Mitte des 14. Jahrhunderts eine solche Ideologie des Glaubenskampfes im osmanischen Umfeld zu verbreiten begann. Neben zahlreichen anderen Gründen mag auch die Herausbildung von „Markgrafengeschlechtern" (*uç bey*) dafür verantwortlich gewesen sein, die gerade an der Wende vom 14. zum 15. Jahrhundert die osmanische Expansion vorantrieben. Für sie scheint die Religion ein besseres Legitimationsmuster für ihr Handeln und auch eine effektivere Klammer für den Zusammenhalt ihrer Truppen gewesen sein als die osmanische Dynastie, deren Angehörige nur in den großen Feldzügen an der Spitze der Truppen standen. Das *gaza*-Verständnis fand aber auch Anwendung in den militärischen Kampagnen gegen muslimische Fürstentümer in Anatolien. Diese Feldzüge wurden beispielsweise damit gerechtfertigt, dass der Widerstand anatolischer Fürsten gegen die osmanische Dynastie den Glaubenskampf gegen christliche Herrschaften gefährden würde. Daher gelte es, gegen diesen „Verrat" vorzugehen. Es waren Mehmet I. (1413-1421) und Murat II. (1421-1444/1446-1451), die das *gazi*-Ideal bis dahin am intensivsten pflegten. Hier werden nun ähnliche Prozesse greifbar, wie sie auch in der katholischen

Welt zu beobachten waren. Die verstärkte Betonung des Gazitums der Dynastie bedeutete gleichzeitig eine Intensivierung der Abgrenzung von der christlichen Welt. Dazu haben, ähnlich wie 100 Jahre davor in den südanatolischen Fürstentümern, die Kämpfe mit vorwiegend christlich-katholischen Gegnern beigetragen. Auch Murat II. hatte die Bedrohung durch ein Kreuzfahrerheer erfahren, das 1444 bei Varna besiegt werden konnte. Davor hatte sich eine Atmosphäre existentieller Bedrohung auch in der Hauptstadt Edirne verbreitet und sogar eine Fluchtbewegung hochrangiger Würdenträger nach Bursa eingesetzt. In dieser angespannten Situation fand auch eine der ersten größeren Verfolgungen und Hinrichtungen von Personen statt, die als Häretiker gebrandmarkt wurden. Sie entstammten meist dem heterodoxen Derwischtum, dessen Einfluss auf den osmanischen Herrscher und dessen Umfeld nun immer stärker von der entstehenden Gruppe der Religionsgelehrten herausgefordert wurde. Während also im lateinischen Christentum der Kampf um die kirchliche Einheit tobte, setzte im osmanischen Herrschaftsgebiet der Aufbau eines vorwiegend sunnitisch geprägten institutionalisierten Islam ein. Die Bemühungen, einen religiösen Zentralismus durchzusetzen, scheinen maßgeblich zu Abgrenzungsprozessen beigetragen zu haben. Ähnlich wie in der *antemurale*-Vorstellung wurden Grenzräume diskursiv aufgeladen und dadurch auch zu idealisierten virtuellen Räumen. Bereits der Chronist Ahmedi schuf im späten 14. Jahrhundert das imaginäre Bild von heldenhaften Glaubenskämpfern, die dort den reinen und wahren Islam praktiziert hätten.

Im 14. und 15. Jahrhundert hatten sich damit in der Staatenwelt des lateinischen Christentums und in den islamischen Diskursen innerhalb des osmanischen Herrschaftsgebietes Grenzvorstellungen herausgebildet, die auch einen stark virtuellen Charakter aufwiesen. Beweglich in Raum und Zeit konnten sie sowohl als Begründungsmuster für politisches Handeln innerhalb der jeweiligen Herrschaftsgebilde als auch für außenpolitisches Handeln eingesetzt werden. Wie verhielten sich jedoch solche vor allem nach Innen wirkenden Abgrenzungsmodelle zu den Entgrenzungsprozessen, die an der Wende vom 15. zum 16. Jahrhundert wieder verstärkt einsetzten?

4 Das Osmanische Reich und die Entgrenzung Europas im 16. Jahrhundert

Dieser neue Schub politischer Entgrenzung ist im südlichen Europa von Atlantik- und Mittelmeeranrainerstaaten getragen worden, von denen Portugal, das habsburgische Spanien und das Osmanische Reich als die wichtigsten Träger anzusehen sind. Bereits davor hatten iberische Herrscher die Hoffnung gehegt, die Reconquista in die muslimischen Gebiete Nordafrikas hineinzutragen. Nun griff sie aber in die „Neue Welt" ebenso wie auf den afrikanischen Kontinent aus, wo andalusische Adlige erste Stützpunkte an der Küste errichteten. Melilla (1497) und Mers-El-Kebir (1505) gehören zu den bekanntesten Eroberungen. 1510 wurden Algier in ein Vasallitätsverhältnis gezwungen und Tripolis erobert. Spanien hatte damit die nordafrikanische Küste im westlichen Mittelmeerraum mit Ausnahme von Tunis weitgehend unter seine Kontrolle gebracht. Der symbolträchtige Vertrag von Tordesillas (1494) versinnbildlicht die einsetzende „Globalisierung" europäischer Politik, wodurch die Frage nach den Grenzen Europas in neue Kontexte gestellt wurde. Dieser Aspekt soll am Beispiel des östlichen Motors dieser Bewegung diskutiert werden, dem Osmanischen Reich. Das Imperium der Sultane begann an der Wende vom 15. zum 16. Jahrhundert ebenfalls deutlich über seine bisherigen Grenzen hinauszugreifen. Die ersten Träger der osmanischen Expansion in den nordafrikanischen Raum waren Piraten, die dann als Korsaren im Namen des Sultans ebenfalls Stützpunkte an der Küste einrichteten. Für die Frage nach der Bedeutung der beschriebenen Abgrenzungsmodelle erlangten jedoch die Eroberungen Selims I. (1512-1520) eine große Bedeutung, der zwischen 1516 und 1518 mit dem Sieg über die Mameluken nicht nur Syrien und Ägypten, sondern auch Mekka und Medina unter seine Kontrolle gebracht hatte, und fortan die Bezeichnungen „Beschützer der heiligen Stätten" und „Beschützer der Pilgerfahrt" in seiner Titulatur führte. Insgesamt sah sich der osmanische Herrscher nun stärker in der Rolle eines Verteidigers des Islam, und zwar des aus osmanischer Perspektive wahren sunnitischen Islam. Wenn auch dessen Auslegung nicht in allen religionsrechtlich relevanten Bereichen uneingeschränkte Anwendung fand, so band diese Differenzierung das Osmanische Reich in gesamteuropäische Prozesse ein. Innerkonfessionelle Spaltungen verliehen den politischen und gesellschaftlichen Konflikten eine zusätzliche Brisanz und bewirkten, dass Europa in ein bis zur Mitte des 17. Jahrhunderts andauerndes Zeitalter religiös legitimierter Kriege hineinschlitterte. Mit Blick auf das Osmanische Reich wurde die „innerkonfessionelle Spaltung" zwischen sunnitischem und schiitischem Islam zu einer Legitimations- und zumindest teilweise Motivationsfolie für die weitere Machtausdehnung. Dies galt insbesondere für die Kriege gegen das Reich der Safawiden (1553-1555, 1578-1590, 1603-1612, 1615-1618, 1623-1639), in dem die Schia dominierte. Die Kämpfe wurden von einer scharfen Polemik osmanischer Religionsgelehrter begleitet, die teilweise den Kampf gegen die „Verräter" und „Häretiker" für wichtiger ansahen als Kriege gegen nichtmuslimische Feinde. Die militärischen Auseinandersetzungen gingen mit der Verfolgung, Deportation und Hinrichtung von *kızılbaş* in Anatolien einher. Das östliche Anatolien bildete in dieser Zeit trotz der Machtausdehnung in Gebiete des heutigen Iran und Irak einen Grenzraum, in dem das Ideal des Glaubenskrieges eine politische und gesellschaftliche Tiefenwirkung erzielt hatte. Immerhin waren die Friedensschlüsse mit den safawidischen Schahs die einzigen Abkommen mit fremden Herrschern, in denen theologische Fragen aufgegriffen wurden. Weitaus schwieriger war die Rechtfertigung des Krieges gegen die Mameluken, die selbst dem sunnitischen Islam angehörten. Selim I. ließ daher Rechtsgutachten erstellen, in denen den Mameluken vorgeworfen worden ist, sie würden Muslime unterdrücken und hätten ein Bündnis mit den häretischen Safawiden abgeschlossen. Dadurch seien sie selbst zu Häretikern geworden. Ein „Kreuzzugsgedanke" gegen erklärte innerislamische Feinde war das vorgegebene Deutungsschema, das den Entgrenzungsschub im östlichen Mittelmeerraum begleitete und gleichzeitig die osmanische Herrschaft im Inneren, nämlich dem östlichen Anatolien, festigen sollte.

Während ein solches Abgrenzungsmodell die unmittelbare Erweiterung des Territoriums legitimierte und dabei in Grundzügen die bisherigen Expansionsmechanismen fortführte, eignete es sich kaum für einen global ausgerichteten Entgrenzungsschub. Vielmehr dominierten im 16. Jahrhundert Wahrnehmungs- und Deutungsmodelle von Herrschaft, die eine globale politische Perspektive im Zentrum hatten. Süleyman I. ist gerade unter dem Großwesirat von Ibrahim Pascha (1523-1536) und unter dem Einfluss des Astrologen Remmal Haydar in eschatologische Weltbilder, wie sie zu dieser Zeit vom Atlantik bis zum Indus anzutreffen waren, eingebunden und zumindest bis zu den frühen 1550er Jahren als endzeitlicher Herrscher dargestellt worden. Eine universalistische Dimension enthielten auch die religiösen Titel eines Kalifen und „Beschützer der Heiligen Stätten des Islam", die nun zu zentralen Bausteinen einer propagierten kulturellen Geographie wurden, wie sie der osmanischen Entgrenzung und der damit ansatzweise verbundenen „Überseepolitik" zugrunde lagen. In diese kulturelle Geographie waren die Morisken auf der iberischen Halbinsel ebenso eingebunden wie die im Raum des Indik liegenden islamischen Herrschaftsgebilde, auf die insbesondere die Großwesire Ibrahim Pascha und Mehmet Pascha Sokolović (1565-1579) zurückgriffen. Durch den Verweis auf die Zugehörigkeit zum sunnitischen Islam und der Funktion des osmanischen Sultans als Kalif waren sie bemüht, ein gemeinsames militärisches Vorgehen gegen Portugal zu realisieren, das im Indischen Ozean sein *stato da mar* aufgebaut hatte. Mit dem Tod des Großwesirs Sokolović im Jahre 1579 neigte sich diese Phase osmanischer „Überseepolitik" dem Ende entgegen, auch wenn die geknüpften politischen und wirtschaftlichen Kontakte noch für einige Jahre weiterwirkten.

5 Von der Binnen- zur Außengrenze? Das Osmanische Reich auf dem Weg zum Objekt der Entgrenzung

Bereits während des 16. Jahrhunderts war diese Ausrichtung osmanischer Politik, die den Aufbau eines maritimen Imperiums bedeutet hätte, keineswegs unumstritten. Der Großwesir Rüstem Pascha (1546-1561) sah das Osmanische Reich weniger als eine Seemacht und förderte einen Zeitgeist, der durchaus Ansätze eines osmanischen Patriotismus enthielt. Damit zeichnete sich bereits die politische Wende ab, die nach dem Machtverlust der „Seefraktion" eintrat. Wenn in den Ausführungen zum 16. Jahrhundert die Namen der Großwesire häufiger erwähnt werden als die der Sultane, spiegelt dies strukturelle Veränderungen innerhalb der Eliten in Istanbul wider, die an den politischen Entscheidungsfindungsprozessen beteiligt waren. Zu den entscheidenden Machtfaktoren entwickelten sich immer mehr die Haushalte hoher Amts- und Würdenträger, die als dynamische Klientelsysteme zu verstehen sind. Es waren daher vor allem die Haushalte und die mit ihnen verbundenen Interessengruppen aus dem Seefahrer- und Kaufleutemilieu um Ibrahim Pascha und Mehmet Pascha Sokolović, die eine osmanische „Überseepolitik" umsetzten. Ein genauerer Blick verdeutlicht, dass eine Vielzahl hochrangiger Akteure aus der Zentralverwaltung von den wirtschaftlichen Perspektiven einer Machtausdehnung in den Indischen Ozean hinein zu profitieren versuchte. Dieser Aspekt erscheint bedeutsam im Hinblick auf gesamteuropäische Perspektiven, da mit dem Ausscheiden des Osmanischen Reichs und dem zunehmenden machtpolitischen Bedeutungsverlust der iberischen Großmächte jene Staaten in der entstehenden Kolonialpolitik an Einfluss verloren, die den Entgrenzungsschub im südlichen Europa getragen und stark auf religiöse Begründungsmuster aufgebaut hatten. Dem Kreuzzugs- und Missionierungsideal Spaniens und Portugals hatte das Gaza-Motiv des Osmanischen Reiches entsprochen. Deren Stelle als Motoren der europäischen Entgrenzung nahmen nun die am Atlantik gelegenen protestantischen Seemächte England und die Niederlande ein, die ebenso wie Frankreich vor allem durch Handelsgesellschaften ihre Überseeexpansion betrieben und gleichzeitig aber auch von einer religiösen Triebkraft beeinflusst wurden. Es bleibt eine rein spekulative Frage, ob das Osmanische Reich einen vergleichbaren Weg eingeschlagen hätte, wenn es seine maritime Politik fortgesetzt hätte. Zumindest wies die „maritime Fraktion" strukturelle Ähnlichkeiten mit den Expansionsmechanismen der neu aufkommenden Überseemächte, insbesondere mit Frankreich, auf.

Die Entscheidung Istanbuls, kein maritimes Imperium anzustreben, und die im Verlauf des 17. Jahrhunderts nachlassenden Spannungen mit dem Safawidenreich lassen wieder stärker innereuropäische Grenzräume in den Vordergrund rücken, die das Osmanische Reich von seinen Nachbarn (Polen-Litauen, Habsburger Monarchie und Venedig) trennte. Diese geostrategische Positionierung der Hohen Pforte wirkte sich auch auf die Wahrnehmung und die politische Bedeutung der Territorien aus, in denen die vier genannten Großreiche aneinandergrenzten. Im Gegensatz zu den Mächten, die eine global ausgerichtete „Überseepolitik" betrieben, trugen weder Polen-Litauen noch die Habsburger oder die Osmanen ihre Konflikte auch auf Kriegsschauplätzen außerhalb des Kontinents aus. Jeder Krieg musste daher zwangsläufig mit dem Verlust von Territorien einhergehen, die vom jeweiligen Gegner als zugehörig zum eigenen Reichsgebiet betrachtet wurden. Territoriale Ansprüche und wirtschaftliche Interessen konnten somit auch nicht unter Rückgriff auf „Überseegebiete" kompensiert oder entschärft werden. Unter diesen geopolitischen Rahmenbedingungen setzte der Prozess einer innereuropäischen Entgrenzung ein, dessen Ausrichtung zunächst keineswegs klar erkennbar war. Die militärischen Auseinandersetzungen („Langer Türkenkrieg/1593-1606; „Großer Türkenkrieg/1683-1699) beschränkten sich auf Südosteuropa und blieben regionale Kriegshandlungen. Nur der letzte große Konflikt mit der Markusrepublik (Kretakrieg/1645-1670) wurde an mehreren Fronten auf der Balkanhalbinsel ausgefochten. Der venezianisch-osmanische Krieg besaß aber auch eine in die Zukunft weisende Bedeutung, denn erstmals verlor das Imperium der Sultane ein Territorium endgültig an eine christliche Macht. Der Serenissima gelang es im Jahre 1648 die osmanische Festung Klis zu erobern und die nachfolgende Vertreibung der dortigen muslimischen Bevölkerung deutete bereits die blutige Seite des kommenden innereuropäischen Entgrenzungsprozesses an. Der definitive Verlust eines Gebietes an einen christlichen Gegenspieler sollte sich erst wieder mit dem Friedensschluss von Sremski Karlovci/Karlowitz (1699) ereignen, als fast alle Territorien nördlich der Donau-Save-Linie aufgegeben werden mussten.

In den „Türkenkriegen" manifestierte sich bereits die Mehrschichtigkeit des einsetzenden innereuropäischen Entgrenzungsprozesses, dessen Objekt zunehmend das Osmanische Reich wurde. Zum einen bestand er aus territorialen Verlusten, welche die Hohe Pforte hinnehmen musste. Zum anderen bedeutete er aber auch die diplomatische Integration des Imperiums der Sultane in die sich herausbildende europäische Staatengemeinschaft, die bereits mit den „Italienischen Kriegen" begonnen hatte. In dieser Hinsicht lässt sich von einer *Greater Western World* im frühneuzeitlichen Europa sprechen, um einen Begriff Daniel Goffmans zu verwenden. Deren zwischenstaatliche Kommunikation war von weitgehend anerkannten Symboliken, Praktiken und Gepflogenheiten geprägt, wie die Akzeptanz längerer und schließlich auch unbefristeter Laufzeiten von Friedensverträgen durch die Osmanen beispielhaft zeigt. Schließlich symbolisieren die Friedensverhandlungen in Karlowitz selbst die *Greater Western World* in der Sphäre der Diplomatie. Die Gespräche wurden von Großbritannien und den Niederlanden vermittelt, die am Tagungsort eine Nachbildung des Gebäudes errichten ließen, in dem sie 1697 bereits den Frieden von Rijswijk eingefädelt hatten. Die bauliche Konstruktion bot den Vorteil, dass die Abordnungen den Tagungsraum durch verschiedene Türen betreten konnten. Dies war bedeutsam, denn erstmals handelten Vertreter des Osmanischen Reiches mit mehreren christlichen Mächten gleichzeitig einen Friedensschluss aus.

Die Verdichtung des diplomatischen Austausches durch regelmäßige Gesandtschaften und ständige Vertretungen, die das Osmanische Reich offiziell aber erst im 19. Jahrhundert etablieren sollte, trug auch wesentlich dazu bei, religiöse Gegensätze in den politischen Beziehungen zu verringern. Im Osmanischen Reich haben die ausbleibenden militärischen Erfolge und das im Verlauf des 17. Jahrhunderts zunehmende Bedrohungs- und Krisengefühl dazu geführt, dass sich Diskussionen über die Ursachen dieser Entwicklung zu intensivieren begannen. Dieser Binnendiskurs beeinflusste auch die Werke osmanischer Geographen. Katib Çelebi (1609-1657) sah eine Ursache der nun offensichtlichen Probleme darin, dass sich die Muslime zu wenig für ihre Gegner interessieren würden. Mit seinem Werk *Cihannüma* (Sicht der Welt) wollte er insbesondere den politischen Entscheidungsträgern einen Wissensfundus zur Verfügung stellen. Katib Çelebi löste sich ebenso wie der 1691 verstorbene Ebu Bekr Dimişki in seinem *Al Fath al-Rahmani fi Tarz-i Devlet-i Osmani* zunehmend von Weltbildern, die bis dahin geographische Diskurse bestimmt hatten. Beide waren bemüht, ein möglichst genaues Bild der Grenzräume zu liefern, indem sie die Festungsanlagen und die administrativen Strukturen wiedergaben. Auch wenn deren Werke von der höfischen Öffentlichkeit noch nicht eingehend zur Kenntnis genommen worden sein dürften, so lässt sich dennoch erkennen, dass aufgrund der geostrategischen und militärischen Gegebenheiten sachliche Informationen über die Grenzräume sowie in zunehmenden Maße auch über die christlichen Staaten selbst im Vordergrund standen. Ab dem 18. Jahrhundert wurden Gesandte explizit mit dem Auftrag entsandt, Berichte über Institutionen und Strukturen ihrer Gastländer zu verfassen, um deren Anwendbarkeit oder Nützlichkeit für das Osmanische Reich zu diskutieren. Diese politische oder besser strukturpolitische Verankerung in einer europäischen Staatenwelt ließ die Bedeutung von Religion in der zwischenstaatlichen Kommunikation zurückgehen. Das Gazi-Ideal war nun nicht mehr als eine Reminiszenz an eine idealisierte und propagandistisch bemühte Vergangenheit, die, wie der Reisebericht des Evliya Çelebi (1611-ca. 1685) am Beispiel der osmanisch-habsburgischen Grenze in Ungarn zeigt, der Gesellschaft vor allem auch als Spiegel vorgehalten wurde.

Eine ähnliche Entwicklung lässt sich etwa gleichzeitig in den habsburgischen Landen beobachten, wo trotz oder gerade wegen der Kriege das religiöse Moment in der Wahrnehmung des Osmanischen Reiches und in den politischen Kontakten mit Istanbul kaum noch eine Rolle spielte. Während das „Türkenbild" im 16. Jahrhundert von Angst und Neugier geprägt gewesen war, stieg nun das Interesse an möglichst realistischen und genauen Informationen. In Zeitungen, Flugblättern und Einblattdrucken zeichnete sich der neue Duktus ab, als selbst während der Kriege weniger Berichte über „Türkengreuel", sondern vermehrt Ortsbeschreibungen oder Abbildungen von Festungen aus dem jeweiligen Kriegsgebiet im Vordergrund standen. Daneben wurden die Kämpfe zwar immer noch in religiöse und eschatologische Deutungsmuster verortet, jedoch verloren solche Denkfiguren in dem Maße an Bedeutung, wie die aus christlichen Herrschaftsgebieten zusammengesetzten Armeen militärische Erfolge feiern konnten. Spätestens mit dem aus Habsburger Sicht erfolgreichen Ende des „Großen Türkenkrieges" im Jahre 1699 zerbröckelte das barocke Weltbild mit seiner theologisch-biblizistischen Geschichtskonzeption und es begann sich immer mehr ein politisch-säkulares durchzusetzen, wenngleich ein temporäres Aufleben des Barockkatholizismus unter Karl VI. (1711-1740) stattfand. Der Europabergriff ersetzte in den politischen Schriften den der Christenheit, wenn es galt, eine Gegengröße zum Osmanischen Reich zu entwerfen. Welche Asymmetrien in der Gleichsetzung Europas mit dem Christentum enthalten sind, ist in der historischen Forschung bereits eingehend diskutiert worden. Als Analysekategorie für die politischen Entwicklungen in den beiden folgenden Jahrhunderten eignet sich Religion nicht, vielmehr zeigt sich deren Widersprüchlichkeit mehr als deutlich. Der engen Einbindung des Osmanischen Reiches in die diplomatischen Strukturen der sich herausbildenden europäischen Staatengemeinschaft steht eine realpolitische Entwicklung entgegen, in der die christlichen Großmächte zunehmend versuchen, ihre Konflikte „mit Hilfe" des osmanischen Imperiums – vorwiegend im Sinne territorialer Kompensationen auf Kosten des Osmanischen Reichs - zu lösen, ohne sich dabei eben selbst beschädigen zu müssen. Damit ist die nach „Übersee" gerichtete Entgrenzungspolitik auch in Europa selbst angekommen, das in Teilen nun zunehmend beginnt, eine innereuropäische „Überseepolitik" zu betreiben. Der Beginn dieses Prozesses im späten 17. Jahrhundert bedeutet jedoch nicht, dass damit der Niedergang des Imperiums der Sultane eingesetzt hätte. Vielmehr haben im 18. Jahrhundert noch die Dynamiken einer, um mit Jürgen Osterhammel zu sprechen, inklusiven Europazentrik der christlichen Staatenwelt überwogen und das Osmanische Reich konnte seinen Territorialbestand noch weitgehend bewahren.

6 Von der inklusiven zur exklusiven Europazentrik

Die „Versachlichung" in der diplomatischen Kommunikation entsprach einer politischen Atmosphäre im europäischen Staatensystem des 18. Jahrhunderts, das Jürgen Osterhammel als wertneutralen Mechanismus der Austarierung von Machtbalancen definiert. In dieser außenpolitischen Arena agierte auch die Hohe Pforte. So lange das Osmanische Reich die eigene Diplomatie mit einer entsprechenden militärischen Stärke unterstützen konnte, galt es als Bestandteil der europäischen Staatenwelt. Die Kriege gegen das Haus Habsburg in der ersten Hälfte des 18. Jahrhunderts boten immer noch ausreichend Argumente für eine solche Sichtweise. Istanbul musste zwar im Frieden von Passarowitz (1718) auf das Banat, Oltenien sowie auf Teile bosnischer und serbischer Gebiete verzichten, jedoch brachte der Sieg bei Banja Luka (1737) zumindest einen teilweisen Rückgewinn. Im Frieden von Belgrad (1739) sah sich Wien gezwungen, Oltenien sowie Teile der bosnischen Provinz und nordserbische Regionen an das Osmanische Reich zurückgeben. Es überrascht daher nicht, dass in zahlreichen historiographischen und staatskundlichen Werken das Osmanische Reich als Teil Europas betrachtet wird. Dies sollte sich erst im letzten Drittel des 18. Jahrhunderts zu verändern beginnen, als sich Stimmen mehrten, die auf vermeintliche kulturzivilisatorische Unterschiede und auf eine Andersartigkeit der „Türken" verwiesen. Autoren wie Herder bemühten Ansätze humanistischer Topoi, wenn sie in den „Türken" Eindringlinge nach Europa sahen, die sich in keine höhere Kultur einfügen können. Dabei unterschieden sie in einem immer stärkeren Maße zwischen einer europäischen und einer asiatischen Türkei. Im Gegensatz zu Anatolien galt der Balkan durchaus als Teil Europas, so dass nun vermehrt eine zwischen beiden Reichshälften verlaufende Grenze gezogen wurde. Gleichzeitig regten sich Gedanken, die auf eine „Befreiung" der „unterjochten Völker" abzielten. Jedoch zeigt ein erweiterter Blick in das östliche Europa, dass auch der größte Gegner des Osmanischen Reiches ab dem letzten Drittel des 18. Jahrhunderts aus der gleichen Perspektive einer „europäischen Wertegemeinschaft" gesehen wurde, die die Welt mit dem Gefühl einer kulturzivilisatorischen Überlegenheit zu betrachten begann. Geographen markierten zunächst den Don als Grenze zwischen einem europäischen und asiatischen Russland, ehe der Ural ab den 1770er Jahren diese Funktion zugesprochen bekam. Bereits über weite Strecken der Frühen Neuzeit hatte das Reich der Romanows darüber hinaus auch als eine gegnerische „orientalische" Macht gegolten. Im letzten Drittel des 18. Jahrhunderts, als die Habsburger als militärischer Gegenspieler der Hohen Pforte von der Bühne europäischer Politik abtraten, übernahm dessen Rolle das Zarenreich. Nach dem Ende der militärischen Auseinandersetzungen mit Spanien, Portugal, Venedig und der Habsburger Monarchie hatte die innereuropäische Entgrenzung schließlich dazu geführt, dass die beiden immer stärker ausgegrenzten Mächte um die Vorherrschaft im südosteuropäisch-anatolischen Raum zu ringen begannen. Die Waffengänge zwischen beiden Reichen verliefen für das Osmanische Reich desaströs. Katharina II. (1762-1796) setzte die seit Peter dem Großen (1689-1725) voranschreitende Ausdehnung des Russischen Reiches in die südliche Steppe fort, und es gelang ihr im russisch-osmanischen Krieg von 1768-1774 die Krim unter die Oberhoheit der Zaren zu stellen. Mit dem Verlust dieses Gebietes, dessen Khan sich in einem bis zum 17. Jahrhundert nicht immer engen Vasallitätsverhältnis zum Sultan befunden hatte, war das Schwarze Meer kein osmanisches Binnengewässer mehr. Auch in Südosteuropa ging die Machtausdehnung der Romanows weiter, als ihr Herrschaftsgebiet nach dem Frieden von Iași (1792) bis an den Dnister reichte. Dieser 1787 ausgebrochene Krieg war übrigens der letzte gegen das Osmanische Reich, an dem auch das Haus Habsburg teilgenommen hat. Für den einst mächtigsten Gegner der Osmanen endete er allerdings glücklos.

7 Die Phase der binnenimperialen Entgrenzung

Als sich im Verlauf des 18. Jahrhunderts in der protestantischen und katholischen Staatenwelt die Diskurse über eine territoriale und kulturelle Geographie eines als kulturzivilisatorisch angesehen Europa verfestigten, sollte dies nicht ohne Rückwirkungen auf die beiden Kontrahenten bleiben, durch die Europa seine östlichen Grenzen verlaufen ließ. Innerhalb der russischen Elite herrschte spätestens seit der Wende vom 17. zum 18. Jahrhundert das gleiche Selbstverständnis vor, dessen Projektionsfläche „Asien" war. Islam und Nomadentum galten als Zeichen einer rückständigen Kultur und daraus leitete sich der Anspruch ab, eine *mission civilicatrice* übernehmen zu müssen. Im Kern stand das Ansinnen, die als minderwertig betrachteten Nomaden einer höheren Kultur näherzubringen. Die politische Umsetzung dieser Weltsicht setzte in der zweiten Hälfte des 18. Jahrhunderts ein und erreichte mit der maßgeblich von Speranskij erarbeiteten „Verwaltungsordnung für Sibirien" und insbesondere dem „Statut über die Verwaltung der inorodcy" einen Höhepunkt. Die Nomaden galten nun als „Fremdlinge" (inorodcy) und wurden in drei Gruppen eingeteilt, je nach der ihnen zugeschriebenen Zivilisationsstufe.

Einen ähnlichen Weg schlug auch das Osmanische Reich in der Mitte des 19. Jahrhunderts ein, als die exklusive Europazentrik eine Antwort der osmanischen Politik erforderte. Wie die multiethnischen Imperien der Romanows und der Habsburger sah sich auch das Haus Osman mit den politischen Folgen des

Nationalstaatsgedankens konfrontiert, die im 19./20. Jahrhundert zu einem allmählichen Zusammenbruch der osmanischen Herrschaft in Südosteuropa führten. Bis 1830 gab es ein faktisch autonomes serbisches Fürstentum und einen unabhängigen Staat Griechenland. Diese neu entstehenden Herrschaftsgebilde verdankten ihre Existenz vor allem den geostrategischen Interessen der Großmächte, zu denen allerdings auch immer noch das Osmanische Reich gehörte. Der Krimkrieg (1853-1856), in dem die Hohe Pforte Teil einer antirussischen Mächtekoalition war, verdeutlicht die Ambivalenz der politischen Situation, der sich Istanbul in der Mitte des 19. Jahrhunderts gegenübersah. Im Friedensschluss von Paris (1856) wurde das Osmanische Reich ein formales Mitglied des europäischen Mächtekonzerts, und gleichzeitig blieb es in den Augen der anderen Staaten kein vollwertiger Partner. Neben dem bereits mehrfach erwähnten Blick auf das Reich der Sultane konnte Istanbul – im Gegensatz zum frühen 18. Jahrhundert – seine diplomatischen Schritte nicht mehr militärisch flankieren. Diesem realpolitischen Machtverlust auf der internationalen Bühne stand ein Machtgewinn des Staates im Inneren gegenüber. Im späten 18. und frühen 19. Jahrhundert hatten lokale Notabeln (*ayan*) in vielen Fällen eine autonome Stellung im Machtgefüge des Imperiums erlangt, und diese Entwicklung konnte im Gefolge der Tanzimat in regional unterschiedlicher Intensität beendet oder geschwächt werden. Der stärker gewordene Staat musste nun auf die ambivalente außenpolitische Stellung als formal gleichberechtigtes, aber realpolitisch ausgegrenztes Mitglied der europäischen Staatengemeinschaft und auf die Idee des Nationalstaats bzw. des Nationalismus reagieren. Im Gegensatz zum Zarenreich, wo zunehmend die russische Nation identitätsstiftend wurde, entwickelten osmanische Reformer das Konzept des Osmanismus (*osmanlılık*) und erhoben somit die Dynastie zum Bindeglied des Reiches. Es galt also, ähnlich wie in der Donaumonarchie, einen Reichspatriotismus zu schaffen. Dieses Modell diente als Alternative zum Nationalismus und sollte es allen Bewohnern des Reiches, unabhängig ihrer religiösen und ethnischen Zugehörigkeit, ermöglichen, zu Bürgern des Osmanischen Reiches zu werden. Mit dem Staatsbürgerschaftsgesetz von 1869 konnten Untertanen des Hauses Osman zu Bürgern des Imperiums werden. Aus dem Reich der Osmanen ist nun das Osmanische Reich geworden, das sich jetzt aber auch immer schneller in einen Nationalstaat verwandelte. Es ist daher kein Zufall, dass in der zweiten Hälfte des 19. Jahrhunderts in offiziellen osmanischen Dokumenten der Begriff Türkei als Bezeichnung für das eigene Reich erscheint. Dennoch bleibt festzuhalten, dass bis zu den Balkankriegen 1912/13 der Osmanismus stets eine ernst zu nehmende politische Option darstellte. Dieses Konzept implizierte auch die Übernahme einer eurozentristischen Weltsicht, mit der osmanische Reformer und die neuen bürokratischen Eliten auf die ambivalente Stellung unter den Großmächten reagierten. Wie in Russland wurden auch Bevölkerungsgruppen benannt, die aus Sicht der Zentralregierung einer Zivilisierung bedurften. Die osmanischen „Fremdlinge" bildeten Nomaden und Gesellschaftssegmente, die tribal oder sippenverbändisch strukturiert waren. Dies galt für nordalbanische Stämme und Stammesföderationen, die nun plötzlich als wild und unzivilisiert galten. Die Mehrheit solcher Bevölkerungsgruppen befand sich jedoch in den arabischen Provinzen. In den Memoiren osmanischer Verwaltungsangehöriger, die in Palästina ihren Dienst verrichteten, finden sich Zeugnisse eines kulturzivilisatorischen Überlegenheitsgefühls. Sie distanzierten sich deutlich von den „Arabern" und vermieden auch engere soziale Beziehungen zur lokalen Bevölkerung. Als Schlüsselwörter der osmanischen *mission civilizatrice* lassen sich Disziplinierung und Erziehung festmachen, wodurch die betroffene Bevölkerung auf eine höhere Zivilisationsstufe gebracht werden sollten. Die osmanische Regierung stellte ihren Staat nun selbst als eine Kolonialmacht dar und überlegte, den zum osmanischen Reichsgebiet gehörenden Yemen in eine Kolonie umzuwandeln. Die Mechanismen der europäischen Entgrenzung waren nun in das Selbstverständnis und die Politik eines ihrer Objekte, des Osmanischen Reichs, eingegangen. Dadurch wurde das Reich der Sultane aber auch wieder zu einem Subjekt des Entgrenzungsprozesses, wenngleich in einem sehr eingeschränkten Maße. Die Limitierung der Handlungsfähigkeit im Inneren des eigenen Herrschaftsgebietes resultierte letztlich aus dem Zusammenprall der innerosmanischen und der europäischen Entgrenzung. Immer wieder mussten die osmanischen Behörden die regionale Implementierung von Reformmaßnahmen und andere administrative oder militärische Vorhaben mit den vor Ort präsenten Konsuln der europäischen Großmächte absprechen, die mit der Hohen Pforte um die politische Raummacht in verschiedenen Regionen des Osmanischen Reiches konkurrierten. Ein entscheidender Hebel, um unmittelbar in die Belange vor Ort eingreifen zu können, war das Selbstverständnis christlicher Staaten, sich als „Schutzmächte" nichtmuslimischer Bevölkerungsgruppen im Osmanischen Reich zu begreifen. Die Auswirkungen einer solchen politischen Haltung lassen sich am Beispiel der blutigen Auseinandersetzungen zwischen muslimischen Drusen und christlichen Maroniten im Libanongebirge beobachten, die sich in der Mitte des 19. Jahrhunderts zu einem Problem der internationalen Politik entwickelt hatten. Eine administrative Neuordnung, die zur Stabilisierung der Region beitragen sollte, fand schließlich nach den Vorgaben der europäischen Diplomaten statt. Mit dieser Politik eines *soft imperialism*, deren Ursprünge in den Privilegien zu finden sind, die seit dem 15. Jahrhundert Untertanen und Schutzgenossen anderer Staaten gewährt worden waren, wurden darüber hinaus auch Teile der osmanischen Bevölkerung dem Zugriff der Behörden entzogen und dadurch die Souveränität des Staates eingeschränkt. Gerade im 19. Jahrhundert hatte sich die Zahl osmanischer Untertanen stetig erhöht, die von anderen Staaten Schutzbriefe erhielten.

1863 wollte die Regierung in Istanbul schließlich die Vergabe solcher Dokumente durch die diplomatischen Vertretungen beschränken, und auch das Staatsbürgerschaftsgesetz von 1869 diente dazu, sich dieser Form des *soft imperialism* zu widersetzen.

Die Erfahrungen der europäischen und binnenimperialen Entgrenzungsprozesse sollten schließlich auch in die 1923 gegründete Republik Türkei hineinreichen. Die Mehrzahl der „Gründerväter" entstammte dem Umfeld oder gehörte direkt zu den Teilen der jungtürkischen Bewegung, die im Sultan Abdülhamid II. (1876-1909) stürzten. Die meisten von ihnen kamen aus den noch übriggebliebenen balkanischen Provinzen des Osmanischen Reiches und/oder waren dort in der Provinzverwaltung oder in der Armee tätig. Sie hatten als junge Männer die Politik des *soft imperialsm*, die Entstehung der südosteuropäischen Nationalstaaten und schließlich in den Balkankriegen 1912/13 auch das Schicksal der Vertreibung erfahren. Diesen Erfahrungsschatz brachten sie nun in den Aufbau eines Nationalstaates ein, dessen Kern der anatolische Raum bildete. Einem Territorium, das den meisten dieser neuen politischen Elite fremd und weithin unbekannt war. Die dargelegten Entgrenzungsprozesse beeinflussten aber nicht nur die politischen Handlungsmuster in der frühen Republik Türkei, sondern sie entfalten ihre Wirkungsmacht bis in die Gegenwart.

Literatur

Casale, G 2010, *The Ottoman Age of Exploration*, Oxford University Press, Cambridge.
Clewing, K & Schmitt, OJ (Hg.) 2011, *Geschichte Südosteuropas. Vom frühen Mittelalter bis zur Gegenwart*, Pustet, Regensburg.
Goffman, D 2003, *The Ottoman Empire and Early Modern Europe*. Cambridge University Press, Cambridge.
Imber, C 2005, *The Ottoman Empire, 1300-1650: The Structure of Power*, Palgrave Macmillan, Houndmills, Basingstoke, Hampshire.
Kappeler, A 2008, *Rußland als Vielvölkerreich. Entstehung, Geschichte, Zerfall*, Beck, München.
Osterhammel, J 1998, *Die Entzauberung Asiens. Europa und die asiatischen Reiche im 18. Jahrhundert*, Beck, München.
Reinkowski, M 2005, *Die Dinge der Ordnung. Eine vergleichende Untersuchung über die osmanische Reformpolitik im 19. Jahrhundert*, R. Oldenbourg, München.
Schmitt, OJ 2009, *Skanderbeg. Der neue Alexander auf dem Balkan*, Pustet, Regensburg.
Schorn-Schütte, L 2010, *Konfessionskriege und europäische Expansion. Europa 1500-1648*, Beck, München.
Winkler, HA 2009, *Geschichte des Westens. Von den Anfängen in der Antike bis zum 20. Jahrhundert*, Beck, München.

Markus Koller
Europe and the Ottoman Empire

1 The Dynamics of De-borderisation in the 13th Century

In his "History of the West", which was published in 2009, Heinrich August Winkler cites the Viennese historian Gerald Stourzh, who describes his understanding of Europe with the following words: "Europe is not (only) the West. The West extends beyond Europe. But: Europe also extends beyond the West." Winkler considers the core region of the historical West to be in those parts of the continent whose spiritual centre is Rome and whose cultural characteristics are primarily anchored in the Judeo-Christian tradition. In the 12th and 13th centuries, however, this Europe finally extended beyond the West in the sense of a political de-borderisation (*Entgrenzung*)[1] and began to configure its cultural identity, not least in the encounter with Islam. Such a perspective places structural characteristics and dynamics in the foreground which make visible a political de-borderisation of European history. The areas of Islamic rule on the Iberian peninsula or the Sicilian rulers connected the continent in many ways e.g. with the Islamic-dominated world of North Africa. In the aftermath of the Fourth Crusade, the Latin dominions had political ties, although these were temporary and regionally disparate, to the areas in southern Europe which belonged to varying degrees to the Byzantine Empire in southeastern Europe. But the dynamics of de-borderisation also extended far beyond the purely political dimension, as can be seen e.g. in the pilgrimages to Jerusalem or in trade activities not only with northern Italian cities such as Pisa, Genoa or Venice. The politics of the Venetian Republic in the 13th century suggest a further component of European history which was to increasingly determine developments from the 14th century on. Through the Crusade of 1204 the Signoria began establishing "overseas possessions" (*stato da mar*) in the eastern Mediterranean, particularly in the Aegean Sea, through which also parts of the Balkans were integrated into a maritime empire. The Latin Empire (1204-1261) was almost continuously under Venetian supremacy, and Venice furthermore controlled numerous ports in the Levant, which allowed

---

[1] *De-borderisation* is the English equivalent for the German *Entgrenzung*, a term used to denote moving borderlands, i.e. the fluidity and reshaping of political boundaries. (cf. Pierre Hassner, "Fixed Borders or Moving Borderlands: A New Type of Border for a New Type of Entity", in Zielonka, J (ed.) 2002, *Europe Unbound: Enlarging and Reshaping the Boundaries of the European Union*, Routledge, London.

access to the Crusader states. Venice's imperial policy pointed the way to political and religious de-borderisation in southern Europe, which was now increasingly associated with the emergence of large empires, the dynamics of which can first be observed in the simultaneous processes which were taking place on the Iberian and Balkan peninsulas.

2 Structural Features of the Area of Southeastern Europe and Asia Minor from the 13th to the Middle of the 15th Century

With the disintegration of the Almohad Caliphate, which began after the defeat in 1212 against Christian crusaders, one of the last attempts failed to integrate *Al-Andalus* into an Islamic caliphate that included the Strait of Gibraltar. The subsequent repeated fragmentation into small territorial entities facilitated the further advance of the *reconquista*, until finally in 1291 only Granada under Nasridian rule remained. Granada's fall in 1492 meant the end of the *reconquista*; at least on Iberian soil, and the extension of the Catholic world of states to the southern coast of Portugal and of Spain, which was emerging as a nation.

In many respects, the southeastern European-Anatolian area presented a comparable picture. The Byzantine restoration attempt of 1261, which was not successful everywhere, and the civil wars raging in the Eastern Roman Empire in the 14th century, which coincided approximately with the decay of the Seljuk Empire in Anatolia and the loss of power of the local Mongol overlords there, especially in the first half of the 14th century, bestowed a high degree of political fragmentation on the entire area, albeit in varying intensity both regionally and temporally. Among these numerous territorial entities, a territory in northwestern Anatolia was ruled by an Ottoman or Ataman, as the name can also be read. Under the dynasty originating with him, the Ottomans consolidated much of these areas in the following centuries. At first glance it seemed to be a rapid expansion. The first phase was in a period when the Catholic states of the European continent not only expanded to the southwestern periphery, but also began to increasingly attack areas in the Balkans and Asia Minor. Both movements met for the first time in the Byzantine Civil War (1341-1354) between John Cantacouzenos and the party of John V Palaiologos. With Genoa and Venice, two powers were competing for supremacy in the Aegean Sea and surrounding region. The small states of the southeastern European-Anatolian area were also involved. Unstable alliances were consolidated through political marriages. John Cantacouzenos married off his daughter to Orhan, the son of Osman, whose soldiers contributed significantly to the temporary victory of Cantacouzenos. The involvement in the inner-Byzantine turmoil was the basis for the occupation of the Gallipoli peninsula (1354) by Orhan's troops; in the same year Ankara also fell under their control. In the next decades, the de-borderisation processes of the Catholic states continued in the southeastern European region. The Signoria intensified its contacts to the Balkan states, and the dynasty of Anjou aspired to greater influence on the Balkan peninsula. Meanwhile, the Ottomans succeeded in conquering Philippopel/Plovdiv (1363) and Adrianopel/Edirne (1363), which became the capital of the emerging empire. In 1371, in a battle at the Marica River, the Ottoman armies were victorious against the united forces of the Serbian dominions, which had emerged from the remains of the Nemanjic empire that had broken apart in 1355. Ottoman armies reached the Kingdom of Bosnia in 1388 and after the Battle of Kosovo (1389), the Ottomans extended their sphere of power northward. In 1393 the Bulgarian Tsarist city of Tărnovo fell. At the turn of the 14th and 15th century, the struggle for supremacy on the southern periphery of the continent reached a new dimension when the two main actors – Venice and the Ottoman Empire – skidded into an existential crisis. In the War of Chioggia (1378-1381) the Venetian Republic found itself up against a coalition of Genovese, Hungarian, Austrian and Italian rulers, which almost brought it to the edge of ruin. While the conflicting interests of the expansive Catholic powers culminated in these struggles, the claims to power of two predominantly Islamic empires erupted at the southeastern end of the European periphery for supremacy in Anatolia in the Battle of Ankara (1402), in which Bayezid I (1389-1402) suffered a crushing defeat by the Mongolian conqueror Timur (c. 1328-1405) and subsequently died in captivity in Timurid. This defeat plunged the Ottoman Empire into a "fratricidal war" between the sons of Bayezid, out of which Mehmed I (1413-1421) emerged as victor in 1413. The restoration of Venetian sovereignty over the eastern coast of the Adriatic Sea and the consolidation of Ottoman rule over the territories that had been conquered up to 1402 were now the main focus, so that the Ottomans could not begin to take up their expansionist foreign policy again on a larger scale until 1420.

3 Border Conceptions and Perceptions in Southeastern-Anatolian Europe

In the armed conflicts up to the early 15th century it is now essential to distil the border conceptions and perceptions from the contemporary internal and external perspective, in order to take into account the complexities experienced during this period, at least partially. The reflections could begin with the question whether and to what extent this area was integrated and/or intertwined with the Catholic and Islamic world which surrounded it. Researchers have usually assumed such a perspective and thus almost inevitably considered southeastern Europe and Anatolia to be more or less separate spatial units. With regard to historical structure, such an approach in observing this period should be critically questioned, and religiously defined categories are only appropriate to a limited extent. First, it is noticeable that the beginning of Ottoman expansion came at a time when an apparent political weakness of the Holy See was observed due to the "Babylonian captivity" of the popes in Avignon (1309-1377) and the Great Western Schism (1378-1417). This, however, was offset by a strong centralisation within the Church, which in the truly literal sense took to the field even more forcefully against these groups, which in their view threatened church unity. Within the framework of this in no way new policy, the Curia defined a number of predominantly intra-Christian "enemies", which in the course of the 14th century was expanded to include the "Turks". The war propaganda of those powers on the periphery of the Catholic states, which in contrast to the 13th century were turning inward, contributed to this development significantly. For example, Sigismund of Luxembourg, who was crowned Hungarian king in 1387, continued the expansive foreign policy of his predecessors from the House of Anjou with a thrust to the south. His troops repeatedly invaded the Bosnian kingdom, which at the same time was pressured in the south by the Ottomans. Sigismund presented his campaigns as crusades, which he led against "Turks, Manichees and heretics [...] and against the schismatics, who live in Bosnia". He was referring to the followers of the Bosnian Church, which was regarded by Rome as heretical, although Sigismund's hidden agenda was to gain the Bosnian crown. In southern Europe the crusade idea was only implemented externally in the *realpolitik*, when a power at the edge of the Catholic world wanted to expand its area of domination. The Portuguese incursions into Ceuta (1415) and Tangier (1471) fit into this picture as well as the crusade led by Hungary in 1396, which ended in a defeat against the Ottoman troops at Nicopolis. The composition of the troops of the Sultan shows how fluid the political conflict situation was. The Balkan and Anatolian princes continued to apply the hitherto practiced political mechanisms. Balkan nobles recruited the aid of Ottoman troops to defeat their respective opponents in their numerous feuds. Serbian principalities, just like Anatolian *beyliks*, continued the tradition of political marriages, but now also with the Ottoman dynasty.

    Nevertheless, contours of "border experiences" can be determined, as were observable in the southeastern European-Anatolian area. In many cases the Orthodox Balkan nobility had a twofold political orientation when families split into two branches. One was made up of family members who converted to Islam and served the empire in high administrative and military positions. The other branch opposed the new overlords. For example, both a commander of the Swiss Guard under Julius II (1503-1513) as well as an Ottoman commander came from the Albanian noble family of Araniti. Such "border experiences" were increasingly common in persons connected to the Holy See, who came from the southeastern European-Anatolian and Iberian regions to Rome and to other cities of the Apennine peninsula. The Borgian Pope Callixtus III (1455-1458), who as Cardinal of Valencia had experienced the late *reconquista* first hand, belonged to the most famous examples, along with Cardinal Bessarion, who originated from the empire of Trapezunt. It may therefore have not been a coincidence that particularly under Callixtus III, terms from the Catholic areas of southeastern Europe were ultimately adopted, which have become synonyms for border conceptions. This is especially true for the term "bulwark", which Dubrovnik used in 1454, as it stylised itself to be the bulwark "of our Kingdom of Dalmatia", to defend its position in relation to other Christian rulers. It did not, however, refer to the advancing Ottoman troops who conquered Bosnia, Herzegovina and great parts of what is today Albania in the second half of the 15th century. Thus, they also directly threatened Ragusa, which was required to pay a tribute, but was not directly occupied. The Dalmatian coastal town also applied a similar rhetoric to Skanderbeg, who in the Albanian region fought a battle with changing outcomes against the Ottomans between 1443 and 1468, probably due to a vendetta. The council of the city characterised Skanderbeg in 1452 as a "mirror and model for all Christians, the princes and all people". Like Callixtus III, Pius II (1458-1464) attempted to politically implement the idea of the crusades again, although such plans of the Holy See were not well received among the rulers of Latin Europe. Against this background, the Curia promoted the ideal of a frontier fighter in the person of Skanderbeg, who was first mentioned in 1457 in a papal writ as "true athlete and champion of the Christian name" and was presented as role model for Renaissance Europe. A year later, the image of a "solid wall" was transferred to him. Skanderbeg consciously adapted himself to this conceptual world view and refers implicitly to the understanding of the border concept, which was entirely in the sense of the crusade idea behind this rhetoric. He presented himself as fighter against the enemies of Catholic Christianity. The idea of the "propugnaculum christianitatis" (bulwark of Christianity) spread throughout Europe and continues to be found in the concept of history of not just a few nation states. The border thus also became a virtual space, and the contemporary discourses on religion, society and politics were reflected in the contemporary constructions of "border heroes" such as Skanderbeg or the population living in the border region.

At about the same time a concept of the border which was in many respects equivalent was formed in the Islamic-dominated discourse within the Ottoman dominions, the genesis of which is controversial due to the difficult source situation in historiography. The focus is on the content and political meaning of the term *gaza* (*gazi* as the person who practices *gaza*). Until the end of the 13th century this concept in western Anatolia was applied less to battles against Byzantium and more to battles against the Mongolian overlords. At this time, especially in the southern principalities such as Aydın or Menteşe, the term had a connotation of an anti-Christian faith struggle, which involved conflicts with the Knights of St. John or Venetians, in particular through piracy. The available sources suggest that from the middle of the 14th century on, such a faith struggle ideology began to spread in the Ottoman environment. In addition to numerous other reasons, the emergence of dynasties of landed nobles (*uç bey*) may have been responsible for driving Ottoman expansion, which occurred particularly at the turn of the 14th to 15th century. For them, religion appears to have been a better model of legitimation for their actions and also have provided a more effective instrument for the cohesion of their troops than the Ottoman dynasty, whose members only stood at the head of the troops during great campaigns. But the concept of *gaza* was also used in the military campaigns against Muslim principalities in Anatolia. For instance, these campaigns were justified by the premise that the resistance of the Anatolian princes against the Ottoman dynasty would endanger the religious war against the Christian rulers. That is why it was necessary to take action against this "betrayal". Mehmed I (1413-1421) and Murad II (1421-1444/1446-1451) were the ones who most intensively nourished the *gazi* ideal. Here similar processes were at work as in the Catholic world. The increased emphasis on *ghazawat* (battles) of the dynasty at the same time meant a more intensive delimitation from the Christian world. Like 100 years before in the southern Anatolian principalities, the battles against primarily Catholic-Christian opponents contributed to this. Murad II had also experienced the threat of a Crusader army, which could be defeated in 1444 at Varna. Prior to that, an atmosphere of an existential threat had spread even to the capital Edirne, causing high-ranking dignitaries to flee to Bursa. In this tense situation one of the first major persecutions and executions of persons branded as heretics took place. They mostly originated from the heterodox dervishes, whose influence on the Ottoman ruler and his environment was increasingly challenged by the emerging group of religious scholars. While in Latin Christianity the struggle raged for church unity, in the Ottoman dominions a mainly Sunni-dominated, institutionalised Islam began to take hold. Efforts to enforce a religious centralisation appear to have contributed significantly to differentiation processes. Similar to the *antemural* concept, border areas were discursively charged and thus also became idealised virtual areas. Already in the late 14th century the chronicler Ahmedi created imaginary figures of heroic fighters for the faith, who had been practicing the pure and true Islam.

Thus, in the 14th and 15th centuries, concepts of boundaries which also had a strong virtual character emerged in the states of Latin Christianity as well as in the Islamic discourses within the Ottoman dominions. Flexible in space and time, they could be used both as justification for political actions within the respective ruled entity as well as for actions of foreign policy. But how did such models of demarcation – which had a mainly internal effect – relate to the processes of de-borderisation, which increasingly began to occur at the turn of the 15th to 16th century?

4 The Ottoman Empire and the De-borderisation of Europe in the 16th Century

This new thrust of political de-borderisation was carried out in southern Europe by the Atlantic and Mediterranean countries, of which Portugal, Habsburg Spain and the Ottoman Empire are regarded as the main conveyors. Already prior to that, Iberian rulers had harboured the hope of importing the *reconquista* into the Muslim areas of North Africa. Now, the thrust of de-borderisation extended to the "New World" as well as onto the African continent, where Andalusian nobles built first bastions on the coast. Melilla (1497) and Mers-El-Kebir (1505) are among the most famous conquests. In 1510 Algiers was forced into a vassal relationship and Tripoli was conquered. Spain had thus gained control over almost the entire North African coast in the western Mediterranean with the exception of Tunis. The Treaty of Tordesillas (1494) symbolises the onset of globalisation of European politics, in which the question of Europe's borders was placed in new contexts. This aspect shall be discussed using the eastern impetus of this movement, the Ottoman Empire, as an example. At the turn of the 15th to 16th century, the empire of the sultans also began to strive to expand significantly beyond its previous borders. Pirates were the vanguard of Ottoman expansion in the North African region, who then as corsairs on behalf of the sultan likewise established bases on the coast. The conquests of Selim I (1512-1520) were of great importance for the demarcation models described above. Between 1516 and 1518, with the victory over the Mameluks, Selim I not only gained control over Syria and Egypt but also over Mecca and Medina. Henceforth he included the designations "Protector of the Holy Places" and "Protector of the Hajj" among his titles. Overall, the Ottoman ruler saw himself more in the role of a defender of Islam, and namely from the Ottoman perspective the defender of the true Sunni Islam. Even if its interpretation was not fully applied in all legal areas relevant to religion, this differentiation integrated the Ottoman Empire into European processes as a whole. Interdenominational divisions additionally gave high relevance to the political and social conflicts and caused Europe to slide into an era of religiously legitimised wars that lasted more or less continuously until the middle of the 17th century. In the Ottoman Empire the division between the Sunni and the Shiite branches of Islam provided a legitimation or at least a motivation pattern for the further expansion of power. This was especially true for the wars against the empire of the Safavids (1553-1555, 1578-1590, 1603-1612, 1615-1618, 1623-1639) in which the Shia dominated. The battles were accompanied by a sharp polemic of Ottoman religious scholars, who partially viewed the struggle against the "traitors" and "heretics" as more important than wars against non-Muslim enemies. The military conflicts were accompanied by the persecution, deportation and execution of Kizilbash in Anatolia. Despite the expansion of power into areas that are now Iran and Iraq, during this period eastern Anatolia was a border area, in which the ideal of religious war had attained a profound political and social effect. Indeed, the peace treaties with the Safavid shahs were the only agreements with foreign rulers in which theological issues were addressed. Far more difficult was the justification for the war against the Mameluks, who themselves belonged to Sunni Islam. Selim I therefore ordered a *fatwa*, in which the Mameluks were accused of oppressing Muslims and of having entered an alliance with the heretical Safavids, thus becoming heretics themselves. The idea of a "crusade" against declared enemies within Islam was the given interpretation schema that accompanied the thrust to expand borders in the area of the eastern Mediterranean and at the same time to consolidate Ottoman rule in the interior, in eastern Anatolia.

While such a demarcation model legitimised the direct expansion of the territory and in principle continued the recent expansion mechanisms, it hardly lent itself to a globally oriented attempt of a thrust of de-borderisation. Rather, perceptive and interpretive models of domination prevailed in the 16th century which had a global political perspective at its centre. Particularly under the Grand Vizier Ibrahim Pasha (1523-1536) and under the influence of the astrologist Haydar-i Remmal, Süleyman I played a role in the eschatological world views that were to be found during this period from the Atlantic Ocean to the Indus River. At least until the early 1550s he was portrayed as an eschatological ruler. A universalist dimension was also contained in the religious titles of a caliph and "Protector of the Holy Places of Islam", which now became key building blocks of a propagated cultural geography, as they formed the basis of the Ottoman de-borderisation and thus to some extent the basis of the related "overseas policy". The Moors on the Iberian peninsula were also incorporated into this cultural geography as were the Islamic dominions in the area of the Indian Ocean, which were in particular claimed by the Grand Viziers Ibrahim Pasha and Mehmet Pasha Sokolović (1565-1579). Through the reference to the affiliation to Sunni Islam and the role of the

Ottoman sultan as caliph, they attempted to implement a joint military action against Portugal, which had established its *stato da mar* in the Indian Ocean. With the death of the Grand Vizier Sokolović in 1579, this phase of the Ottoman "overseas policy" drew to a close, even if the associated political and economic contacts continued to resonate for several years.

5 From the Internal to the External Border? The Ottoman Empire on the Way to Becoming the Object of De-borderisation

Already during the 16th century this orientation of Ottoman policy that tended towards establishing a maritime empire was by no means uncontroversial. The Grand Vizier Rüstem Pasha (1546-1561) perceived the Ottoman Empire to be less a naval power and promoted a spirit which indeed contained elements of Ottoman patriotism. This already signalled the political change which occurred after the loss of power of the "naval faction". When in the commentaries on the 16th century the names of the grand viziers are named more frequently than the sultans, this reflects structural changes within the elites in Istanbul who were involved in the decision-making processes. More and more households of high official dignitaries, who are to be understood as dynamic clientele systems, became crucial factors of power. Therefore, mainly the households and the associated interest groups from the seafaring and merchant milieu led by Ibrahim Pasha and Mehmet Pasha Sokolović were the groups that implemented an Ottoman "overseas policy". A closer look shows that a number of high-ranking stakeholders from the central administration attempted to profit from the economic perspectives of an expansion of power into the region around the Indian Ocean. This aspect appears to be significant in terms of the perspectives of Europe as a whole. With the withdrawal of the Ottoman Empire and Spain's and Portugal's increasing loss of significance as political powers, those states that had borne the thrust of de-borderisation in southern Europe and justified this on religious grounds lost influence as colonialism developed. The crusading and missionising ideal of Spain and Portugal had corresponded to the *gaza* motif of the Ottoman Empire. Their place as generators of European de-borderisation was now assumed by England and the Netherlands – Protestant naval powers situated at the Atlantic – which like France carried out their overseas expansion primarily through merchant companies but which at the same time were also driven by religious motives. It remains purely speculative whether the Ottoman Empire would have followed a similar trajectory if it had continued its maritime policy. At least the "maritime faction" had structural similarities with the expansion mechanism of the emerging overseas powers, especially France.

Istanbul's decision not to seek to become a maritime empire, and the declining tensions with the Safavid Empire allowed a stronger focus on intra-European border areas that separated the Ottoman Empire from its neighbours (Poland-Lithuania, the Habsburg monarchy and Venice). This geostrategic positioning of the Sublime Porte had an impact on the perception and the political significance of the territories bordered by the above-mentioned four empires. In contrast to the powers that carried out a globally oriented "overseas policy", neither Poland-Lithuania nor the Habsburgs nor the Ottomans fought their conflicts in war zones outside the continent. Every war was thus inevitably associated with the loss of territories, which were regarded as belonging to its own imperial territory by the respective opponents. Territorial claims and economic interests thus could not be compensated or defused by resorting to "overseas territories". Under these geopolitical conditions the process of an intra-European de-borderisation began, whose orientation initially was not at all clear. The military conflicts (Long Turkish War/1593-1606; Great Turkish War/1683-1699) were limited to southeastern Europe and remained regional wars. Only the last major conflict with the Venetian Republic (Crete War/1645-1670) was fought on several fronts on the Balkan Peninsula. The Venetian-Ottoman War was also significant for the future because for the first time the empire of the sultans lost a territory permanently to a Christian power. The Serenissima succeeded in conquering the Ottoman fortress of Klis in 1648, and the subsequent expulsion of the Muslim population there heralded the bloody side of the coming intra-European de-borderisation process. The definitive loss of an area to a Christian opponent was not to happen again until the peace settlement of Sremski Karlovci/Carlowitz (1699), when almost all territories north of the Danube-Sava line had to be surrendered.

In the "Turkish Wars" the complexity of the beginning intra-European de-borderisation process became manifest, whose object increasingly became the Ottoman Empire. On the one hand, it consisted of territorial losses, which the Sublime Porte had to accept. On the other hand, it also meant the diplomatic integration of the empire of the sultans into the emerging community of states, which had already begun with the "Italian Wars". In this respect one can speak of a *Greater Western World* in Early Modern Europe, to use a term of Daniel Goffman. Their inter-state communication was marked by widely recognised symbols, practices and customs, as the acceptance of longer and eventually indefinite periods of peace treaties by the Ottomans exemplifies. Finally, the peace negotiations in Carlowitz themselves symbolise the *Greater Western World* in the sphere of diplomacy. The peace talks were mediated by Great Britain and the Netherlands, who had a replica of the building erected at the conference venue, in which they in 1697 had already negotiated the Peace of Rijswijk. The structural design had the advantage that the delegations could enter the meeting room through different doors. This was important because for the first time representatives of the Ottoman Empire negotiated a peace settlement with several Christian powers simultaneously.

The increase in diplomatic exchanges through regular envoys and permanent consulates, which however the Ottoman Empire was not to officially establish until the 19th century, contributed significantly to reducing the religious differences in the political relations. In the Ottoman Empire the lack of military successes and the increasing sense of crisis and of being threatened led to an increasingly intensive debate about the causes of this development. This internal discourse also influenced the works of Ottoman geographers. Katib Çelebi (1609-1657) saw one cause of the now apparent problems in the lack of interest the Muslims showed for their opponents. With his work *Cihannüma* (View of the World) he particularly wanted to provide policy makers with a knowledge base. Just like Ebu Bekr Dımeşki (d. 1691) had written in his *Al Fath al-Rahmani fi Tarz-i Devlet-i Osmani,* Katib Çelebi detached himself more and more from views of the world which had hitherto determined the geographical discourses. Both geographers attempted to provide the most accurate picture of the border areas by rendering the fortifications and the administrative structures. Even though the nobles at court did not yet take sufficient notice of their works, it is nevertheless apparent that due to the geo-strategic and military situation, factual information about the border areas and increasingly also about the Christian states stood in the foreground. From the 18th century on, envoys were explicitly sent with the order to write reports on institutions and structures of their host countries in order to discuss their applicability or usefulness for the Ottoman Empire. This political or rather structural-political anchoring in a world of European states allowed the importance of religion to diminish in the communication between states. The *gazi* ideal was now nothing more than a reminiscence of an idealised and propagandised past, which was held up to the society as a mirror, as the travelogue of Evliya Çelebi (1611 – c. 1685) demonstrates using the example of the Ottoman-Habsburg border area in Hungary.

A similar development can be observed about the same time in the lands under Habsburg rule, where despite or perhaps because of the wars, the religious factor hardly played a role in the perception of the Ottoman Empire and in the political contacts with Istanbul. While in the 16th century the image of the Turks had been characterised by fear and curiosity, now there was growing interest to obtain information that was as realistic and accurate as possible. In newspapers, pamphlets and broadsheets a new tone became apparent. Even during the wars they contained fewer reports about "Turkish atrocities", but rather increasingly contained local descriptions or illustrations of fortresses from the respective war zone. In addition, although the fights were still interpreted in religious and eschatological stereotypes, this mode of thinking became less and less dominant as the armies from the Christian-ruled areas were able to gain military victories. From the Habsburg perspective, at the latest with the successful conclusion of the Great Turkish War in 1699, the Baroque world view with its theological-biblicistic conception of history crumbled, and an increasingly political-secular conception began to prevail, although a temporary revival of Baroque Catholicism took place under Charles VI (1711-1740). In political writings, "Europe" replaced "Christianity" as counterpart to the Ottoman Empire. Which asymmetries arise from equating Europe with Christianity has already been discussed in detail in historical research. Religion is not appropriate as a category of analysis for the political developments in the following two centuries; rather, the contradictions of religion as category become more than clear. The close ties of the Ottoman Empire to the diplomatic structures of the emerging European community of states stand in contrast to a pragmatic development in which the major Christian powers increasingly try to solve their conflicts "with the aid" of the Ottoman Empire – mainly in terms of territorial compensation at the expense of the Ottoman Empire – without thereby damaging themselves. Thus, the policy of de-borderisation directed at the "overseas areas" now was applied in Europe itself, which in part began to pursue an intra-European "overseas policy". However, the beginning of this process in the late 17th century does not mean that with it the decline of the empire of the sultans had been set in motion. Rather, in the 18th century the dynamics of an inclusive Eurocentrism – to use the term coined by Jürgen Osterhammel – still predominated, and the Ottoman Empire could still retain its territories to a great extent.

6 From Inclusive to Exclusive Eurocentrism

"Objectivity" in diplomatic communications corresponded to a political atmosphere in the European state system of the 18th century which Jürgen Osterhammel defines as a value-neutral balancing of power. The Sublime Porte was also active in this foreign policy arena. As long as the Ottoman Empire was able to support its own diplomacy with a corresponding military strength, it was considered part of the European states. The wars against the House of Habsburg in the first half of the 18th century still offered sufficient arguments for such a view. Although in the Peace of Passarowitz (1718) Istanbul had to give up the Banat,

Oltenia and parts of the Bosnian and Serbian areas, through the victory at Banja Luka (1737) Istanbul was able to regain at least part of the lost territory. In the Treaty of Belgrade (1739) Vienna was forced to return Oltenia and parts of the Bosnian province and northern Serbian regions to the Ottoman Empire. It is thus not surprising that in many historiographical and political science works, the Ottoman Empire is considered part of Europe. This was not to begin to change until the last third of the 18th century, when increasingly voices were heard that pointed to alleged differences in culture and civilisation and the "otherness" of the "Turks". Authors like Johann Gottfried von Herder utilised a humanistic topos when they depicted the "Turks" as invaders to Europe who were unable to adapt to a higher culture. Increasingly, they differentiated between a European and an Asian Turkey. In contrast to Anatolia, the Balkans were considered part of Europe, so that now increasingly a border was drawn between the two halves of the Empire. At the same time the idea arose which aimed to "liberate" the "oppressed peoples". However, an expanded view into eastern Europe shows that also the greatest enemy of the Ottoman Empire from the last third of the 18th century on was seen from the same perspective of a "Europe with common values", which began to view the world with a sense of superiority with regard to culture and civilisation. Geographers long viewed the Don River as the border between European and Asian Russia, before the Ural Mountains were attributed this function from the 1770s on. Furthermore, over long stretches of the Early Modern Period the empire of the Romanovs had been considered an enemy "oriental" power. In the last third of the 18th century, when the Habsburgs as military opponents of the Sublime Porte left the stage of European politics, the Tsarist Empire took over this role. After the end of military conflicts with Spain, Portugal, Venice and the Habsburg monarchy, the intra-European de-borderisation ultimately led to the result that the two increasingly marginalised powers began to contend for supremacy in the southeastern European-Anatolian area. The armed conflicts between the two empires turned out to be disastrous for the Ottoman Empire. Catherine II (1762-1796) continued the progressive expansion of the Russian Empire into the southern steppe, which was begun by Peter the Great (1689-1725). In the Russian-Ottoman War of 1768-1774 she succeeded in placing the Crimea under tsarist sovereignty. With the loss of this territory, whose khan had not always been in a close vassal relationship to the sultan until the 17th century, the Black Sea was no longer an inland body of water in the area under Ottoman rule. Also in southeastern Europe, the expansion of the Romanovs progressed, and their dominion after the Treaty of Jassy (1792) extended to the Dniester River. This war which erupted in 1787 was also to be the last war against the Ottoman Empire in which the House of Habsburg took part. However, for the once most powerful opponent of the Ottomans, it resulted in an unfortunate end.

7 The Phase of the Intra-imperial De-borderisation

In the course of the 18th century, the discourses in the Protestant and Catholic states developed into a common view of Europe's territorial geography and European cultural civilisation. This was not to be without repercussions for the two adversaries at Europe's eastern borders. Since the turn of the 17th to 18th century at the latest, the same superior self-image prevailed within the Russian elite, but it was projected instead on "Asia". Islam and nomadism were considered a sign of backward culture and from this the claim was derived for the necessity to undertake a *mission civilisatrice*. In essence, the notion was to introduce higher culture to the nomads, who were considered inferior. The political implementation of this ideology began in the second half of the 18th century and culminated with the "Administrative Code for Siberia", which was mainly composed by Speransky, and especially in the "Statutes on the Administration of the Inorodtsy". The nomads were now considered as "non-Russians, of different descent/nation" (*inorodtsy*) and were divided into three groups, depending on the level of civilisation attributed to them.

The Ottoman Empire also took a similar approach in the middle of the 19th century, when the exclusive Eurocentrism required a response from the Ottoman policy. Like the multi-ethnic empires of the Romanovs and the Habsburgs, the House of Ottoman was confronted with the political consequences of the nation-state concept, which led to a gradual collapse of Ottoman rule in the 19th/20th century. Until 1830 a de facto autonomous Serbian principality and an independent state of Greece existed. These emerging entities primarily owed their existence to the geostrategic interests of the major powers, to which however the Ottoman Empire still belonged. The Crimean War (1853-1856), in which the Sublime Porte was part of an anti-Russian coalition of powers, underlines the ambivalence of the political situation Istanbul faced in the middle of the 19th century. In the Peace of Paris (1856) the Ottoman Empire became a formal member of the European concert of powers, while at the same time in the eyes of the other states it was still not considered a full partner. Besides the already mentioned look at the empire of the sultans, Istanbul was no longer able to accompany its diplomatic steps with military action – in contrast to the early 18th century. This de facto loss of political power on the international stage was balanced by a gain in the power of the state in interior matters. In the late 18th and early 19th century local notables (*ayan*) had in many cases attained an autonomous position in the power structure of the empire, and this development was halted or weakened in the aftermath of the Tanzimat with regionally varying intensity. The strengthened state now had to react to the ambivalent foreign policy position as a formally equal but de facto excluded member of the concert of European states and to the idea of the nation-state and/or nationalism. In contrast to the Tsarist Empire, where the national identity was increasingly dominated by the Russian nation, the Ottoman reformers developed the concept of Ottomanism (*osmanlılık*) and thus elevated the dynasty to become the integrative link of the empire. The aim was to create an imperial patriotism like in the Danube monarchy. This model served as an alternative to nationalism and was to allow all inhabitants of the empire, regardless of their religious and ethnic affiliation, to become citizens of the Ottoman Empire. With the Citizenship Act of 1869 the subjects of the house of Osman could become citizens of the Empire. The empire of the Ottomans now became the Ottoman Empire, which was transforming itself ever more rapidly into a nation state. It is therefore no coincidence that in the second half of the 19th century the term Turkey appeared in official Ottoman documents as reference to the empire. Nevertheless, it must be noted that up to the Balkan Wars in 1912/13, Ottomanism always posed a serious policy option. This concept also implied the adoption of a Eurocentric view of the world, with which Ottoman reformers and the new bureaucratic elites reacted to the ambivalent position among the great powers. Like in Russia, population groups were designated which in the view of the central government needed to be civilised. The Ottoman "foreigners" consisted of nomads or segments of society that had a tribal or clan-like structure. This was true for the northern Albanian tribes and tribal federations, which were now suddenly regarded as wild and uncivilised. The majority of such population groups, however, were found in the Arab provinces. In the memoirs of Ottoman administration members who performed their duties in Palestine, there is evidence of a feeling of superiority with regard to culture and civilisation. They distanced themselves clearly from the "Arabs" and avoided close social relations with the local population. The keywords of the *mission civilisatrice* were discipline and education, through which the respective population should be led to a higher level of civilisation. The Ottoman government itself presented its state as a colonial power and considered transforming Yemen, which belonged to the Ottoman imperial area, into a colony. The mechanisms of European de-borderisation now became integrated into the self-image and the policy of one of its objects, the Ottoman Empire. Thus, the empire of the sultans once again became a player in the process of de-borderisation, albeit to a very limited extent. The limitation of the ability to act within its own dominion ultimately resulted from the clash of intra-Ottoman and European de-borderisation. Repeatedly, the Ottoman authorities had to coordinate the regional implementation of reform measures and other administrative or military plans with the local consuls of the European powers, which competed with the Sublime Porte for political supremacy in various regions of the Ottoman Empire. A crucial lever to intervene directly in local concerns was the self-image of Christian states as "protective powers" of non-Muslim population groups in the Ottoman Empire. The effects of such a political attitude can be observed e.g. in the bloody conflicts between Muslim Druze and Christian Maronites in the Lebanon Mountains, which developed into a problem of international politics in the mid-19th century. An administrative reorganisation that intended to contribute to the stabilisation of the region finally took place according to the precepts of European diplomats. Due to this policy of a *soft imperialism*, whose origins are to be found in the privileges that had been granted since the 15th century to subjects and protected members of other states, parts of the Ottoman population were also beyond the reach of the authorities, and thus the sovereignty of the state was restricted. Especially in the 19th century the number of Ottoman subjects steadily increased who received protection letters from other states. In 1863 the government in Istanbul finally restricted the awarding of such documents by the diplomatic missions, and the Citizenship Act of 1869 also served to resist this form of *soft imperialism*.

The experiences of the European and intra-imperial processes of de-borderisation were ultimately also to affect the Republic of Turkey, which was founded in 1923. The majority of the "founding fathers" came from the environment or belonged directly to the parts of the Young Turk movement that overthrew Sultan Abdul Hamid II (1876-1909). Most of them came from the still remaining Balkan provinces of the Ottoman Empire and/or worked there in the province administration or in the army. As young men, they had experienced the policy of *soft imperialism*, the emergence of the southeastern European nation-states and finally, in the Balkan Wars of 1912/13 also the fate of expulsion. They now brought this wealth of experience into the structure of a nation state, whose core formed the Anatolian region – a territory that was foreign to most of this new political elite and was largely unknown. However, the processes of de-borderisation described here not only influenced the patterns of political action in the early Republic of Turkey, but unfold their impact up to the present day.

Translated from the German by Carol Oberschmidt and Thomas Oberschmidt

Bibliography

Casale, G 2010, *The Ottoman Age of Exploration*, Oxford University Press, Cambridge.
Clewing, K & Schmitt, OJ (ed.) 2011, *Geschichte Südosteuropas. Vom frühen Mittelalter bis zur Gegenwart*, Pustet, Regensburg.
Goffman, D 2003, *The Ottoman Empire and Early Modern Europe*. Cambridge University Press, Cambridge.

Imber, C 2005, *The Ottoman Empire, 1300-1650: The Structure of Power*, Palgrave Macmillan, Houndmills, Basingstoke, Hampshire.
Kappeler, A 2008, *Rußland als Vielvölkerreich. Entstehung, Geschichte, Zerfall*, Beck, Munich.
Osterhammel, J 1998, *Die Entzauberung Asiens. Europa und die asiatischen Reiche im 18. Jahrhundert*, Beck, Munich.
Reinkowski, M 2005, *Die Dinge der Ordnung. Eine vergleichende Untersuchung über die osmanische Reformpolitik im 19. Jahrhundert*, R. Oldenbourg, Munich.
Schmitt, OJ 2009, *Skanderbeg. Der neue Alexander auf dem Balkan*, Pustet, Regensburg.
Schorn-Schütte, L 2010, *Konfessionskriege und europäische Expansion. Europa 1500-1648*, Beck, Munich.
Winkler, HA 2009, *Geschichte des Westens. Von den Anfängen in der Antike bis zum 20. Jahrhundert*, Beck, Munich.

Alberto Masoero
La Russia tra Europa e Asia

1 Un impero dai confini incerti

La collocazione transcontinentale è una costante nella storia dello stato russo. Favorì una pluralità di apporti religiosi, culturali e istituzionali in gran parte spontanei e pluridirezionali, non necessariamente riconducibili a una chiara dicotomia tra Oriente e Occidente. Europa e Asia, del resto, significarono cose diverse in secoli diversi. Come una grande spugna, la Russia assorbì dal tedesco il lessico militare e dal cinese mandarino la parola *čaj* per indicare il tè, la seconda bevanda nazionale. Questa posizione intermedia condizionò l'evoluzione dei confini, ma influenzò anche le rappresentazioni identitarie e l'ideologia dello stato. A partire dal Cinquecento il regno di Mosca iniziò la propria espansione verso est con la conquista degli stati tatari di Kazan' e Astrachan, ereditando in una certa misura il retaggio della sovranità mongola. Si consolidò respingendo a ovest l'invadenza della Confederazione polacco-lituana, uno stato che era allora più prestigioso e potente. Avrebbe rivendicato, dopo le spartizioni polacche del Settecento, anche il titolo di re di Polonia. Il processo secolare di espansione territoriale, diretto di volta in volta verso regioni diverse dell'Europa e dell'Asia, subì le principali battute d'arresto in concomitanza di alcuni periodi di profonda crisi politica, sociale ed economica, accompagnati da gravi perdite di territori e dalla discontinuità dinastica o della forma di stato. Tali furono il Periodo dei Torbidi (1598 -1613) e il ciclo guerra mondiale-rivoluzioni-guerra civile del 1914-21, oltre che la fase storica inaugurata dalla fine dell'Unione Sovietica nel 1991 e dalla nascita degli stati post-sovietici.

Il problema dell'auto-identificazione con le forme di stato e le ideologie europee divenne una questione significativa quando la Russia entrò in contatto, a partire dalle guerre e dalle riforme di Pietro il Grande, con l'assetto politico e la modernità dell'Europa settecentesca. Dipendeva non solo dall'intensificazione delle relazioni, iniziata già nel corso del Seicento, ma anche dal fatto che nel secolo XVIII gli stati europei stavano diventando qualcosa di diverso ed esprimevano una coscienza più marcata della loro superiorità nei confronti del resto del mondo. L'ambizione di svolgere un ruolo internazionale di gran lunga più impegnativo, simboleggiato dall'assunzione del nuovo titolo di *imperator* (parola straniera) aprì un lungo periodo caratterizzato dalla ricezione di idee che il contesto europeo avrebbe offerto nelle fasi storiche successive, dall'Illuminismo al nazionalismo moderno o al socialismo, idee che di volta in volta furono reinterpretate e utilizzate ai fini della legittimazione dello stato, ma anche dei suoi confini quanto meno progettati e perseguiti.

Sarebbe però fuorviante misurare l'oscillazione russa tra Oriente e Occidente, dal Settecento al Novecento, con il metro di una maggiore o minore europeizzazione, punto di vista che presuppone implicitamente il rapporto tra un soggetto docente e uno discente, un perenne apprendistato di cui la storiografia non potrebbe che misurare i progressi o le lacune rispetto a un modello dato. Al contrario, ed è il primo punto che occorre sottolineare, l'ideologia della monarchia zarista, le sue antitesi rivoluzionarie ottocentesche e poi il progetto sovietico – insieme geopolitico e ideologico – espressero di volta in volta una ricezione complessa di modelli europei o extraeuropei sempre unita all'ambizione di una forza propulsiva autonoma, di essere cioè il centro e non una periferia del mondo. In modi diversi, queste declinazioni dell'idea di stato esprimevano la volontà di superare la stessa contrapposizione tra Oriente e Occidente, tra Europa e Asia. Erano animate dalla volontà di costituire un punto di irradiazione politica e culturale, articolato di volta in volta con un vocabolario universalistico o internazionalista.

Questa proiezione fu accompagnata da una seconda, fondamentale continuità, cioè dallo scarto tra grandiosità dei fini e limitatezza dei mezzi disponibili relativamente alle condizioni di ciascuna epoca storica. Lo stato che nel secolo XV si immaginò come la "Terza Roma", cioè come l'erede diretto – senza dover passare attraverso la legittimazione europea – dell'impero più prestigioso della storia allora presa in considerazione, era un piccolo principato slavo-orientale. Nel corso dei secoli l'espansione su uno spazio smisurato divenne un mito fondante della monarchia. L'ampliamento dei confini assunse il significato di sanzione simbolica della maestà del sovrano e poi della grandezza nazionale, ma rese difficile governare popolazioni estremamente eterogenee e mobilitare le risorse di regioni remote. Nonostante il consolidamento della burocrazia durante il secolo XIX, lo stato era soggetto a un apparato amministrativo sempre relativamente gracile e rarefatto che, anche in epoca sovietica, suscitava il timore di perdere il controllo su territori difficili da difendere e da presidiare. Le condizioni geologiche e climatiche ostacolarono lo sviluppo di un'agricoltura produttiva. Nei momenti della massima potenza internazionale, quando le sue truppe sfilarono a Parigi e Berlino dopo le guerre napoleoniche e la II guerra mondiale, l'economia russa era inferiore a quella dei nemici che aveva sconfitto, anche se in campo militare e soprattutto culturale il divario era assai più sottile.

Questa tensione tra ambizioni universali e risorse limitate non precluse affatto la crescita territoriale, economica e politica di uno stato che, a metà del Novecento, si presenterà sulla scena internazionale come una delle due superpotenze mondiali, ma ne condizionò lo sviluppo storico. Essa generava al tempo stesso insicurezza geopolitica e l'abitudine a rispecchiarsi e a cercare legittimazione nei modelli più prestigiosi di ciascuna epoca, non solo e non necessariamente europei. Lo scarto tra mezzi e fini stimolò il dibattito ottocentesco sul divario tra la Russia e le società più progredite, l'urgenza della modernizzazione staliniana e poi l'obiettivo chruščëviano di "raggiungere e superare" gli Stati Uniti del secondo dopoguerra. Imperi davvero sicuri di sé, come quello cinese o britannico all'apice della loro potenza, non si sarebbero mai auto-rappresentati mediante il confronto con uno stato più avanzato. Ambizioni espansionistiche e difficoltà nel controllo delle periferie conferivano un valore particolare all'integrità territoriale, cioè la ricerca di un confine immodificabile, ma contemporaneamente producevano il suo contrario, cioè una perdurante indeterminatezza del limite esterno. La Russia ebbe sempre a est, sud e ovest delle ambigue *okrainy* ovvero regioni "prossime al confine" e dallo *status* incerto, terre "altre", ma percepite come "proprie", di cui immaginare di volta in volta l'incorporazione per annessione o, meglio, per spontanea, entusiastica adesione.

2 Una potenza europea nel secolo dei lumi?

Fu Vasilij Tatiščev, intellettuale e geografo vicino a Pietro il Grande, a "scoprire" e a fissare negli Urali un confine tra Europa e Asia che attraversava l'Impero al suo interno, prolungandosi con più controversa incertezza verso il Mar Caspio. La nuova delimitazione sostituiva quella precedente rappresentata dal fiume Don, che collocava gran parte dell'odierna Russia europea in "Asia" e che fino alla fine del Seicento non aveva suscitato particolari dibattiti o interesse. Nel momento in cui la Russia si espandeva verso Occidente, dopo aver sconfitto gli Svedesi nella Guerra del Nord (1721), la cultura geografica sentiva il bisogno di ampliare la propria demarcazione europea e distinguerla meglio, anche culturalmente, da possedimenti asiatici abitati da "selvaggi" o sudditi "di altra fede" (*inovercy*). Dire che l'Impero era diviso in una parte europea e in una asiatica corrispondeva alla rivendicazione dello *status* di una potenza europea dotata di vastissimi possedimenti extraeuropei, come l'Inghilterra, la Spagna o il Portogallo dell'epoca. Una capitale costruita *ex novo* secondo i modelli architettonici barocchi poteva essere pensata come il centro metropolitano di uno stato imperiale che proiettava le proprie ambizioni espansionistiche fino all'Estremo Oriente. Per questa via le esplorazioni geografiche ordinate da Pietro giungevano a scoprire il Pacifico settentrionale e le coste del Nordamerica (più tardi l'Alaska degli zar), percepite fino a fine Settecento come un'estensione dei possedimenti russi in Asia, una propaggine dell'Oriente.

Quando Caterina II affermava perentoriamente che "la Russia è una potenza europea" constatava un dato di fatto, cioè il ruolo da protagonista che l'Impero zarista aveva assunto nel gioco militare e diplomatico all'epoca della Guerra dei Sette anni. Il suo documento politico più importante, il *Nakaz* o Istruzione del 1767, disegnava un modello di stato attingendo copiosamente ai testi dell'Illuminismo, ma l'importazione presentava alcuni significativi slittamenti semantici. Laddove Montesquieu aveva classificato la forma di governo degli stati di grandi dimensioni con la definizione di un "dispotismo" prevalentemente orientale, l'imperatrice lo correggeva e traduceva "potere autocratico" (art. 10 del *Nakaz*), a rimarcare non soltanto la rispettabilità delle proprie fonti di legittimazione, ma anche la continuità con l'accezione originaria del termine "autocrate", ovvero un sovrano che non è vassallo di nessun altro. La ricezione ignorava il principio della separazione dei poteri, centrale invece ne *L'esprit des lois*. Ricavava da Montesquieu il concetto di corpi intermedi, retaggio di antiche autonomie nobiliari che dovevano limitare il potere in una monarchia ben ordinata. Ma il modello di stato tratteggiato da Caterina non applicava questa definizione a quegli istituti dello stato russo che più verosimilmente avrebbero potuto essere assimilati a corpi cetuali titolari di autonomi diritti, ad esempio la Duma dei boiari soppressa nel 1707. "Poteri intermedi" erano definiti il Senato e le magistrature dello "stato regolare" creato da Pietro I (*Nakaz*, art. 18, 20), ovvero poteri amministrativi più che corpi politici distinti dal potere esecutivo. Il concetto di Montesquieu assumeva perciò un significato opposto a quello originario: articolazioni dello stato assoluto preposte alla traduzione pratica della volontà imperiale, più che alla sua limitazione per legge.

Il "progetto greco" della conquista di Costantinopoli elaborato negli anni delle guerre russo-turche del 1768-1774 e 1787-1892, tema esplorato magistralmente da Andrej Zorin, rivela il legame profondo e ambiguo tra ricezione della cultura illuministica ed espansione dei confini imperiali, oltre che la difficoltà di collocare tale ricezione sull'asse orizzontale di una progressiva europeizzazione, lungo un percorso ideale che procederebbe univocamente da ovest verso est. Le nuove acquisizioni territoriali andavano ben al di là di obiettivi strategici pure importanti, come il consolidamento di un approdo sul Mar Nero e quindi dell'accesso al Mediterraneo. Fu uno dei progetti di politica estera più grandiosi, dettagliati e ambiziosi mai concepiti dallo stato russo. Esso era accompagnato da un apparato simbolico attentamente costruito e sorvegliato. Dopo la conquista della "città perduta dai Greci" e dell'Impero ottomano, lo stato dei Romanov avrebbe dovuto dividersi in due imperi alleati, quello settentrionale di Pietroburgo e quello meridionale di Costantinopoli. Sul trono di questi due stati russi dovevano sedere i nipoti di Caterina, Alessandro e Costantino, i cui nomi erano ostentatamente associati alle gesta di Costantino il Grande e di Alessandro Magno. Lo spostamento dei confini avrebbe dovuto procedere verso sud e poi idealmente verso la Persia, lungo la direttrice espansionistica dei grandi stati ellenistici. Fu contemplata anche la conquista di Gerusalemme, culla della Russia cristiana, e dell'Etiopia.

Caterina e il suo favorito Grigorii Potëmkin erano sinceramente convinti che tutto ciò rappresentasse un ritorno verso le radici elleniche e "ateniesi" della Russia. Era, beninteso, il simbolo politico di una Atene depurata delle sue connotazioni repubblicane e sovrapposta ambiguamente allo spirito conquistatore di Alessandro Magno, una Grecia dei filosofi intesa come rafforzamento e complemento, non come antitesi della Bisanzio cristiana. Vi era una sottile ma sostanziale differenza tra questa concezione espansionistica e le argomentazioni eurocentriche con cui negli stessi anni Voltaire spronava Caterina a combattere la barbarie, a far la guerra contro i "nemici delle arti e gli oppressori delle donne" per liberare i popoli dal dispotismo orientale del sultano e dalla superstizione dell'Islam. Occupare o liberare Costantinopoli significava piuttosto ricongiungersi alle fonti della civiltà da cui era scaturita la ragione europea, fonti rivendicate come originariamente proprie. Questa prospettiva grandiosa – una vera e propria utopia di stato inestricabilmente congiunta alla *Realpolitik* espansionistica – capovolgeva la genealogia secondo cui i "lumi" sarebbero migrati storicamente da Atene a Roma, da qui a Parigi e poi a Pietroburgo, capitale di una *tabula rasa* ai margini nord-orientali d'Europa nell'immagine suggerita da Leibniz. Al contrario, ritornando al luogo-idea di origine la Russia rivendicava la discendenza diretta dalla culla della civiltà europea. L'Impero zarista giungeva a pensare se stesso come il più autentico interprete dei "lumi", non già come allievo della ragione europea: i Russi discendevano dai "Greci" e in quanto tali rappresentavano non la periferia, ma il centro dell'Illuminismo settecentesco.

Per questo la Nuova Russia delle steppe meridionali e la penisola di Crimea, risultato parziale di uno scarto macroscopico tra ambizioni visionarie e realtà politico-militari, assunsero già allora una valenza ideologica intensissima, ben al di là della propaganda legittimante o delle pubbliche relazioni tra teste coronate. Queste nuove regioni russe (in realtà tatare e greche) non rappresentavano solo territori occupati e poi effettivamente popolati durante la prima metà dell'Ottocento per brama di conquista o interesse economico. Dovevano essere segnate simbolicamente da toponimi greci, come il governatorato di Tauride e Odessa, la città di Odisseo. La Crimea doveva offrire lo scenario di un giardino ordinato dalla ragione, un paradiso in terra in cui non solo e non tanto i "russi" (l'imperatrice era una principessa tedesca convertita), ma tutte le popolazioni convivevano armoniosamente sotto lo scettro della Minerva sul trono. Nell'ode di Vasilij Petrov a Potëmkin del 1778 si elencavano senza distinzioni qualitative "l'Oriente e l'Occidente, il Nord e il Sud", così come "il Moldavo, l'Armeno, l'Indiano o il Greco, o il nero Etiope". La Crimea occupava una posizione centrale in questa geografia politica in quanto specchio della grandezza imperiale, prova vivente di un Illuminismo concretamente realizzato dall'Impero.

3 La Russia e l'Europa nell'età delle rivoluzioni

Il dibattito ottocentesco tra partigiani e avversari del carattere europeo della Russia, solo superficialmente riassunto in una contesa tra "slavofili" e "occidentalisti", fu in parte influenzato dalla diversa sensibilità dell'età romantica, animata dal desiderio di definire l'identità dei popoli e i loro destini storici, impegnata a tracciare le differenze tra grandi civiltà e i loro principi ispiratori reali o presunti, ad esempio ciò che differenziava il mondo slavo da quello romano-germanico. Ammiratori e detrattori di un'Europa astratta e stilizzata polemizzavano tra loro utilizzando le categorie filosofiche di Schelling e di Hegel o le argomentazioni storiografiche di Guizot e Tocqueville, prova di un'appartenenza di fatto al contesto intellettuale europeo. La discussione storico-filosofica sull'antitesi tra Russia ed Europa avveniva contemporaneamente all'elaborazione di una nuova ideologia nazionale della monarchia, la cosiddetta "nazionalità ufficiale" riassunta nella triade Ortodossia, Autocrazia, Nazionalità. Questi fenomeni paralleli esprimevano la ricerca di una risposta alle nuove idee di cittadinanza e di sovranità popolare scaturite dalle rivoluzioni tardo-settecentesche. Erano la reazione a un contesto politico che nel frattempo era mutato profondamente, e che non corrispondeva più a quello dell'assolutismo illuminato.

La ricezione russa giunse con un certo ritardo. Nei primi anni del suo regno (1801-1825) Alessandro I si avvaleva della collaborazione di uno statista francofilo dalle idee radicali, Michail Speranskij, e poteva ancora immaginare se stesso e suoi giovani amici del Comitato segreto come "giacobini sul trono", in continuità con l'idea di un Impero intento a realizzare le idee più innovative d'Europa. Anche dopo il 1815 il concerto europeo della Restaurazione e l'ideologia della Santa Alleanza consentivano allo zar di presentarsi come un monarca solidale con gli altri sovrani europei del tempo, in sintonia con il re di Prussia e l'imperatore asburgico. La crisi del paradigma di una Russia come potenza europea fu innescata da tre eventi che si susseguirono in un breve arco di tempo tra il 1825 e il 1830. Il primo fu l'insurrezione decabrista del 14 dicembre 1825, che costrinse Nicola I (1825-1855) a salire al trono con l'ansia di un sovrano che aveva appena dovuto sedare un moto risorgimentale. La minaccia era maturata al centro dello stato, tra i giovani ufficiali dei reggimenti della Guardia acquartierati a poca distanza dal Palazzo d'Inverno. Il secondo evento fu la rivoluzione polacca del 1830-31, che scoppiò nella più prestigiosa tra le periferie annesse durante l'espansione settecentesca. La Polonia del Congresso aveva goduto fino ad allora del massimo grado di autonomia che l'autocrazia zarista fosse disposta a concedere a una provincia, al punto da tollerare il paradosso di una costituzione nobiliare negli anni in cui il pensiero politico russo, a partire dalla *Memoria sulla Russia antica e moderna* (1812) di Nikolaj Karamzin, iniziava ad associare l'identità nazionale con le prerogative autocratiche. Il terzo evento ebbe luogo anch'esso nel 1830 e si svolse fuori dai confini dello stato, nella Francia dei "lumi". La rivoluzione di luglio scuoteva lo *status quo* post-napoleonico e inaugurava un periodo storico in cui l'Europa sarebbe apparsa in Russia, agli intellettuali come ai sovrani, con il volto delle due maggiori ideologie del suo lungo Ottocento: il socialismo e il nazionalismo. I tre eventi anticipavano tendenze che si sarebbero prolungate in Europa occidentale, così come al centro dell'Impero e alla sua periferia: la rivoluzione paneuropea del 1848, la seconda rivoluzione polacca del 1863 e la lunga stagione del movimento rivoluzionario russo, che a partire dal 1859-61 avrebbe sfidato lo stato zarista. Questa fase di rielaborazione tra il 1825 e il 1855 corrispose a un periodo di relativa pace e di attenuazione della proiezione espansionistica. Il lungo conflitto caucasico può essere interpretato come un rafforzamento difensivo del confine meridionale. Esso accompagnò uno sforzo di consolidamento interno dello stato e delle sue istituzioni, dalla codificazione legislativa al rafforzamento della burocrazia.

La concezione dell'alterità russa rispetto all'Europa prendeva forma in risposta alle sollecitazioni di queste sfide, reali o percepite. La conclusione disperante con cui Pëtr Čaadaev notava l'assenza di una cultura russa autoctona nella prima delle sue *Lettere filosofiche* (1836) emergeva contemporaneamente allo sconforto con cui Sergej Uvarov esplicitava per la prima volta, in una lettera a Nicola I del marzo 1832, la dottrina della nazionalità ufficiale. Uvarov parlava di "eventi di importanza enorme" che avevano avuto "un'influenza funesta sullo sviluppo della cultura nella nostra patria", minato la fiducia di chi credeva nel "progresso" e nel "futuro dei popoli", costringendo "a dubitare di noi stessi". Da qui partiva il ragionamento che illustrava il progetto di una "religione nazionale e popolare" (*narodnaja religija*) da inculcare dall'alto, attraverso istituzioni universitarie potenziate, allo scopo di dare coesione e senso comune ai sudditi di uno stato che appariva pericolosamente "scosso nelle sue fondamenta politiche, morali e religiose".

I primi a contrapporre Russia ed Europa in quanto civiltà fondate su principi qualitativamente opposti furono i teorici di questa ideologia monarchica post-illuministica e post-rivoluzionaria. Negli *Aforismi storici* del 1827 lo storico di corte Michail Pogodin contrapponeva seccamente un'Europa cresciuta mediante la logica della "conquista" e della "rivoluzione" a uno stato russo segnato geneticamente dal principio diverso e superiore della "sottomissione volontaria" al potere. Presupposto di tale nazionalismo ufficiale era una visione profondamente pessimistica della società russa, cioè l'idea di un "magnifico popolo russo, ma magnifico ancora solo in potenza" poiché "all'atto pratico è vile, incontrollabile, bruto" senza il potere disciplinante dell'autocrazia.

Il dibattito tra gli intellettuali, seppur limitato a piccole cerchie prive di influenza politica, nasceva in risposta a questi stimoli. Gli occidentalisti affermavano il carattere europeo della Russia per sostanziare speranze riformatrici. La Russia era un paese essenzialmente europeo, temporaneamente deviato o ostacolato nel suo sviluppo da alcuni fattori storici: la parentesi ritardante del giogo mongolo o – nell'interpretazione storico-geografica di Sergej Solovëv – la vastità di spazi sconfinati difficilmente difendibili, i quali avevano rallentato la penetrazione della civiltà occidentale e favorito la formazione di un potere centralizzato e militarizzato. La logica hegeliana permetteva di rileggere l'assolutismo settecentesco da Pietro il Grande in poi come il momento intermedio di una dialettica storica, presupposto di una successiva affermazione della ragione consapevole e del diritto. Storici occidentalisti come Konstantin Kavelin avrebbero interpretato la liberazione dei contadini del 1861 come il passo ulteriore in una sequenza di emancipazioni dall'alto iniziata con la liberazione della nobiltà dal servizio di stato da parte di Pietro III nel 1762, e da proseguire con diritti politici e costituzionali. La prospettiva europeizzante, tuttavia, non garantiva un esito liberale o democratico. In occidentalisti come lo storico e giurista Boris Čičerin si traduceva invece in un diverso sostegno alle prerogative autocratiche, riassunto nella formula "potere forte e misure liberali", prima di una lunga serie di metafore usate in seguito per legittimare il modello di una modernizzazione autoritaria.

Il punto di vista alternativo degli slavofili non metteva in discussione il principio dell'autocrazia, accettata come forma naturale di governo della Russia. Però nello sforzo di affermare la dignità della cultura nazionale rispetto a quella europeo-occidentale essi innovavano in modo sostanziale il concetto di "popolo russo". A differenza di apologeti della monarchia come Pogodin o Egor Kankrin, i quali avevano proposto seriamente di chiamare lo stato "Petrovia" per sottolineare che la nazione era una creazione diretta dello zar, gli slavofili mettevano l'accento sull'esistenza di una società pre-petrina culturalmente autonoma. Essi costruivano retrospettivamente una tradizione nazionale individuata in una civiltà religiosa, piuttosto che nella persona del sovrano. Ostili a ogni definizione contrattualistica dello stato, essi contrapponevano alla razionalità "pietroburghese", artificiale e imposta, il concetto "moscovita" di un popolo inteso come *ecuméne* cristiano-ortodossa armoniosa e corale, portatrice di valori indipendenti dall'educazione disciplinante dell'Impero. La focosa polemica slavofila non esprimeva necessariamente un rifiuto della moderna società industriale.

Aleksej Chomjakov si presentò all'Esposizione internazionale di Londra del 1851, vetrina e celebrazione del progresso positivistico, con un progetto di macchina a vapore; e slavofili saranno anche molti imprenditori moscoviti di metà Ottocento. Da questa critica scaturiva la visione di un popolo russo tutt'altro che antimonarchico e tuttavia né "incontrollabile" né "bruto", rappresentato come un'entità collettiva dotata di di creatività e capacità espansionistica.

Anche il socialismo russo inaugurato da Aleksandr Herzen, che della monarchia zarista avrebbe rappresentato l'antitesi, maturò da una risposta alle rivoluzioni sociali e nazionali d'Europa, in questo caso attraverso una riflessione critica sugli eventi del 1848. Egli modificava in senso etico-sociale il concetto slavofilo di popolo ortodosso. Nelle pagine scritte in tedesco dal conservatore prussiano August Haxthausen egli scopriva la comune contadina russa o *obščina*, modello dello stato futuro fondato sull'autonomia federale e sulla gestione democratica delle risorse collettive. Emigrato a Londra, Herzen scriveva spesso in francese per un pubblico cosmopolita di fuoriusciti. Il suo socialismo assumeva il significato di un'ideologia nazionale dai toni messianici: una replica a chi affermava l'inconsistenza o l'inferiorità della civiltà russa e contemporaneamente la vocazione a una liberazione universale capace, in prospettiva, di superare l'esito fallimentare della rivoluzione d'Europa, "vecchio mondo decrepito" contrapposto all' "energia selvaggia, fresca ... di popoli nuovi" (così in *Epilogo del 1848*, pubblicato nel 1849).

Nel primo proclama rivoluzionario *Alla giovane generazione*, circolato anonimo all'università di Pietroburgo nell'autunno del 1861, Michail Michajlov e Nikolaj Šelgunov contrapponevano ai "giardinetti e boschetti tedeschi", metafora della mediocrità benpensante, le determinazione russa di "dividere il nostro campo ... come si divideva la terra nell'antichità, quando c'era posto per tutti", cioè nell'*ager publicus* della repubblica romana. Questa variante dell'idea di una discendenza diretta dalla grandezza classica era spesso accompagnata dal paragone con la giovanile freschezza extra-europea degli Stati Uniti. Il dibattito russo sviluppava in modo autonomo il parallelo di Tocqueville tra Russia e America come popoli del futuro. Nell'articolo *La Russie* (1849), in cui tirava le somme della rivoluzione europea e delineava il progetto politico populista, Herzen citava i celebri versi di Goethe (*Amerika, du hast es besser*) e aggiungeva subito dopo che tale definizione *s'aplique fort bien à la Russie*.

4 Colonialismo europeo o impero eurasiatico?

Ideologia autocratica e riformismo occidentalizzante, nazionalismo e socialismo intersecarono nella seconda metà dell'Ottocento un'ulteriore espansione verso Oriente. La sconfitta nella guerra di Crimea (1853-56) intensificò la percezione di un ritardo da colmare e stimolò un lungo periodo di progetti riformatori. Negli stessi anni lo stato zarista completava la pacificazione della Transcaucasia, annetteva le vaste regioni dell'Ussuri e dell'Amur in Estremo Oriente (1860) e penetrava in Asia centrale (1865). Mentre il Congresso di Berlino del 1878 frustrava le aspirazioni di egemonia panslava e balcanica, a est le truppe russe assumevano il controllo del Turkestan con i protettorati di Samarcanda e di Buchara (1885), giungendo a lambire le conquiste britanniche in Afghanistan. Dopo la rivolta dei Boxer in Cina (1900) l'Impero occupò parte della Manciuria, mentre altri progetti di espansione durante la prima guerra mondiale avrebbero preso di mira la Persia settentrionale, le coste meridionali del Mar Nero e il Bosforo. Fino a quale punto queste acquisizioni territoriali potevano dirsi l'opera di un grande stato europeo intento a partecipare alla conquista di colonie extraeuropee?

La geografia delle regioni annesse – oltre la catena del Caucaso e la Steppa della fame in Asia centrale – rendeva fino a un certo punto plausibile, e per molti versi lusinghiera, l'identificazione con il colonialismo occidentale. Funzionari e orientalisti studiavano con attenzione il modo in cui i Francesi governavano l'Algeria musulmana e gli Inglesi avevano affrontato la rivolta dei Sepoys in India. Come gli slavofili avevano scoperto il nazionalismo attraverso Schelling, così la conoscenza dell'Oriente russo si sviluppò attraverso la mediazione intellettuale della *Erdkunde* di Carl Ritter, tradotta a partire dal 1856. La letteratura coloniale europea, ad esempio *De la colonisation chez les peuples modernes* di P.-P. Leroy-Beaulieu del 1874 (tradotto in russo nel 1877), offriva classificazioni utili per interpretare le acquisizioni recenti. Lo slancio patriottico che aveva ispirato l'abolizione della servitù della gleba nel 1861, residuo "scandaloso" che impediva alla Russia di considerarsi una nazione moderna e quindi compiutamente europea, alimentava allo stesso tempo la visione di una grandiosa missione civilizzatrice verso Oriente. Dopotutto, a metà Ottocento ogni potenza europea degna di questo nome aveva o cercava di acquisire delle colonie.

Nonostante ciò la cultura zarista fu sempre restia ad adottare compiutamente il paradigma coloniale. La storia del colonialismo europeo presentava un'ampia gamma di movimenti secessionisti più o meno riusciti, dalla crescente autonomia dei *dominions* britannici ai movimenti indipendentistici in America latina, per non parlare del caso esemplare della rivoluzione statunitense. La prospettiva di un destino russo in Asia maturava nel momento in cui il rischio della secessione si materializzava nella rivolta polacca del 1863 e nel coevo movimento autonomistico siberiano. La consapevolezza di una capacità di governo del territorio assai limitata (a metà Ottocento era più facile, partendo da Pietroburgo, raggiungere New York che Vladivostok) si sovrapponeva a una preoccupazione quasi ossessiva per l'integrità del territorio statuale inteso come eredità dinastica. Il principio autocratico inibiva l'adozione di una gerarchia metropoli-colonia che potesse prefigurare anche solo implicitamente una frammentazione futura o cessioni di sovranità. Perciò appariva inopportuno definire colonie asiatiche il Turkestan o l'Amur. "Noi non abbiamo colonie", affermò perentoriamente il ministro degli interni Dmitrij Tolstoj a metà degli anni '80 dell'Ottocento. Nel lessico ufficiale si parlava piuttosto di "ampliamento incessante dello stato imperiale russo" (in ogni direzione) seguito dall'assimilazione graduale di "regioni prossime al confine".

Dagli anni '60 dell'Ottocento alle riforme di Stolypin del 1906-1911 settori importanti della burocrazia si posero il problema di superare l'isolamento delle periferie per promuovere la coesione dello stato. Essi perseguirono in modo ondivago, e con risultati disuguali, politiche di assimilazione demografica, linguistica e istituzionale, ad esempio cercando di sostituire le cariche vicereali dei governatorati generali periferici – segno legale di una condizione di alterità provvisoria – con circoscrizioni amministrative più simili a quelle del centro russo-europeo. Negli esponenti più illuminati come il ministro delle finanze Nikolaj Bunge la politica asiatica era intesa non tanto come una russificazione delle conquiste territoriali, quanto come costruzione di un impero-nazione attraverso un processo di integrazione reciproca tra russi e non russi, sulla base di leggi e istituzioni comuni. Al principio del Novecento era ormai diffusa l'idea che il baricentro dello stato si stesse spostando verso est. Una commissione ufficiale presieduta da Dmitrij Mendeleev calcolò nel 1905 il "centro demografico" e il "centro geografico" della Russia, suggerendo che il primo, collocato nei pressi di Tambov a sud di Mosca, fosse destinato a spostarsi progressivamente fino a coincidere con il secondo, a nord di Omsk in Siberia occidentale.

La cultura non ufficiale rafforzava questi punti di vista e iniziava a sfumare il significato di una differenza culturale tra la Russia europea e l'Asia. Ancora nel 1893 Pëtr Semenov-Tjan' Šanskij definiva la colonizzazione russa come uno "spostamento del confine etnografico d'Europa verso oriente", ma questa prospettiva occidentalistica era contestata da più parti. Autori dall'orientamento ideologico eterogeneo mettevano in discussione il parallelo tra conquiste zariste ed espansione coloniale europea. Ne *La Russia e l'Europa* del 1869 Nikolaj Danilevskij metteva in questione il confine settecentesco tra una parte europea e una parte asiatica dello stato, fino ad allora dominante. Egli capovolgeva la geografia petrina di Tatiščev e negava il significato degli Urali come limite tra continenti. In questa prospettiva la Russia diventava il centro di una massa terrestre, una "regione naturale" unitaria di fronte alla quale l'Europa occidentale retrocedeva allo *status* di promontorio dell'Asia. Considerata in questa luce, l'avanzata verso Oriente perdeva i connotati della conquista europeizzante di terre straniere e diventava un processo naturale, ambiguamente interno. Vladimir Lamanskij sistematizzò ulteriormente questa visione in *Tre mondi del continente eurasiatico* del 1892, in cui argomentava l'esistenza di un mondo intermedio russo radicalmente distinto dall'Europa e dall'Asia, un'unica "patria" estesa anche a Oriente senza soluzioni di continuità, soggetta a un processo di riappropriazione più che di occupazione esterna. Autori socialisti come Sergej Južakov sviluppavano l'idea populista del contadino come portatore della russicità e teorizzavano la penetrazione russa in Oriente sulla base di un principio "popolare" e comunitario, in contrapposizione all'imperialismo capitalista britannico. L'orientalista Esper Uchtomskij, assai vicino allo zar Nicola II, si spingeva oltre e teorizzava l'origine mongola dell'Impero: lo zar non discendeva da Bisanzio ma da Gengiz Khan, e quindi la Russia si rapportava ai popoli dell'Oriente con i tratti dell'affinità culturale, della convivenza pacifica e del rispetto delle tradizioni locali. A differenza degli stati europei, ansiosi di depredare la Cina, l'Impero zarista agiva sulla scena mondiale con la specificità di una potenza non-coloniale per eccellenza.

Le teorie dell'asiaticità russa adattavano al contesto coloniale alcuni motivi tradizionali dell'ideologia monarchica zarista. L'affermazione dell'affinità tra Russia e Oriente proiettava sulla politica dei confini in Asia il principio di una "sottomissione volontaria" al potere come tratto distintivo della diversità russa rispetto all'Europa. L'idea di una spontanea fedeltà dei sudditi allo zar, declinata sotto Nicola I in opposizione alle rivoluzioni quarantottesche, veniva tradotta in senso spaziale e applicata al rapporto tra centro pietroburghese e popoli-regioni d'Oriente. Se i Russi erano gli eredi dell'Orda d'oro, espandere i confini in Asia significava ritornare a casa. In Uchtomskij, ad esempio, la tesi della discendenza mongola sfociava nel progetto visionario di un'unione volontaria tra Cina e Russia, popoli affini, sotto lo scettro dello "zar bianco". Nel 1902 il generale Alekseev citò argomentazioni simili nel telegramma con cui proponeva di prolungare l'occupazione della Manciuria.

La definizione eurasiatica della Russia non approdava però veramente al concetto di una civiltà delimitata da confini chiari e riconosciuti, nazionali o multinazionali che fossero. Il contorno di questo spazio culturale immaginato rimaneva altamente indefinito e andava ben oltre la frontiera dello stato imperiale del tempo. Per il panslavista Lamanskij i limiti del mondo russo si estendevano a gran parte dell'Europa orientale, alla Turchia occidentale e alla costa mediterranea della Siria. Uchtomskij pensava che, procedendo oltre il Caspio e il lago Bajkal, "non possiamo incontrare un confine chiaramente definito ... oltre il quale si interrompe il nostro territorio legittimo". Questa indeterminatezza produsse effetti molto concreti negli anni della crisi zarista: la sconfitta nella guerra con il Giappone del 1904, in parte esito del destino asiatico coltivato nei decenni precedenti, si riverberava sulla stabilità politica del centro contribuendo allo scatenamento della rivoluzione del 1905.

5 Socialismo europeo, rivoluzione mondiale e confini della potenza sovietica

La diffusione del marxismo dagli anni '80 dell'Ottocento può essere considerata come un'europeizzazione provvisoria del socialismo russo. Protagonisti del movimento rivoluzionario come Plechanov paragonarono la polemica tra populisti e marxisti a un prolungamento del dibattito tra occidentalismo e slavofilia. Adottare le categorie marxiane come scienza della rivoluzione comportava una considerazione della differenza russa rispetto all'Europa alla luce del ritardo in un processo scandito da stadi comuni. Pëtr Struve attribuiva a questo punto di vista il significato di una pedagogia europeizzante: "riconosciamo la nostra arretratezza e andiamo alla scuola del capitalismo" (*Note sullo sviluppo economico della Russia*, 1894). Scegliere la guida teorica di Marx ed Engels significava riconoscere l'egemonia culturale della socialdemocrazia tedesca, assumerne la denominazione partitica (il Partito operaio socialdemocratico russo di Lenin e Martov) e condividere l'appartenenza istituzionale alla Seconda internazionale. Nasceva in tale contesto la denominazione del socialismo pre-marxista in "populismo" (*narodničestvo*), con l'accezione peggiorativa di un socialismo romantico, contadino e provinciale, privo di adeguata consapevolezza teorica. In verità, in quegli anni i socialisti di ispirazione neopopulista come Viktor Černov cercavano una propria strada per rapportarsi all'identità europea. Essi distinguevano all'interno dell'Europa una tipologia geografica e sociale delle periferie contadine che accomunava la Russia a paesi come l'Ungheria e l'Italia, e in tal modo permetteva ai russi di pensarsi come un tipo particolare di europei.

L'adozione di una concezione "monistica" della storia (alla Plechanov) non scioglieva però il dilemma della rivoluzione proletaria in un paese ancora prevalentemente agrario. Come pensare la costruzione del socialismo in un mondo contadino che il marxismo ortodosso classificava come "piccolo-borghese", categoria sociale conservatrice e quindi spazio inesorabilmente arretrato della storia europea? Lenin risolveva il problema con un'operazione intellettuale per molti aspetti speculare a quella di Černov che però, a differenza di questa, sottolineava il primato mondiale, e non soltanto europeo, della Russia. Invece di differenziare il centro capitalistico dalle sue periferie agrarie egli associava il futuro della Russia ai due maggiori esempi di modernità del primo Novecento, cioè la

Germania e gli Stati Uniti, forme di sviluppo riassunte nei concetti di una "via prussiana" e di una "via americana" alla rivoluzione. Alla più indiretta "via prussiana" (di un'evoluzione capitalistica delle tenute nobiliari e della proletarizzazione dei contadini) egli preferiva la "via americana", cioè una rottura rivoluzionaria che avrebbe spezzato ogni residuo feudale e liberato l'accesso alle risorse fondiarie dello spazio imperiale, trasformando il contadino "semi-asiatico" in un agricoltore moderno e in un protagonista della storia.

Gli appunti su *Capitalismo e agricoltura negli Stati Uniti d'America* (1915) riassumevano la logica di questa interpretazione. La modernità statunitense rappresentava "un modello. Avanti a tutti. Più libero di tutti, ecc. (...) Confronta l'America con la Russia, se si desse la terra ai contadini". Grazie all'identificazione con la "rivoluzione dei *farmers*", la *jacquerie* contadina diventava una componente della rivoluzione democratico-borghese. Le potenzialità future della Russia erano per di più assimilate al tipo ideale dell'agricoltura più moderna del tempo, cresciuta nei grandi spazi extra-europei delle praterie. Lenin si ispirava in parte a *L'operaio americano* di Karl Kautsky (una serie di articoli tradotti in sette edizioni russe con il titolo *L'operaio russo e l'operaio americano*), nei quali il leader della socialdemocrazia tedesca affrontava l'"enigma" della differenza euro-americana discusso da Werner Sombart, ovvero *Perché negli Stati Uniti non c'è il socialismo* (1905). Colpito dalla radicalità della rivoluzione russa del 1905, Kautsky rappresentava la Russia e l'America come due specchi incompleti del futuro europeo, caratterizzati rispettivamente dal vigore rivoluzionario e dal massimo grado di sviluppo della razionalità produttiva capitalistica. Lenin si appropriava della comparazione triangolare tra Germania-Europa, Stati Uniti e Russia, ma la modificava sottilmente per disegnare un destino storico che sottolineava il significato centrale della Russia. Egli immaginava la rivoluzione socialista nell'impero contadino degli zar come un'accelerazione della storia che avrebbe permesso di ricongiungere le due metà extra-europee, realizzando contemporaneamente il primato del socialismo e della modernità: non solo "il soviet", quindi, ma altresì "l'elettrificazione" di cui Lenin studiava con attenzione le applicazioni negli Stati Uniti.

La rivoluzione bolscevica fu concepita in una prospettiva mondiale, più che europea. Ciò influenzava la rappresentazione dello stato futuro e della sua collocazione geopolitica, ancor prima che nascesse l'Unione Sovietica. All'inizio della guerra mondiale Lenin rifletteva sulla futura configurazione degli stati al termine del conflitto, in previsione di un ciclo di rivoluzioni ritenute allora imminenti o probabili. Prevedeva il dissolvimento degli imperi d'Austria, Germania e Russia, ma rifiutava di ipotizzare al loro posto la nascita di una repubblica federale europea che avrebbe significato una spartizione di colonie nel resto del mondo. Immaginava piuttosto il fine ultimo di "Stati Uniti del mondo (e non della sola Europa)", preceduti da una fase in cui uno o più paesi socialisti si sarebbero scontrati con altri paesi ancora capitalisti (*Sulla parola d'ordine degli Stati uniti d'Europa*, 1915).

La nascita dell'Unione Sovietica avrebbe messo in relazione queste rappresentazioni della centralità russa con la concretezza storica di uno stato, della sua potenza diplomatico-militare e dei suoi confini. La Guerra civile (1918-1921) realizzò la riconquista di gran parte dello spazio post-zarista, a partire dal nucleo centrale di un territorio poco più ampio della Moscovia storica e sullo sfondo di una crisi economica, sociale e alimentare gravissima. La nuova classe dirigente bolscevica riuscì a riprendere il controllo del territorio, ad eccezione delle regioni più occidentali, sconfiggendo una serie di progetti alternativi di ricostituzione statuale di segno politico eterogeneo. Di volta in volta incoraggiò nelle periferie sfuggite al suo controllo insurrezioni nazionali "proletarie" e represse movimenti nazionali ostili, per poi assumere nel 1922 la configurazione di una federazione di repubbliche socialiste dotate di propri confini istituzionalizzati, ma soggette alla gerarchia centralizzata del partito comunista.

La tesi del "socialismo in un solo paese" riconosceva il fallimento dell'ipotesi di una rivoluzione post-bellica nei maggiori paesi europei e quindi l'impossibilità, almeno nell'immediato futuro, di un ruolo della Russia socialista come guida di un processo di costruzione socialista paneuropeo. La svolta imposta da Stalin dal 1929 rispondeva alla percezione di fragilità, insieme interna ed esterna, di un paese uscito dalla guerra civile con forti fenomeni di regressione economica. Uno stato che perseguiva ambizioni globali dovette fare i conti con risorse ancor più limitate di quelle accessibili alla Russia pre-rivoluzionaria. Collettivizzazione delle campagne e Grande terrore, cioè la repressione di quinte colonne dissidenti reali o potenziali, procedevano parallelamente all'industrializzazione accelerata, perseguita in larga parte per prepararsi a uno scontro bellico. Erano accompagnate dall'uso dell'Internazionale comunista come strumento indiretto della politica estera, tanto nel contesto politico europeo che in quello dei movimenti anticoloniali extraeuropei. La duplice prospettiva di una patria del socialismo e di una grande potenza, alla fine degli anni '30 associata in modo più esplicito ai simboli patriottici della grandezza statuale zarista, si traduceva nell'ampliamento ulteriore dei confini di stato.

L'alleanza con la Germania nazista tra il 1939 e il 1941 permise l'annessione di territori dell'ex-Impero zarista perduti nel corso della crisi rivoluzionaria. Lo stato sovietico acquisì la Bessarabia, trasformata in Repubblica sovietica di Moldavia, e la Bucovina settentrionale, associata all'Ucraina socialista insieme alla Galizia orientale e alla Volinia. Incorporò la Polonia orientale, inserita nella Bielorussia sovietica, e le repubbliche baltiche di Lituania, Lettonia ed Estonia. Soltanto una resistenza imprevista nella Guerra d'Inverno (1939-1940) impedì che la Finlandia entrasse a far parte completamente della sfera di influenza sovietica, pur perdendo parte della Carelia. Con poche variazioni minori questi confini esterni uscirono consolidati al termine della II guerra mondiale, durante la quale l'Unione sovietica sconfisse, con costi umani colossali, il progetto di conquista e unificazione europea del Terzo Reich.

Anche dopo il 1945, tuttavia, il limite politico della sovranità conservò una geometria multipla e sfuggente, una perdurante indeterminatezza tra il 'dentro' e il 'fuori', tra proprio e altrui che rappresenta uno dei fattori di continuità secolare della storia russa. L'ambiguità derivava non solo dalla collocazione storica a cavallo tra Europa e Asia, ma soprattutto dall'ideologia di uno stato che trovava la propria ragion d'essere nell'ambizione di giocare un ruolo egemonico mondiale, e in questo senso oltre l'Europa e oltre l'Asia. L'Unione sovietica trionfante era uno stato prevalentemente russo guidato da un leader georgiano (Josif Džugašvili), unito ai numerosi popoli sovietici dall'identità sovranazionale del partito. La sua ideologia ufficiale si ispirava a due autori tedeschi, Marx ed Engels, le cui opere erano diventate materia obbligatoria di studio in tutte le scuole, fino ai villaggi più remoti dell'Asia centrale e dell'Estremo oriente. Nonostante questa ispirazione indiscutibilmente europea, l'Unione sovietica mirava a rappresentare un modello per i tanti, nuovi stati usciti dal processo di decolonizzazione in Asia, Africa e America Latina, una alternativa su scala globale alle declinanti potenze europee e alla crescente superpotenza nordamericana.

Non era affatto chiaro dove iniziasse e dove terminasse l'ambito di potere effettivo di questa ulteriore variante di 'stato russo'. L'ideologia internazionalistica suscitava fedeltà nei partiti comunisti di tutto il mondo e quindi permetteva di influenzare la politica interna di altri stati. Vi era una frontiera interna e ufficiale della Repubblica federale russa (a sua volta composta da innumerevoli repubbliche nazionali autonome) e un'ulteriore frontiera che separava, a Occidente, l'Unione sovietica e le democrazie popolari est-europee. Al di là vi era l'"impero esterno", lo spazio aggiuntivo di una sovranità indiretta, ma molto concreta che si estendeva fino al muro fisico e politico di Berlino. Altri confini separavano circa quaranta aree urbane all'interno del territorio sovietico, dove l'accesso era limitato a causa della presenza di installazioni militari o industriali sensibili, secondo il criterio della sicurezza e della fedeltà politica. Una di queste "città chiuse" era Sebastopoli, simbolo potentissimo del patriottismo russo nelle sue diverse declinazioni storiche e tuttavia luogo a cui i cittadini sovietici, inclusi i parenti dei residenti, potevano accedere solo con una procedura paragonabile alla richiesta del visto d'ingresso per un paese straniero. In ogni caso non era l'Europa ad aver 'occidentalizzato' la Russia. Era lo stato russo ad aver esteso il proprio potere – contemporaneamente ideologico, politico e militare – su quasi metà del continente europeo.

Bibliografia

Bassin, M 1991, "Russia between Europe and Asia: the Ideological Construction of Geographical Space", *Slavic Review*, vol. 50, no.1, pp. 1-17.
Kappeler, A 2001, *Russland als Vielvölkerreich. Entstehung, Geschichte, Zerfall*, Beck, Munich.
Laruelle, M 1999, *L'idéologie eurasiste russe ou Comment penser l'empire*, l'Harmattan, Paris-Montréal.
Masoero, A 2000, "La funzione dell'esempio americano in Herzen e Černyševskij" in *Il pensiero sociale russo. Modelli stranieri e contesto nazionale*, eds A Masoero & A Venturi, F. Angeli, Milan, pp. 33-93.
Masoero, A 2013, "Territorial Colonization in Late Imperial Russia: Stages in the Development of a Concept", *Kritika: Explorations in Russian and Eurasian History*, vol. 14, no. 1, pp. 59-91.
Rossiya i Vostok 2000, eds SM Ivanova & BN Melnikhenko, Izd.vo S.-Peterburgskogo universiteta, St. Petersburg.
Schimmelpenninck van der Oye, D 2010, *Russian Orientalism. Asia in the Russian Mind from Peter the Great to the Emigration*, Yale University Press, New Haven.
Venturi, A 1997, "*Russko-italyanskaya model V.M. Chernova (1899-1902)*" in *Russkaya emigratsiya do 1917 goda - laboratoriya liberalnoy i revolyutsionnoy mysli*, Evropeysky Dom (Rossiyskaya Akademiya Nauk - Maison des sciences de l'homme), St. Petersburg, pp. 21-30
Walicki, A 1973, *Una utopia conservatrice. Storia degli slavofili*, Einaudi, Turin.
Wortman, RS 1995, *Scenarios of Power: Myth and Ceremony in Russian Monarchy*, Princeton University Press, Princeton.
Zorin, A 2004, *Kormya dvuglavogo orla. Literatura i gosudarstvennaya ideologiya v Rossiy v posledney treti XVIII – pervoy treti XIX veka*, Novoe literaturnoe obozrenie, Moscow.

Alberto Masoero
Russia between Europe and Asia

1 An Empire with Uncertain Boundaries

The transcontinental location of the Russian state is a constant factor throughout its history. It fostered a multiplicity of religious, cultural and institutional relations, largely spontaneous and pluridirectional, and not necessarily implying a clear dichotomy between East and West. After all, Europe and Asia meant different things in different centuries. Like a sponge, Russia absorbed its military vocabulary from German and the word *chay* for tea – the second most popular national drink – from Mandarin Chinese. This intermediate position affected the evolution of its borders, but also influenced representations of national identity and the ideology of the state. In the sixteenth century the Tsardom of Russia began its eastward expansion by conquering the Tatar states of Kazan and Astrakhan, and to some extent it inherited the legacy of Mongol rule. It consolidated its power in the West, resisting the interference of the Polish-Lithuanian Commonwealth, a more prestigious and powerful state at the time. The Tsar would also, after the partitions of Poland in the eighteenth century, claim the title of King of Poland. The centuries-old process of territorial expansion, directed towards different regions of Europe and Asia at different times, encountered its main setbacks during periods of profound political, social and economic crisis, accompanied by significant losses of territory and by discontinuities in dynasties and in the form of the state. This happened during the Time of Troubles (1598-1613) and the cycle of world war-revolution-civil war of 1914-1921, as well as in the historical phase that began with the collapse of the Soviet Union in 1991 and the birth of the post-Soviet states.

Identification with European forms of state and ideologies became an important issue when Russia came into contact with the political structure and modernity of eighteenth-century Europe, at the time of the wars and reforms of Peter the Great. The question of Russia's Europeanness depended not only on an intensifying of relations, which had already begun in the seventeenth century, but also on the fact that in the eighteenth century the European states were changing in nature and expressing a greater awareness of their superiority to the rest of the world. The ambition to play a far more influential international role, symbolised by the assumption of the new title of *imperator* (a foreign word), began a long period characterised by the reception of ideas provided by the European context in the ensuing historical phases, ideas as diverse as the philosophy of the Enlightenment, modern nationalism and socialism. These intellectual influences were reinterpreted according to the prevailing circumstances of each period. They were used to affirm the legitimacy of the state and define the borders of its sovereignty, borders established or imagined as a purpose of political action.

It would be misleading, however, to judge the Russian oscillation between East and West, from the eighteenth century to the twentieth century, by the measure of greater or lesser Europeanisation. This point of view implicitly presupposes a teacher-pupil relationship, a perpetual apprenticeship with respect to which historiography could only measure progress and lacunae with reference to a given model. On the contrary – and this is the first point that must be emphasised – the ideology of the Tsarist monarchy, its nineteenth-century revolutionary antitheses and later the Soviet project (both geopolitical and ideological) expressed at different times a complex reception of European and extra-European models always combined with the ambition to be an autonomous driving force – that is, to be the centre, not a peripheral area, of the world. In different ways, these variations in the idea of the state expressed the desire to overcome the contrast between East and West, between Europe and Asia. They were animated by the desire to constitute a point of political and cultural irradiation, expressed in a universalistic or internationalist vocabulary, in accordance with the circumstances of the different periods.

This projection was accompanied by a second, fundamental continuity – that of the contrast between the grand aims and the limited means available with respect to the conditions of each historical age. The state which imagined itself in the fifteenth century as the "Third Rome" – the direct heir, without any need for European legitimisation – of the most prestigious empire in history taken into consideration at the time, was a small eastern Slavic principality. Down the centuries, expansion over a boundless space became a founding myth of the monarchy. The widening of state boundaries took on the significance of a symbolic sanction of the sovereign's majesty and later of national greatness, but made it difficult to govern extremely heterogeneous populations and to mobilise the resources of remote regions. Despite the consolidation of the bureaucracy during the nineteenth century, the state was governed by a still relatively thin and rarefied administrative apparatus, which, even in the Soviet era, aroused the fear of losing control over territories that were difficult to guard and defend. The geological and climatic conditions hindered the development of a productive agriculture. At the times of greatest international power, when its troops paraded in Paris and Berlin after the Napoleonic wars and the Second World War, Russia's economy was inferior to that of the enemies it had defeated, even though in the military and especially the cultural field the gap was much narrower.

This tension between universal ambitions and limited resources did not preclude the territorial, economic and political growth of a state which, in the mid-twentieth century, would emerge on the international scene as one of the two world superpowers, but it did affect its historical development. It generated both geopolitical insecurity and a tendency on the part of the elite to mirror themselves and seek legitimacy in the most prestigious models of every age, and not necessarily only European ones. The disparity between the means available and the ends aspired to prompted the nineteenth-century debate about the gap between Russia and more advanced societies, the urgency of Stalinian modernisation and later the Krushchevian slogan of "catching up with and overtaking" the United States after the Second World War. Truly self-confident Empires, like the Chinese or British empires at the height of their power, would never have represented themselves through a comparison with a more advanced state. Expansionist ambitions and difficulties in controlling the peripheries conferred a particular value on territorial integrity – the quest for an unalterable boundary – but at the same time also produced its contrary: a perpetual indeterminacy of the outer limit. Russia always had to its east, south and west ambiguous *okrainy*, or regions "close to the border" and of uncertain status, lands that were "other" but perceived as "its own", which it could imagine itself incorporating by annexation, or, preferably, by spontaneous, enthusiastic adhesion.

2 A European Power in the Age of the Enlightenment?

It was Vasily Tatishchev, an intellectual and geographer close to Peter the Great, who "discovered" and selected the Urals as a boundary between Europe and Asia which ran across the Empire in its interior, continuing, with a more controversial uncertainty, towards the Caspian Sea. The new line replaced the previous one represented by the River Don, which had put a large part of modern European Russia in "Asia", and which until the end of the seventeenth century had not aroused any particular debate or interest. When Russia expanded eastwards, after defeating the Swedes in the Great Northern War (1721), geographers felt the need to widen its European demarcation and distinguish it more clearly, not only in a geographical but in a cultural sense, from Asian possessions inhabited by "savages" or subjects "of different faith" (*inovertsy*). To say that the Empire was divided into two parts, a European one and an Asian one, constituted a claim to the status of a European power endowed with vast extra-European possessions, like Britain, Spain or Portugal at that time. A capital built from scratch according to Baroque architectural models could be seen as the metropolitan centre of an imperial state which projected its expansionist ambitions right into the Far East.

In this way the geographical explorations ordered by Peter the Great discovered the north Pacific and the coasts of North America (later the tsars' Alaska), which until the end of the eighteenth century were regarded as an extension of Russian possessions in Asia, an offshoot of the East.

When Catherine II stated peremptorily that "Russia is a European power", she was simply recording a fact – the significant role that the Tsarist Empire had taken in the military and diplomatic game during the Seven Years' War. Her most important political document, the *Nakaz*, or "Instruction", of 1767, described a model of the state which drew copiously on the texts of the Enlightenment. Yet the borrowing also involved some notable semantic shifts. Whereas Montesquieu had described the form of government of a large state as a predominantly oriental "despotism", the Empress corrected him and translated "autocratic power" (art. 10 of the *Nakaz*), to highlight not only the respectability of her sources of legitimisation, but also the continuity with the original meaning of the term "autocrat" – a sovereign who is no one else's vassal. The reception ignored the principle of the separation of powers which is central to *L'esprit des lois*. Admittedly, it borrowed from Montesquieu the concept of intermediate bodies – the heritage of ancient aristocratic autonomies which were supposed to limit power in a well-ordered monarchy. But the model of the state sketched out by Catherine did not apply this definition to those institutions of the Tsarist state which could most plausibly have been compared to estate bodies possessing autonomous rights, such as the Boyar Duma, which had been suppressed in 1707. The term "intermediate powers" was used of the Senate and the magistratures of the "regular state" created by Peter I (*Nakaz*, art. 18, 20) – that is, they were considered to be administrative institutions, rather than political bodies distinct from the executive power. Thus Montesquieu's concept took on a meaning which was the opposite of the original one: sectors of the absolute state which were responsible for the implementation of imperial will, rather than for its limitation by law.

The "Greek project" of the conquest of Constantinople formulated during the Russo-Turkish wars of 1768-1774 and 1787-1892, a theme magisterially explored by Andrey Zorin, reveals the profound and ambiguous link between the Tsarist reception of European Enlightenment and the expansion of imperial boundaries. The theme also shows the difficulty of placing this reception on the horizontal axis of progressive Europeanisation, along an ideal itinerary which proceeded unequivocally from west to east. The new territorial acquisitions were much more than strategic objectives, such as the consolidation of a Black Sea harbour and therefore of access to the Mediterranean. The Greek project was one of the grandest, most detailed and most ambitious foreign policy plans ever conceived by the Russian state. It was accompanied by a carefully constructed and supervised symbolic system. After taking the "city lost by the Greeks" and defeating the Ottoman Empire, the Romanov state would have to split up into two allied empires, the northern one of Petersburg and the southern one of Constantinople. The thrones of these two Russian states would be occupied by Catherine's grandsons, Alexander and Konstantin, whose names were ostentatious allusions to the deeds of Constantine the Great and Alexander the Great. The shift in the boundaries would have to proceed southwards and then ideally towards Persia, according to the expansionist plan of the great Hellenistic states. Also envisaged was the taking of Jerusalem – the cradle of Christian Russia – and Ethiopia.

Catherine and her favourite Grigory Potëmkin were genuinely convinced that all this would represent a return to Russia's Hellenic and "Athenian" roots. Their Athens was a political symbol cleansed of its republican connotations and ambiguously superimposed on the conquering spirit of Alexander the Great; their Greece was a nation of philosophers seen as a reinforcement and completion of Christian Byzantium, not an antithesis to it. There was a subtle but significant difference between this expansionist conception and the Euro-centric arguments with which Voltaire urged Catherine to combat barbarism, to make war on the "enemies of the arts and the oppressors of women" in order to free the peoples from the oriental despotism of the sultan and the superstition of Islam. Rather, occupying or liberating Constantinople meant a return to the sources of the civilisation from which European reason had originated, sources that the Empire claimed as its own. This grand perspective – a state utopia inextricably linked to expansionist *Realpolitik* – turned on its head the genealogy whereby the sources of reason had historically migrated from Athens to Rome, from there to Paris and then to Petersburg, the capital of a *tabula rasa* on the north-eastern margins of Europe, in the image suggested by Leibniz. On the contrary, returning to its ideaplace of origin, Russia claimed direct descent from the cradle of European civilisation. The Tsarist empire came to think of itself as the most authentic interpreter of the "lights of reason", not as a pupil of European philosophers: the Russians descended from the Greeks, and as such represented not the periphery but the core of the eighteenth-century Enlightenment.

Therefore the New Russia of the southern steppes and the Crimean peninsula, the partial result of a macroscopic disparity between visionary ambitions and military reality, assumed already at that time an intense ideological importance, going far beyond justificatory propaganda or public relationships between crowned heads. These new Russian (though in reality Tatar or Greek) regions did not represent only territories first occupied and then populated in the first half of the nineteenth century out of a desire for conquest or economic interest. They had to be symbolically designated with Greek toponyms, such as the governorate of Tauris and Odessa, the city of Odysseus. Crimea had to offer the scenario of a garden planned by reason, an earthly paradise where not only 'Russians' (the

Empress was a converted German princess) but all populations lived harmoniously together under the sceptre of ruling Minerva. Vasily Petrov's *Ode to Potëmkin* (1778) listed without qualitative distinctions "the East and the West, the North and the South", as well as "the Moldavian, the Armenian, the Indian or the Greek, or the black Ethiopian". The Crimea occupied a central position in this political geography as a mirror of imperial greatness, living proof of an Enlightenment concretely realised by the Tsarist Empire.

3 Russia and Europe in the Age of Revolutions

The nineteenth-century debate between proponents and adversaries of the European nature of Russia, only superficially described as a contest between "Slavophiles" and "Westernisers", was to some extent influenced by the different sensibility of the Romantic age, with its characteristic desire to define the identity of peoples and their historical destinies. Romantic culture attempted to trace the differences between major civilisations and their real or supposed underlying principles, such as the characteristics that distinguished the Slavic from the Romano-Germanic world. The admirers and detractors of an abstract, stylised Europe argued among themselves on the basis of the philosophical categories of Schelling and Hegel or employed the historiographical arguments of Guizot and Tocqueville – proof that they did in fact belong to the European intellectual context. The historical and philosophical debate about the antithesis between Russia and Europe was contemporaneous with the emergence of a new national ideology of the monarchy, the so-called "official nationality" summed up in the triad Orthodoxy, Autocracy and Nationality. These parallel developments were part of a search for a response to the new ideas about citizenship and popular sovereignty that had arisen from the revolutions of the late eighteenth century. They were a reaction to a political context which in the meantime had changed profoundly and no longer corresponded to that of enlightened absolutism.

The Russian reception came rather late. In the early years of his reign (1801-1825), Alexander I availed himself of the help of a Francophile statesman with radical ideas, Mikhail Speransky, and still imagined himself and his young friends of the Secret Committee as "Jacobins on the throne", in continuity with the idea of an Empire intent on realising the most innovative European ideas. Even after 1815 the concert of Europe in the restoration period and the ideology of the Holy Alliance enabled the Tsar to present himself as a monarch allied with the other European sovereigns of the time, in harmony with the King of Prussia and the Habsburg Emperor. The crisis of the paradigm of Russia as a European power was triggered by three events which occurred in a short period of time, from 1825 to 1830. The first was the Decembrist uprising of 14 December 1825, which forced Nicholas I (1825-1855) to ascend the throne with the anxiety of a sovereign who had just put down a Risorgimento-like insurrection. The threat had developed in the centre of the state, among the young officers of the regiments of the Imperial Guard stationed a short distance away from the Winter Palace. The second event was the Polish Revolution of 1830-1831, which took place in the most prestigious of the peripheral regions that had been annexed during the eighteenth-century period of expansion. Congress Poland had hitherto enjoyed the highest degree of autonomy that the Tsarist autocracy was prepared to grant to a province, to the point of tolerating the paradox of an aristocratic constitution in the years when Russian political thought, starting with Nikolay Karamzin's *Memoir on Ancient and Modern Russia* (1812), was beginning to associate the national identity with autocratic prerogatives. The third event also took place in 1830, but outside the boundaries of the state, in France, the cradle of the Enlightenment. The July Revolution shook the post-Napoleonic status quo and initiated a historical period in which Europe would appear in Russia, to intellectuals and sovereigns alike, in the guise of the two most important ideologies of its long nineteenth century: socialism and nationalism. The three events anticipated tendencies that would continue in western Europe, as well as in the centre of the Empire and on its periphery, as evinced in the pan-European revolution of 1848, the second Polish revolution of 1863 and the long period of the Russian revolutionary movement, which began to challenge the Tsarist state in 1859-1861. This phase of re-elaboration in the years 1825-1855 corresponded to a period of relative peace, when the impulse towards expansion was attenuated. The long Caucasian conflict may be interpreted as a defensive reinforcement of the southern border. It accompanied an attempt to consolidate the state and its institutions internally, from legislative codification to the reinforcement of bureaucracy.

The concept of Russian otherness with respect to Europe took shape in response to the demands of these real or perceived challenges. The despairing conclusion with which Pëtr Chaadayev noted the absence of an autochthonous Russian culture in the first of his *Philosophical Letters* (1836) appeared contemporaneously with the dismay with which Sergey Uvarov expounded for the first time, in a letter to Nicholas I in March 1832, the doctrine of official nationality. Uvarov spoke of "events of enormous importance" which had had "a baleful influence on the development of culture in our homeland", undermined the confidence of those who believed in "progress" and in the "future of the peoples", compelling Russians "to doubt ourselves". This premise supported the argument for the project of a "national and popular religion" (*narodnaya religiya*) to be inculcated from above, through the expansion of university education. The new official ideology was meant to give cohesion and a sense of collective identity to the subjects of a state which appeared dangerously "shaken in its political, moral and religious foundations".

The first authors to contrast Russia and Europe as civilisations based on qualitatively opposite principles were the theorists of this post-Enlightenment and post-Revolutionary monarchic ideology. In his *Historical Aphorisms* (1827) the court historian Mikhail Pogodin starkly contrasted a Europe which had grown through the logic of "conquest" and "revolution" with a Russian state genetically characterised by the different and superior principle of "voluntary submission" to power. The presupposition behind this official nationalism was a deeply pessimistic vision of Russian society – the idea of a "magnificent Russian people, but one that is still magnificent only in power" because "in practice it is vile, uncontrollable, brutish" without the disciplining power of autocracy.

The debate between the intellectuals, though limited to small circles devoid of political influence, arose in response to these stimuli. The Westernisers asserted the European nature of Russia to substantiate hopes of reform. Russia was an essentially European country, which had been temporarily diverted or obstructed in its development by certain historical factors: the retarding interval of the Mongol yoke or – according to the historico-geographical interpretation of Sergey Solovëv – the vastness of immense and not easily defensible spaces, which had slowed down the penetration of western civilisation and favoured the formation of a centralised and militarised power. Hegelian logic made it possible to reinterpret eighteenth-century absolutism, from Peter the Great onwards, as an intermediate phase in the historical dialectic, the precondition for a subsequent affirmation of conscious reason and law. Westernising historians such as Konstantin Kavelin would interpret the liberation of the peasants in 1861 as the next step in a sequence of emancipations from above which had begun with the abolition of compulsory state service for the nobility by Peter III in 1762, and which was to be followed by political and constitutional rights. The Europeanising perspective, however, did not guarantee a liberal or democratic outcome. In Westernisers such as the historian and jurist Boris Chicherin it translated into a different kind of support for autocratic prerogatives, summed up in the formula "strong power and liberal measures", only the first in a long series of metaphors subsequently used to legitimise the model of an authoritarian modernisation.

The alternative view of the Slavophiles did not question the principle of autocracy, which they accepted as the natural form of government for Russia. However, in their effort to emphasise the dignity of national culture with respect to western European culture they substantially modified the concept of "the Russian people". Unlike apologists of the monarchy such as Pogodin or Egor Kankrin, who had seriously suggested calling the state "Petrovia" to emphasise that the nation was a direct creation of the Tsar's, the Slavophiles stressed the existence of a culturally autonomous pre-Petrine society. They retrospectively constructed a national tradition identified with a religious civilisation, rather than with the person of the sovereign. The Slavophiles opposed any social-contract definition of the state. They rejected an artificially imposed "Petersburgian" rationality and contrasted it with the "Muscovite" concept of a people seen as an inherently harmonious, choral, Orthodox Christian world, a society capable of expressing values independent of the disciplining education of the Empire. The fiery Slavophile polemic did not necessarily express a rejection of modern industrial society. Aleksey Khomyakov appeared at the Great Exhibition of 1851 in London, a showcase for and celebration of positivist progress, with a project for a steam engine; and many Muscovite entrepreneurs of the mid-nineteenth century would also be Slavophiles. This vision fomented the view of a Russian people that was far from antimonarchical and yet neither "uncontrollable" nor "brutish", rather a collective entity capable of creativity and territorial expansion.

The Russian socialism founded by Alexander Herzen, which would become the antithesis of Tsarist monarchy, also originated as a response to the social and national revolutions of Europe, in this case through critical reflection on the events of 1848. He modified the Slavophile concept of an "Orthodox people" in an ethical and social direction. In the German writings of the Prussian conservative August Haxthausen he discovered the Russian peasant commune or *obshchina*, the model for the future state based on federal autonomy and on the democratic management of collective resources. After emigrating to London, Herzen often wrote in French for a cosmopolitan emigré readership. His socialism took on the meaning of a national ideology with messianic tones. It was a reply to those who spoke of the insignificance or inferiority of Russian civilisation and at the same time a declaration of faith in Russia's destiny of carrying a message of universal liberation. The Russians appeared capable, in the future, of overcoming the failed outcome of the revolution of Europe, "a decrepit old world", contrasted with the "savage, fresh energy ... of new peoples" (as he writes in *Epilogue of 1848*, published in 1849).

In the first revolutionary proclamation *To the Younger Generation*, circulated anonymously at the University of Petersburg in autumn 1861, Michail Mikhailov and Nikolay Shelgunov contrasted a metaphor for conformist European mediocrity ("little German gardens and woods") with the Russian determination to "divide our field ... as land was divided in antiquity, when there was room for everyone" – that is, in the *ager publicus* of the Roman republic. This variant of the idea of direct descent from classical greatness was often accompanied by a comparison with the youthful extra-European freshness of the United States. The Russian debate autonomously developed Tocqueville's parallel between Russia and America as peoples of the future. In his article *La Russie* (1849), in which he assessed the European revolution and delineated the populist political project, Herzen quoted Goethe's famous line *Amerika, du hast es besser*, and added immediately afterwards that this definition *s'applique fort bien à la Russie*.

4 European Colonialism or Eurasian Empire?

Autocratic ideology and westernising reformism, nationalism and socialism intersected with further expansion towards the east during the second half of the nineteenth century. Defeat in the Crimean War (1853-1856) intensified the awareness of needing to make up ground, and prompted a long period of reformist projects. During the same years the Tsarist state completed the pacification of Transcaucasia, annexed the vast regions of Ussuri and Amur in the Far East (1860) and penetrated into central Asia (1865). Although the Congress of Berlin (1878) thwarted its ambitions of Pan-Slavic and Balkan hegemony, in the east the Russian troops took control of Turkestan, with the protectorates of Samarkand and Bukhara (1885), reaching the edge of the territory conquered by Britain in Afghanistan. After the Boxer Rising in China (1900), the Tsarist Empire occupied part of Manchuria, while other expansionist projects during the First World War would target northern Persia, the southern coasts of the Black Sea and the Bosphorus. To what extent could these territorial acquisitions be described as the work of a great European state determined to participate in the conquest of extra-European colonies?

The geography of the annexed regions – beyond the Caucasus Mountains and the Hungry Steppe – made the identification with western colonialism to a certain extent plausible, and in many respects flattering. Functionaries and orientalists carefully studied the ways in which the French governed Muslim Algeria and the British had dealt with the Sepoy Mutiny in India. Just as the Slavophiles had discovered nationalism through Schelling, so the knowledge of the Russian East developed through the intellectual mediation of Carl Ritter's *Erdkunde*, published in Russian translation from 1856 onwards. European colonial literature, for example *De la colonisation chez les peuples modernes* by P.-P. Leroy-Beaulieu, published in 1874 (and in Russian translation in 1877), provided classifications useful for interpreting the recent acquisitions. The patriotic fervour that had inspired the emancipation of the serfs in 1861, a "scandalous" residue which prevented Russia from considering itself a modern and hence completely European nation, at the same time fostered the vision of a great civilising mission towards the East. After all, in the mid-nineteenth century every European power worthy of the name had, or was trying to acquire, colonies.

Nevertheless, Tsarist culture was always reluctant to adopt the colonial paradigm in its entirety. The history of European colonialism presented numerous secessionist movements which had met with varying degrees of success, from the increasing autonomy of the British dominions to independence movements in Latin America, not to mention the exemplary case of the American Revolution. The perspective of a Russian destiny in Asia developed at a time when the risk of secession was materialising in the Polish revolt of 1863 and in the contemporaneous Siberian autonomist movement. The awareness of a very limited capacity for governing the territory (in the mid-nineteenth century it was easier, starting from Petersburg, to reach New York than Vladivostok) was accompanied by an almost obsessive concern for the integrity of the state territory seen as a dynastic heritage. The autocratic principle inhibited the adoption of a metropolis-colony hierarchy which might foreshadow, albeit implicitly, future political fragmentation and the devolution of sovereignty. So it seemed inadvisable to describe Turkestan or the Amur region as Asian colonies. "We have no colonies", the Interior Minister declared peremptorily in the mid-1880s. The official language referred rather to an "incessant expansion of the Imperial Russian state" (in every direction) followed by the gradual "assimilation of regions near the border".

From the 1860s to Stolypin's reforms in the years 1906-1911 important sectors of the bureaucracy set themselves the task of overcoming the separateness of the peripheries in order to promote the cohesion of the state. They pursued in a wavering manner, and with uneven results, policies of demographic, linguistic and institutional assimilation, trying, for example, to replace the viceroyal authority of peripheral governors-general – a legal token of a state of temporary otherness – with administrative regions more similar to those of the European Russian centre. In the more enlightened exponents, such as the Finance Minister Nikolay Bunge, Asian policy was understood less as a Russification of territorial conquests than as the construction of a nation-empire through a process of mutual integration between Russians and non-Russians, on the basis of common laws and institutions. At the beginning of the twentieth century the idea that the hub of the state was shifting eastwards was already widespread. In 1905 an official commission chaired by Dmitry Mendeleyev calculated the "demographic centre" and the "geographical centre" of Russia, suggesting that the former, located near Tambov, south of Moscow, was destined to move progressively until it coincided with the latter, north of Omsk, in western Siberia.

Unofficial culture reinforced these views and began to blur the meaning of a cultural difference between European Russia and Asia. As late as 1893, Pëtr Semenov-Tyan Shansky described Russian colonisation as a "shifting of the ethnographic boundary of Europe towards the east", but this Westernising view was contested in many circles. Authors of different ideological persuasions challenged the parallel between the Tsarist conquests and European colonial expansion. In *Russia and Europe* (1869) Nikolay Danilevsky questioned the hitherto dominant eighteenth-century distinction between a European part and an Asian part of the state. He turned Tatishchev's Petrine geography on its head and denied the significance of the Urals as a boundary between continents. In this perspective Russia became the centre of a terrestrial mass, a unitary "natural region" with respect to which western Europe was reduced to the status of a promontory of Asia. Considered in this light, the eastward advance lost the character of a Europeanising conquest of foreign lands and became a natural, ambiguously internal process. Vladimir Lamansky systematised this view further in *Three Worlds of the Eurasian Continent* (1892), in which he argued for the existence of an intermediate Russian world radically distinct from both Europe and Asia, a single "homeland" which extended uninterruptedly eastwards too and was subject to a process of reappropriation rather than of external occupation. Socialist authors such as Sergey Yuzhakov developed the populist idea of the peasant as a vector of Russianness and analysed Russian penetration into the East on the basis of a "popular", communitarian principle, in contrast to British capitalist imperialism. The orientalist Esper Ukhtomsky, who was closely associated with Tsar Nicholas II, went further and argued for the Mongol origin of the Empire: the Tsar did not descend from Byzantium but from Genghis Khan, so Russia was bonded to the peoples of the East by the traits of cultural affinity, peaceful coexistence and respect for local traditions. Unlike the European states, which were anxious to plunder China, the Tsarist Empire acted on the world stage as a pre-eminently non-colonial power.

The theories of Russia's Asianness adapted certain traditional motifs of Tsarist monarchic ideology to the colonial context. The affirmation of the affinity between Russia and the East projected onto the politics of borders in Asia the principle of "voluntary submission" to power as a distinctive feature of Russia's difference from Europe. The idea of the subjects' spontaneous loyalty to the Tsar, developed under Nicholas I in opposition to the 1848 revolutions, was reframed in spatial terms and applied to the relationship between the Petersburg centre and the regions and peoples of the East. If the Russians were the heirs of the Golden Horde, to expand the state borders in Asia was to return home. In Ukhtomsky, for example, the theory of Mongol descent gave rise to the visionary project of a voluntary union between China and Russia, as related peoples, under the sceptre of the "white Tsar". In 1902 General Alekseyev cited similar arguments in the telegramme with which he recommended prolonging the occupation of Manchuria.

The Eurasian definition of Russia did not evolve into the notion of a civilisation surrounded by clear and accepted boundaries, whether national or multinational. The outer edge of this imagined cultural space remained open-ended and went well beyond the borders of the existing Imperial state. For the Pan-Slavist Lamansky the limits of the Russian world extended to much of eastern Europe, western Turkey and the Mediterranean coast of Syria. Uchtomsky thought that, proceeding beyond the Caspian and Lake Baikal, "we cannot find a clearly defined border … beyond which our rightful land ceases to be". This indeterminacy produced very concrete effects in the years of the Tsarist crisis: defeat in the war with Japan in 1904, partly a result of the Asian destiny cultivated in the preceding decades, had repercussions on the political stability of the centre, contributing to the outbreak of the 1905 revolution.

5 European Socialism, World Revolution and the Boundaries of Soviet Power

The spread of Marxism from the 1880s onwards may be considered a temporary Europeanisation of Russian socialism. Leaders of the revolutionary movement such as Plekhanov compared the polemic between populists and Marxists to a continuation of the debate between Westernism and Slavophilism. Adopting Marxist categories as a science of revolution implied treating the difference between Russia and the rest of Europe as a case of the former lagging behind in a process interspersed with common stages. Pëtr Struve interpreted this approach as a kind of Europeanising pedagogy: "let us acknowledge our backwardness and go to the school of capitalism" (*Critical Notes on the Economic Development of Russia*, 1894). To accept the theoretical guidance of Marx and Engels was to recognise the cultural hegemony of German social democracy, adopt its party name (the Russian Social Democratic Workers' Party of Lenin and Martov) and adhere to the Second International. In this context, pre-Marxist socialism came to be termed "populism" (*narodnichestvo*), with the pejorative connotation of a Romantic, peasant, provincial socialism, lacking an adequate theoretical consciousness. In reality, during those years socialists of neo-populist inspiration such as Viktor Chernov were seeking their own way of relating to the European identity. They posited the social and geographical typology of a peasant periphery within Europe which included Russia as well as such countries as Hungary and Italy, thereby making it possible for the Russians to think of themselves as a type of Europeans.

However, the adoption of a "monistic" conception of history (like that of Plekhanov) did not solve the dilemma of proletarian revolution in a still predominantly agrarian country. How could one think of building socialism in a peasant world that orthodox Marxism classified as "petit-bourgeois", a conservative social category and therefore an inevitably retarded space in European history? Lenin solved the problem with an intellectual operation which was in many ways a mirror image of that of Chernov but which, unlike the latter's theory, emphasised Russia's primacy in the world, not just in Europe. Instead of differentiating the capitalist centre from its agrarian peripheries he associated the future of Russia with the two greatest examples of modernity in the early twentieth century, Germany and the United States – forms of development summed up in the concepts of a "Prussian path" and an "American path" towards revolution. Rather than the more indirect "Prussian path" (involving a capitalist evolution of noble estates and a proletarianisation of peasants) he preferred the "American path" – a revolutionary departure that would eliminate all feudal remnants and give access to the landed resources of the imperial space, transforming the "semi-Asiatic" peasant into a modern farmer and a protagonist of history.

The notes on *Capitalism and Agriculture in the United States of America* (1915) summarised the logic of this interpretation. American modernity represented "a model. Ahead of everyone. Freer than everyone, etc. [...] Compare America with Russia, if land were given to the peasants." Thanks to this identification with the "revolution of farmers", the peasant *jacquerie* became a component of the democratic-bourgeois revolution. More than that, the future potential of Russia could be associated with the ideal type of the most advanced agriculture of the time, developed in the wide, extra-European spaces of the prairies. Lenin was to some extent inspired by Karl Kautsky's *Der amerikanische Arbeiter* (a series of articles translated in seven Russian editions with the title *The Russian Worker and the American Worker*), where the leader of German social democracy dealt with the "enigma" of the difference between Europe and America discussed by Werner Sombart, in *Warum gibt es in den Vereinigten Staaten keinen Sozialismus?* (1905). Struck by the radical nature of the Russian revolution of 1905, Kautsky represented Russia and America as two incomplete mirrors of the European future, characterised respectively by revolutionary vigour and the highest degree of development of capitalist productive rationality. Lenin adopted the triangular comparison between Germany-Europe, the United States and Russia, but subtly modified it to delineate a historical destiny which emphasised the central significance of Russia. He imagined the socialist revolution in the Tsar's peasant empire as an acceleration of history which would make it possible to bring the two extra-European halves together, realising the primacy of socialism and modernity simultaneously: not only "the soviet", then, but also "electrification", whose applications in the United States Lenin studied attentively.

The Bolshevik revolution was conceived in a worldwide perspective, rather than a European one. This influenced the representation of the future state and its geopolitical position, even before the creation of the Soviet Union. At the beginning of the First World War Lenin reflected on the future configuration of the states at the end of the conflict, taking into account the various revolutions which were then thought to be imminent or probable. He foresaw the dissolution of the empires of Austria, Germany and Russia, but refused to hypothesise, in place of them, the rise of a European federal republic, which would have entailed the sharing out of colonies in the rest of the world. Rather, he imagined the ultimate goal of a "United States of the world (not just of Europe)", preceded by a phase in which one or more socialist countries would clash with other countries which were still capitalist (*On the Slogan for a United States of Europe*, 1915).

The creation of the Soviet Union would link these representations of Russian centrality with the historical concreteness of a state, its diplomatic and military power as well as its borders. The Civil War (1918-1921) realised the reconquest of most of the post-Tsarist space, starting from the central nucleus of a territory not much larger than historical Muscovy and against the background of a very serious economic and social crisis and food shortages. The new Bolshevik elite succeeded in regaining control of the territory, except for the westernmost regions, defeating a series of alternative state-building projects of heterogeneous political types. In the peripheries that had eluded its control it encouraged, at various times, "proletarian" national insurrections and repressed hostile national movements, until in 1922 it took on the configuration of a federation of socialist republics, each with its own institutionalised borders but subject to the centralised hierarchy of the communist party.

The theory of "socialism in one country" acknowledged the failure of the hypothesis of post-war revolution in the major European countries and therefore the impossibility, at least in the immediate future, of a leading role for socialist Russia in a process of pan-European socialist construction. The change in direction imposed by Stalin from 1929 onwards was a response to the perception of the fragility, both internal and external, of a country which had emerged from the civil war suffering from the effects of significant economic regression. A state pursuing global ambitions had to cope with resources even more limited than those available to pre-revolutionary Russia. The collectivisation of the countryside and the Great Terror – the repression of real or potential dissident fifth columns – proceeded in parallel with accelerated industrialisation, pursued chiefly in preparation for another war. These were accompanied by the use of the communist international as an indirect tool of foreign policy, both in the European political context and in that of the anticolonial movements outside Europe. The dual prospect of a homeland of socialism and of a great power, associated more explicitly in the late 1930s with the patriotic symbols of Tsarist state greatness, was translated into the further expansion of state borders.

Alliance with Nazi Germany in the years 1939-1941 made possible the annexation of some territories of the former Tsarist empire that had been lost in the course of the revolutionary crisis. The Soviet state acquired Bessarabia, which became the Soviet republic of Moldavia, and northern Bukovina, which was linked with socialist Ukraine, along with eastern Galicia and Volhynia. It absorbed eastern Poland, which was absorbed into Soviet Belorussia, and the Baltic republics of Lithuania, Latvia and Estonia. Only unexpected resistance in the Winter War (1939-1940) prevented Finland from coming completely within the Soviet sphere of influence, though it lost part of Carelia. With a few minor variations, these outer boundaries emerged unchanged at the end of the Second World War, during which the Soviet Union defeated, at a colossal human cost, the Third Reich's plan to conquer and unify Europe.

Even after 1945, however, the political limit of sovereignty maintained a multiple and elusive geometry, a continuing indeterminacy between "inside" and "outside", between what what was one's own and what was of others, which is a constant feature of centuries of Russian history. This ambiguity derived not only from Russia's historical position midway between Europe and Asia, but particularly from the ideology of a state which found its *raison d'être* in the ambition to play a hegemonic role on the world stage, and therefore beyond Europe and beyond Asia. The triumphant Soviet Union was a predominantly Russian state directed by a Georgian leader (Iosif Dzhugashvili), and united with the numerous Soviet peoples by the party's supra-national identity. Its official ideology was inspired by two German authors, Marx and Engels, the study of whose works had become compulsory in all schools, even in the remotest villages of Central Asia and the Far East. Despite this indisputably European inspiration, the Soviet Union aimed to represent a model for the many new states that had emerged from the process of decolonisation in Asia, Africa and Latin America, an alternative on a global scale to the declining European powers and the growing North American superpower.

It was not at all clear where the actual boundaries of power of this further variant of the "Russian state" lay. The internationalist ideology aroused loyalty in communist parties all over the world and so made it possible to influence the internal politics of other states. There was an internal and official frontier of the Russian Federal Republic (which in its turn comprised numerous autonomous national republics), and a further frontier which separated, in the west, the Soviet Union and the East European popular democracies. Beyond that was the "outer empire", the additional space of an indirect but very concrete sovereignty which extended as far as the physical and political wall of Berlin. Other borders delimited about forty urban areas within the territory of the Soviet Union according to the criteria of security and political loyalty, because of sensitive military or industrial installations. One of these "closed cities" was Sevastopol, a powerful symbol of Russian patriotism in its different historical declinations. Soviet citizens, including residents' relatives, could only enter by means of a procedure comparable to a visa application for a foreign country. In any case, there was no question of Europe having "westernised" Russia. On the contrary, the Russian state had extended its ideological, political and military power over almost half the European continent.

Translated from the Italian by Jonathan Hunt

Bibliography

Bassin, M 1991, "Russia between Europe and Asia: the Ideological Construction of Geographical Space", *Slavic Review*, vol. 50, no.1, pp. 1-17.
Kappeler, A 2001, *Russland als Vielvölkerreich. Entstehung, Geschichte, Zerfall*, Beck, Munich.
Laruelle, M 1999, *L'idéologie eurasiste russe ou Comment penser l'empire*, l'Harmattan, Paris-Montréal.
Masoero, A 2000, "La funzione dell'esempio americano in Herzen e Černyševskij" in *Il pensiero sociale russo. Modelli stranieri e contesto nazionale*, eds A Masoero & A Venturi, F. Angeli, Milan, pp. 33-93.
Masoero, A 2013, "Territorial Colonization in Late Imperial Russia: Stages in the Development of a Concept", *Kritika: Explorations in Russian and Eurasian History*, vol. 14, no. 1, pp. 59-91.
Rossiya i Vostok 2000, eds SM Ivanova & BN Melnikhenko, Izd.vo S.-Peterburgskogo universiteta, St. Petersburg.
Schimmelpenninck van der Oye, D 2010, *Russian Orientalism. Asia in the Russian Mind from Peter the Great to the Emigration*, Yale University Press, New Haven.
Venturi, A 1997, "*Russko-italyanskaya model V.M. Chernova (1899-1902)*" in *Russkaya emigratsiya do 1917 goda - laboratoriya liberalnoy i revolyutsionnoy mysli*, Evropeysky Dom (Rossiyskaya Akademiya Nauk - Maison des sciences de l'homme), St. Petersburg, pp. 21-30.
Walicki, A 1973, *Una utopia conservatrice. Storia degli slavofili*, Einaudi, Turin.
Wortman, RS 1995, *Scenarios of Power: Myth and Ceremony in Russian Monarchy*, Princeton University Press, Princeton.
Zorin, A 2004, *Kormya dvuglavogo orla. Literatura i gosudarstvennaya ideologiya v Rossiy v posledney treti XVIII – pervoy treti XIX veka*, Novoe literaturnoe obozrenie, Moscow.

John H. Elliott
Europe and the Atlantic

1 Plus Ultra

Borrowing an idea from the Greek poet Pindar, Dante warns in his *Inferno* that men should not stray beyond – *più oltre* – the Pillars of Hercules. The narrow straits between the rock of Gibraltar and the coast of North Africa were traditionally seen as the western boundaries of Europe, beyond which lay the unnavigable ocean. In 1516 an Italian humanist invented a device for the young Charles of Ghent, now king of Spain and soon to be elected Holy Roman Emperor as the Emperor Charles V. In a direct contradiction of Dante's admonition the device showed the two pillars of Hercules entwined with a banderole bearing the Latin motto *Plus Ultra* - "further yet". When first invented, the image and the motto seem primarily to have been intended as a general statement of the infinite possibilities open to the young monarch for expanding his power and his dominions, but they soon came to acquire a specific geographical connotation inspired by a changing vision of the world.

This was not surprising. By the time of Charles's election as Emperor in 1519 Iberian mariners had moved far beyond the pillars of Hercules. The Portuguese had penetrated deep into the southern Atlantic, settling the uninhabited Azores from the 1430s and making their way down the West African coast and from there into the Indian Ocean. Down the African coastline they established occasional trading posts and fortresses, but these were no more than small European enclaves on the edge of a vast continent which would remain beyond the limits of European territorial occupation until the nineteenth century. The Castilians, for their part, had seized the Canary islands from the hands of their Guanche inhabitants, and it was from the Canaries that Columbus had launched out into the Atlantic in 1492 to find a new and inhabited world of Caribbean islands, and subsequently a mainland whose population would become, under the new dispensation, subjects of the monarchs of Castile and of Spain's expanding "empire of the Indies".

In the space of little more than half a century, therefore, Europeans had decisively broken the taboo of the pillars of Hercules and opened up an Atlantic world which, through conquest and colonisation, they would aspire to make their own. Their expansionist aspirations were by no means new, but hitherto they had primarily been directed eastwards, towards Asia and the world of Islam. Now, however, they were for the first time seriously directed westwards as well as eastwards, even if westwards expansion was initially driven by the desire to find an alternative route to the riches of Asia, take the Ottoman empire in the rear, and spread the Christian gospel round the globe.

In moving westwards, voyagers, conquerors and colonists became engaged in a centuries-long process of extending the geographical boundaries of Christendom and transforming the Atlantic into a European ocean. Once they possessed the necessary navigational and technical skills there was little to stand in their way. Neither the indigenous populations of western Africa nor those of the Americas possessed the capacity or the desire to organise large-scale overseas voyages for the purpose of acquiring new territory, discovering new markets, or propagating their own religious beliefs and value-systems. The only obstacles that confronted Europeans, other than the winds and the waves, were the challenges posed by environmental and climatic conditions to which they were unaccustomed, a possible insufficiency of domestic resources, and their own internal disputes. The resolution of these disputes would, from the beginning, generate new conflicts and lead to the imposition of new boundaries in place of the notional boundary formerly created by the pillars of Hercules.

2 Closed and Opened Seas

The first such disputes created by Atlantic expansion were those that arose in the late fifteenth century between the kingdom of Portugal and a newly united Spain over the possession of new-found islands and lands. Assuming the legitimacy of the overthrow of their indigenous rulers – a legitimacy open to question – to whom, for instance, did the Canary islands, claimed by both powers, belong? Both turned to the papacy as the traditional arbiter of intra-European disputes and the nominal regulator of relations between Christian and non-Christian peoples. In doing so, they sought to legitimise their overseas activities in terms of the obligation of Christian princes to assist the Church of Rome in bringing the faith to those who had either rejected or never heard of the Christian gospel. The papacy responded by drawing a vertical arbitration line down the Atlantic which would separate the respective zones of expansion to be allocated to the Spaniards and the Portuguese – a line subsequently redrawn by agreement between the two powers in the Treaty of Tordesillas of 1494.

If Tordesillas was an attempt to partition between the competing Iberian powers the Atlantic basin and its extensions, with a western zone reserved for the Spaniards and an eastern zone for the Portuguese, it was also an attempt, even more dubious, to turn an open sea into a *mare clausum*. In both instances, medieval European notions of borders and sovereignty, themselves still embryonic, were being imposed on non-European spaces and peoples. Since the restriction of navigation on the high seas flew in the face of doctrines of natural law about the right of humans to navigate and trade freely, it was problematic in theory and proved unenforceable in practice. In spite of this exercise of papal sovereignty it quickly became clear that the Atlantic was to become a European, rather than an exclusively Iberian, lake.

The allocation to the monarchs of Spain and Portugal of recently discovered lands and islands, together with those still to be discovered, proved equally controversial. What right had the papacy to carve up the world in this way? As Francis I of France famously remarked to the Imperial ambassador, he would like to see what was written in Adam's last will and testament. By then French traders had made numerous incursions into Brazil, still unknown to European voyagers when the Tordesillas demarcation line was agreed, and which unexpectedly proved to fall within the zone of expansion allocated to the Portuguese crown. By then, too, the Spaniards had acquired a vast American empire, following the conquest of Mexico and central America in the 1520s and Peru in the 1530s. The subsequent discovery of rich silver mines in both regions gave Spanish monarchs financial resources on a scale far beyond anything available to their European rivals, and helped make Spain the most formidable military power in Europe, and one well able to protect its silver-fleets and the American mainland from attack by its enemies.

In the long run, however, the policy of total exclusion adopted by the Iberian powers proved unsustainable. The silver and gold of the New World inevitably provoked a determination among the excluded to seize their share of the spoils. French and English attacks on Spanish transatlantic shipping were accompanied by attempts to secure bases in the Antilles from which to launch more effective raids on Spanish shipping and transatlantic ports and cities. These were followed by moves to imitate the Spanish example by founding colonies on those parts of the American mainland well away from areas settled by Spaniards and in outlying Caribbean islands that Spain was unable to protect. These colonising initiatives meant in effect the first real extension of Europe into North America, with the founding of the English settlement of Virginia in 1607, of French Quebec in 1608, and of the New England colonies in the 1620s and 1630s. The Dutch, having successfully achieved their independence from Spain, not only began moving into Portuguese Brazil in the 1620s and 1630s, but also established settlements on Manhattan Island, in the upper Hudson Valley and along the New Jersey shore.

Many of the first colonising attempts on the North American mainland proved abortive, but enough early settlements survived and prospered to encourage over the seventeenth and eighteenth centuries a mass migratory movement of

Europeans across the Atlantic. Between 1500 and 1800 one and a half million of them settled in the New World in pursuit of new lands and better lives. Under the pressure of new arrivals all the settlements, whether Iberian or north European, pushed the boundaries of Europe westwards, unleashing the prospect of almost unlimited further expansion of European dominion over new regions and peoples to the shores of the Pacific and beyond. In 1571 the Philippines became an extension of Spain's Mexican viceroyalty when a Spanish expeditionary force seized Manila. The occupation of the Philippines allowed the inhabitants of Mexico City to boast that it had become the centre of the world – a world that now seemed to have been created without boundaries as imperialist Europeans scrutinised their globes. Bishop Berkeley was doing no more than echo an old refrain when, in the 1730s, he composed his famous lines: "Westward the Course of Empire takes its way".

3 The Imposition of New Boundaries

The presence of European settlements and the imposition of European governance on large swathes of territory in the Americas and beyond do not, however, necessarily mean that Europe had automatically acquired an unlimited transatlantic extension of itself. The pillars of Hercules might have been transformed from a boundary into a passage, but in reality other boundaries, internal and external, would constrict Europe's transatlantic domains and hold back European control at numerous points. Many of these boundaries were physical, but others were of a more indefinable character, and proved still more difficult to transcend.

Some of the physical boundaries were created by topographical features, like the dense tropical forests of central and southern America, or the Appalachian Mountains, which for a time halted the westward movement of British and continental European settlers in the Carolinas, Virginia, Maryland and Pennsylvania. Other barriers, which often proved to be even more daunting, were created by the presence of hostile or unsubdued indigenous tribes and nations. Here the significant variations in the patterns of settlement adopted by the different European nations led to differing results. The Portuguese in Brazil stayed for a long time close to the Atlantic seaboard, and would only by degrees push their way into the vast Brazilian interior, crushing and enslaving Indian tribes that stood in their way and extending the agrarian frontier as they opened up the land for European-style development. The Spanish conquistadores, by contrast, fanned out across central and southern America, overcoming formidable logistical and topographical obstacles in their advance, founding towns and cities, and bringing often densely settled indigenous populations under Spanish rule. Spanish control over the indigenous communities was frequently more nominal than real, and in some areas, like the Yucatán of the Mayas, the inhabitants successfully held out for a long time against Spanish encroachments. Over vast areas, however, Spanish methods of conquest and settlement led to the effective incorporation of large populations into Spain's American empire.

The edges of that empire, on the other hand, saw the creation of boundaries, some more porous than others. Boundaries, after all, were points of contact as well as of conflict, and became zones of mutual influence that proved conducive to the mingling of peoples and cultures. In these areas hybrid societies developed, drawing both on European and non-European cultural practices and ways of behaviour. Some boundaries, however, were more impermeable than others. In Chile and northern Mexico the Spaniards came up against societies which they proved unable to subjugate by force of arms, and they had particular difficulty when facing the moving frontiers of nomadic peoples like the North American Comanches. These "barbarous" Indians remained a problem for the Spanish imperial authorities right through the eighteenth century.

Mainland North America, largely colonised by the English, the French and the Dutch, for long consisted of little more than a string of European settlements hugging the Atlantic seaboard, although French settlers, taking advantage of the St. Lawrence river, penetrated deeper into the interior than their British rivals, who lacked waterways that could carry them in inland. All were faced, however, by Indian tribes and polities, many of which proved to be formidable adversaries as the colonists sought to extend the areas of land under their control. As a result, even by the second half of the eighteenth century some two thirds of North America north of Mexico still remained outside European control. Borders between European and Indian territories were constantly shifting in response to pressures from one side or another, and there were large middle zones of mutual interaction which left even nominal borders ill-defined. When in 1763 the British imperial government sought to draw its famous "Proclamation Line", demarcating British and Indian territory in its bid to avoid antagonising the Indian nations of the interior, the line turned out to be little more than a cartographic fiction as waves of settlers continued to surge westwards in their eagerness to occupy new land.

New World frontiers, however, were not confined to physical barriers, or to imaginary lines drawn on maps. There were also more indefinable frontiers - frontiers of the mind, creating walls of separation between Europeans and non-Europeans. The non-Europeans included not only the indigenous peoples of the Americas, but also the black population of slaves imported in increasing numbers by

Europeans from Africa. They also included, at least in some degree, a growing population of people of mixed blood, straddling racial divides and never quite belonging to any of their ethnic groups of origin. All these, in European eyes, had somehow to be brought and kept within the fold of Christendom.

Medieval Christendom, threatened by the advance of Islam, not only saw itself as engaged in a great crusade to halt and throw back its Moslem enemies, but also as being divinely endowed with a mission to convert infidels and carry the Christian gospel to the ends of the earth. Although at the time of the overseas voyages Christendom was slowly evolving into a recognisably modern Europe, the sense of mission remained strong. It inspired the papal bulls of the fifteenth century that sought to regulate Iberian overseas expansion, and served to justify and give shape to the transatlantic activities of the Iberian colonising powers. Although the Protestant Reformation would involve the rejection of papal authority in many parts of Europe, the English and other Protestant peoples equally saw themselves as engaged in a divinely authorised enterprise as they embarked on the process of colonisation and responded in greater or lesser degree to the obligation to convert the native inhabitants of the lands into which they had moved.

Unlike the more secular and less centrally organised colonising activities of the Protestant peoples, the incorporation of American lands and their inhabitants into the Spanish and Portuguese empires was a combined church-state enterprise, with the religious orders driving forward the process of conversion and religious indoctrination. But as the friars came up against resistance or sheer incomprehension it quickly became apparent that religious instruction and baptism were not of themselves sufficient. Christianity, it transpired, had to go hand in hand with "civility". In other words, the indigenous peoples not only needed to absorb European belief-systems, but would also have to assimilate a whole range of European attitudes and values if they were to become true Christians whose conversion was more than skin-deep. This would involve, among other major changes, the abandonment of polygamy, the imposition of European notions of decency in questions of dress and undress, and also – although there was disagreement on this point – the adoption by indigenous peoples of the language of their conquerors, in view of the difficulty found by preachers in using native languages and vocabulary to convey even the fundamental points of Christian doctrine.

"Civility", therefore, meant the imposition of European norms on the non-European peoples of the Americas. This "civilising" process, first seriously undertaken in Spanish America, would eventually transmute into "the white man's burden" of the nineteenth and early twentieth centuries, the self-imposed mission of the great imperial powers to inculcate into the non-European peoples of the world European, and – in due course – western, values. Inevitably, even in its initial transatlantic manifestation, this proved an uphill task. Some European methods and activities were eagerly embraced, and there was much selective appropriation, particularly of those European products, animals and technology that could be seen as improving long-established native life-styles. But, especially where the rejection of traditional customs and beliefs was involved, there was also strong opposition, or, at best, superficial conformity with the new spiritual and cultural requirements. In effect, the indigenous peoples of the Americas set up internal barriers, which European belief-systems and cultural expectations could not easily transcend.

4 Frontiers of Inclusion and Exclusion

On the whole, in those areas where European domination became a reality on the ground, Spain's American empire was more successful in breaking down these barriers than the empires of other European powers. Spain's Atlantic enterprise was based on integrationist policies, designed to incorporate the large sedentary populations that came under its control within a capacious imperial fold, in which European and non-European communities had their own allotted space within what was conceived of as an organic society. The frontiers of that society, at least in intention, were frontiers of inclusion, whereas the English, after the failure of initial tentative efforts at incorporation, moved increasingly towards the creation of frontiers of exclusion. This involved marginalising the indigenous inhabitants and increasingly pushing them to the edges of the areas of European settlement and deeper into the interior. It involved, too, the adoption of segregationist policies, which created in British colonies new internal barriers defined by colour and race. Iberian America was by no means exempt from such internal divisions, but its racial complexities were greater, and the lines of demarcation correspondingly more fluid.

Such variations between the Iberian-American and Anglo-American societies had their roots in the variations of historical development and experience in their European homelands. Europe itself, after all, was far from being a homogenous society. Fragmented as it was into a plurality of polities and possessing a diversity of faiths, its colonisation of America was inevitably characterised by a similar diversity. The new colonial societies naturally expressed many of the features of the societies from which they sprang, thus giving British, French or Iberian America their own identities and their own religious, cultural and linguistic characteristics. These have lasted, although with local transmutations, from the moment of foundation until today.

Yet underlying all the diversity was a shared commonality which would make the New World of America distinctively, although by no means exclusively, "European". Over large areas of the New World the indigenous peoples of the conquered and colonised lands, along with millions of imported Africans, would participate, either voluntarily or, more frequently, under compulsion, in the building of the new societies. These societies, however, were built to a European design. Certain common features of European civilisation had impelled, and made, the Atlantic crossing and were quick to reassert themselves in the new American environment: the sense of mission, for example, based on a growing belief in the superiority of European values and ideals, or the urge to acquire territory and exploit the land and labour of others in the pursuit of riches and power. Dominion and subjection seemed to be built into the European genetic code, although so also, on the reverse side of the coin, was the belief in the existence of a higher, natural, law which decreed that all members of the human race, irrespective of race and creed, were entitled to enjoy certain fundamental rights.

At every point, however, the fragmented character of Europe impinged on the development of its transatlantic extension as a uniform European enterprise. Europe's inter-state and inter-faith rivalries were endemic, spurring competition and confrontation both on the high seas and in the western hemisphere as a whole. The desire for the acquisition of the precious metals produced by the American mines was, and remained, a bitter source of enmity, but as the newly colonised lands began to reveal their potential for adding to the wealth of the mother country through the production of tobacco, sugar and other commodities, so the urge to acquire more of the New World's land and resources intensified. This intensification in turn led to an intensification of conflict between the rival European powers, and to the organisation of what in effect were at once commercial as well as territorial empires, all of them aspiring to maximise the profitability of the mother country's Atlantic possessions. The colonial trades and the safety of their transatlantic shipping lanes became a major concern of imperial governments, while Dutch, British, and French traders, often acting in collusion with the local agents of empire, made concerted and increasingly successful efforts to breach the Iberian monopoly and penetrate the lucrative Hispano-American market.

Commercial and territorial rivalries in the Americas added fuel to the flames of international conflict. Wars that began in Europe were carried over with increasing frequency into the Caribbean and onto the American mainland, where local disputes along the frontiers of empire were subsumed into the wider struggle for European and Atlantic hegemony. The development of military and naval technology made possible the planning and organisation of campaigns that could be conducted thousands of miles from home, turning the entire Atlantic basin into a potential theatre of conflict. As a result, the North American continent became in the eighteenth century the setting for full-scale confrontation between the rival empires of Britain, France and Spain – a confrontation that, following their victory in the Seven Years War of 1756-1763, would see the British emerge as the dominant power in European North America, as large new areas of territory fell under British rule.

These international rivalries led to the imposition, or at least the attempted imposition, of European-style frontiers in the Americas as statesmen in the European capitals tried to draw demarcation lines on what were likely to be grossly inadequate maps. The Amazonian frontier regions separating the Spanish and Portuguese empires remained for a long period *terra incognita*, and the geography of most of the North American interior continued to be the subject of intense speculation and surmise into the nineteenth century. The drawing of frontiers, however, was not confined to attempts at imperial demarcation. The mainland British colonies engaged in endless boundary disputes with one another – disputes that would be carried over after the American Revolution into the newly created United States. Spain's enormous American empire, for its part, was divided into distinctive administrative and judicial units, although these did not prevent it, at least in the colonial period, from being articulated by personal, family and economic relationships that transcended regional distinctions and gave it a degree of internal coherence. With the coming of independence, however, and the fragmentation of the empire into eighteen embryonic nation-states, newly drawn boundaries, roughly based on those of the old administrative units, became acutely contested and gave rise to innumerable frontier disputes and to wars between neighbouring republics which had previously formed part of a single imperial complex.

The independence movements in Iberian and North America at the turn of the eighteenth and nineteenth centuries may to some extent, therefore, be seen as further evidence of the Europeanisation of the western hemisphere, in the sense that the Americas now replicated the European model of territorial and national division, and its consequent national rivalries. Territoriality and incipient nationalism bore witness to the closeness of the bonds linking Europe and the Americas – bonds that were tightened in the course of the eighteenth century as imperial governments took an increasingly close interest in the management of their transatlantic possessions and as tidal waves of European emigrants crossed the ocean, constantly replenishing in the process not only the original racial stock of settlers, but also the stock of European customs, ideas and practices on the farther shores of the Atlantic.

The transatlantic transfer of European culture was visible throughout the Americas. It was visible, for instance, in the careful imitation of European styles of art, architecture and the latest fashions in dress. The growing taste for classicism among eighteenth-century European elites was promptly replicated in American houses and furniture. A flourishing transatlantic book trade meant the speedy imitation of European literary styles and genres by American writers, and the emergence of an American reading public avid for the latest works of European authors. People and books kept colonial elites informed of changing European ideas about law, administration and the ordering of society; and as the Enlightenment of the eighteenth century spread through the Atlantic world, it introduced to the Americas fresh approaches to rational and scientific inquiry – approaches that would challenge and undermine traditional modes of thought and behaviour.

Yet the progressive Europeanisation of the colonial societies was paradoxically accompanied by a process that would lead them in the contrary direction - towards their progressive Americanisation. The tightening of some of the bonds between Europe and America went hand in hand with the loosening of others. It is possible to detect over the course of the eighteenth century a psychological distancing between increasingly mature "creole" societies and the Europe that had given birth to them. The creoles – white immigrants and their descendants – naturally developed over time an attachment to the lands they had made over in their own image, and pride in their own achievements and those of their forefathers. Moreover, in adapting to life in a non-European environment and to the presence of non-European peoples, they had developed their own distinctive forms of social behaviour. These, together with cultural and linguistic deviations from European norms, came to seem perfectly natural to them, but helped to make them appear somehow different in the eyes of newly arrived Europeans, who, as a result, tended to look down on them as being in some way inferior. Resentful of the slights to which Europeans were subjecting them, creoles in both Iberian and British America responded, while still turning to Europe for models to imitate, by beginning to think of themselves as "Americans" and treating the name "American" as a badge of honour.

5 Manifest Destiny?

A growing awareness of their distinctive American identity was one of the motivating forces behind the American Revolution and the Latin American wars of Independence. "European" and "American" were ceasing to be one and the same. The sheer fact of having fought for, and won, independence from their imperial masters gave the new sense of collective identity an assertiveness born of success in war. One expression of this was the enunciation of the Monroe Doctrine, which in effect signalled that the new United States was turning its back on the old Europe and claiming the western hemisphere as an all-American preserve.

Above all, however, the sense of collective identity was driven, as far as the United States was concerned, by its great continental thrust of the nineteenth century, as streams of settlers and new immigrants opened up the North American interior and pushed the new republic's frontiers relentlessly westwards until they reached the Pacific Ocean. In 1893 Frederick Jackson Turner, the great historian of the American frontier, would end his famous lecture on *The Significance of the Frontier in American History*, with the following words: "What the Mediterranean Sea was to the Greeks, breaking the bond of custom, offering new experiences, calling out new institutions and activities, that, and more, the ever retreating frontier has been to the United States directly, and to the nations of Europe more remotely. And now, four centuries from the discovery of America, at the end of a hundred years of life under the Constitution, the frontier has gone, and with its going has closed the first period of American history".

The effect of a century of westward expansion was to create through the Atlantic world an image of the United States as a land of unbounded opportunities, making it a magnet for millions of European immigrants in search of a better life. But it was not only in the United States that frontiers were being pushed forward. There were still vast unoccupied spaces in the southern regions of the hemisphere, and other great steams of emigrants, especially from southern Europe, joined the Atlantic migration to exploit the still unrealised opportunities offered by Latin America. It was the United States, however, that was the great success story of the nineteenth century, as a process of massive industrialisation accompanied and followed the process of continental expansion.

The sheer scale of its success in conquering the interior and forging a continental nation born of an unprecedented constitutional experiment encouraged a sense among the citizens of the United States of the uniqueness of their country as possessing a divinely ordained "manifest destiny". This sense of American exceptionalism set the United States apart not only from the rest of the Americas but also from Europe. Blithely ignoring the large African population in their midst, and the Native American peoples who were ruthlessly corralled into reservations as the frontier advanced inexorably westwards, its citizens had no difficulty in envisaging their country as preeminently the land of the free. The young republic, as a functioning democracy with a built-in system of rights, was in its own eyes a blessed land offering equal opportunities to all those willing to work – a land that allowed freedom of thought and expression to all its citizens, and one in which property was sacrosanct and the individual was master of his fate.

In reality these concepts had their roots in Europe, but in their North American manifestation they found uninhibited expression. As the frontier closed at the turn of the nineteenth and twentieth centuries, and the United States transformed itself into a great industrial power, its intensified nationalism had a double effect. The combination of newly assertive consciousness and economic muscle encouraged the development of imperialist pretensions, in the form of growing interventionism in hemispheric affairs, and a further westward expansion, this time far into the Pacific in the wake of the Spanish-American war of 1898. In effect the United States had now joined the ranks of the Great Powers, although it would long be reluctant to accept the implications of its newly acquired status. For the second, and contrary, result of the changes that came with the closing of Turner's "first American century" was to sharpen the cultural and psychological divisions between the United States and Europe, making the United States seem sufficient unto itself, and thus reinforcing its inherently isolationist instincts.

The Atlantic, however, was by now too small to make isolationism a permanent possibility, as became all too clear in 1917 when the United States was drawn into the First World War and found itself involved in sorting out the affairs of Europe. The involvement was both inspired by, and found its justification in, an idealism which saw it as America's destiny to bring into being a new world order that would end international conflict and in due course bring to all the peoples of the world the virtues of freedom, democracy and national self-determination that had made the United States the great nation it had become.

This first experiment in reordering the world would end in failure, but the guidelines had been laid down, and would be taken up by a new generation in the Second World War and its aftermath, as the balance between American isolationism and interventionism tilted one more in favour of the latter. The term "the West" seems for the first time to have been used in place of "European" in the late nineteenth century to describe the civilisation of Europe and the Americas in its totality. As the twentieth century proceeded, American and European values, which themselves were shared values even if with sometimes differing emphases, were gradually subsumed into a set of "western" values, which the United States and the free nations of post-war Europe joined forces to defend in a great transatlantic alliance, that would be institutionalised in the North Atlantic Treaty Organisation. Beneath the shelter of NATO's umbrella the Atlantic itself thus became the heart and centre of the free world, developing and promoting around the globe the principles of liberal democracy and open market economies.

The paradoxical effect of the various successes enjoyed by the "West" in the second half of the twentieth century was to reduce the centrality of the Atlantic to a world that was fast being globalised. There was, however, nothing very new about this decentralising process. Ever since the breaching of the pillars of Hercules the Atlantic had been a frontierless sea, from which Europeans had voyaged into the Indian and Pacific Oceans and made their way around the world. Spain's viceroyalty of Peru, bordering the Pacific Ocean, nevertheless became an integral part of the Atlantic world as Spanish fleets shipped the riches of its silver mines back to Europe. Its Mexican viceroyalty, while closely linked to the Iberian peninsula, simultaneously looked outwards across the Pacific to China and Japan. Freed of its traditional constraints by its conquest of the waters of the Atlantic, Renaissance Europe was poised to embark on what would prove an only partly successful endeavour to reshape the world in its image. As the twentieth century gave way to the twenty-first, there were strong indications that, after five centuries of mixed success and failure, the age of the European Atlantic was finally over, and that of the Pacific was about to begin.

Bibliography

Bailyn, B 2005, *Atlantic History. Concept and Contours*, Harvard University Press, Cambridge, Mass.
Billington, RA (ed.) 1961, *Frontier and Section. Selected Essays of Frederick Jackson Turner*, Prentice-Hall, Englewood Cliffs, N.J.
Canny, N & Morgan, P (eds) 2011, *The Oxford Handbook of the Atlantic World, 1450-1850*, Oxford University Press, Oxford.
Elliott, JH 1970, *The Old World and the New, 1492-1650*, Cambridge University Press, Cambridge.
Elliott, JH 2006, *Empires of the Atlantic World. Britain and Spain in America, 1492-1830*, Yale University Press, New Haven.
Gruzinski, S & Wachtel, N (eds) 1996, *Le Nouveau Monde. Mondes Nouveaux. L'expérience américaine*, École des Hautes Études en Sciences Sociales, Paris.
Headley, JM 2008, *The Europeanization of the World. On the Origins of Human Rights and Democracy*, Princeton University Press, Princeton.
Meinig, DW 1986, *The Shaping of America: Vol.1 Atlantic America, 1492-1800*, Yale University Press, New Haven.
Pagden, A 2001, *Peoples and Empires. Europeans and the Rest of the World from Antiquity to the Present*, Weidenfeld and Nicolson, London.
Tracy, JD (ed.) 1990, *The Rise of Merchant Empires. Long-Distance Trade in the Early Modern World*, Cambridge University Press, Cambridge.
Weber, DJ 1992, *The Spanish Frontier in North America*, Yale University Press, New Haven.

Massimo L. Salvadori
L'Europeizzazione del mondo e il suo declino

1 La sovrastante potenza dell'Europa e la combinazione dei suoi fattori

Quando si guarda a Roma nel periodo compreso tra la fine delle guerre puniche e la morte di Costantino - nel corso del quale essa andò affermando tutta la sua potenza, che la mise in grado di conquistare in misura sempre maggiore, assoggettare e ordinare quello che ai suoi occhi era tout court il mondo - è dato vedere come i fattori di questa potenza, che le conferì una posizione di forte superiorità rispetto ai soggetti politici, sociali e istituzionali con i quali Roma entrò gradualmente in urto, costituissero un *unicum*, un qualcosa senza riscontri nella scena geopolitica formata dai territori compresi nell'impero. Questo *unicum* era la combinazione di una cultura politica e giuridica, di un'architettura istituzionale che dal centro si articolava a livello delle province, di un governo disciplinatore sia delle parti sociali collocate nel nucleo dominante sia delle molteplici popolazioni organizzate gerarchicamente all'interno dell'impero in espansione, di un alto livello di capacità produttiva e di conoscenze tecnologiche, di strutture militari dotate di una efficacia offensiva e difensiva in grado di garantire un'incontrastata supremazia, di una efficiente rete di comunicazioni intese a favorire gli scambi commerciali e la dislocazione delle forze armate preposte ad assicurare la difesa all'interno dell'ordine costituito, la protezione dei confini e la loro dilatazione. Questo fu dunque il convergere di fattori che rese possibile la romanizzazione del mondo antico in Occidente fino alla sua crisi e poi al crollo definitivo.

Quella "combinazione di potenza" che aveva caratterizzato Roma dominatrice scomparve nella sua forma piena dalla scena del Vecchio continente per oltre mille anni. Essa si protrasse o si riprodusse, ma in una maniera soltanto parziale in ambiti territoriali limitati, nell'impero bizantino, nell'impero islamico dell'epoca d'oro, nell'impero ottomano, in Persia, nell'India del Gran Mogol: imponenti costruzioni politiche e istituzionali, dotate bensì di capacità di dominio, di forza ordinatrice e anche di un dinamismo espansionistico di grandissimo vigore, tutte però prive della forza risolutiva che aveva consentito a Roma di acquisire – ecco il punto – un incontrastato monopolio di potenza. Neppure l'impero cinese poté sostenere il paragone, a causa delle ondate di gravissime turbolenze e divisioni interne, delle ricorrenti convulsioni intestine, della lotta delle etnie per la prevalenza, dei conflitti tra le dinastie.

La combinazione tornò a riproporsi in Europa tra il Settecento e la seconda metà dell'Ottocento in una forma - rispetto al modello romano – per un verso assai simile, per l'altro assai differente: anzi del tutto contrastante. La somiglianza era data dai molteplici e importanti elementi di unità; il contrasto da una frammentazione di Stati che si accompagnava a continue guerre intestine.

Come Roma, anche l'Europa aveva acquistato una forte identità che ne segnava la diversità rispetto al resto del mondo. Essa era caratterizzata nel suo caso specifico dalla comune matrice cristiana, seppure dilaniata dalle contrapposizioni tra cattolici, protestanti e ortodossi; da una cultura politica, giuridica, letteraria e scientifica che, al di là delle molteplicità e diversità delle sue correnti ed espressioni, costituiva un patrimonio comune delle sue élites; da forti istituzioni statali; da un'economia in espansione cui il processo di industrializzazione a partire dagli ultimi decenni del XVIII secolo impresse un crescente dinamismo; da progressi senza eguali nel campo del sapere scientifico e delle applicazioni tecnologiche; da una sovrastante potenza dei suoi apparati militari rispetto al resto del globo. Furono questi gli elementi che permisero all'Europa di acquisire una superiorità a mano a mano maggiore nei confronti dei grandi imperi ottomano e asiatici, che tra Cinque e Seicento erano ancora stati in grado di contrastare quella superiorità. E fu quest'ultima che consentì all'Europa di dare - dopo il primo grande ma pur sempre parziale "assalto" in direzione degli altri continenti a iniziare dalla fine del Quattrocento con la conquista delle Americhe - un rinnovato e ancor più vigoroso assalto al resto del mondo e di imporre quella che venne chiamata la sua "centralità", destinata a durare sino alla prima guerra mondiale. Occorre però notare che tale centralità mostrò i primi segni di significativo indebolimento nella seconda metà del XIX secolo in conseguenza del rapido rafforzamento economico e politico degli Stati Uniti e degli inizi della modernizzazione istituzionale e militare del Giappone.

Ne *Lo spirito delle leggi* Montesquieu espresse compiutamente la coscienza che gli europei avevano maturato della propria posizione dominante. Due affermazioni riescono in proposito particolarmente illuminanti: l'una riguarda la posizione acquisita dal Vecchio continente nel mondo, l'altra quella tenuta da alcuni paesi nel continente stesso. Montesquieu prima scrive che "l'Europa ha raggiunto un grado così elevato di potenza da non trovar riscontro nella storia"; poi, con riferimento specifico agli indici probanti di maggior dinamismo al suo stesso interno, nota che, se "l'Europa svolge il commercio e i traffici marittimi delle altre tre parti del mondo", Francia, Inghilterra e Olanda "svolgono quasi tutto il commercio e la navigazione dell'Europa". Egli offriva così una chiave decisiva per comprendere per un verso le caratteristiche più generali del rapporto tra l'Europa e il resto del mondo e per l'altro la gerarchia stabilitasi in campo economico tra i paesi in prima fila e quelli in seconda o terza fila. Un altro elemento che contribuiva a conferire all'Europa la sua netta superiorità Montesquieu lo individua negli effetti della rivoluzione scientifica che, con radici riconducibili al Quattro-Cinquecento, era andata dispiegandosi con vigore crescente a partire dal Seicento. In una delle *Lettere persiane* egli fa dire allo stupito Usbek che in Europa vi sono filosofi che "seguono in silenzio le tracce della ragione umana" e che non vi è da credere "fino a dove li ha condotti questa guida. Essi hanno decifrato il Caos, e con una semplice meccanica hanno spiegato l'ordine dell'architettura divina".

Fu anche Voltaire nel *Saggio sui costumi e lo spirito delle nazioni* a sottolineare come il convergere di cultura e progressi scientifici e tecnologici avessero conferito all'Europa strumenti di potere quali non si erano mai avuti in epoche precedenti e non si davano in altre zone del mondo. Ma la notazione in lui più tipica fu l'insistere, come si vede bene ne *Il secolo di Luigi XIV*, sul fatto che "nonostante le guerre, e nonostante le diversità di religione", era andata stabilendosi una "repubblica letteraria", una "grande società degli spiriti" che legava gli intellettuali mediante un comune linguaggio culturale e civile. Si trattava di un *Leitmotiv* condiviso, al di là di tutte le loro personali diatribe, da Rousseau; tanto che il primo poteva affermare che l'Europa era unita dagli "stessi principi politici e di diritto pubblico e di politica; ignoti nelle altre parti del mondo" e il secondo che in Europa era venuta costituendosi una "società di popoli", la quale univa in un "sistema" operante "attraverso la stessa religione, il medesimo diritto delle genti, i costumi, le lettere, il commercio, e mediante una sorta di equilibrio che è la conseguenza necessaria di tutto ciò".

All'incirca un secolo dopo, un altro grande intellettuale, l'inglese John Stuart Mill, nel suo celebre saggio *Sulla libertà* rifletteva - in un'epoca ormai pienamente investita dagli effetti del processo di industrializzazione che aveva più che mai il suo centro propulsore nel Vecchio continente – su "che cosa ha reso le nazioni europee un settore dell'umanità che si evolve e non resta statico" e quindi sulla loro "superiorità - che, quando esiste, è un effetto e non una causa –". A spiegazione, faceva riferimento alla mancanza di uniformità, all'affermarsi di una molteplicità di caratteri e di correnti culturali, alla capacità di praticare "una gran quantità di vie", allo sperimentalismo, tal che "i tentativi reciproci di impedir il progresso altrui hanno raramente avuto un successo definitivo, e a lungo andare tutti hanno avuto la possibilità di recepire i risultati positivi altrui". La conclusione suonava: "l'Europa deve a questa pluralità di percorsi tutto il suo sviluppo progressivo e multiforme". Al che però Mill faceva seguire la significativa considerazione che occorreva domandarsi fino a quando essa sarebbe stata in condizione di godere di questa "dote".

2 Il culmine della "centralità" europea tra Sette e Ottocento

Voltaire e Rousseau parlarono di un'unità culturale e civile che era andata affermandosi in Europa nonostante le sue divisioni interne, i contrasti politici e religiosi e le guerre. Orbene, chi guardi alla storia del continente tra la fine del Quattrocento e l'Ottocento non fa fatica a vedere come, in contrasto con quegli elementi di unità, essa fu segnata da ricorrenti ondate di violenze messe in atto dai maggiori Stati europei, che, dotati di imponenti apparati militari, tentarono, singolarmente o con la loro rete di alleanze, di assumere - nella forma sia del dominio diretto sia dell'egemonia - una posizione di primato: tentativi tutti infine falliti dopo successi solo parziali e temporanei. Giusto quindi il detto di Kant che le paci raggiunte tra le potenze europee, dando una sostanza precaria ai periodi di "equilibrio" da queste convenuti, risultavano unicamente "tregue" tra una guerra e l'altra. I più consistenti tentativi di stabilire il predominio nel periodo sopra indicato furono in successione quelli nella seconda metà del Cinquecento di Filippo II, nella prima metà del Seicento degli Asburgo d'Austria e di Spagna, a cavallo tra Sei e Settecento di Luigi XIV, a cavallo tra Sette e Ottocento della Francia rivoluzionaria e napoleonica; tentativi cui seguì infine nella seconda metà del XIX secolo quello culminato negli scontri della Germania bismarckiana prima con l'Austria e poi con la Francia di Napoleone III conclusisi con l'emergere della prima a maggiore potenza dell'Europa continentale. In questo quadro la Gran Bretagna - che, resa straordinariamente forte a partire dalla rivoluzione industriale di cui fu il centro irradiatore e il nucleo più vigoroso, con l'effetto di consentirle uno sviluppo commerciale e industriale senza confronti per circa un secolo - tenne costantemente parte a sé. Essa era tesa a preservare e a difendersi dalle invasioni esterne, a far valere tutto il peso della sua incontrastata prevalenza navale, a spostare la propria forza nei conflitti tra gli Stati europei avendo quale fine costante di impedire che nell'Europea continentale l'intento di questa o di quella potenza di acquisire il predominio assumesse il carattere di una duratura stabilità.

La storia d'Europa a partire da quelli che si considerano gli inizi dell'età moderna era stata la storia di grandi guerre tra le maggiori potenze, che avevano messo in sempre maggiore evidenza la crescente efficienza dei rispettivi apparati bellici. Sennonché nei secoli XVI e XVII questa efficienza non aveva ancora raggiunto nei confronti degli eserciti terrestri e delle flotte dell'impero ottomano e degli imperi asiatici un grado di incomparabilità: che venne invece raggiunta in maniera via via più accelerata nel corso del secolo XVIII. Fu allora che la bilancia a livello mondiale andò irresistibilmente pendendo a favore della maggiori potenze europee, le quali - dopo che Spagna e Portogallo erano entrate in una fase di crescente decadenza - si erano ridotte a quattro: la Gran Bretagna, la Francia, l'Austria e la Russia, la quale ultima era entrata nel concerto dei grandi Stati del continente grazie al processo di modernizzazione energicamente avviato da Pietro. Ad affacciarsi al loro fianco, era salita, ma ancora in una posizione di relativa minorità, la Prussia. Sennonché nel cerchio più ampio delle potenze europee era andato nettamente delineandosi un nucleo più ristretto. Il quale era composto da Gran Bretagna e Francia, i due paesi più sviluppati economicamente e più forti militarmente, i quali congiuntamente ma in maniera concorrenziale nella seconda metà del secolo diedero un fortissimo impulso - con il concorso secondario ma significativo della Russia e quello certo non trascurabile di altri Stati europei - a quello che si può definire l' "assalto al mondo". Procedevano così parallelamente i conflitti di potenza all'interno dell'Europa e la congiunta lotta per l'assoggettamento, nella duplice specie dell'acquisizione di influenza e della conquista, di parti crescenti dei continenti extraeuropei. Ora l'impulso all'europeizzazione del mondo conobbe una vigorosa accelerazione, nella forma del moderno imperialismo-colonialismo, che, mentre mostrava appunto la comune matrice europea, era messo in atto dai grandi Stati rivali. Venivano esportati e imposti - secondo le caratteristiche tipiche di ciascuna potenza - culture politiche, istituzioni giuridiche, apparati burocratici e modalità organizzative, tecniche produttive, merci, anche costumi, e stabilite le élites dominanti a cui era affidato il compito di esercitare il potere e il controllo sui territori assoggettati. Può dirsi che le frontiere dell'Europa, superando quelle propriamente geografiche, andarono via via allargandosi alle parti del mondo in cui questa estendeva la propria influenza nei suoi molteplici aspetti.

La "centralità" europea raggiunse il suo culmine tra la seconda metà del XVIII secolo e la prima metà del XIX. Allora essa fu piena e incontrastabile, dopo di che si protrasse ancora per poco più di sessant'anni; ma - come si è già osservato - vide però levarsi contro la sua superiorità a Occidente la potenza produttiva degli Stati Uniti, divenuti agli inizi del Novecento la maggiore singola economia a livello mondiale e a Oriente il "risveglio" del Giappone: potenza degli uni e risveglio dell'altro entrambi - si badi - tributari dell'influenza dell'Europa e dell'importanza dei rapporti con essa, ma anche espressioni della volontà di mettere ormai in discussione una supremazia che non poteva più essere quella di un tempo. Gli Stati Uniti erano per molteplici e determinanti aspetti figli dell'Europa, che aveva loro trasmesso cultura, essenziali punti di riferimento politici e istituzionali cui ispirarsi e con i quali confrontarsi, scienza e tecnologia; e sotto questo aspetto la loro storia costituiva un capitolo significativo dell' "europeizzazione del mondo". Ma al tempo stesso fin dalle origini del loro costituirsi in Unione, del formarsi delle loro istituzioni politiche e sociali e della elaborazione di un loro proprio "spirito nazionale", si erano posti su posizioni persino aspramente critiche nei confronti della "madre Europa". Si pensi in proposito al dibattito sulla Costituzione e in particolare agli articoli di Hamilton e di Madison nei *Federalist Papers*, dove la madre appariva per molti versi come un contromodello e una "matrigna": che intendeva dominare il mondo, imporre i propri interessi su quelli altrui, che, nella varietà delle scene offerte dai suoi molti paesi, dava deplorevoli esempi di regimi dispotici, di avversione ai principi di libertà degli individui e delle collettività, di abissali iniquità economiche e sociali, di rigide barriere di classe, di guerre tra le opposte parti della società e tra gli Stati. Lo spirito degli americani fu sin dalle origini quello di figli ribelli, che - specie dopo la guerra civile che ne rinsaldò fortemente il vincolo unitario - diedero vita ad una comunità capace sia di una crescente autonomia dall'Europa sia di dotarsi di una cultura dai tratti originali sia di intraprendere la strada di un accelerato sviluppo economico che affiancava un apparato industriale in espansione ad una possente agricoltura sia di diventare la terra pronta ad accogliere milioni di poveri e migliaia di rifugiati politici desiderosi di fuggire dalla durezze del Vecchio mondo. Fu così che gli americani giunsero a concepire, mediante un processo di rovesciamento, un senso di decisa superiorità non solo più morale ma ormai anche materiale nei confronti di quello.

Pressoché in parallelo corse il risveglio del Giappone, il paese che nella prima metà del XIX secolo dovette far fronte, seppure in forme meno umilianti e drammatiche della Cina, alle pretese e ingiunzioni per un verso di russi, inglesi e olandesi e per l'altro degli americani. Furono in particolare questi ultimi, arrivati nel 1846 e soprattutto nel 1853 con le loro navi, a umiliare maggiormente i giapponesi, a renderli consapevoli della loro incapacità di resistere. Il che li indusse, per reazione, ad avviare quel processo di modernizzazione economica, istituzionale e militare che nel giro di meno di quarant'anni li avrebbe messi in grado di sconfiggere nella guerra del 1904-1905 la Russia. Fu però ancora un segno del prestigio e dell'influenza dell'Europa il fatto che il governo imperiale nipponico, per apprendere le vie della propria modernizzazione e formare i quadri ad essa necessari, si rivolgesse alla Gran Bretagna, alla Francia e alla nuova Germania. Ma segno dei tempi era che gli apprendisti andassero a scuola dei loro insegnanti europei per sottrarsi quanto più rapidamente possibile alle imposizioni dei bianchi del Vecchio Mondo (e anche del Nuovo). La potenza ormai dispiegata e destinata ad una sempre maggiore ascesa degli Stati Uniti e del Giappone costituì la testimonianza dell'inizio della crisi della centralità di quell'Europa che per circa due secoli si era eretta a padrona del globo e largamente lo era stata: centralità che sarebbe letteralmente naufragata nel 1914-1918, quando apparve che sì nel corso del suo predominio essa aveva diffuso al di là dei propri confini cultura, istituzioni, scienza e tecnica, ma contemporaneamente aveva insegnato ad altri paesi come impadronirsi della potenza che aveva a lungo costituito un monopolio europeo e come da ultimo spezzarla, ponendo così fine all' "europeizzazione del mondo".

3 Tappe dell'ascesa e del declino della centralità dell'Europa nel mondo moderno

Punto decisivo della fase ascendente della centralità dell'Europa nel mondo moderno fu costituito dalla cosiddetta "Guerra dei sette anni", che, dispiegatasi tra il 1756 e il 1763, ebbe il carattere di un grande conflitto combattuto sia all'interno del Vecchio continente sia nelle Americhe sia in Asia. Essa mostrò appieno come la potenza europea si manifestasse al tempo stesso nelle guerre tra i suoi Stati e nella spinta espansionistica esterna di cui furono allora protagoniste la Gran Bretagna e la Francia; e a quale grado di forza e di efficienza fossero giunte le macchine belliche europee, le uniche ormai capaci di confrontarsi reciprocamente. Si trattava di una superiorità che sarebbe stata ulteriormente ed enormemente accresciuta dagli effetti della rivoluzione industriale. La Guerra dei sette anni fu quella che si può definire propriamente la prima guerra mondiale dell'età moderna, in quanto combattuta su tre continenti. Le sue conseguenze più importanti furono da un lato il riconoscimento e il consolidamento della Prussia quale nuova potenza europea e dall'altro la posizione preponderante acquistata in campo coloniale dalla Gran Bretagna, che distrusse l'impero francese nell'America settentrionale ed eliminò le posizioni acquisite della Francia in India, dove consolidò un'autorità destinata ad estendersi e a affermarsi sempre più ampiamente e profondamente. Sicché tanto nell'America del Nord quanto in India l'europeizzazione assunse il volto di una "europeizzazione inglese".

Occorre a questo punto notare che il fenomeno di enorme portata che definiamo europeizzazione del mondo ebbe per un verso un volto bensì unitario in relazione ai tratti comuni che la civiltà europea nelle sue componenti presentava, ma per l'altro verso quello impresso nel loro rapporto con le altre parti del mondo dalle molteplici specificità giuridiche, economiche, culturali, ideologiche e anche religiose dei singoli Stati colonialistici e imperialistici. Nel periodo in cui l'Europa nel suo insieme fece valere al massimo la sua potenza e la sua centralità, si ebbe quindi una pluralità di "europeizzazioni": al primo posto vi fu l'inglese, al secondo la francese, seguite da quella olandese e belga, per limitarci a segnalare le maggiori. Sotto questo profilo nel Sette-Ottocento queste europeizzazioni si posero in continuità con quelle di cui nei secoli precedenti erano state la spagnola e la portoghese.

Si è detto che la più importante delle molteplici europeizzazioni fu l'inglese. E infatti essa si dispiegò in tutti i continenti extraeuropei nella forme vuoi dell'assoggettamento diretto, vuoi delle formazioni giuridiche e politiche che sarebbero culminate nel *Commonwealth* basato su principi di relativa autonomia, vuoi dell'egemonia stabilita su Stati sottoposti alla sua influenza politica ed economica. Fu un processo che portò alla creazione di un gigantesco impero che per ampiezza territoriale e profondità della penetrazione non aveva precedenti nella storia. Di peso grandissimo fu anche l'europeizzazione francese, che si estese anch'essa - con una progressiva accelerazione nel secolo XIX a partire dalla conquista dell'Algeria nel 1830 - in tutti i continenti extraeuropei; mettendo in evidenza la prevalente volontà di assimilazione diretta dei territori d'oltremare nell'ambito della "più grande Francia".

È un dato acquisito che aspetto comune, seppure manifestato in gradi diversi, della centralità dell'Europa fu la costruzione dell'ideologia della superiorità degli europei; che, ancora una volta, aveva i suoi precedenti nei più vecchi imperi di Spagna e Portogallo. In essa, intesa a dare una legittimazione ai vari atti di conquista, all'esercizio del dominio e al diritto degli europei a fare valere la loro guida sui popoli "inferiori" del mondo, si intrecciavano, obbedendo sia a convinzioni sia a intenti meramente strumentali, morale, religione, diritto, pseudoscienza. Il razzismo costituì l'espressione più cruda e vistosa di quella costruzione.

Bisogna d'altra parte sottolineare che l'europeizzazione del mondo non si espresse unicamente con il colonialismo e l'imperialismo, con la conquista territoriale, il duro e persino crudele assoggettamento dei popoli giudicati inferiori. Essa ebbe altresì aspetti che possiamo senza esitazioni definire "progressisti". Fu dall'Europa che gli altri continenti presero le più avanzate conoscenze scientifiche e le tecnologie prodotte dalla rivoluzione industriale e dai suoi sviluppi. Può dirsi che il treno e la nave a vapore furono forse i maggiori simboli dell'europeizzazione modernizzatrice del mondo. Dal Vecchio continente vennero anche le grandi correnti culturali, i modelli istituzionali e politici e i miti ideologici che diventarono patrimoni importanti e decisivi per la formazione delle élites degli altri continenti. Dall'Europa si diffusero nelle altre parti del globo, con effetti suscettibili di diverso giudizio, illuminismo, idealismo, positivismo, materialismo storico, liberalismo oligarchico-conservatore e liberalismo democratico, nazionalismo democratico e nazionalismo autoritario, neocesarismo, socialismo e comunismo.

Si sono già sottolineate, a proposito del rapporto tra questa e il resto del mondo, l'importanza e l'originalità del caso degli Stati Uniti. La nascita degli Stati Uniti venne salutata da numerosi intellettuali e ideologi europei come una sorta di nuovo inizio del mondo e come annuncio di una libertà destinata a uscire dai loro confini. La celebrarono con toni entusiastici grandi poeti come Byron,

Shelley e Goethe, che si trovarono concordi nell'esaltare la giovinezza prometeica degli americani rispetto alla vecchiezza degli europei. Ma più dense di intelligenza storica furono le considerazioni di un Hegel e di un Cousin; il primo dei quali nelle *Lezioni sulla filosofia della storia*, tenute tra il 1821 e il 1831, parlò dell'America come del "paese dell'avvenire", e il secondo nella *Introduzione alla storia della filosofia* del 1845 di un potente soggetto emergente candidato a raccogliere la successione dell'Europa. Dal canto suo Tocqueville nella prima parte de *La democrazia in America*, pubblicata nel 1835, in un passo celeberrimo - prefigurando un'Europa (il riferimento era palesemente all'Europa ad occidente della Russia) ancora padrona della terra ma destinata ad andare incontro a un processo di decadenza - profetizzava l'ascesa parallela dei russi e degli americani, che "entrambi sembrano chiamati da un disegno segreto della Provvidenza a tenere un giorno nelle loro mani i destini di metà del mondo", servendosi gli uni dei mezzi offerti dalla servitù e gli altri di quelli della libertà. Fu Tocqueville a diffondere nella cultura europea quest'idea della futura grandezza del colosso americano e di quello russo. Ma essa non era di per sé originale. La troviamo, ad esempio, già nettamente formulata nelle parole dello slavofilo russo Kireevskij, il quale nel 1829 contrapponeva alla corrodente vecchiezza dell'Europa occidentale il futuro di grandezza che attendeva l'America e la Russia, i cui popoli erano "giovani e non logorati".

Quando vennero avanzate, le previsioni e profezie degli Hegel, dei Cousin, Kireevskij e Tocqueville apparivano ed erano, in relazione allo stato delle cose, mere ipotesi, frutti dell'immaginazione. Erano al tempo stesso testimonianze, seppure ancora assai minoritarie, della consapevolezza - in palese e netta controcorrente rispetto al senso di una intangibile sicurezza nella superiorità dell'Europa la quale continuava a caratterizzare il pensiero e i sentimenti prevalenti delle sue élites intellettuali e politiche - che il primato dello stesso nucleo costituito dai paesi più vigorosi e dinamici del Vecchio continente doveva essere visto alla luce dei cicli che avevano e avrebbero scandito la storia universale. Come si è detto, quelle erano ancora ipotesi, immaginazioni; e infatti la centralità dell'Europa e la sua capacità di influenza e di dominio nel mondo non avevano allora neppure raggiunto l'apice. Questo venne infatti toccato nel ventennio tra gli anni Cinquanta e Ottanta dell'Ottocento dall'Europa capitalistica e borghese, postasi alla testa di un processo di modernizzazione economica che non aveva eguali, dotata di una potenza finanziaria, di apparati industriali, di una rete di comunicazioni e capace di una penetrazione commerciale senza pari: una superiorità che fece da impulso ad una ulteriore fase della conquista e della colonizzazione di nuovi immensi territori. Le Esposizioni universali di Londra del 1851 e di Parigi del 1855 e del 1889 furono le grandiose vetrine della persistente superiorità europea, pur prossima in quest'ultima data ad essere ormai sfidata in campo economico dall'impetuosa ascesa degli Stati Uniti.

4 Crisi e crollo della centralità europea

La spinta espansionistica che portò le potenze europee negli ultimi decenni che precedettero il 1914 a dilatare ulteriormente, e sovente in reciproco contrasto, le frontiere di imperi già immensi fu insieme lo specchio da un lato della loro persistente comune potenza e dall'altro delle loro debolezze e fratture; le quali si sarebbero pienamente dispiegate, rivelandosi catastrofiche, durante la prima guerra mondiale e nel dopoguerra. Il periodo di pace intercorso tra la guerra franco-prussiana e l'inizio del grande conflitto aveva solo malamente mascherato le fratture. Infatti, la tregua durata poco meno di mezzo secolo aveva visto il riaccendersi della rivalità tra la Francia e la Germania unificata; il balzo in avanti di quest'ultima trasformatasi con una crescente intensità in un paese industriale in grado di sfidare e superare la Gran Bretagna per capacità di organizzazione dei fattori produttivi, modernità degli impianti e dinamismo commerciale, e di costruire la più efficiente e possente macchina militare del mondo; il consolidarsi infine degli schieramenti formati per un verso dalla Triplice Intesa tra Gran Bretagna, Francia e Russia e per l'altro dalla Triplice Alleanza fra Germania, Austria e Italia. L'esito fu prima l'esplosione delle antitesi e poi il crollo della centralità europea. Il fatto del tutto nuovo fu che - mentre nel corso dell'età moderna l'Europa era stata bensì la sede di grandi guerre intestine susseguitesi in continue ondate, ma queste non avevano mai messo in discussione la sua complessiva superiore potenza economica, tecnologica e militare, che era andata anzi costantemente aumentando, costituendo il presupposto dell'europeizzazione del mondo - ora si arrivò alla fine di quel ciclo storico.

La crisi della centralità europea aveva avuto, come si è già avuto modo di ricordare, le sue eloquenti avvisaglie nella vertiginosa ascesa economica degli Stati Uniti e in quella parallela del Giappone, dotatosi, oltre che di un ragguardevole apparato produttivo, anche di possenti forze armate e nel fatto che entrambi i paesi erano entrati con slancio sulla scena delle contese imperialistiche. Ciò nonostante, prima del 1914 quella crisi si presentava pure sempre relativa, in quanto il Vecchio continente continuava a concentrare nell'insieme delle sue componenti la maggiore forza industriale, una soverchiante superiorità militare e il possesso o il controllo di sterminati territori extraeuropei. Ma, e questo costituiva un punto cruciale, a differenza che nei secoli precedenti, esso non era più in grado di comunicare al mondo esterno quell'impulso che abbiamo chiamato "progressista" costituito dall'espandersi della sua più avanzata cultura, della sua scienza e della sua tecnologia. Sempre maggiori zone del mondo esterno si erano rese e andavano rendendosi capaci di sviluppare risorse proprie.

Un tale profondo cambiamento non veniva ancora percepito nella sua importanza e nelle sue potenziali implicazioni dalle classi dirigenti dei maggiori Stati del Vecchio continente, rimaste chiuse in un inamovibile e arrogante senso di superiorità e rassicurate da una soverchiante potenza militare, ritenuta una invalicabile barriera da parte del resto del mondo. Tra gli intellettuali che per contro mostravano a quel punto piena coscienza dell'approssimarsi di una svolta epocale si trovava in prima fila Georges Sorel, il quale, quando ormai l'Europa andava correndo verso l'immane conflitto, affermò che un'intera stagione della sua storia si era chiusa, in quanto essa non aveva più nulla di grande da dare al resto del mondo e che - scriveva – "una sola idea unisce l'Europa" ovvero: "l'idea della guerra".

Gli avvenimenti svoltisi in Europa nel corso della prima guerra mondiale tra il 1914 e il 1918 mostrarono, come se al vaso di Pandora che li racchiudeva fosse stato improvvisamente tolto il coperchio, tutte le divisioni e tutti i contrasti che erano andati maturando nel Vecchio continente, opponendo tra loro gli Stati e le nazionalità, le classi, gli schieramenti politici, le ideologie e i sentimenti. Nel crogiolo incandescente del conflitto, gli ultimi residui dell'originaria idea illuministica e prima ancora erasmiana della repubblica degli spiriti europei venne sepolta da una spaventosa, mai vista carneficina, dalle macerie materiali che distrussero l'economia del continente, in un contesto di odi furiosi condivisi dalle masse popolari e dalle élites culturali - al cui interno i celebratori della *Kultur* si contrapposero a quelli della *Civilisation* - e di scatenamento di una lotta senza quartiere dei nazionalisti imperialisti e autoritari contro i nazionalisti democratici e gli internazionalisti, dei socialisti fautori dell'abbattimento dello Stato borghese contro sia i socialisti moderati sia i liberali e sia i reazionari, dei movimenti anticapitalistici contro i difensori del capitalismo. Nell'apocalisse che produsse la sua autodistruzione l'Europa gettò nella grande fornace tutte le risorse umane, economiche e militari che aveva accumulato nel quarantennio della pace.

La fine della guerra ebbe conseguenze di portata storica universale. La più evidente di tutte fu il crollo definitivo della centralità europea. Infatti, la guerra spezzò irrimediabilmente quel moto ascendente dell'Europa che, iniziato nel XV secolo, venne ora drasticamente interrotto.

Nel corso della guerra si produssero cinque avvenimenti cruciali, il cui significato deve essere colto nei loro nessi reciproci. Il primo, il più clamoroso e simbolico, fu il fatto senza precedenti - si trattò del canto del cigno perverso della centralità dell'Europa - che le grandi potenze europee le quali avevano dato inizio al grande conflitto non erano state in grado di finirlo. Perché finisse, e in un certo modo, fu necessario che intervenissero nel 1917 gli Stati Uniti, erettisi a grande potenza oltre che economica anche militare. Fu infatti il loro apporto dapprima economico e finanziario e in seguito direttamente militare che soltanto consentì agli avversari degli Imperi centrali di resistere e infine di vincere. A esprimere la coscienza della svolta epocale erano le eloquenti parole indirizzate ai suoi compatrioti nel settembre 1919 dal presidente Wilson, con le quali rivendicava l'avvento di un nuovo primato: quello americano: "Nel volto dell'America si rispecchia il futuro e, miei concittadini, nel progetto dell'America si rispecchia il futuro del mondo". Era un modo per affermare chiaramente che il ruolo preponderante esercitato dai vecchi "lupi" europei negli affari internazionali apparteneva al passato.

Il secondo avvenimento fu il messaggio rivoluzionario universalistico lanciato da Lenin nel corso della guerra prima e dopo la presa del potere da parte dei bolscevichi in Russia nell'ottobre 1917, secondo il quale la vecchia Europa, in un quadro contraddistinto dal prorompere sulla scena di nuovi soggetti statali, nazionali, politici e sociali, era destinata a perdere il ruolo che aveva occupato in passato nella scena del mondo. Si era giunti al termine del secolare ciclo storico fondato sul primato nel mondo delle maggiori potenze europee e dei loro imperi, al quale andava sostituendosi quello della rivoluzione sociale e anticoloniale internazionale. Componente essenziale del discorso di Lenin era l'appello ai popoli coloniali, semicoloniali o comunque ancora soggetti agli Stati europei, alla rivolta contro i loro dominatori, invitati a unirsi a quella degli eredi di Spartaco che vivevano nei paesi più avanzati oppressi dallo sfruttamento capitalistico. Tanto Wilson quanto Lenin, pur da opposti punti di vista, convergevano nel registrare che la multisecolare centralità dell'Europa e quindi l'europeizzazione del mondo era andata incontro ad un crollo senza ritorno.

Il terzo avvenimento che nel dopoguerra fece da spia al crollo della centralità del Vecchio continente fu la distruzione della potenza della Germania, il cui impetuoso sviluppo economico, scientifico, tecnologico e militare era stato il dato più significativo della storia europea nel quarantennio precedente il 1914: potenza che agli inizi del secolo XX - quando pure gli Stati Uniti erano ormai ascesi al vertice della gerarchia mondiale in quanto più forte paese industriale - collocava quel paese, divenuto a sua volta il maggiore paese industriale in Europa, al primo piano nel mondo per l'eccellenza della sua macchina produttiva e per la capacità di far interagire organizzazione del lavoro, scienza e tecnologia. La "pace cartaginese" imposta da inglesi e francesi ai tedeschi nel 1919 costituì la tragica testimonianza che l'Europa, travolta dai suoi incomponibili conflitti intestini, brancolava in uno stato di completa cecità nella considerazione del proprio futuro: cecità manifestata dalla determinazione di Gran Bretagna e ancor più della Francia - vincitrici per interposta persona – di strangolare definitivamente la Germania. Quale fosse lo spirito dominante dei capi francesi e inglesi, su cui gravava principalmente il compito della difficilissima rimozione delle macerie che seppellivano il continente, lo espresse con parole di fuoco indirizzate a Clemenceau e a Lloyd George Keynes nel suo celebre saggio *Le conseguenze economiche della pace*: "La vita futura dell'Europa non li riguardava; i suoi mezzi di sopravvivenza non davano loro alcuna ansietà. Le loro preoccupazioni, buone e cattive ad un tempo, si riferivano alle frontiere e alle nazionalità, all'equilibrio delle forze, agli ingrandimenti imperialistici, al futuro indebolimento di un nemico forte e pericoloso, alla vendetta e a riversare dalle spalle dei vincitori su quelle dei vinti gli insostenibili pesi finanziari".

Il quarto avvenimento fu il crollo dell'impero zarista cui fece seguito l'ascesa al potere dei bolscevichi in Russia e il disfacimento dell'impero multinazionale austro-ungarico. Il primo ebbe l'effetto di scatenare dagli Urali alle coste dell'Atlantico una guerra ideologica, politica e sociale che per la violenza delle contrapposizioni aveva precedenti comparabili unicamente nelle guerre civili e religiose causate dalla Riforma protestante e nello scontro tra la Francia rivoluzionaria e napoleonica e il variegato e contraddittorio schieramento degli Stati ad essa ostili. La differenza era che quelle contrapposizioni e quei conflitti, pur tanto laceranti, avevano approdato alla ridefinizione e all'assestamento di nuovi rapporti all'interno di un'Europa che dal regolamento dei contrasti epocali scatenatisi nelle epoche della Riforma e Controriforma e della gigantesca lotta tra la Grande Nazione e i suoi nemici non vide messe in discussione le proprie energie complessive e quindi anche la sua capacità di dare un sempre maggiore impulso al processo di europeizzazione del mondo. Per contro la violenta contrapposizione tra il comunismo posto al servizio degli interessi del nuovo Stato sovietico e l'Europa capitalistica e borghese - scoppiata con estrema virulenza proprio in un dopoguerra in cui a occidente di Mosca si dispiegava il grande disordine generato dalle irragionevoli imposizioni delle potenze vincitrici alle potenze vinte - costituì un ulteriore dirompente fattore e segnale che la centralità dell'Europa era giunta alla sua fase terminale. Sennonché la coscienza troppo spesso non è in grado di rispecchiare la realtà dei fatti: la Gran Bretagna e la Francia - in ciò rafforzate dalla scelta degli Stati Uniti di tornare all'isolazionismo e confortate e compiaciute nelle loro ambizioni imperialistiche in particolare dalla posizioni recentemente acquisite in Medio Oriente per effetto del dissolvimento dell'impero ottomano - ritennero di poter ancora erigersi a rappresentanti e tutrici di una centralità europea divenuta nei fatti ormai del tutto illusoria.

Il quinto elemento che stava a testimoniare del chiudersi della parabola che aveva visto l'Europa esercitare il ruolo preponderante nelle vicende del mondo era riconducibile al posto occupato sulla scena mondiale dagli Stati Uniti e dal Giappone. Non si trattava più, come a cavallo tra Otto e Novecento, di un iniziale moto ascendente, bensì di potenze consolidate in grado di strappare al Vecchio continente quello che alla vigilia della grande guerra era stato l'ultimo suo monopolio: l'assoluta superiorità militare.

Della portata degli sconvolgimenti avvenuti espresse piena consapevolezza nel 1923 il conte austriaco Coudenhove-Kalergi, che, ardente fautore di una ricostruzione federalistica dell'Europa, con uno spirito al contempo realistico e utopistico, osservava: "Oggi l'Europa non è più il centro della terra (...) Il mondo si è emancipato dall'Europa. (...) Può l'Europa nella sua frammentazione politica ed economica mantenere la sua pace e la sua indipendenza di fronte alle crescenti potenze mondiali extra-europee o essa è costretta, per conservare la propria esistenza, ad organizzarsi in federazione di Stati?".

5 Il tentativo dell' "Attila moderno" e la definitiva "esplosione" dell'Europa

Il decennio seguente la pace di Versailles fu un periodo di relativa ripresa dell'Europa, assestatasi però su basi che si sarebbero rivelate assai precarie; poi sopravvenne lo sconvolgimento economico provocato dalla grande crisi che, partita nel 1929 dagli Stati Uniti, dilagò anche nel Vecchio continente con esiti devastanti. Gli anni della relativa ripresa avevano avuto due principali fondamenti: costituiti l'uno dalla preponderanza delle due potenze vincitrici, la Gran Bretagna e la Francia, e dalla capacità del capitalismo continentale di resistere all'assalto rivoluzionario guidato da Mosca rimasta infine isolata, dove Stalin aveva imposto una politica di raccoglimento nazionale; l'altro, dopo il caos economico del 1923, dalla ricostruzione dell'apparato industriale della Germania grazie al piano di investimenti americani varato nel 1924, che consentì al paese di raggiungere per alcuni anni una certa stabilità politica e istituzionale.

Quale fosse tutta l'importanza dello spostamento del centro dell'economia mondiale dal Vecchio al Nuovo Mondo fu mostrato dalla crisi del 1929. Il che in effetti era già pienamente emerso durante la guerra. Solo infatti in virtù dell'aiuto finanziario e delle forniture di mezzi prima e in seguito dell'intervento militare diretto degli Stati Uniti, Gran Bretagna, Francia e Italia erano riuscite ad aver ragione della Germania e dell'Austria-Ungheria; e sempre solo in virtù di rinnovati aiuti e del vigoroso moto ascendente che negli anni Venti aveva caratterizzato l'economia americana - giunta a detenere verso la fine del decennio oltre il 40 per cento della produzione industriale mondiale - il continente aveva potuto risalire la china. La crisi partita da Wall Street e subito dilagata in Europa fu la prova del nove, questa volta in chiave negativa, che il benessere o il malessere europeo dipendevano direttamente dallo stato di salute degli Stati Uniti.

Nei dieci anni che precedettero lo scoppio della seconda guerra mondiale quello che era parso un barlume di ordine europeo - l'ordine imposti dai paesi risultati vincitori nel 1918 - andò gradualmente logorandosi fino a anche nel settembre 1939 non si giunse alla vera e propria deflagrazione dell'Europa. La Germania era stata il paese più drammaticamente investito dalle conseguenze della crisi partita dall'America. La faticosamente raggiunta stabilità politica e istituzionale andò in frantumi. I partiti comunista e nazionalsocialista – nemici giurati l'uno dell'altro ma uniti dall'odio verso la repubblica nata a Weimar nel 1919, che, nonostante la loro aggressività, erano rimasti modeste minoranze in termini di consenso popolare e di rappresentanza parlamentare – dopo il 1929 andarono vertiginosamente crescendo, così da indebolire sempre più socialdemocratici, cattolici del Centro e liberaldemocratici, fino a che i nazisti guidati da Hitler, preso il sopravvento insieme sui comunisti e sui sostenitori delle istituzioni democratiche e parlamentari, nel gennaio 1933 non ascesero al potere, allargando le frontiere del fascismo internazionale, tenuto a battesimo in Italia da Mussolini nel 1922, e più in generale dei regimi autoritari che a mano a mano erano andati dilagando e sarebbero ancora dilagati nel continente. Nei sei anni che seguirono la presa del potere da parte di Hitler in Germania, la mappa geopolitica dell'Europa fu caratterizzata: dalla rapida e forte ripresa della potenza industriale e militare tedesca e dall'avvicinamento via via più stretto dell'Italia alla Germania, dalla esplicitata volontà di quest'ultima di mettere in radicale discussione mediante una politica aggressiva gli equilibri frutto della pace del 1919; dalla debolezza nei suoi confronti da parte di Gran Bretagna e Francia; dal processo di modernizzazione industriale e militare dell'Unione Sovietica, uscita in misura rilevante dalla posizione di precedente debolezza e assurta a soggetto di primo piano della politica internazionale. L'Europa fu così divisa in tre centri dominanti: quello nazi-fascista guidato da Germania e Italia e animato da intenti aggressivi ed espansionistici, quello democratico rappresentato da Gran Bretagna e Francia segnato da non secondarie differenze e da una palese arrendevolezza in politica estera, e quello costituito dall'Unione Sovietica, la quale, oltre che sull'accresciuta forza dello Stato, poteva contare sull'appoggio dei partiti comunisti europei, seppure, con l'unica rilevante eccezione del Partito comunista francese, questi fossero deboli o persino ridotti a entità marginali, perseguitati quando non cancellati dalla scena politica. L'idea e la presunzione della superiorità era tornata con tragica forza in Europa ad opera del nazionalsocialismo, sia nel razzismo che proclamava il diritto al predominio degli ariani e perseguiva l'oppressione tanto della nemica "razza ebraica", di cui auspicava l'annientamento, quanto di tutte le razze e popolazioni "inferiori" che intendeva ridurre a uno stato di soggezione semischiavistica (il veleno razzistico trovò un terreno fertile di diffusione in Francia, in Polonia, in altri paesi dell'Est - dove aveva radici antiche - e nell'Italia fascista che nel 1938 adottò leggi razziali), sia nella convinzione propria di Hitler e dei suoi seguaci di poter riaffermare nel mondo la centralità dell'Europa mediante i successi della potenza tedesca.

L'Europa aveva accumulato un potenziale esplosivo tale per cui, quando fosse stata accesa la miccia, essa sarebbe diventata, per la seconda volta nel Novecento e in un grado molto maggiore, un cumulo di macerie. La miccia venne accesa nel settembre 1939 con l'aggressione alla Polonia da parte della Germania e la sua spartizione tra questa e l'Unione Sovietica. La guerra civile spagnola - allargatasi ad affare internazionale - aveva poco prima già documentato a qual punto fossero arrivati i contrasti intereuropei. È altamente significativo che ai tempi delle sue iniziali folgoranti vittorie militari la Germania nazista ritenne che esse ponessero le basi del ritorno, cui sopra si è accennato, alla centralità dell'Europa nel mondo. Questo sogno era nutrito dall'idea che si potesse costruire l'alleanza planetaria tra le razze superiori di cui gli ariani erano chiamati a costituire il fondamento sotto la guida di un'Europa rigenerata da "un ordine nuovo" - avente come presupposto la distruzione dell'Unione Sovietica e la riduzione degli slavi a popolo servo - alla testa del quale doveva esservi il Terzo Reich millenario. Fu questo il tentativo di unificazione dell'Europa e di rilancio del suo primato messo in atto da Hitler, che Einaudi con un'espressione pregnante avrebbe poi definito "l'Attila moderno".

Il suo fallimento provocò da un lato la drammatica "esplosione" dell'Europa, che si trovò nel 1945 in uno stato di devastazione materiale e sociale senza precedenti, dall'altro lo spostamento dello scettro della forza nelle mani del colosso americano e di quello euro-asiatico. Il fatto che ancora una volta, come già nel 1918, la Gran Bretagna e la Francia - questa disastrosamente sconfitta nel 1940 dalla Germania - si fossero trovate dalla parte dei vincitori non nascondeva il significato della loro definitiva retrocessione a potenze di secondo rango, entrate nella sfera di influenza della superpotenza occidentale e incapaci di difendersi dalla superpotenza orientale se non ponendosi sotto l'ombrello protettivo statunitense. Altro segno del crollo europeo fu che la ricostruzione economica dei paesi rimasti nell'area capitalistica fu resa possibile, in misura ancora più determinante di quanto non fosse avvenuto dopo il 1918, unicamente dall'aiuto americano. Infine, a sanzionare il declino del continente che per secoli aveva avuto saldamente nelle proprie mani le chiavi della potenza politica, economica e militare fu la doppia divisione che oppose per quasi mezzo secolo l' "Europa americana" all' "Europa sovietica" e la Germania occidentale alla Germania orientale. I paesi europei non erano più padroni dei loro destini.

La condizione di subalternità cui era giunta l'Europa era riassumibile nei seguenti punti: 1) come già nel 1914, nel 1939 suo perverso privilegio era stato di aver scatenato il conflitto mondiale, ma di essere stata ancora una volta incapace in grado di risolverlo; 2) a differenza della prima guerra mondiale, che aveva pur sempre lasciato Gran Bretagna e Francia nella posizione di potenze di primo livello, la seconda eliminò qualsiasi Stato integralmente europeo dai vertici del potere mondiale; 3) la forza necessaria per dare - comunque fosse - un ordine al globo divenne prerogativa degli Stati Uniti e dell'Unione Sovietica; 4) alla tradizionale rivalità fra gli Stati europei, alle loro alleanze e schieramenti contrapposti si sostituì la subordinazione dell'Europe divisa alle due superpotenze: subordinazione che volle dire per gli europei occidentali cadere sotto l'egemonia americana e per gli orientali subire un dominio totalitario.

In tal modo, con la soggezione dell'Europa resa "provincia" per una parte di una potenza extraeuropea e per l'altra di una potenza euroasiatica, si chiudeva un'epoca della storia. Nel 1945 si profilò non solo la definitiva cancellazione di quelli che ancora potevano apparire gli ultimi quanto mai parziali residui della centralità un tempo esercitata dal Vecchio continente, ma anche la perdita, più o meno radicale a seconda dei vari paesi, delle componenti fondamentali alla base della sovranità degli Stati ovvero il potere di decidere in maniera pienamente autonoma delle proprie istituzioni, delle strategie in materia economica, della politica estera, delle alleanze militari. Nel corso del quarantennio della "guerra fredda" che oppose l'Occidente capitalistico all'Oriente comunista, questa perdita accomunò entrambe le due Europe, come reso platealmente evidente dal fatto che le chiavi della guerra e della pace - elemento tanto cruciale del potere sovrano - vennero del tutto sottratte a ciascuna di esse, diventando prerogativa dei due Stati erettisi a dominatori del mondo. Tant'è che la pace interna di cui finalmente godette il Vecchio continente non fu opera degli europei stessi ma effetto degli equilibri stabiliti dalle superpotenze, le quali imposero loro margini di decisione, favorirono certi tipi di regime, ne promossero e dettarono altri, propagandarono e diffusero le loro ideologie nel quadro dei confliggenti processi di "americanizzazione" e di "sovietizzazione". La fine poi degli imperi coloniali europei dopo il 1945, accompagnata da fallimentari tentativi di mantenerne almeno i residui e da guerre crudeli e ingloriose, volle altresì dire che le frontiere dell'Europa, un tempo tanto allargatesi all'esterno mediante il processo di "europeizzazione de mondo", tornarono a rinchiudersi entro i suoi confini propriamente geografici.

Bibliografia

Bairoch, P 1997, *Victoires et déboires. Histoire économique et sociale du monde du XVI siècle à nos jours*, Gallimard, Paris.
Bracher, KD 1982, *Zeit der Ideologien*, Deutsche Verlags-Anstalt GmbH, Stuttgart.
Dehio, L 1948, Gleichgewicht oder Hegemonie, Scherpe-Verlag, Krefeld.
Fuller, JFC 1961, *The conduct of war 1789-1961*, Eyre Methuen, London.
Galasso, G 2001, *Storia d'Europa*, Laterza, Roma-Bari.
Hughes, HS 1958, *Consciousness and Society. The Reorientation of European Social Thought*, Harvard University Press, Cambridge.
Judt, T 2005, *Postwar. A History of Europe Since 1945*, Penguin Press, New York.
Kennedy, P 1987, *The Rise and Fall of the Great Powers*, Random House, New York.
Landes, DS 1998, *The Wealth and Poverty of Nations*, Norton, New York.
Rossi, P 2007, *L'identità dell'Europa*, il Mulino, Bologna.
Salvadori, ML 1990, *Storia dell'età moderna e contemporanea*, Loescher, Torino.
Salvadori, ML 2001, "Ascesa e crisi della centralità dell'Europa", in *La storia. I Grandi problemi dell'Età Contemporanea. 5*, eds N Tranfaglia & M Firpo, Garzanti, Milano.
Silvestri, M 1977, *La decadenza dell'Europa occidentale, 1890-1939, 3 voll.*, Einaudi, Torino.
Villani, P 1983, *Trionfo e crollo del predominio europeo*, il Mulino, Bologna.

Massimo L. Salvadori
The Europeanisation of the World: Its Rise and Decline

1 The Dominant Power of Europe and the Combination of the Factors that Caused It

When we consider Rome in the period from the end of the Punic wars to the death of Constantine, when it was establishing the power which enabled it to conquer, subjugate and organise what in its eyes constituted the world, we see that the basis of that power – what gave it a position of overwhelming superiority with respect to the political, social and institutional bodies with which it came into conflict – was something unparalleled in the geopolitical scene formed by the territories of the empire. That unparalleled factor was a combination of various elements: a political and legal culture; a system of government based on a division into provinces; an administration which controlled both the social groups in the central nucleus and the many peoples hierarchically organised within the expanding empire; high productivity and technological expertise; armed forces with offensive and defensive capabilities that could guarantee complete supremacy; an efficient network of communications that facilitated trade and the deployment of the armed forces to maintain internal order and protect and extend the borders. This combination of elements underlay the Romanisation of the ancient world in the West until its decline and eventual dissolution.

After that, this "combination of power" which had characterised ancient Rome, in its full form, disappeared from Europe for more than a thousand years. It persisted, or reappeared, in partial forms, in some particular areas – the Byzantine empire, the Islamic empire during the golden age, the Ottoman empire, Persia, and India under the Great Mogul. Although all these great political structures had the capacity for control, organisation and expansion, however, they lacked the decisive strength which had made it possible for Rome to gain an unassailable monopoly on power. Not even the Chinese empire bore comparison, for it was beset by recurrent episodes of turbulence and internal divisions, internecine warfare, a struggle for predominance between ethnic groups, and conflicts between dynasties.

That same combination of factors reappeared in Europe, however, from the eighteenth century to the second half of the nineteenth century, in a form which was in one respect very similar to the Roman model, but in another very different from it, indeed the exact opposite. The similarity lay in its many important elements of unity; the difference lay in the fragmentation of its states and its frequent internal wars.

Like Rome, Europe had acquired a strong identity which distinguished it from the rest of the world. This was based on a number of elements: a common Christian heritage, despite discord between Catholics, Protestants and Orthodox believers; a political, juridical, literary and scientific culture which, though embracing many different traditions and forms, was the common heritage of all European elites; powerful state institutions; an expanding and dynamic economy stimulated by the industrialisation which began in the late eighteenth century; unparalleled progress in the fields of science and technology; and overwhelming military superiority with respect to the rest of the world. These elements enabled Europe gradually to gain the upper hand over the Ottoman and Asian empires, which had rivalled it in the sixteenth and seventeenth centuries. This superiority in turn enabled Europe to launch a new and even more vigorous assault on the rest of the world (after the first important but only partial "assault" which had begun in the late fifteenth century with the conquest of the Americas), and a "centrality" which would remain until the First World War. It should be noted, however, that this centrality had shown earlier signs of decline in the second half of the nineteenth century, as a result of the rapid economic and political growth of the United States and the beginning of the political and military modernisation of Japan.

The Europeans' awareness of their dominant position is well described by Montesquieu in his *De l'esprit des lois*. Two statements in his book are particularly revealing: one concerns Europe's position in the world, the other the position of certain countries within Europe. With respect to the first point, he writes that "Europe has arrived at so high a degree of power that nothing in history can be compared with it"; then he goes on to note, with reference to signs of greater dynamism within Europe, that just as "Europe carries on the trade and navigation of the other three parts of the world", so France, England and Holland "do nearly that of Europe". Montesquieu's words are a vital key to the understanding of the general nature of Europe's relationship with the rest of the world, and of the economic distinction between countries of the first rank and those of the second or third rank. Another factor which contributed to Europe's superiority, according to Montesquieu, was the scientific revolution, which had begun in the fifteenth and sixteenth centuries and grown with increasing vigour since the seventeenth century. In one of the *Lettres persanes* he makes the Usbek note with surprise that there are philosophers in Europe who "follow silently the footprints of human reason" and it is incredible "how far this guide has led them. They have cleared up chaos, and have explained, by a simple mechanism, the order of divine architecture".

Voltaire, too, in his *Essai sur les moeurs et l'esprit des nations*, emphasised that the combination of culture with scientific and technological progress had given Europe instruments of power such as had never existed in previous ages and did not exist in other parts of the world. But he constantly stresses, in such works as *Le siècle de Louis XIV*, the fact that "despite the wars and the diversity of religion", a "literary republic" had been established, a "great society of minds" which linked intellectuals through a common intellectual and political language. This theme was common to both Voltaire and Rousseau, whatever their disagreements on other matters; while the former declared that Europe was united by the 'same principles of public law and politics, unknown in other parts of the world" the latter observed that in Europe there was emerging a "society of peoples' united within a "system" which operated "through the same religion, the same law of peoples, customs, letters and commerce, and a kind of equilibrium which is the necessary consequence of all this".

About a century later, another great intellectual, John Stuart Mill, in his *On Liberty*, reflected – in an age now showing the full effects of the process of industrialisation whose hub was more than ever in Europe – on "what has made the European family of nations an improving, instead of a stationary portion of mankind" and therefore on the "superior excellence in them, which when it exists, exists as the effect, not as the cause". To explain this, he cited their lack of uniformity, their diversity of character and culture, their ability to follow "a great variety of paths", and their experimentalism, noting that "their attempts to thwart each other's development have rarely had any permanent success, and each has in time endured to receive the good which the others have offered. His conclusion was that "Europe is [...] wholly indebted to this plurality of paths for its progressive and many-sided development". He went on, however, to note pointedly that it was doubtful how long Europe would continue to enjoy this "benefit".

2 The Peak of European "Centrality" in the Eighteenth and Nineteenth Centuries

Voltaire and Rousseau, then, spoke of an increasing cultural and political unity in Europe despite internal divisions, political and religious disagreements and wars. Anyone who considers the history of the continent from the late fifteenth century to the nineteenth century, however, cannot fail to notice that, in contrast to the elements of unity, that history was marked by recurrent outbreaks of violence prompted by the major European states, which, with their powerful military machines, attempted to gain control, individually or in alliance with others, either through direct subjugation or through indirect influence; attempts which ultimately failed after partial, temporary successes. Kant was right, therefore, to observe that the peace treaties made between European powers, creating precarious periods of "equilibrium", were really only "truces" between one war and another. The most significant attempts to gain control during this period were those made by Philip II, in the second half of the sixteenth century; the Habsburgs of Austria and Spain, in the first half of the seventeenth century; Louis XIV, in the late seventeenth and early eighteenth centuries; and Revolutionary and Napoleonic France, in the late eighteenth and early nineteenth centuries. These attempts were followed in the second half of the nineteenth century by that which led to Bismarckian Germany's clashes first with Austria and then with the France of Napoleon III, from which Germany emerged as the greatest power in continental Europe. In all these conflicts Great Britain followed an independent line. Its role as the hub and main driving force of the Industrial Revolution had given it unrivalled commercial and industrial development for about a century. As such, its main priorities were defending itself against foreign invasions, exploiting its naval superiority, and shifting its support during conflicts from one European state to another, in order to ensure that no single power achieved lasting dominance in continental Europe.

The history of Europe since the beginning of the modern era had been one of great wars between major powers, which showed the growing effectiveness of the various military machines. In the sixteenth and seventeenth centuries this effectiveness was not yet on a decisively higher level than that of the armies and fleets of the Ottoman empire and the Asian empires; but in the eighteenth century it came ever closer to reaching that level. At that point the balance of power began to swing irresistibly towards the major European countries, of which – Spain and Portugal having gone into decline – there were now four: Great Britain, France, Austria and Russia, the last of which had joined the group of major European powers thanks to the programme of modernisation energetically pursued by Peter the Great. Prussia had also emerged alongside these nations, but was still on a lower level than them. Within this small circle of major European powers there was a smaller nucleus, made up of Great Britain and France, the most highly developed countries in economic terms and the most powerful from the military point of view. These two nations, acting in concert, but also in competition with each other, gave a strong impulse to the "assault on the world" in the second half of the eighteenth century. Smaller but still significant contributions were made by Russia, and to some extent by other European states. Thus the struggle within Europe, and the combined struggle of European powers to subjugate increasing parts of the extra-European continents, proceeded in parallel. The process of Europeanising the world now accelerated, taking the form of modern imperialism and colonialism with a common European matrix, but implemented by rival states. These states exported political traditions, legal systems, bureaucratic machineries and organisational methods, and they imposed not only production methods, but also products, and even customs, according to the characteristics of each colonial country, and established governing elites to exercise power and control over the subject states. It might be said that the boundaries of Europe had extended beyond its strictly geographical borders to the parts of the world over which it spread its variegated influence.

European "centrality", as was mentioned earlier, reached its peak in the late eighteenth century and the first half of the nineteenth century. During this period it was complete and undisputed. It lasted for just over sixty years, but – as we have seen – in the face of growing challenges to its superiority: in the west from the productivity of the United States, which by the beginning of the twentieth century had become the greatest individual economy in the world; and in the east by the "reawakening" of Japan. The power of the former and the reawakening of the latter were, it should be emphasised, in themselves products of European influence and relations with Europe, but also expressions of a resolve to challenge Europe's supremacy. The United States was in many crucial respects a product of Europe, which had given it culture, some key political models, science and technology; and in this respect the history of the United States was itself an important phase in the "Europeanisation of the world". But at the same time, ever since it had begun to coalesce into a Union, formed its own political and social institutions and developed a "national spirit" of its own, the United States had adopted a strongly critical attitude towards "mother Europe". A significant example is the debate on the Constitution, and in particular the articles of Hamilton and Madison in *The Federalist Papers*, where mother Europe is represented in many respects as an antimodel and a "stepmother" – a continent which aimed to conquer the world and impose its own interests on those of others; and which, in the variety of scenarios existing in its many countries, provided many deplorable examples of despotic regimes, opposition to the principles of the freedom of individuals and groups, glaring economic and social inequalities, rigid class barriers, and wars both between different parts of society and between states. From the beginning the Americans were like rebellious children. Especially after the Civil War, which greatly strengthened their sense of unity, they created a community which felt increasingly independent of Europe, developed a culture with original characteristics of its own, and started a process of rapid economic development based on an expanding industrial system and a powerful agriculture; the United States became a haven for millions of poor people and thousands of political refugees wishing to flee the hardships of the Old World. Gradually the tables were turned, and Americans felt a sense not only of moral but of material superiority to Europe.

The awakening of Japan ran almost parallel. In the first half of the nineteenth century Japan had undergone, though on less humiliating terms and on a smaller scale than China, the impositions and intrusions of the Russians, British and Dutch on the one hand and of the Americans on the other. The Americans in particular, who arrived in their ships in 1846 and in greater force in 1853, humiliated the Japanese and made them aware of their defencelessness. This induced Japan, as a reaction, to begin the process of economic, political and military modernisation which in less than forty years would enable it to defeat Russia in the war of 1904-1905. It was a sign of the enduring prestige and influence of Europe that the imperial Japanese government, in order to learn how to bring about its own modernisation and train the staff necessary to implement it, turned to Great Britain, France and the new Germany. But these apprentices studied under their European teachers only in order to be able to escape as soon as possible from the impositions of the white men of the Old (and the New) World.

The new and increasing power of the United States and Japan was evidence of the beginning of a decline in the centrality of Europe, after she had presented itself as, and to a large extent had indeed been, mistress of the world for about two centuries. That centrality would collapse completely from 1914-1918, when it became apparent that although it had disseminated culture, organisational methods, science and technology during the period of its supremacy, it had also taught other countries how to acquire the power that had for so long been a European monopoly, and how ultimately to overcome it, thus putting an end to the "Europeanisation of the world".

3 Phases in the Rise and Decline of the Centrality of Europe in the Modern World

The crucial event in the rise of the centrality of Europe in the modern world was the Seven Years' War (1756-1763), a wide-ranging conflict fought out on the Old Continent, in the Americas and in Asia. It was a vivid illustration of the way European power manifested itself both in internal wars between European states and in the outward expansionist drive led by Great Britain and France. It also showed the strength and effectiveness of the European war machines, which were now far superior to any others. This superiority would be further increased by the effects of the Industrial Revolution. The Seven Years' War, fought on three continents, may fairly be described as the first world war of the modern age. It had two particularly important consequences: first, the emergence of Prussia as a new European power; secondly, the advantage gained in the colonial sphere by Great Britain, which eliminated France's imperial possessions in North America and expelled France from India, establishing an authority there which would continue to grow in extent and power. Both in North America and in India Europeanisation henceforth meant "British Europeanisation".

It should be noted at this point that the highly complex phenomenon which we call the Europeanisation of the world had two aspects: on the one hand unity, in the common features shared by all parts of European civilisation; on the other diversity, in the different legal, economic, cultural, ideological and religious characteristics of the individual colonialist and imperialist states. Consequently, during the period when the power and centrality of Europe was at its height, there was a plurality of "Europeanisations": in first place the British one, followed by the French, and then by the Dutch and Belgian, to mention only the most important. In this sense, the Europeanisations of the eighteenth and nineteenth centuries were a continuation of the Spanish and Portuguese Europeanisations of the preceding centuries.

The most important of these many Europeanisations, the British version, spread throughout all the extra-European continents in one of three forms: first, direct subjugation; secondly, legal and political formations, which would ultimately lead to the Commonwealth, based on principles of relative autonomy; and thirdly, control over states through political and economic influence. This threefold process built up a vast empire whose territorial extent and depth of penetration had no precedents in history. French Europeanisation, too, extended to all the extra-European continents, accelerating in the nineteenth century after the conquest of Algeria in 1830. Its predominant aim was the direct assimilation of overseas territories into the sphere of "greater France".

A feature common to all Europeanisations, though manifested in different degrees, was their construction of an ideology of European superiority, which again had precedents in the earlier empires of Spain and Portugal. This process, whose purpose was to legitimise acts of conquest, the exercise of power and the right of Europeans to impose their leadership on the 'inferior' peoples of the world, was a mixture of sincerely used or manipulated morality, religion, law and pseudo-science. Its crudest and most striking expression was racism.

It should be stressed, however, that the Europeanisation of the world did not only take the form of colonialism and imperialism, territorial conquest, and the harsh, or even cruel, subjugation of peoples judged to be inferior. It also had aspects which may legitimately be described as "progressive". Europe conveyed to the other continents the latest scientific knowledge and the technologies produced by the Industrial Revolution and later developments. The train and the steamship were in a sense the greatest symbols of modernising Europeanisation in the world. Europe also passed on cultural movements, political models and ideological myths which were vital to the training of the elites of other continents. It disseminated, with varying effects, such fundamental concepts as the Enlightenment, idealism, positivism, historical materialism, conservative liberalism and democratic liberalism, democratic nationalism and authoritarian nationalism, neo-Caesarism, socialism and communism.

The importance and singularity of the case of the United States has already been noted. The creation of the United States was greeted by many European intellectuals and ideologues as a new beginning of the world, heralding a freedom that would spread beyond its borders. It was hailed enthusiastically by poets such as Byron, Shelley and Goethe, who contrasted the Promethean youthfulness of the Americans with the decrepitude of the Europeans. More penetrating historical analysis was provided by Hegel and Cousin; the former, in his *Vorlesungen über die Geschichte der Philosophie* (1821-1831), described America as the "country of the future", while the latter, in his *Introduction à l'histoire de la philosophie* (1845), spoke of a powerful emerging country which was destined to be Europe's heir. Meanwhile, Tocqueville, in a celebrated passage from the first part of *Democracy in America* (1835), foresaw a Europe (clearly the meaning Europe west of Russia) which was still mistress of the earth but in a phase of decline. In parallel with this he prophesied the rise of Russia and America, both of which "seem called by some secret design of Providence to hold the destinies of half the world in their hands one day", the former by using the means of serfdom and the latter those of freedom. It was Tocqueville who popularised this idea of the future greatness of the American and Russian giants in European culture. But the idea was not in itself original. We already find it clearly expressed, for example, in 1829 by the Russian Slavophile Kireyevsky, who contrasted the tarnished old age of western Europe with the future greatness that awaited America and Russia, whose peoples were "young and not exhausted".

The predictions of Hegel, Cousin, Kireyevsky and Tocqueville seemed at the time to be, and were indeed – in relation to the existing state of affairs – mere hypotheses, fruits of the imagination. But they were also testimonies, though isolated ones, to an idea which contrasted starkly with the unshakeable confidence in the superiority of Europe which continued to characterise the thoughts and feelings of European intellectual and political elites. This idea was that the period of domination by the nucleus formed by the most vigorous and dynamic countries of the Old Continent was simply one of a series of cycles which had pervaded world history. These were still, however, as we have seen, only hypotheses, ideas; in fact, Europe's centrality and capacity for influence and domination in the world had not even reached its apex at this time. That point would be reached in the 1870s and 1880s by a capitalist, bourgeois Europe, the product of a process of unprecedented economic modernisation, unequalled in the financial power, industrial resources and network of communications it had at its disposal: a superiority which stimulated a further phase of conquest and colonisation of immense new territories. The great exhibitions of London in 1851 and Paris in 1855 and 1889 were shop windows for continuing European superiority, though by the latest of those dates that superiority was close to being challenged in the economic field by the rapid rise of the United States.

4 The Decline and Fall of European Centrality

The expansionist impulse which led the European powers to extend the frontiers of already immense empires further, often in conflict with one another, in the last decades which preceded 1914 was a reflection both of the collective power they still had and of their weaknesses and divisions, which would be revealed with all disastrous effect in the First World War and the years that followed. The interval of peace between the Franco-Prussian War and the beginning of the Great War had only papered over the divisions. During the less than half a century's truce, several things had happened: the rivalry between France and unified Germany had been rekindled; Germany had been transformed in a remarkably short time into a major industrial country whose industry now rivalled or surpassed that of Great Britain in its efficiency, modernity and dynamism, and which possessed the most effective military machine in the world; and two major alliances had formed: the Triple Entente of Great Britain, France and Russia, and the Triple Alliance of Germany, Austria and Italy. The result was in the first place war, in which all these enmities exploded, and then the collapse of European centrality. In the modern age Europe had experienced a series of great internal wars, but those wars had never threatened its superior overall economic, technological and military power; on the contrary, that power had continued to grow, and formed the basis of the Europeanisation of the world. Now, however, it had come to the end of its historical cycle.

There had been, as has already been mentioned, some significant warning signs of a threat to European centrality. Chief among these had been the swift economic rise of the United States and the parallel rise of Japan, which had acquired not only a remarkable production system but powerful armed forces. In addition, both those countries had become involved in imperialist conflicts. Nevertheless, until 1914 the threat was small, for the countries of the Old Continent still had the strongest industries and overwhelming military superiority, as well as possessing, or having control over, vast extra-European territories. But the crucial difference from the situation in previous centuries was that Europe was no longer able to give the external world a "progressive" impulse through its more advanced culture, science and technology. Increasingly large areas of the external world were developing their own resources.

The importance and implications of this change had not yet been perceived by the ruling classes of the major European countries, which still had an over-weening sense of superiority, reassured by their overwhelming military power, which seemed an insurmountable barrier against the rest of the world. Some intellectuals, however, were aware of the profound change that was taking place. One of these was Georges Sorel, who, as Europe rushed towards world war, commented that an entire cycle of its history had ended, for it had nothing important to give the rest of the world any more, and – as he wrote – "one idea alone unites Europe", namely "the idea of war".

The events of the 1914-1918 war suddenly revealed all the divisions and tensions that had been building up in the Old Continent, setting states and nationalities, classes, political alignments, ideologies and sentiments against one another. In the horror of war, the last remnants of the Erasmian and Enlightenment idea of a republic of European minds were swept away by slaughter on an unprecedented scale and material damage which wrecked the economy of the continent. There were deep divisions within both the common people and within the cultural elites (where some defended *Kultur*, others *Civilisation*) and bitter conflict set imperialist, authoritarian nationalists against democratic nationalists and internationalists; socialists who wanted to bring down the bourgeois state against moderate socialists, liberalists and reactionaries; and anti-capitalists against defenders of capitalism. Europe poured all the human, economic and military resources it had accumulated in four decades of peace into a great furnace of self-destruction.

The conclusion of the war revealed a dramatic change in world affairs. The most obvious one was the final collapse of European centrality. The war had put an end to the rise of Europe, which had been a continuous process since the fifteenth century.

There are five crucial, interrelated points about the war that need to be understood. The first, and most symbolic, was the fact that, for the first time, the great European powers which began a war were not able to end it. The reason it ended, and ended in the way it did, was the United States' intervention in 1917. That nation enabled the adversaries of the central empires to hold out and eventually emerge victorious, first by providing economic and financial support and later by direct military action. An awareness of the epochal change that this implied is expressed in President Woodrow Wilson's address to his fellow countrymen in September 1919: "The American face mirrors the future, and, my fellow citizens, the American purpose mirrors the future of the world". In other words, the dominance of the old European powers in international affairs was a thing of the past.

The second factor was the universalistic revolutionary message that was sent out by Lenin during the war both before and after the Bolsheviks' seizure of power in Russia in October 1917. His message was that, with the emergence of new national, political and social forces, the old Europe was destined to lose its former role on the world stage. The long historical cycle during which the major European powers and their empires had dominated the world had come to an end, and was being replaced by international social and anti-colonial revolution. An essential ingredient of Lenin's discourse was an appeal to all colonial and semi-colonial peoples, and to those still subject to European states, to rise up against their oppressors and join the rebellion of the heirs of Spartacus who lived in those countries, oppressed by capitalist exploitation. Both Woodrow Wilson and Lenin, from opposite points of view, were registering the fact that the centrality of Europe, and therefore the Europeanisation of the world too, had come to an end.

The third fact which suggested that the centrality of the Europe had collapsed was the destruction of the power of Germany, whose rapid economic, scientific, technological and military advance had been the most important development in European history in the forty years preceding 1914. By the turn of the twentieth century, when the United States emerged as the strongest industrial country in the world, Germany had become the strongest industrial country in Europe, and was second to none in the world in the efficiency of its production system and its ability to combine organised labour, science and technology. The humiliating terms imposed by the British and French on the Germans in 1919 was tragic evidence that Europe, divided by irreconcilable internal conflicts, was blind to its needs for the future. The blindness showed in the determination of Great Britain, and particularly of France, to crush Germany for good. The mood of the French and British leaders, in the face of the immensely difficult task of repairing the damage that had been done to Europe, was summed up by Keynes's words about Clemenceau and Lloyd George in his celebrated book *The Economic Consequences of the Peace*: "The future life of Europe was not their concern; its means of livelihood was not their anxiety. Their preoccupations, good and bad alike, related to frontiers and nationalities, to the balance of power, to imperial aggrandisements, to the future enfeeblement of a strong and dangerous enemy, to revenge, and to the shifting by the victors of their unbearable financial burdens on to the shoulders of the defeated".

The fourth fact was the collapse of the Tsarist empire, followed by the rise to power of the Bolsheviks in Russia and the dissolution of the Austro-Hungarian empire. The collapse of the empire led to an ideological, political and social war from the Urals to the Atlantic coasts whose ferocity had precedents only in the civil and religious wars arising from the Protestant Reformation and in the wars between Revolutionary and Napoleonic France and the variegated alliance of states that opposed it. But those confrontations and wars, however destructive, had resulted in the formation of new relationships within Europe; and the settling of those earlier conflicts had not impaired Europe's overall strength, and therefore its ability to continue the process of Europeanising the world. By contrast, the violent opposition between Soviet communism and capitalist, bourgeois Europe which broke out in the post-war years was a further source of disruption and a sign that the centrality of Europe had entered its terminal phase. But too often consciousness fails to absorb the reality of events. Great Britain and France were reinforced in their approach by the United States' decision to return to its former isolationism, and encouraged in their imperialistic ambitions by the territories they had recently gained in the Middle East with the break-up of the Ottoman Empire. As a result, the two countries thought they could still act as representatives and guardians of a European centrality which was now in fact purely illusory.

The fifth factor which showed that the period of Europe's preponderance role in world affairs had come to an end was the place now occupied on the world stage by the United States and Japan. These two countries were no longer simply rising powers, as they had been at the turn of the century, but established powers capable of seizing the Old Continent's last monopoly – absolute military superiority.

Full awareness of the extent of the changes that had come about was expressed in 1923 by the Austrian Count Coudenhove-Kalergi, an ardent supporter of the federalist reconstruction of Europe, whose attitude was both realistic and utopian. He wrote: "Today Europe is no longer the centre of the earth [...] The world has broken free of Europe. [...] Can Europe, with its political and economic fragmentation, maintain its peace and independence in the face of the rise of the growing extra-European world powers, or is it compelled to organise itself into a federation of states in order to preserve its own existence?"

5 The Project Launched by the "Modern Attila" and the Final "Explosion" of Europe

The decade following the Treaty of Versailles was a period of relative recovery for Europe, but it did not last long; it ended with the great economic crisis which began in the United States in 1929 and spread to Europe, where it had a devastating effect. The relative recovery rested on two main foundations: one was the dominance of the two victorious powers, Great Britain and France, and the ability of European capitalism to resist the revolutionary assault led by an increasingly remote Moscow, where Stalin had imposed a policy of isolationism; the other, which developed after the economic crisis of 1923, was the reconstruction of the German industrial system thanks to the plan of American investment launched in 1924, which enabled Germany to attain a certain degree of political and institutional stability for a few years.

The effects of the shift of the centre of the world economy from the Old World to the New were felt to the full in 1929. In fact this shift had already become clear, as we have seen, with the importance of American assistance to the allies during the First World War and supply of material first of all and to Germany in the 1920s. Recovery in Europe had also been helped by a vigorous upswing in the American economy in the 1920s: by the end of the decade the United States had more than forty per cent of world industrial production. The Wall Street crisis was further conclusive evidence that European affluence depended directly on the state of health of the United States. In the next ten years, what had seemed to be a vestige of European order, that order imposed by the countries that had been victorious in 1918, was gradually eroded until in September 1939 Europe exploded.

Germany had been the country most seriously affected by the consequences of the Wall Street crisis. Its hard-won political stability was shattered. The Communist Party and the National Socialist Party, though sworn enemies, were united in their loathing of the Weimar republic created in 1919. At first, despite their aggressiveness, they were only small minorities in terms of popular support and parliamentary representation. After 1929, however, support for them grew rapidly, and increasingly weakened the Social Democrats, the Catholic Centre Party and the Liberal Democrats. Finally, in January 1933 the Nazis led by Hitler defeated both the communists and the supporters of parliamentary democracy and came to power, thus widening the frontiers of Fascism – which had been created in Italy by Mussolini in 1922 – in parallel with other authoritarian regimes that were emerging in Europe. In the six years following Hitler's seizure of power in Germany, the geopolitical map of Europe was characterised by several features: a rapid recovery of German industrial and military power; an increasingly close relationship between Italy and Germany; Germany's direct challenge to the equilibrium established under the treaty of 1919 by its aggressive policy; the weak response to Germany made by Great Britain and France; and the industrial and military modernisation of the Soviet Union, which had risen from its previous position of weakness to become a leading figure in international politics.

Thus Europe was divided into three main groups of countries: a Nazi-Fascist group led by Germany and Italy, aggressive and expansionist in its aims; a democratic one centring on Great Britain and France, weakened by internal discord and by the meekness of its foreign policy; and the Soviet Union, which was not only strengthened in itself as a state, but had the support of European communist parties – though except for the French Communist Party these parties were weak or even marginal, being persecuted and in some cases banned from political life. The idea of European superiority had been revived in negative fashion by National Socialism. It could be seen in the brand of racism that proclaimed the Aryans' right to pre-eminence and promoted the oppression of the "Jewish race", which it aimed to annihilate, and of all 'inferior' races and peoples, which it planned to reduce to a state of semi-slavery. These racist ideas found fertile terrain in France, Poland and Eastern European countries – where they had ancient roots – and in Fascist Italy, which passed racist laws in 1938. The idea of European superiority could be seen more specifically in the conviction of Hitler and his followers that they could re-establish European centrality in the world through the achievements of German power.

The Spanish Civil War, which grew into an international conflict, showed the extent of the discord within Europe. The Old continent had accumulated such explosive potential that when the fuse was lit, the results were bound to be devastating. The fuse was lit in September 1939 when Germany invaded Poland and divided it up with the Soviet Union. It is significant that Nazi Germany proclaimed at the time of its first military victories that they were laying the foundations for a revival of European centrality in the world. This dream was based on the idea that it was possible to create a worldwide alliance between the superior races, with the Aryans at its centre, and lead a Europe regenerated by "a new order". The Soviet Union would be destroyed and the Slavs reduced to slavery. The basis of the project would be the thousand-year Third Reich. This was the project for the unification of Europe and the restoration of its primacy launched by Hitler, whom Einaudi, in a telling phrase, would later describe as "the modern Attila".

The failure of the project had two main effects. First, after the great "explosion" Europe was left, in 1945, in a state of unprecedented material and social devastation. Secondly, power shifted into the hands of two great powers – one American, the other Eurasian. The fact that, as in 1918, Great Britain and France – despite the latter's disastrous defeat by Germany in 1940 – emerged on the winning side did not alter the fact that they had been permanently relegated to the status of second-tier powers. They were now simply part of the western superpower's sphere of influence, and their only means of defence against the eastern superpower was to put themselves under the protective umbrella of the United States. Another symptom of the collapse of Europe was that the economic reconstruction of the countries that had remained in the capitalist area was possible, to an even higher degree than had been the case after 1918, exclusively thanks to American aid. Finally, the decline of Europe was sealed by the dual division whereby for nearly half a century "American Europe" was opposed to "Soviet Europe" and West German to East Germany. The European countries were no longer masters of their own destinies.

The condition of subordination which Europe had reached could be summed up in the following points. First, in 1939, as in 1918, the continent had had the doubtful privilege of starting a world war but had been unable to finish it. Secondly, unlike the First World War, which had at least left Great Britain and France as powers of the first rank, the Second removed all wholly European states from the top tier of world power. Thirdly, the power to impart order of any kind on the world became the exclusive prerogative of the United States and the Soviet Union. Fourthly, the traditional rivalries, alliances and alignments of European states were replaced by the subordination of a divided Europe to two superpowers – which in the case of western Europeans meant accepting American hegemony and in the case of eastern Europeans meant subjection to a totalitarian regime.

So ended a period of history, with Europe now reduced to "provincial" status, dependent partly on an extra-European power and partly on a Eurasian one. The end of the war in 1945 erased not only the last traces of the centrality once held by the Old Continent, but also, to a greater or lesser degree in the various countries, the main elements which form the basis of the sovereignty of states, namely the power to choose one's own system of government, economic strategies, foreign policies and military alliances. During the forty years of the "Cold War" between the capitalist west and the communist east, the loss of this power was common to both parts of Europe. The keys to war and peace – a crucial element of sovereign power – were denied to both of them, and became the exclusive prerogative of the two states that now dominated the world. Even the internal peace which the Old Continent at last enjoyed was not a creation of the Europeans themselves but the result of an equilibrium established by the superpowers, by enforcing their own decisions, supporting, promoting or imposing particular kinds of regime and spreading their ideologies, as an integral part of the conflicting processes of "Americanisation" and "Sovietisation". Moreover, the end of the European colonial empires after 1945, accompanied by failed attempts to preserve at least some remnants of them, and by brutal, inglorious wars, was another indication that Europe had finally drawn back to within its geographical boundaries.

Translated from the Italian by Jonathan Hunt

Bibliography

Bairoch, P 1997, *Victoires et déboires. Histoire économique et sociale du monde du XVI siècle à nos jours*, Gallimard, Paris.
Bracher, KD 1982, *Zeit der Ideologien*, Deutsche Verlags-Anstalt GmbH, Stuttgart.
Dehio, L 1948, Gleichgewicht oder Hegemonie, Scherpe-Verlag, Krefeld.
Fuller, JFC 1961, *The conduct of war 1789-1961*, Eyre Methuen, London.
Galasso, G 2001, *Storia d'Europa*, Laterza, Roma-Bari.
Hughes, HS 1958, *Consciousness and Society. The Reorientation of European Social Thought*, Harvard University Press, Cambridge.
Judt, T 2005, *Postwar. A History of Europe Since 1945*, Penguin Press, New York.
Kennedy, P 1987, *The Rise and Fall of the Great Powers*, Random House, New York.
Landes, DS 1998, *The Wealth and Poverty of Nations*, Norton, New York.
Rossi, P 2007, *L'identità dell'Europa*, il Mulino, Bologna.
Salvadori, ML 1990, *Storia dell'età moderna e contemporanea*, Loescher, Torino.
Salvadori, ML 2001, "Ascesa e crisi della centralità dell'Europa", in *La storia. I Grandi problemi dell'Età Contemporanea. 5*, eds N Tranfaglia & MF Garzanti, Milano.
Silvestri, M 1977, *La decadenza dell'Europa occidentale, 1890-1939, 3 voll.*, Einaudi, Torino.
Villani, P 1983, *Trionfo e crollo del predominio europeo*, il Mulino, Bologna.

The Authors

Franco Cardini (1940) is Professor Emeritus of Medieval History at the Scuola Normale Superiore (Pisa); he has also taught at the University of Florence, at the *École des Hautes Études en Sciences Sociales* (Paris), and at other European and international universities (among them Jerusalem, Göttingen, Sao Paulo). His field of studies includes crusades, pilgrimages, and the relationships between Europe and Islam. He has authored several books: *Alle radici della cavalleria medievale* (1981), *Quell'antica festa crudele* (1982), *Europa e Islam: storia di un malinteso* (1999), *In Terrasanta* (2002), *Gerusalemme* (2012), and *Istambul* (2014), among others. His recent work *La società medievale* (2014) has been translated into seven languages.

Sir John Elliott is Regius Professor Emeritus of Modern History in the University of Oxford, and an honorary Fellow of Oriel College, Oxford and Trinity College, Cambridge, where he was a University lecturer from 1957-1968. He was Professor of History at King's College, London, from 1968-1973, then Professor in the School of Historical Studies at the Institute for Advanced Study at Princeton. In 1990 he returned to the UK as Regius Professor of Modern History at Oxford until his retirement in 1997. His works on Spain, Europe and the Americas in the Early Modern period include *Imperial Spain, 1469-1716* (1963); *The Revolt of the Catalans* (1963); *The Old World and the New, 1492-1650* (1970); *The Count-Duke of Olivares* (1986); and *Empires of the Atlantic World, 1492-1830* (2006). He received the Wolfson Prize in 1986, the Prince of Asturias Prize in 1996, and the Balzan Prize in 1999. In 1988 he received the Gran Cruz de Alfonso X el Sabio and in 1996 the Gran Cruz of Isabel la Católica. He was knighted for his services to history in 1994. His most recent book, *History in the Making*, was published in 2012.

Manfred Hildermeier was born in 1948 and studied in Bochum and Tübingen 1966-72, PhD 1976. Stipends to Moscow (1973, 1989) and Stanford (1973-74); Assistant Professor at the Free University of Berlin 1977-83, Habilitation 1983. Professor for Russian and Soviet History at the University of Göttingen since 1985. Research stays at Harvard University (1986), the Historische Kolleg (1985-86), the Institute for Advanced Studies at Berlin (2000-2001) and Oxford University (2003-2004); Chair, Deutscher Historikerverband (2000-2004), Opus Magnum Stipend 2009-10; Co-editor of numerous journals; Member of the Deutsch-Russische Historikerkommission and the Berlin-Brandenburg and Göttingen Academies of Sciences.

Markus Koller is Professor for Ottoman and Turkish History and member of the Board of the Centre for Mediterranean Studies at the University of Bochum. He has published on the social and cultural history of the Ottoman Balkans, the Eastern Mediterranean and European-Ottoman relationships including *Bosnien an der Schwelle zur Neuzeit. Eine Kulturgeschichte der Gewalt (1747-1798)*, Munich 2004, *Eine Gesellschaft im Wandel - die osmanische Herrschaft in Ungarn im 17. Jahrhundert (1606 - 1683)*, Stuttgart 2010 and, together with Andreas Helmedach et.al., *Das osmanische Europa. Methoden und Perspektiven der Frühneuzeitforschung zu Südosteuropa*, Leipzig 2014.

Arnaldo Marcone was educated at Scuola Normale Superiore of Pisa/Pisa University (1973-77). Post-graduate studies: Scuola Normale Superiore of Pisa (1978-1981) "Ricercatore": Scuola Normale Superiore of Pisa (1981-1983), University of Florence (1983-1992). Associate Professor of Social and Economic History of the Ancient World (University of Parma), Full Professor of Roman

History in the University of Udine (2001-2008). Full professor of Roman History in the University Roma 3 since 2008. He was fellow of the Alexander von Humboldt-Stiftung (1986-87) and of the Institute of Advanced Study (2002). He has been member of the editorial board of the journal Rivista Storica Italiana (Torino) since 2010. Current main research-fields: 1) Economic and Social History of the Ancient World; 2) the Late Roman Empire; 3) the modern Historiography on the Ancient World and particularly on the Economic and Social History of the Ancient World, most of all M. Rostovtzeff.

Alberto Masoero teaches Russian history at Ca' Foscari University of Venice. He graduated from the University of Turin and received his M.A. from Princeton University and his Ph.D. from the University of Turin. He has published extensively on Russian cultural and intellectual history, populism, and economic thought. His current research focuses on the representation and transformation of space in Tsarist Siberia. Among his recent publications are *Fracture Lines in the Tsarist Empire. An Overview* (2010, in Italian) and *Territorial Colonization in Late Imperial Russia. Stages in the Development of a Concept*, "Kritika. Explorations in Russian and Eurasian History" (2013).

Pietro Rossi (1930) is Professor Emeritus of Philosophy of History at the University of Turin, member (and former President) of the Turin Academy of Sciences, member of the National Academy of Lincei and of Academia Europaea. He was also Max-Weber-Gastprofessor at the University of Heidelberg and Humboldt Prize recipient in 1999, member of the Committee of *Enciclopedia delle scienze sociali*, published by the Istituto della Enciclopedia Italiana (1991-99), and of the Advisory Board of *International Encyclopedia of the Social and Behavioral Sciences*, published by Elsevier (2001). His work includes books as *Lo storicismo tedesco contemporaneo* (1956/1994³), *Vom Historismus zur historischen Sozialwissenschaft* (1987), *Max Weber. Una idea di Occidente* (2007), *Il senso della storia. Dal Settecento al Duemila* (2012), and the editorship (with C.A. Viano) of the *Storia della filosofia*, published by Laterza (1993-99).

Massimo L. Salvadori is Professor Emeritus of History of Political Thought at the University of Turin. From 1982-83 he was a fellow at the Wilson International Center of Scholars, Washington, D.C., and afterwards Visiting Professor at the Harvard and Columbia universities. In 2006 President Giorgio Napolitano nominated him for the Grande Ufficiale della Repubblica Italiana. His more recent publications include: *Storia dell'età moderna e contemporanea* (1991), *L'utopia caduta. Storia del pensiero comunista da Lenin a Gorbaciov* (1992), *La sinistra nella storia italiana* (1999), *L'Europa degli americani. Dai Padri fondatori a Roosevelt* (2005), *Democrazie senza democrazia* (2009), *Storia d'Italia, crisi di regime e crisi di sistema 1861-1913* (2013). Several of his works have been translated into foreign languages.

Bo Stråth, Professor Emeritus, fil.dr, was from 2007-2014 Finnish Academy Distinguished Professor of Nordic, European and World History and Director of Research at the University of Helsinki. From 1997-2007 he was Professor of Contemporary History at the European University Institute in Florence, and from 1990-1996 Professor of History at the University of Gothenburg. His research focuses on philosophy of history and the political, social and economic theory of modernity, from a conceptual history perspective with special attention to questions of what keeps societies together or divides them and how community is constructed. A special field of interest in this perspective is the history of European integration.

www.ingramcontent.com/pod-product-compliance
Lightning Source LLC
Chambersburg PA
CBHW070609170426
43200CB00012B/2634